D0028657

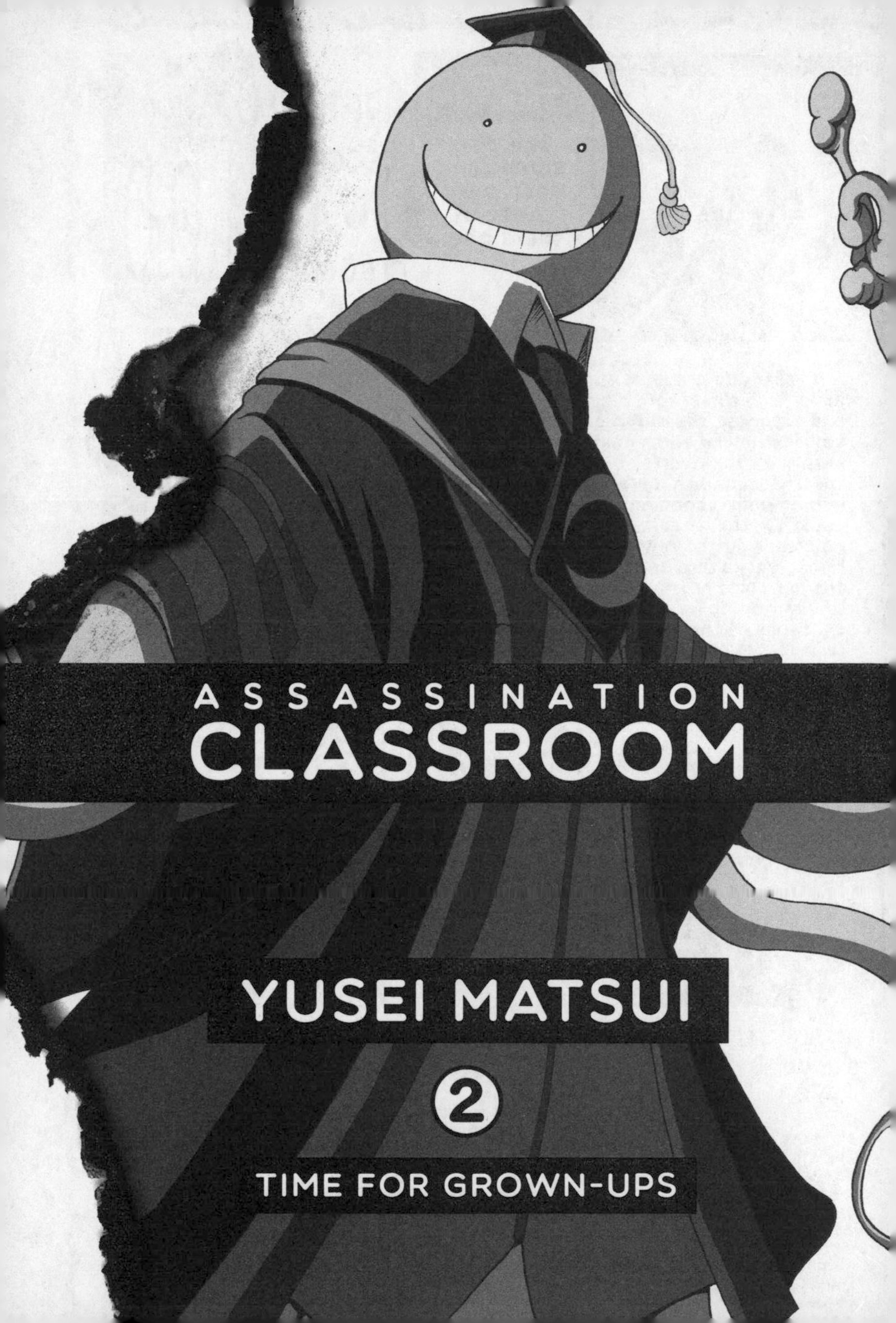

ASSASSINATION CLASSROOM

YUSEI MATSUI

2

TIME FOR GROWN-UPS

Koro Tribune

April Issue

Published by: Class 3-E Newspaper Staff

Our new teacher is a creature who plans to destroy the world...?!

Story Thus Far

One day, something destroyed most of the moon.

I'M THE ONE WHO DISINTEGRATED PART OF THE MOON.
AND NEXT YEAR AT THIS TIME I'M GOING TO DO THE SAME THING TO YOUR PLANET EARTH.
ALSO, I'M YOUR NEW TEACHER. I HOPE WE

A mysterious creature showed up in our junior high classroom claiming that he had attacked the moon and promising to destroy the earth next March. And then...he took over as our teacher. What the-?! Faced with a creature beyond human understanding that no army could kill, the leaders of the world had no choice but to rely on the students of Kunugigaoka Junior High, Class 3-E to do the job. For a reward of ten billion yen (100 million dollars)... SIGN ME UP!! Will the students of the so-called End Class, filled with losers and rejects, be able to kill their target Koro Sensei by graduation...?!

JUS
TAKE A
WOR
OF AD
FROM
TARG

Koro Sensei

A mysterious octopus-like creature whose nickname is a play on the words "koro senai," which means "can't be killed." He is capable of flying at Mach 20 and his versatile tentacles protect him from attacks and aid him in everyday activities. Nobody knows why he wants to teach Class 3-E, but he has proven to be an extremely capable teacher.

He gets revenge on his would-be assassins by fixing them up... literally.

Nagisa Shiota

Class E student. Skilled at information gathering, he has been taking notes on Koro Sensei's weaknesses.

It actually comes in handy!
Koro Sensei's Weakness #1
He messes up when he shows off

Kaede Kayano

Class E student. She's the one who named Koro Sensei. Sits at the desk next to Nagisa, and they seem to get along well.

Ryoma Terasaka

Unsuccessfully used Nagisa in a dangerous bomb attack on Koro Sensei, and ended up being severely scolded for it. Doesn't take his studies very seriously.

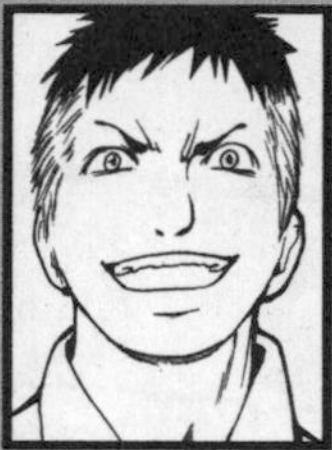

Karma Akabane

Class E student. A quick thinker skilled at surprise attacks. Succeeded in injuring Koro Sensei a few times.

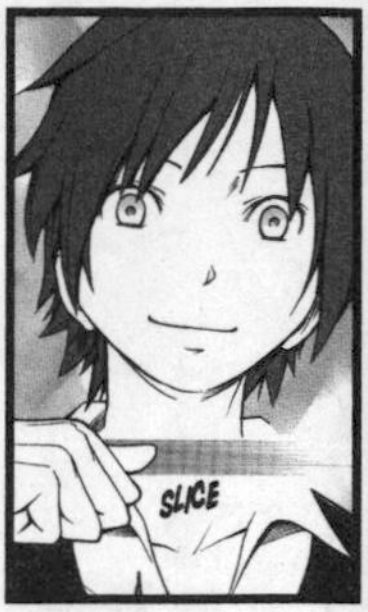
SLICE

Now he's joined the city's Junior High baseball team!

Congratu-lations!

Known as "Slippery Sugino" because of his breaking balls that slip past the batter. The team's starting pitcher. He loves that but hates his nickname.

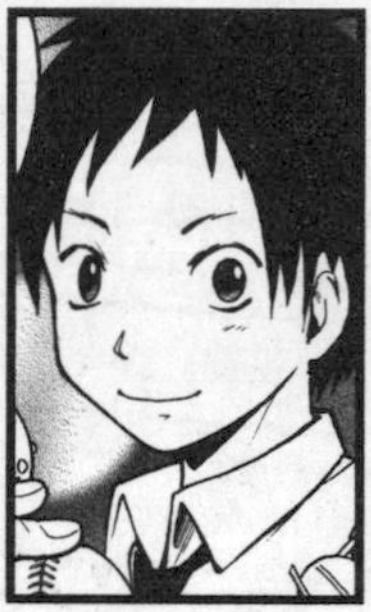

Tomohito Sugino

Class E student. Tried to assassinate Koro Sensei using a baseball (yeah, a baseball). It didn't work out too well, but he rediscovered his love of the game!

Tadaomi Karasuma

Member of the Ministry of Defense. The Class E students' P.E. teacher. Also in charge of managing assassins sent in from the outside.

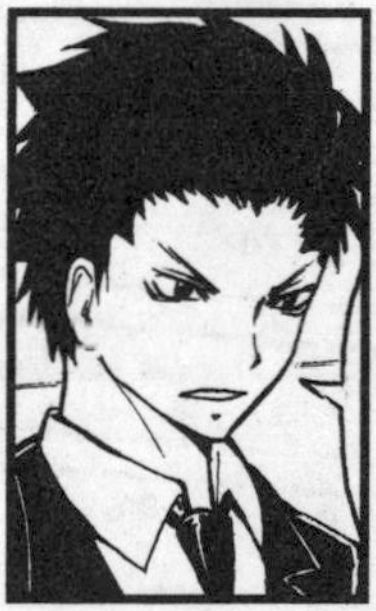

Manami Okuda

Class E student. Receives excellent grades in science and tried to poison Koro Sensei. He subsequently taught her the importance of communication skills in everyday life and assassination attempts.

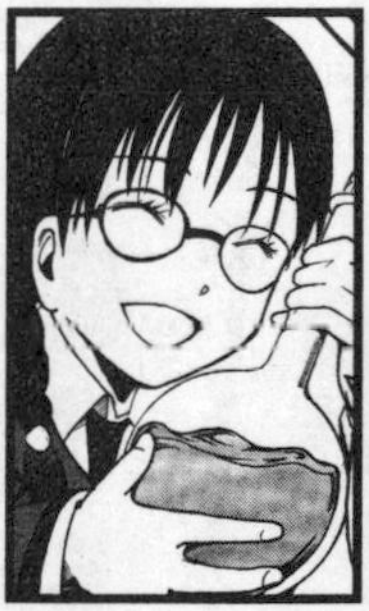

Chalkboard Scratchers **Nail Salon** *Now Open!*

For the busy professional woman! Beautiful nail art in less than a second!!

Men welcome too. ♥

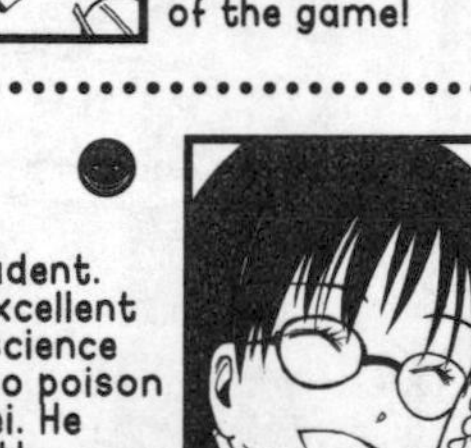
I HAD ENOUGH TIME TO DO YOUR NAILS TOO. YOU LIKE THEM?
!!

ASSASSINATION CLASSROOM 2 CONTENTS

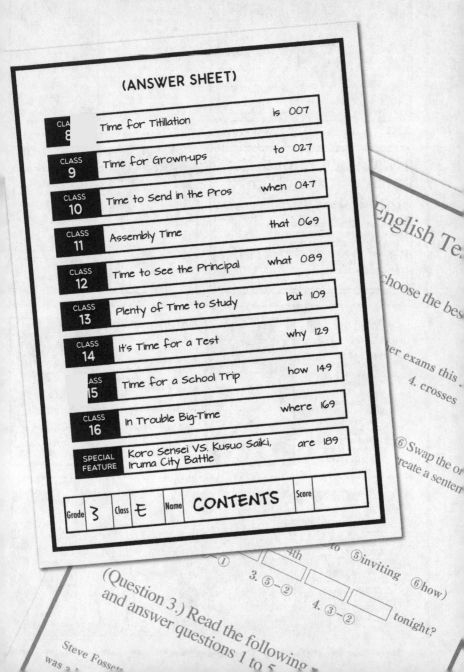

(ANSWER SHEET)

| Grade 3 | Class E | Name CONTENTS | Score |

English Te

choose the bes

her exams this

4. crosses

⑥Swap the or
create a senten

⑤inviting ⑥how)

tonight?

④th

to

3. ⑤－②

4. ③－②

(Question 3.) Read the following
and answer questions 1 to 5

Steve Fosset
was a

Class 8 Time for Titillation

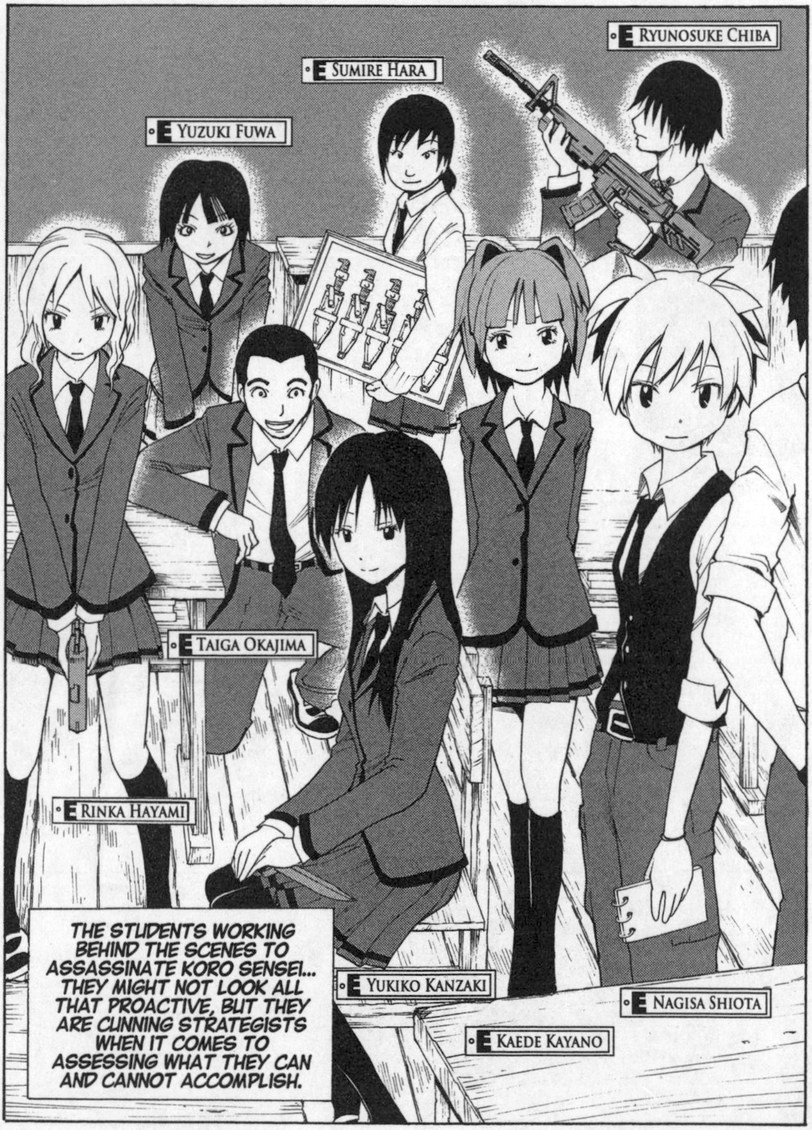
E Ryunosuke Chiba
E Sumire Hara
E Yuzuki Fuwa
E Taiga Okajima
E Rinka Hayami
E Nagisa Shiota
E Kaede Kayano
E Yukiko Kanzaki
THE STUDENTS WORKING BEHIND THE SCENES TO ASSASSINATE KORO SENSEI... THEY MIGHT NOT LOOK ALL THAT PROACTIVE, BUT THEY ARE CUNNING STRATEGISTS WHEN IT COMES TO ASSESSING WHAT THEY CAN AND CANNOT ACCOMPLISH.

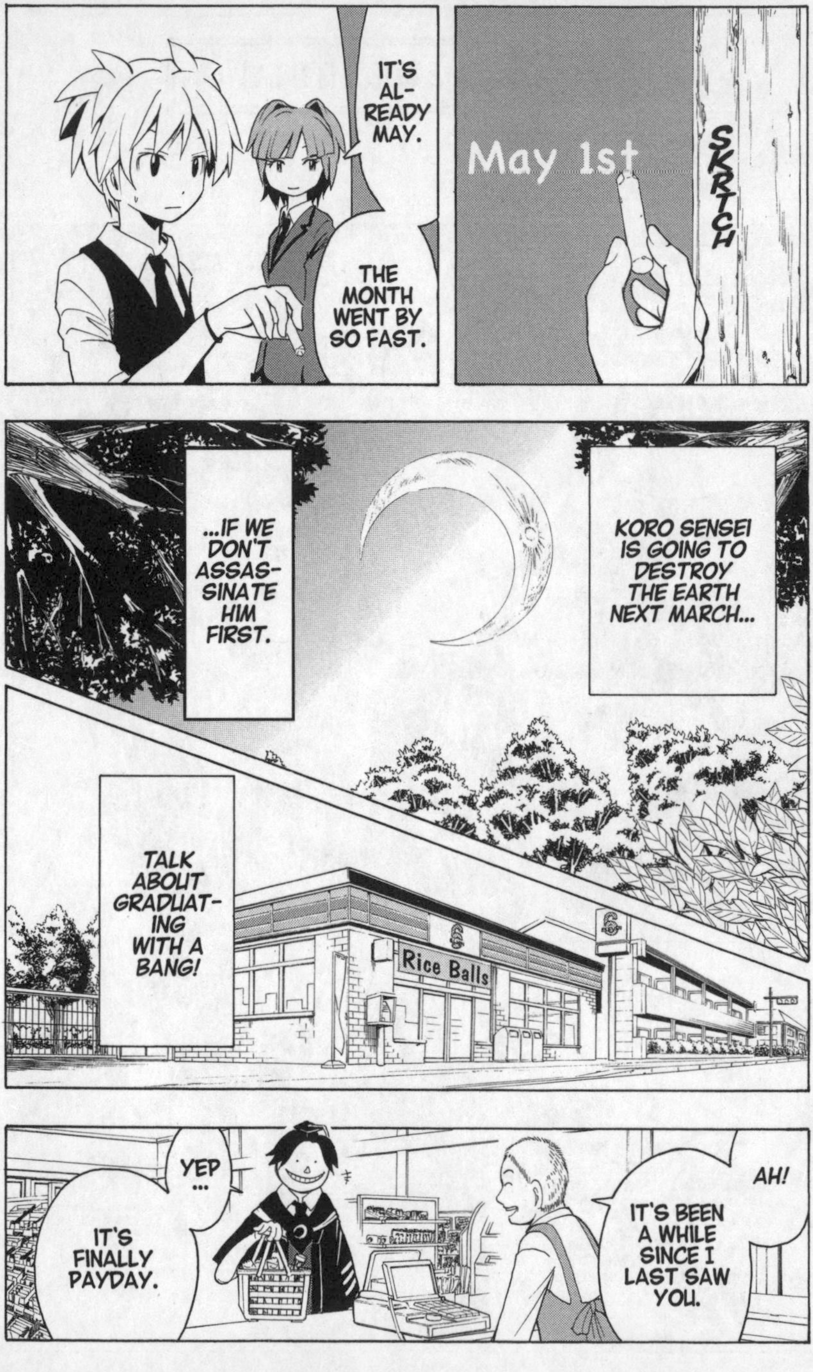
May 1st
SKRTCH
IT'S AL-READY MAY.
THE MONTH WENT BY SO FAST.
KORO SENSEI IS GOING TO DESTROY THE EARTH NEXT MARCH...
...IF WE DON'T ASSAS-SINATE HIM FIRST.
TALK ABOUT GRADUAT-ING WITH A BANG!
Rice Balls
AH!
IT'S BEEN A WHILE SINCE I LAST SAW YOU.
YEP...
IT'S FINALLY PAYDAY.

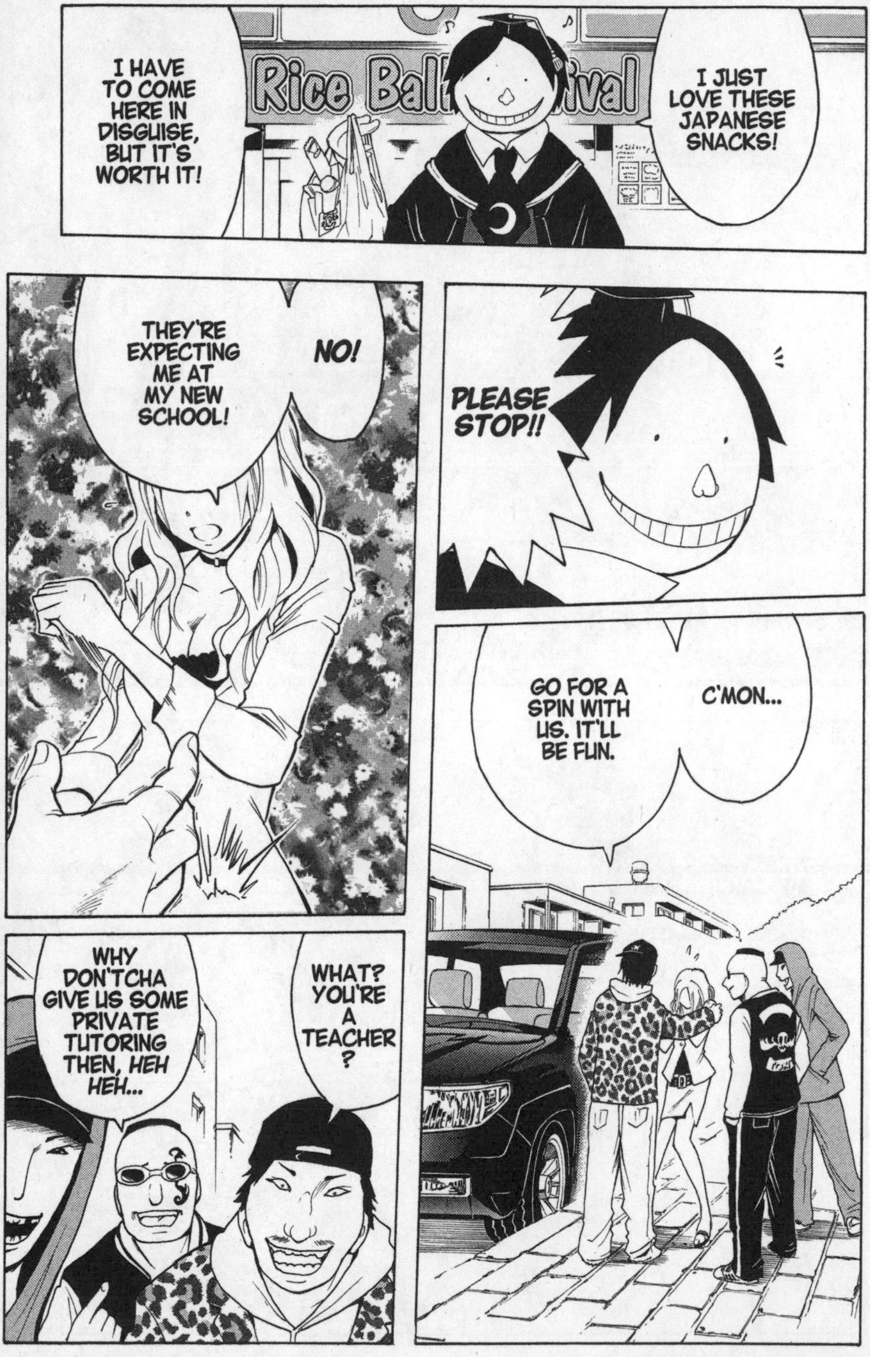
I JUST LOVE THESE JAPANESE SNACKS!
Rice Ball
I HAVE TO COME HERE IN DISGUISE, BUT IT'S WORTH IT!
PLEASE STOP!!
C'MON...
GO FOR A SPIN WITH US. IT'LL BE FUN.
NO!
THEY'RE EXPECTING ME AT MY NEW SCHOOL!
WHAT? YOU'RE A TEACHER?
WHY DON'TCHA GIVE US SOME PRIVATE TUTORING THEN, HEH HEH...

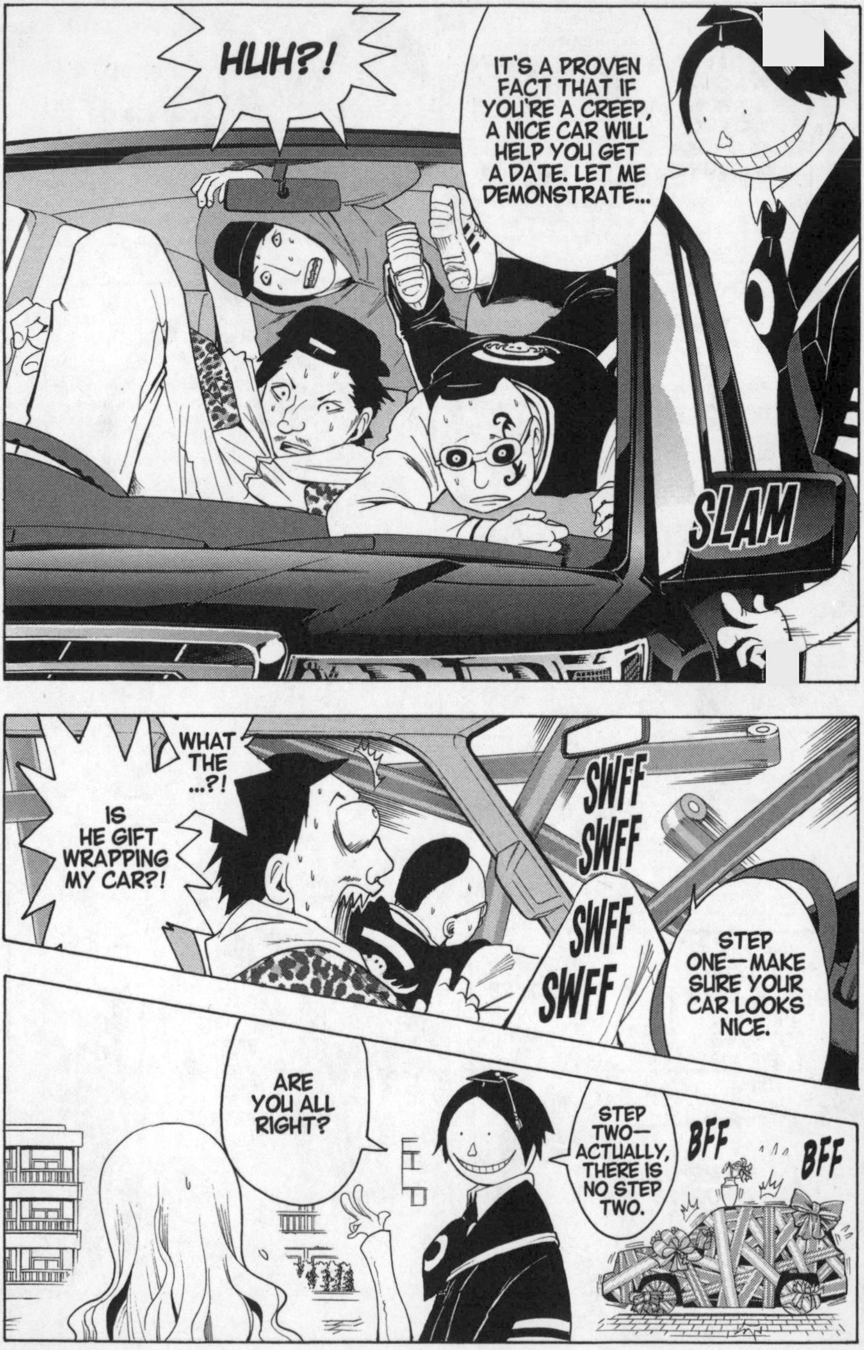
IT'S A PROVEN FACT THAT IF YOU'RE A CREEP, A NICE CAR WILL HELP YOU GET A DATE. LET ME DEMONSTRATE...
HUH?!
SLAM
SWFF SWFF
WHAT THE ...?!
IS HE GIFT WRAPPING MY CAR?!
SWFF SWFF
STEP ONE—MAKE SURE YOUR CAR LOOKS NICE.
BFF
BFF
STEP TWO—ACTUALLY, THERE IS NO STEP TWO.
ARE YOU ALL RIGHT?

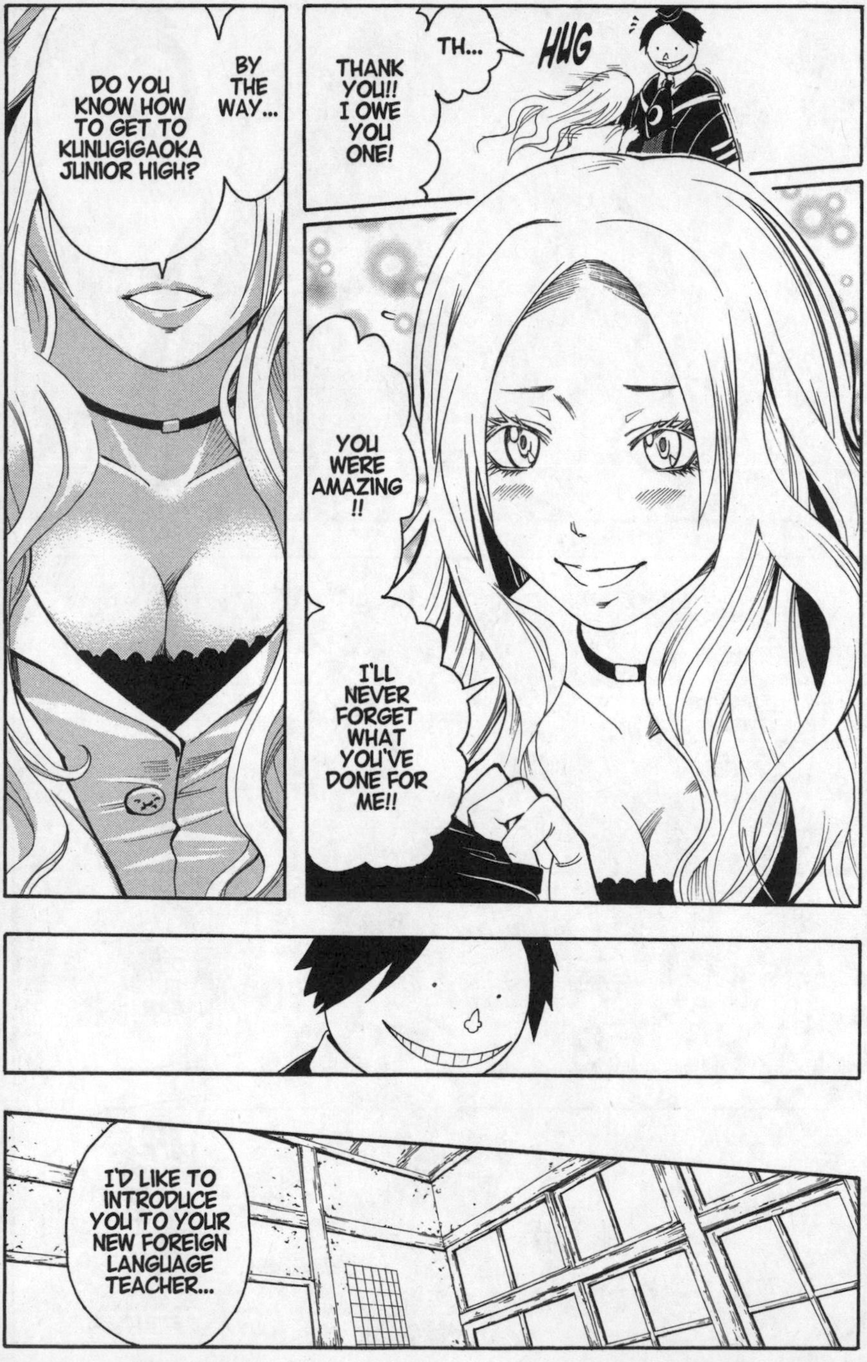
HUG
TH...
THANK YOU!! I OWE YOU ONE!
YOU WERE AMAZING!!
I'LL NEVER FORGET WHAT YOU'VE DONE FOR ME!!
BY THE WAY...
DO YOU KNOW HOW TO GET TO KUNUGIGAOKA JUNIOR HIGH?
I'D LIKE TO INTRODUCE YOU TO YOUR NEW FOREIGN LANGUAGE TEACHER...

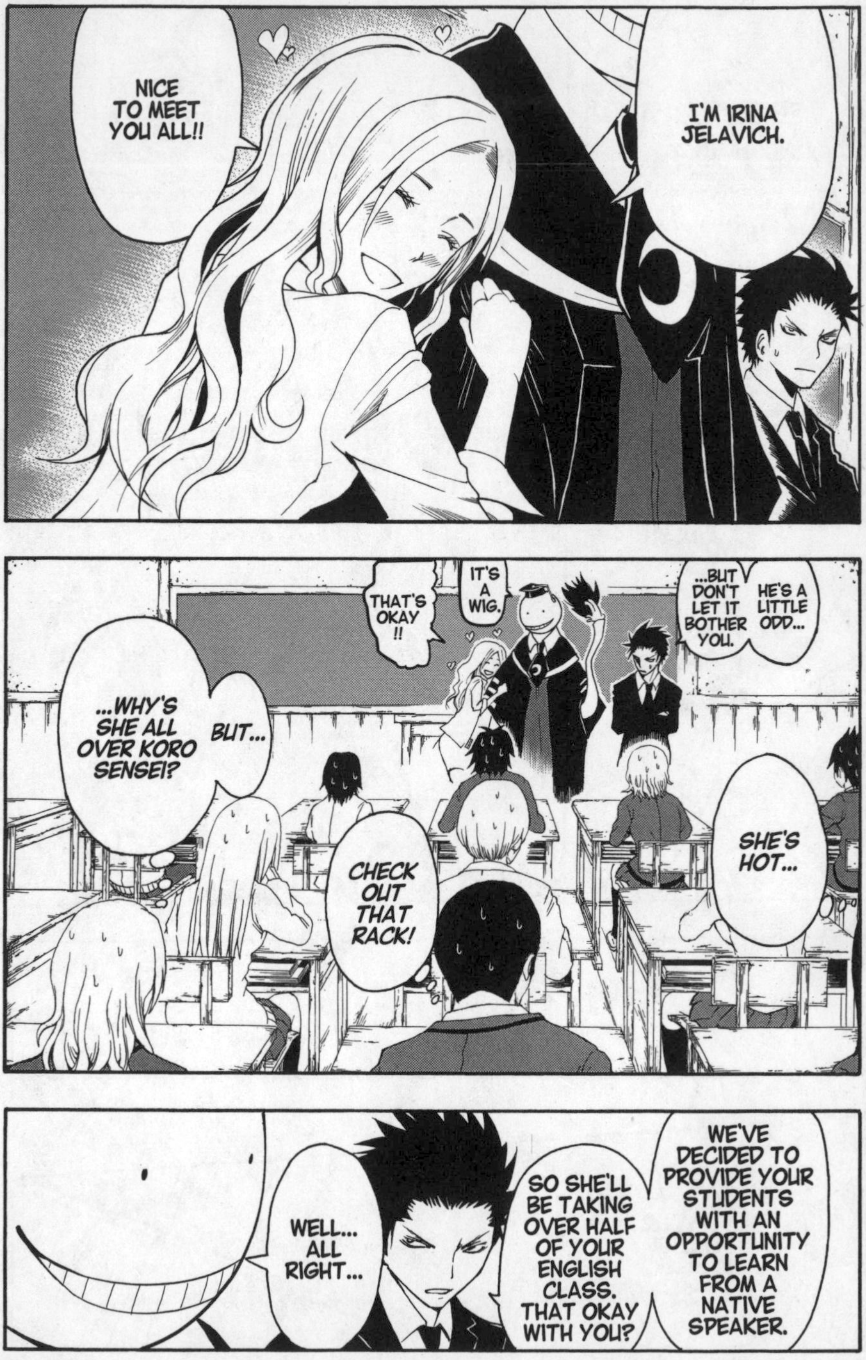
I'M IRINA JELAVICH.
NICE TO MEET YOU ALL!!
HE'S A LITTLE ODD...
...BUT DON'T LET IT BOTHER YOU.
IT'S A WIG.
THAT'S OKAY!!
SHE'S HOT...
BUT...
...WHY'S SHE ALL OVER KORO SENSEI?
CHECK OUT THAT RACK!
WE'VE DECIDED TO PROVIDE YOUR STUDENTS WITH AN OPPORTUNITY TO LEARN FROM A NATIVE SPEAKER.
SO SHE'LL BE TAKING OVER HALF OF YOUR ENGLISH CLASS. THAT OKAY WITH YOU?
WELL... ALL RIGHT...

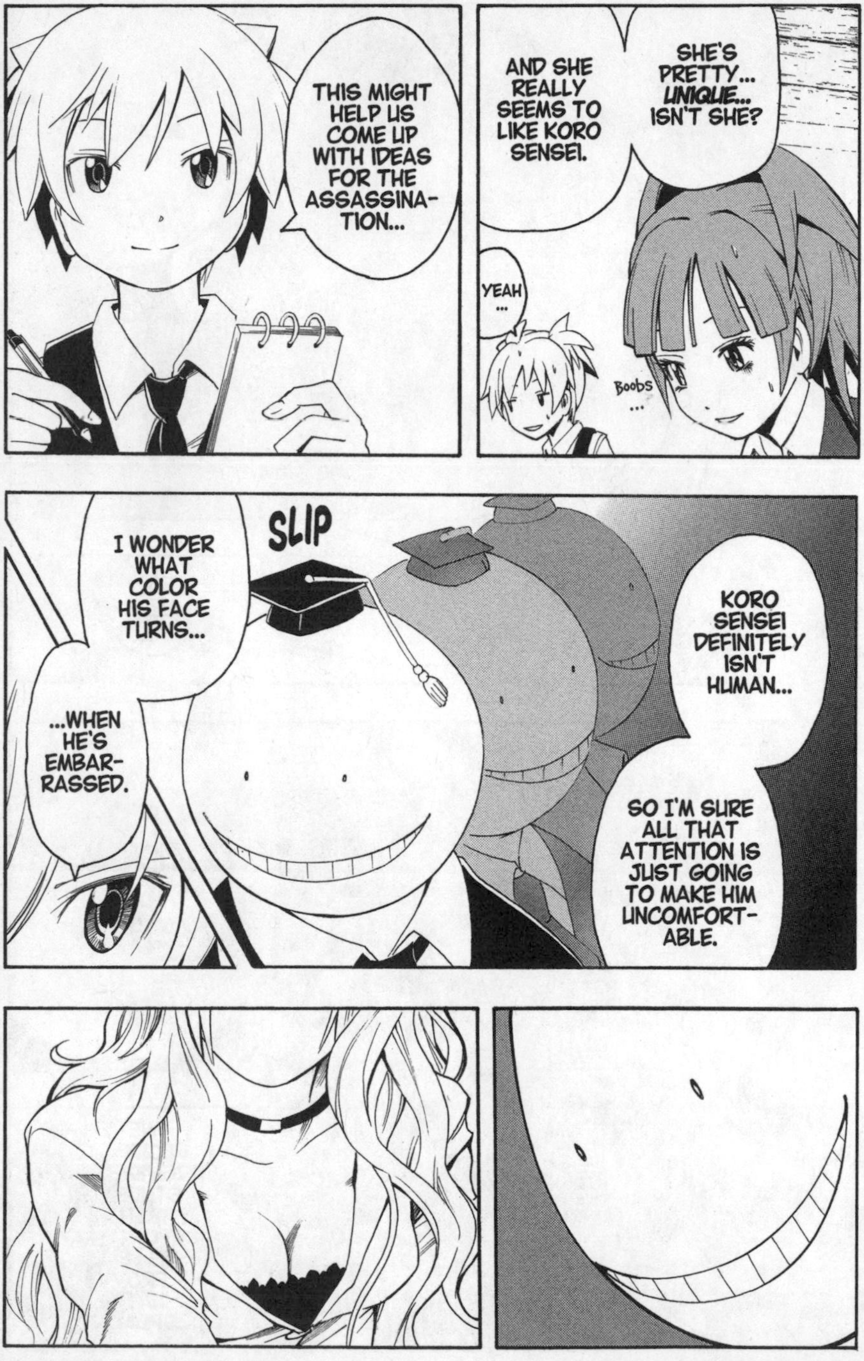
SHE'S PRETTY... UNIQUE... ISN'T SHE?
AND SHE REALLY SEEMS TO LIKE KORO SENSEI.
YEAH...
Boobs...
THIS MIGHT HELP US COME UP WITH IDEAS FOR THE ASSASSINATION...
KORO SENSEI DEFINITELY ISN'T HUMAN...
SO I'M SURE ALL THAT ATTENTION IS JUST GOING TO MAKE HIM UNCOMFORTABLE.
SLIP
I WONDER WHAT COLOR HIS FACE TURNS...
...WHEN HE'S EMBARRASSED.

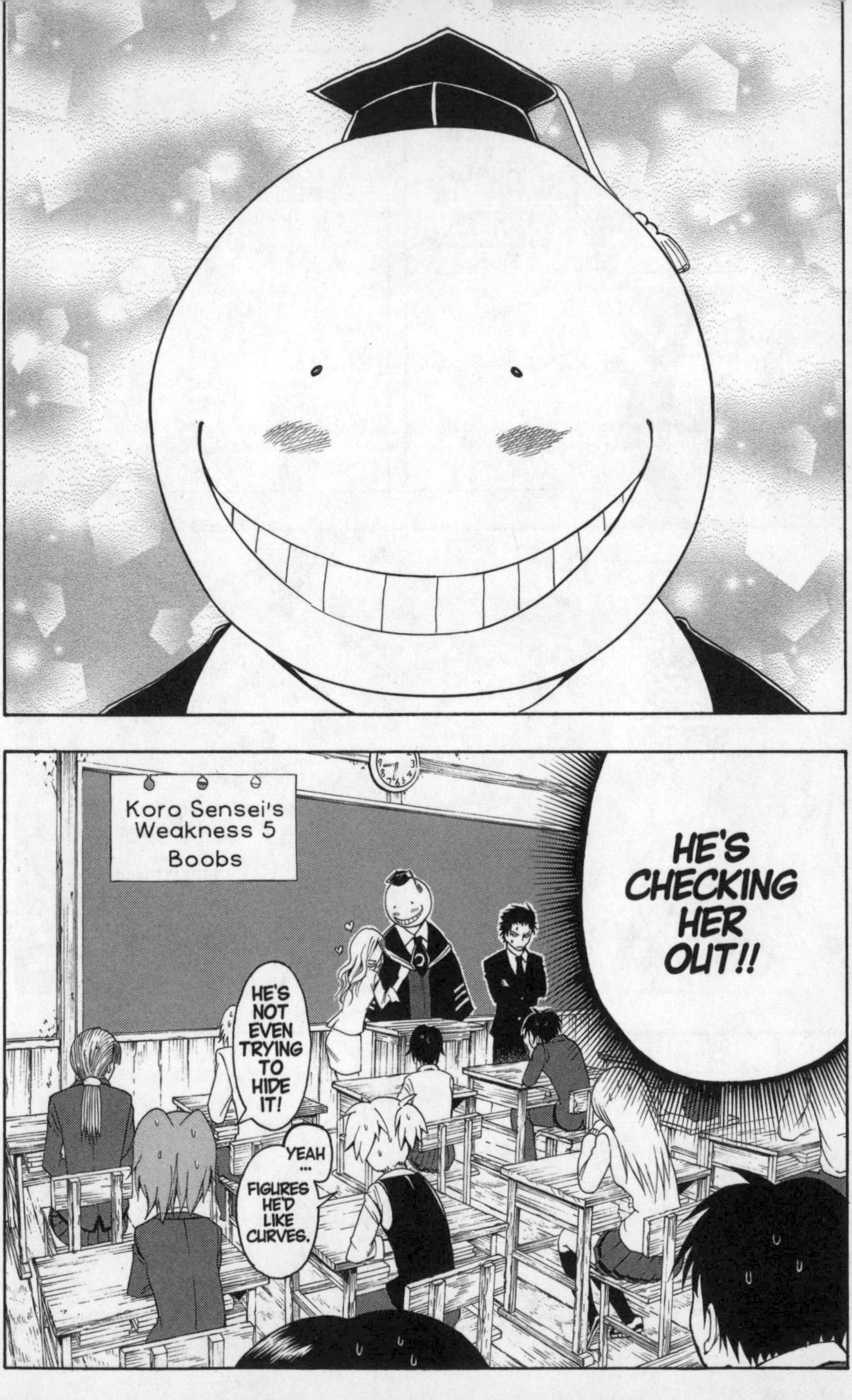
HE'S CHECKING HER OUT!!
Koro Sensei's Weakness 5 Boobs
HE'S NOT EVEN TRYING TO HIDE IT!
YEAH... FIGURES HE'D LIKE CURVES.

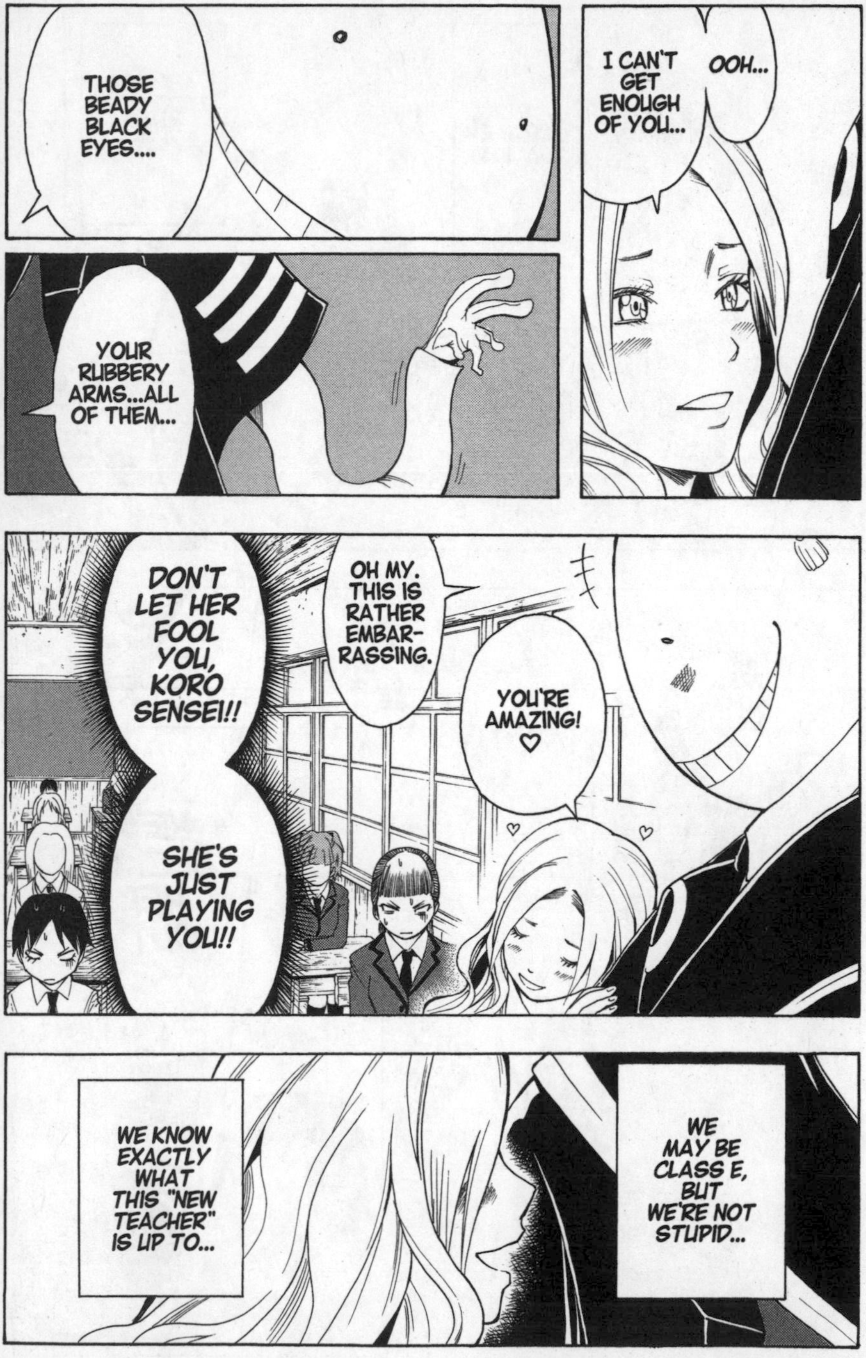
OOH...
I CAN'T GET ENOUGH OF YOU...
THOSE BEADY BLACK EYES....
YOUR RUBBERY ARMS...ALL OF THEM...
YOU'RE AMAZING! ♡
OH MY. THIS IS RATHER EMBARRASSING.
DON'T LET HER FOOL YOU, KORO SENSEI!!
SHE'S JUST PLAYING YOU!!
WE MAY BE CLASS E, BUT WE'RE NOT STUPID...
WE KNOW EXACTLY WHAT THIS "NEW TEACHER" IS UP TO...

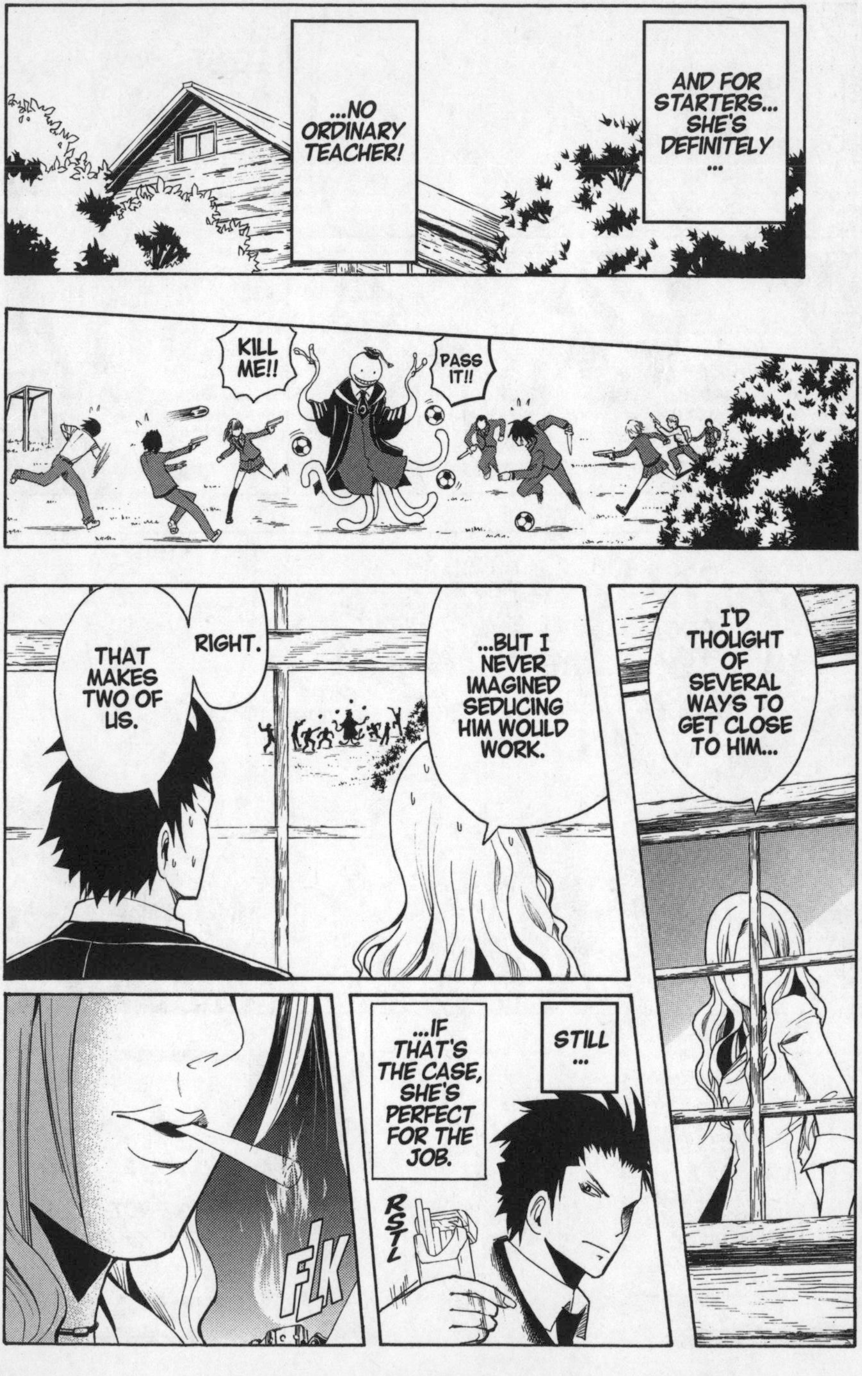
AND FOR STARTERS... SHE'S DEFINITELY ...
...NO ORDINARY TEACHER!
PASS IT!!
KILL ME!!
I'D THOUGHT OF SEVERAL WAYS TO GET CLOSE TO HIM...
...BUT I NEVER IMAGINED SEDUCING HIM WOULD WORK.
RIGHT.
THAT MAKES TWO OF US.
STILL ...
...IF THAT'S THE CASE, SHE'S PERFECT FOR THE JOB.
RSTL
FLK

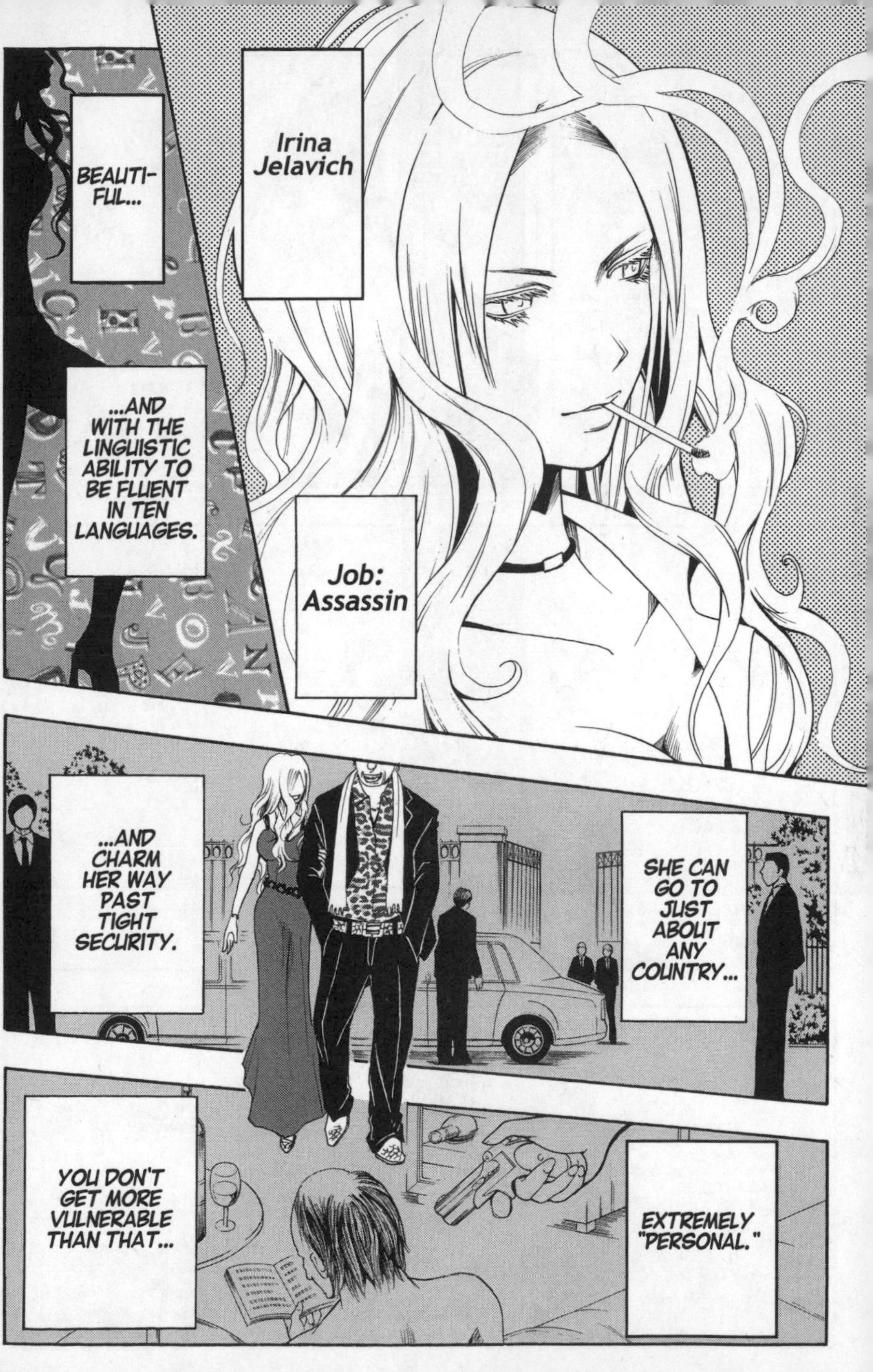
Irina Jelavich
Job: Assassin
BEAUTI-FUL...
...AND WITH THE LINGUISTIC ABILITY TO BE FLUENT IN TEN LANGUAGES.
SHE CAN GO TO JUST ABOUT ANY COUNTRY...
...AND CHARM HER WAY PAST TIGHT SECURITY.
EXTREMELY "PERSONAL."
YOU DON'T GET MORE VULNERABLE THAN THAT...

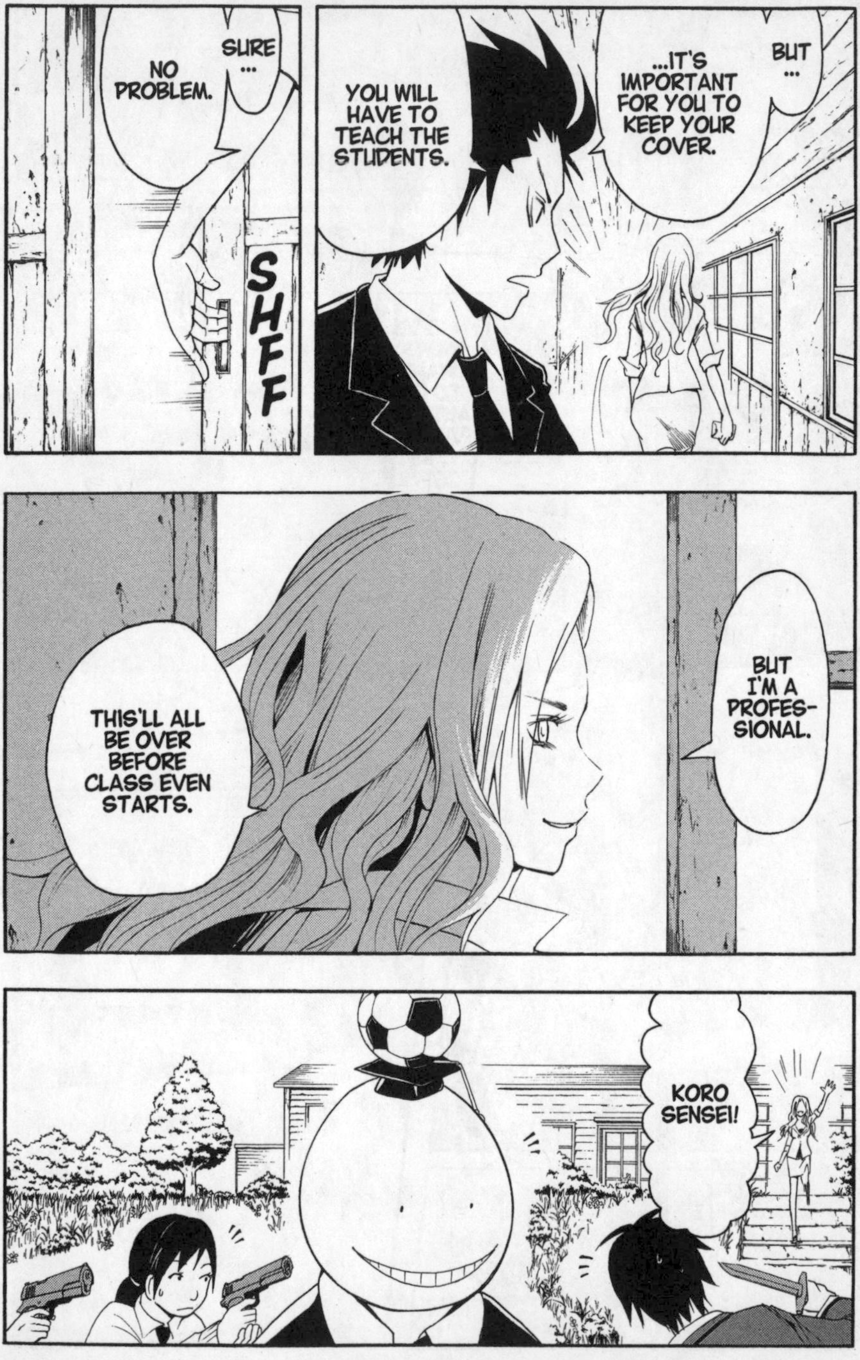
BUT ...
...IT'S IMPORTANT FOR YOU TO KEEP YOUR COVER.
YOU WILL HAVE TO TEACH THE STUDENTS.
SURE ...
NO PROBLEM.
SHFF
BUT I'M A PROFES-SIONAL.
THIS'LL ALL BE OVER BEFORE CLASS EVEN STARTS.
KORO SENSEI!

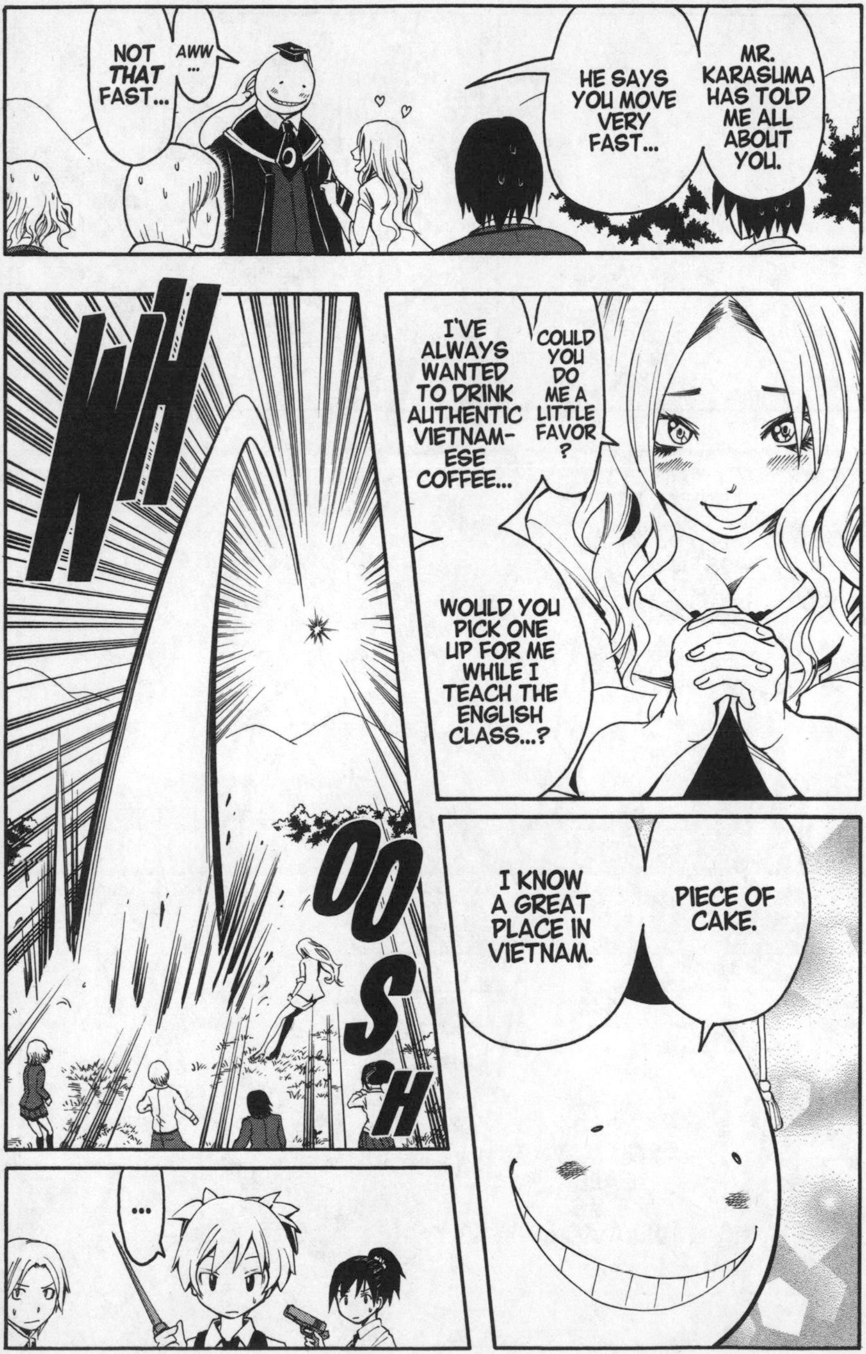
MR. KARASUMA HAS TOLD ME ALL ABOUT YOU.
HE SAYS YOU MOVE VERY FAST...
AWW...
NOT THAT FAST...
COULD YOU DO ME A LITTLE FAVOR?
I'VE ALWAYS WANTED TO DRINK AUTHENTIC VIETNAM-ESE COFFEE...
WOULD YOU PICK ONE UP FOR ME WHILE I TEACH THE ENGLISH CLASS...?
PIECE OF CAKE.
I KNOW A GREAT PLACE IN VIETNAM.
WHOOSH
...

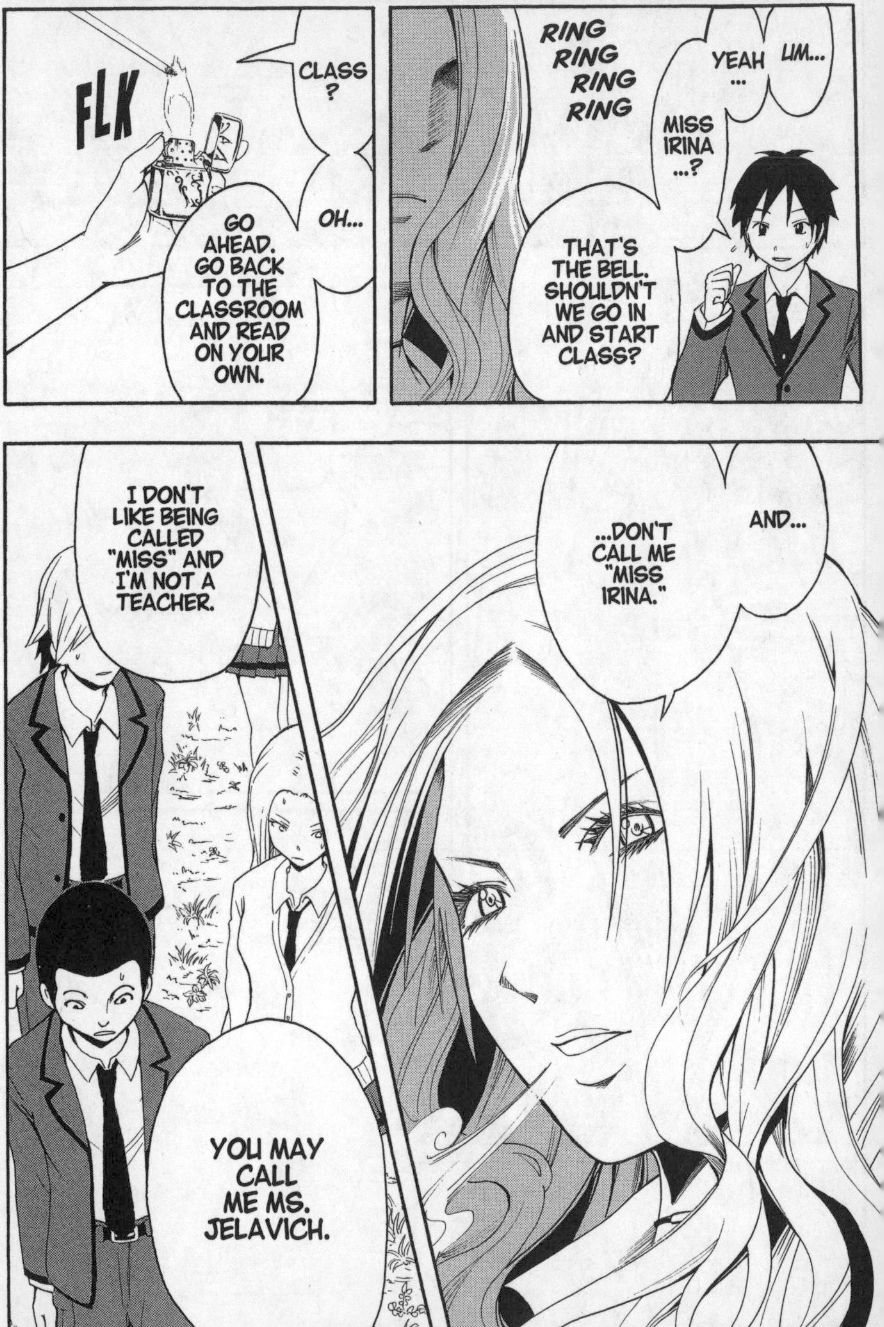
UM...
YEAH...
MISS IRINA...?
RING RING RING RING
THAT'S THE BELL. SHOULDN'T WE GO IN AND START CLASS?
CLASS?
OH...
FLK
GO AHEAD. GO BACK TO THE CLASSROOM AND READ ON YOUR OWN.
AND...
...DON'T CALL ME "MISS IRINA."
I DON'T LIKE BEING CALLED "MISS" AND I'M NOT A TEACHER.
YOU MAY CALL ME MS. JELAVICH.

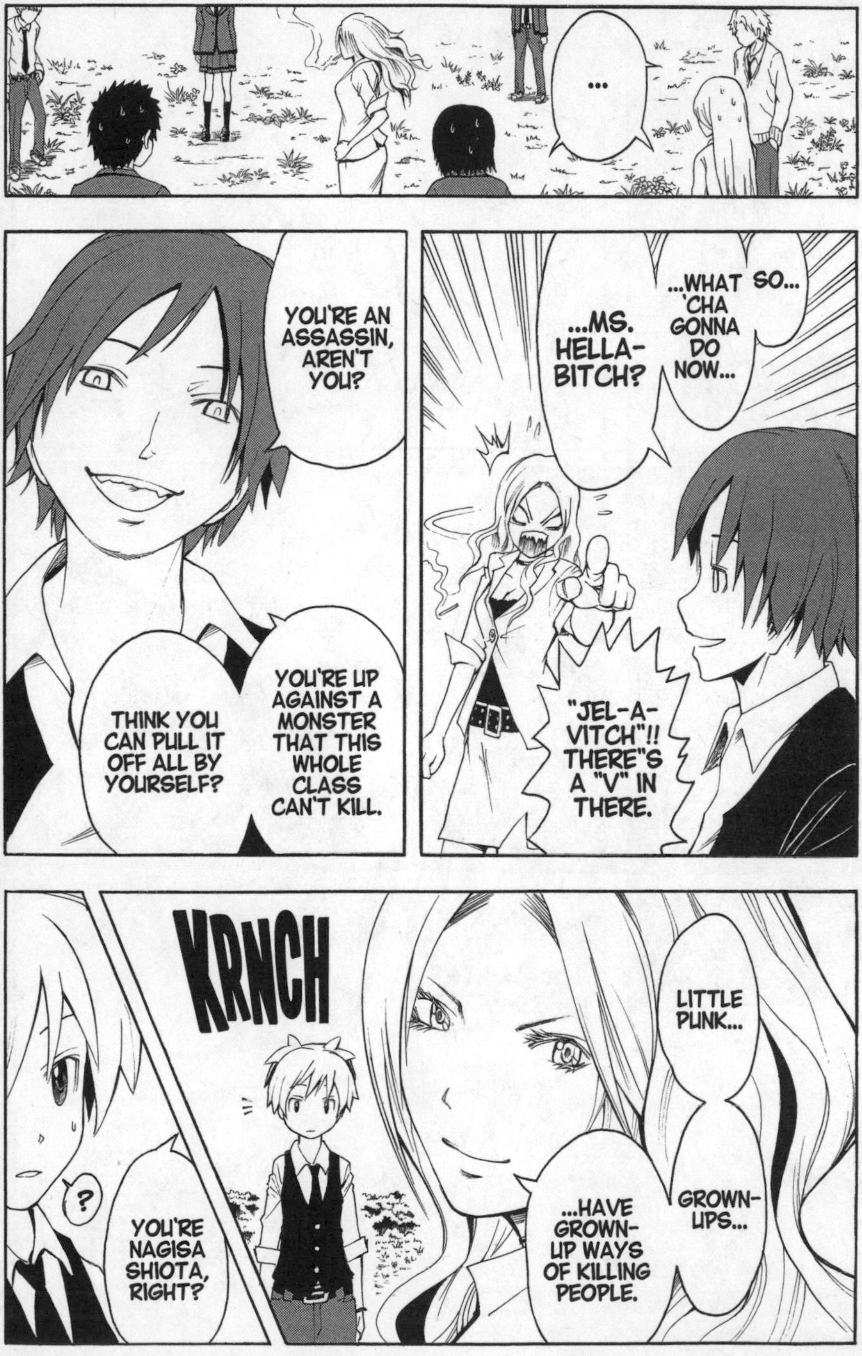
...
SO... ...WHAT 'CHA GONNA DO NOW...
...MS. HELLA-BITCH?
"JEL-A-VITCH"!! THERE"S A "V" IN THERE.
YOU'RE AN ASSASSIN, AREN'T YOU?
YOU'RE UP AGAINST A MONSTER THAT THIS WHOLE CLASS CAN'T KILL.
THINK YOU CAN PULL IT OFF ALL BY YOURSELF?
KRNCH
LITTLE PUNK...
GROWN-UPS...
...HAVE GROWN-UP WAYS OF KILLING PEOPLE.
?
YOU'RE NAGISA SHIOTA, RIGHT?

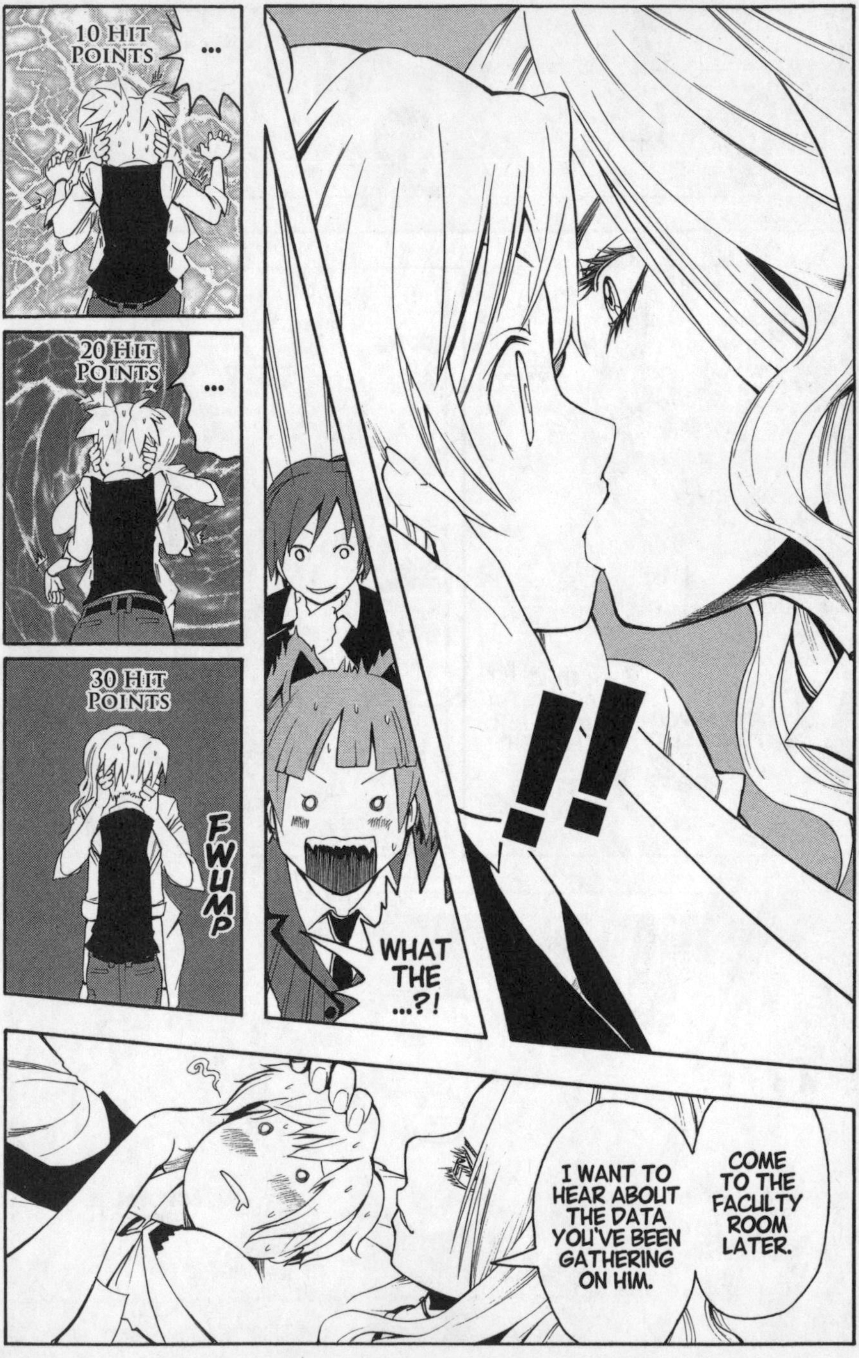
!!
WHAT THE ...?!
10 HIT POINTS
...
20 HIT POINTS
...
30 HIT POINTS
FWUMP
COME TO THE FACULTY ROOM LATER.
I WANT TO HEAR ABOUT THE DATA YOU'VE BEEN GATHERING ON HIM.

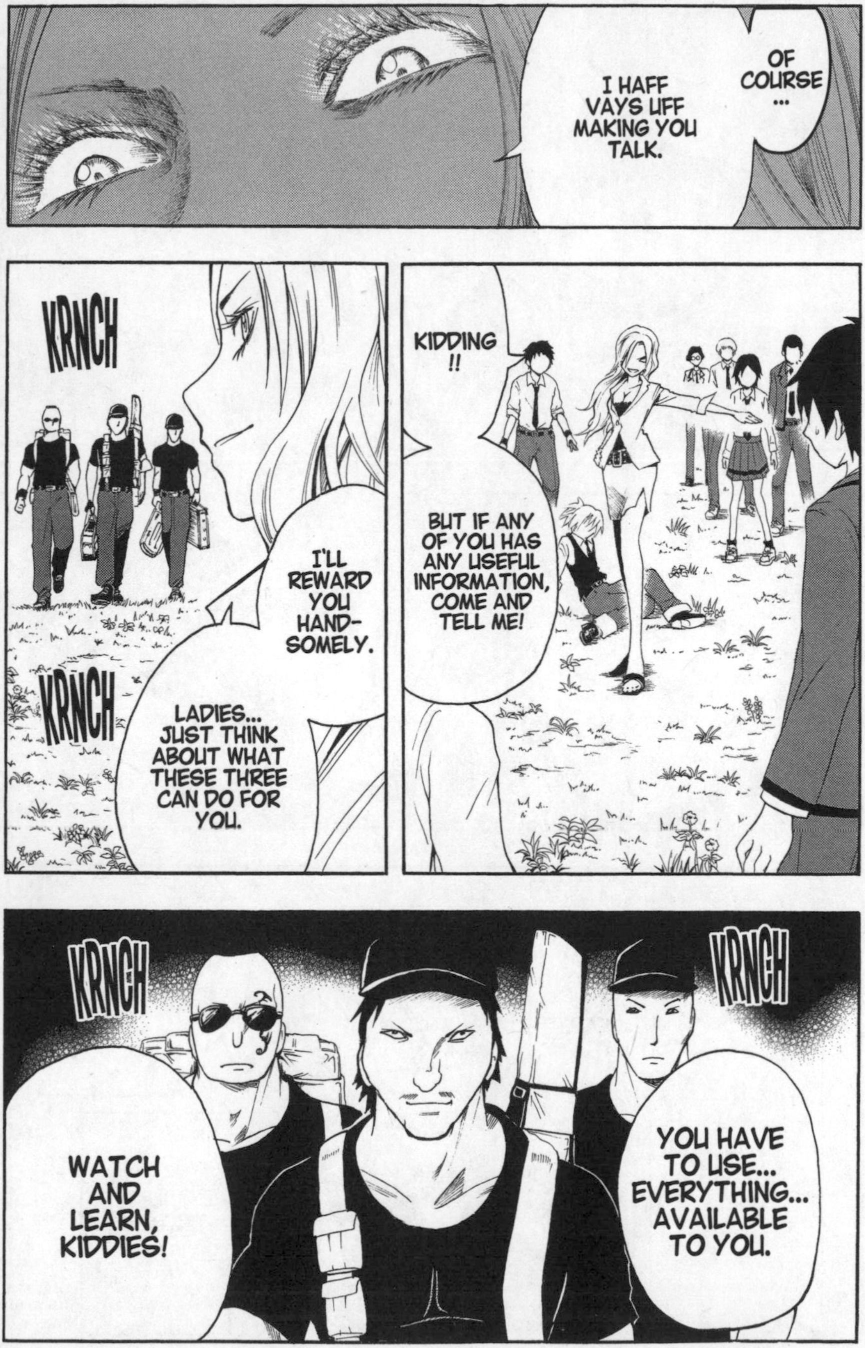
OF COURSE...
I HAFF VAYS UFF MAKING YOU TALK.
KIDDING!!
BUT IF ANY OF YOU HAS ANY USEFUL INFORMATION, COME AND TELL ME!
I'LL REWARD YOU HANDSOMELY.
KRNCH
LADIES... JUST THINK ABOUT WHAT THESE THREE CAN DO FOR YOU.
KRNCH
KRNCH
YOU HAVE TO USE... EVERYTHING... AVAILABLE TO YOU.
KRNCH
WATCH AND LEARN, KIDDIES!

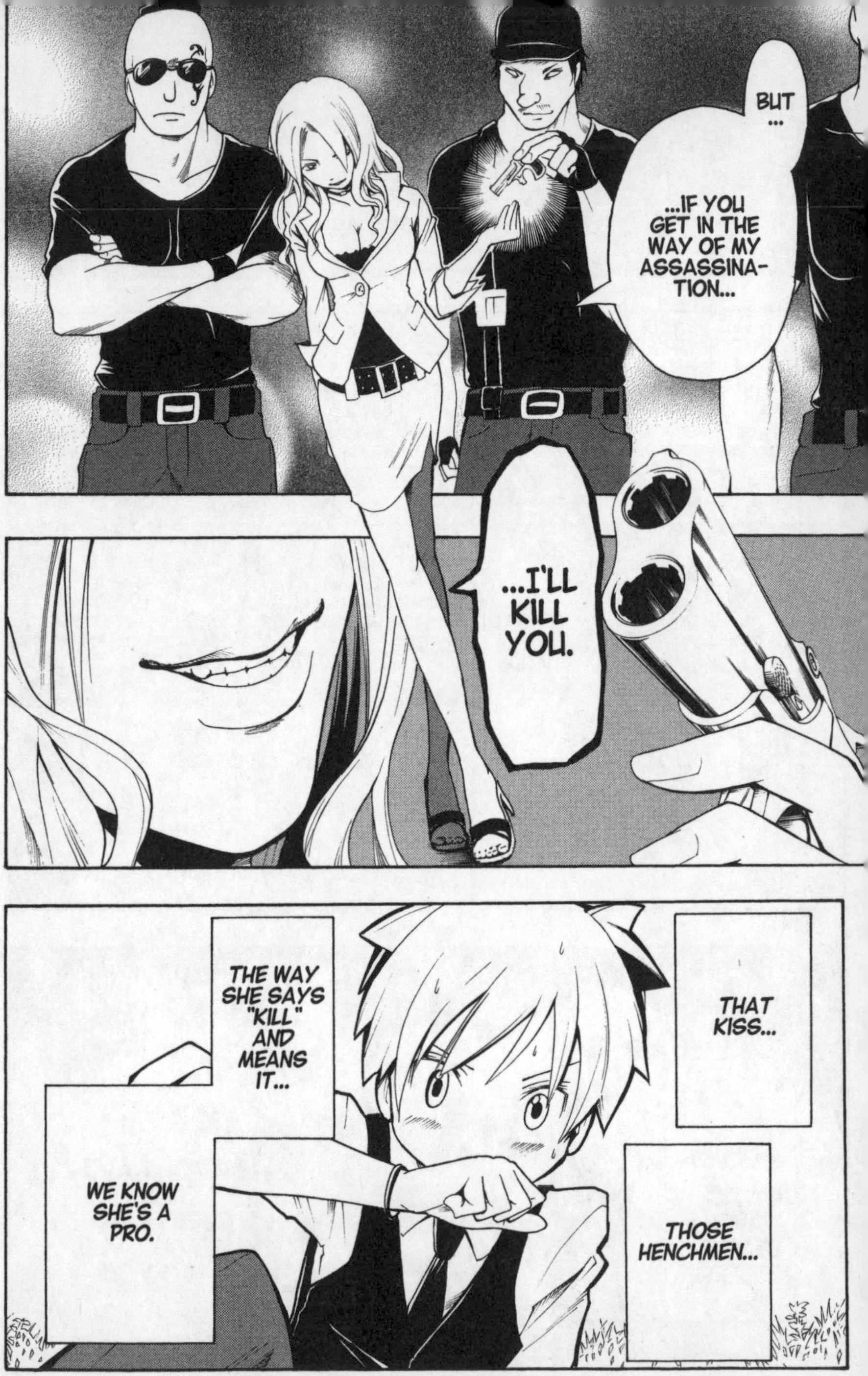
BUT ...
...IF YOU GET IN THE WAY OF MY ASSASSINA-TION...
...I'LL KILL YOU.
THAT KISS...
THOSE HENCHMEN...
THE WAY SHE SAYS "KILL" AND MEANS IT...
WE KNOW SHE'S A PRO.

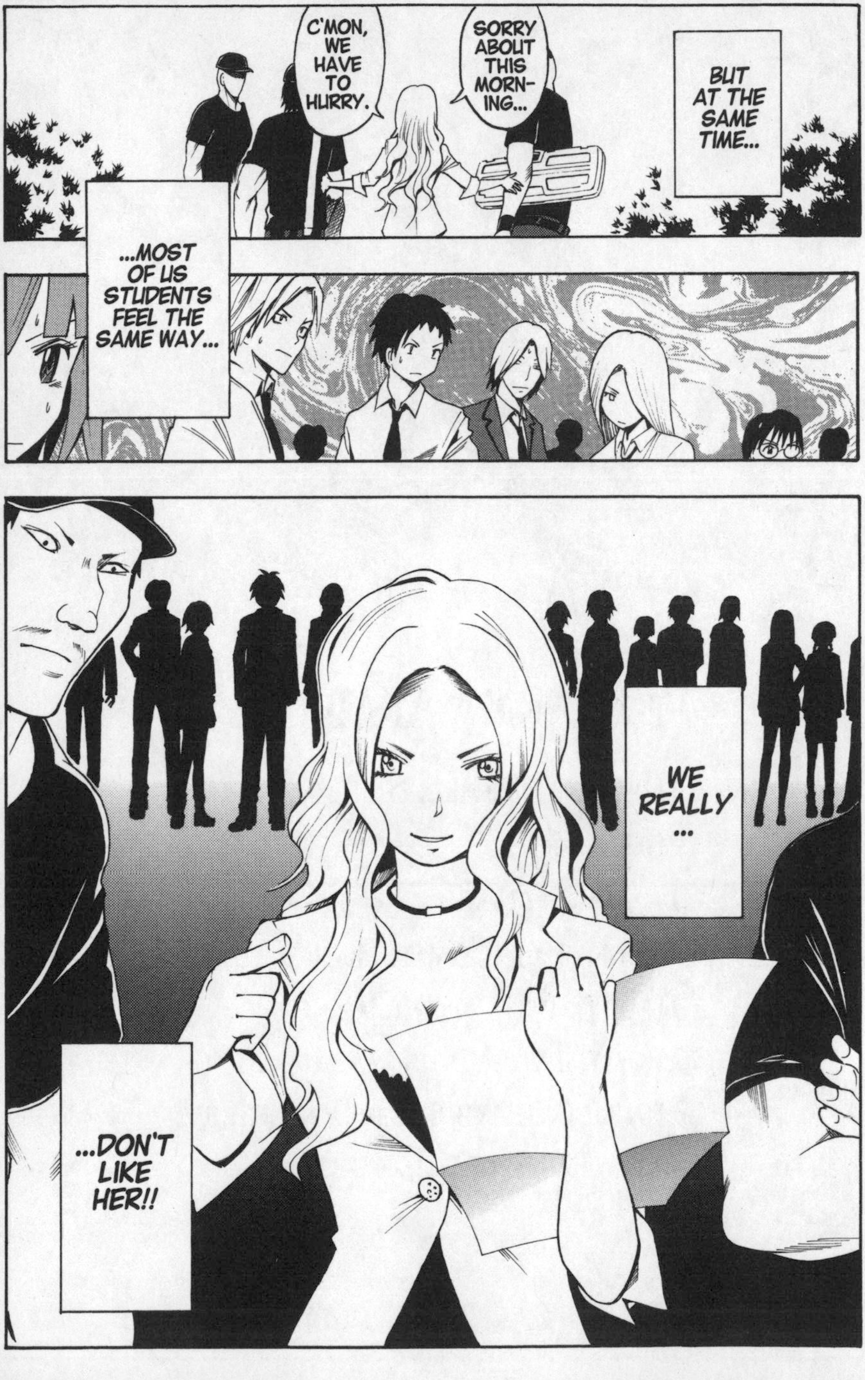
BUT AT THE SAME TIME...
SORRY ABOUT THIS MORNING...
C'MON, WE HAVE TO HURRY.
...MOST OF US STUDENTS FEEL THE SAME WAY...
WE REALLY ...
...DON'T LIKE HER!!

e-1 Karma Akabane

- 🙂 Birthday: December 25
- 🙂 Height: 5' 9"
- 🙂 Weight: 132 lbs.
- 🙂 Favorite Subject: Mathematics
- 🙂 Least Favorite Subject: Japanese
- 🙂 Hobby/Skill: Taunting and Harassing
- 🙂 Future Goal: Evil Government Official
- 🙂 A new illness he'd like to spread: Senioritis

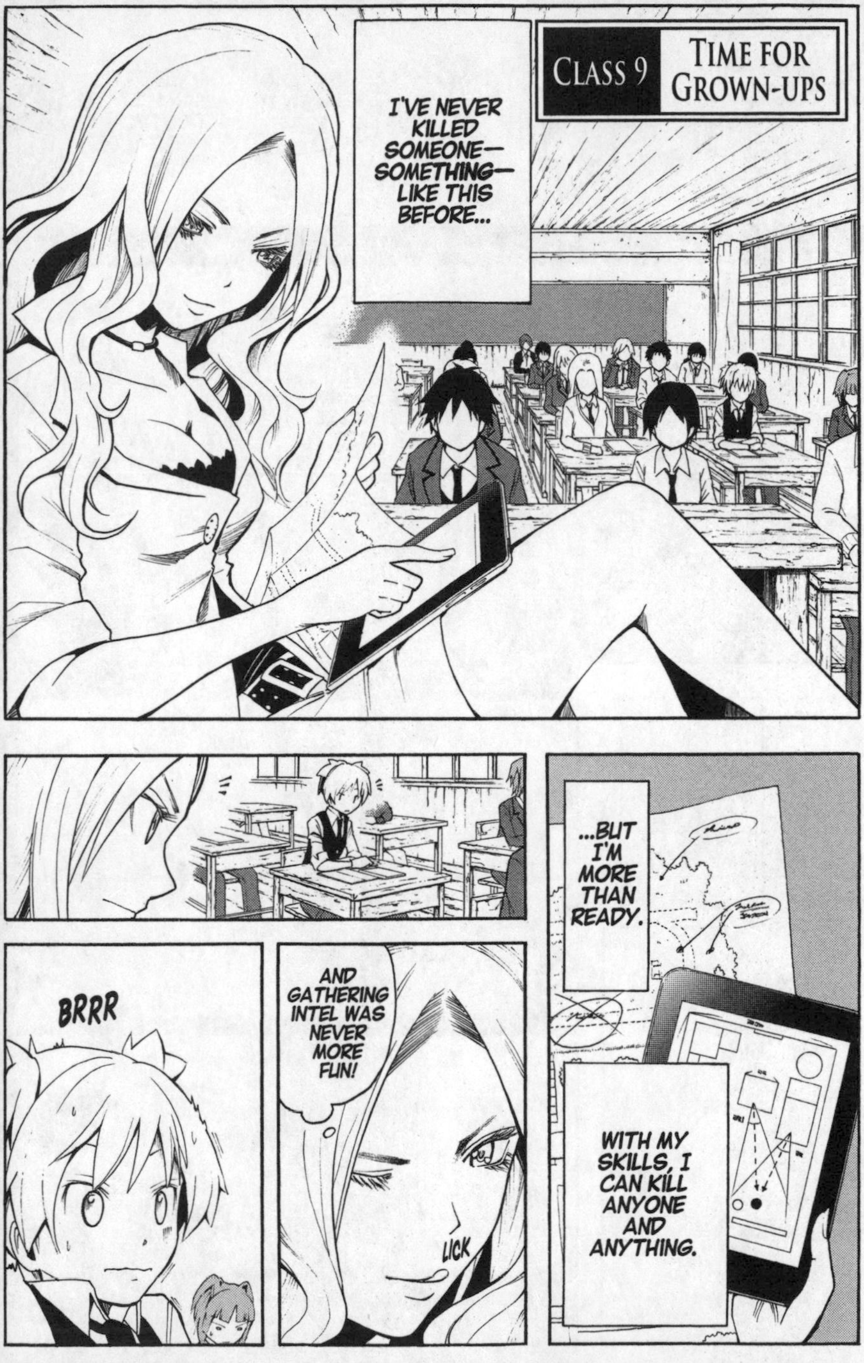
CLASS 9
TIME FOR GROWN-UPS
I'VE NEVER KILLED SOMEONE— SOMETHING— LIKE THIS BEFORE...
...BUT I'M MORE THAN READY.
WITH MY SKILLS, I CAN KILL ANYONE AND ANYTHING.
AND GATHERING INTEL WAS NEVER MORE FUN!
LICK
BRRR

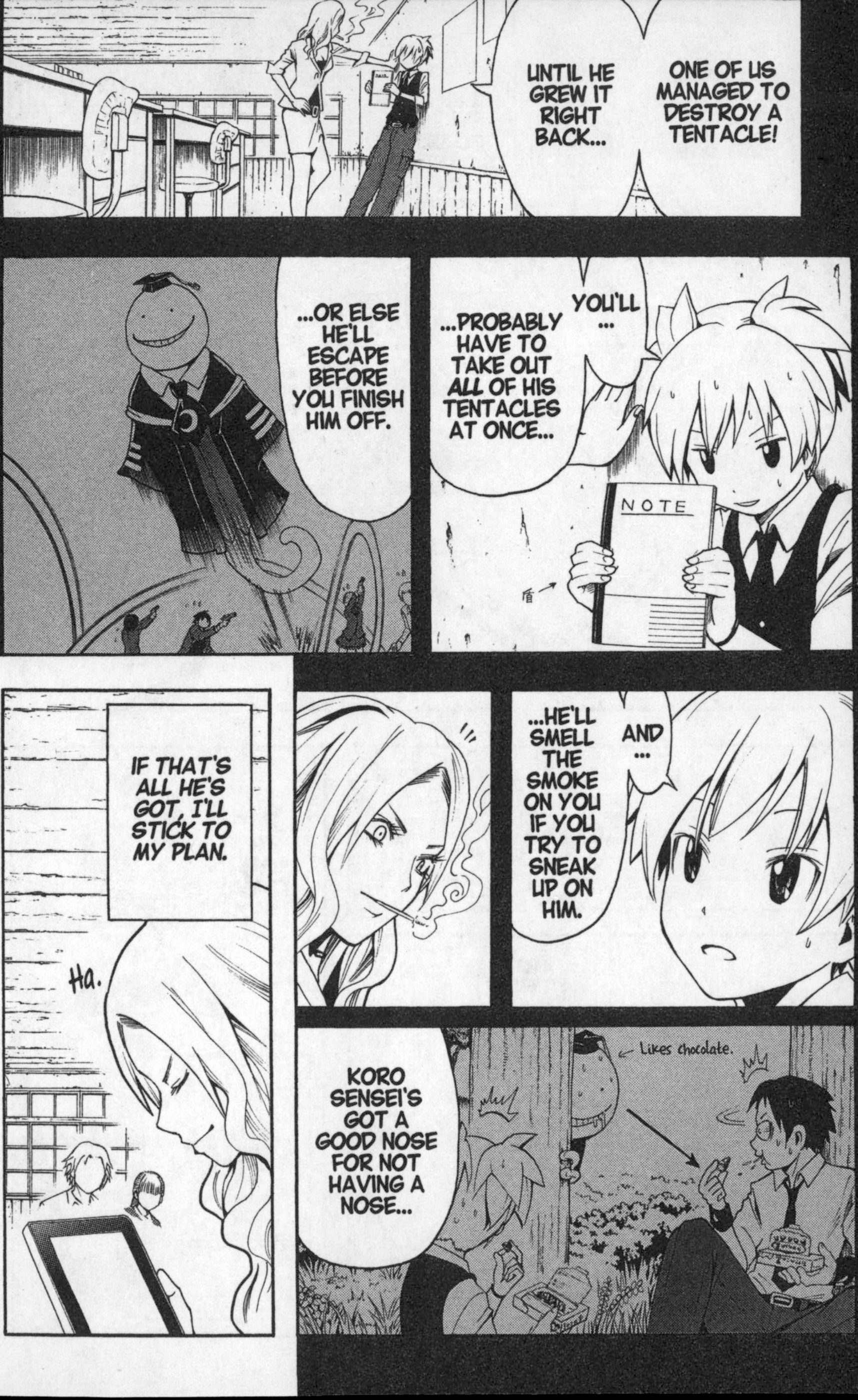
ONE OF US MANAGED TO DESTROY A TENTACLE!
UNTIL HE GREW IT RIGHT BACK...
YOU'LL ...
...PROBABLY HAVE TO TAKE OUT ALL OF HIS TENTACLES AT ONCE...
...OR ELSE HE'LL ESCAPE BEFORE YOU FINISH HIM OFF.
NOTE
AND ...
...HE'LL SMELL THE SMOKE ON YOU IF YOU TRY TO SNEAK UP ON HIM.
KORO SENSEI'S GOT A GOOD NOSE FOR NOT HAVING A NOSE...
Likes chocolate.
IF THAT'S ALL HE'S GOT, I'LL STICK TO MY PLAN.
Ha.

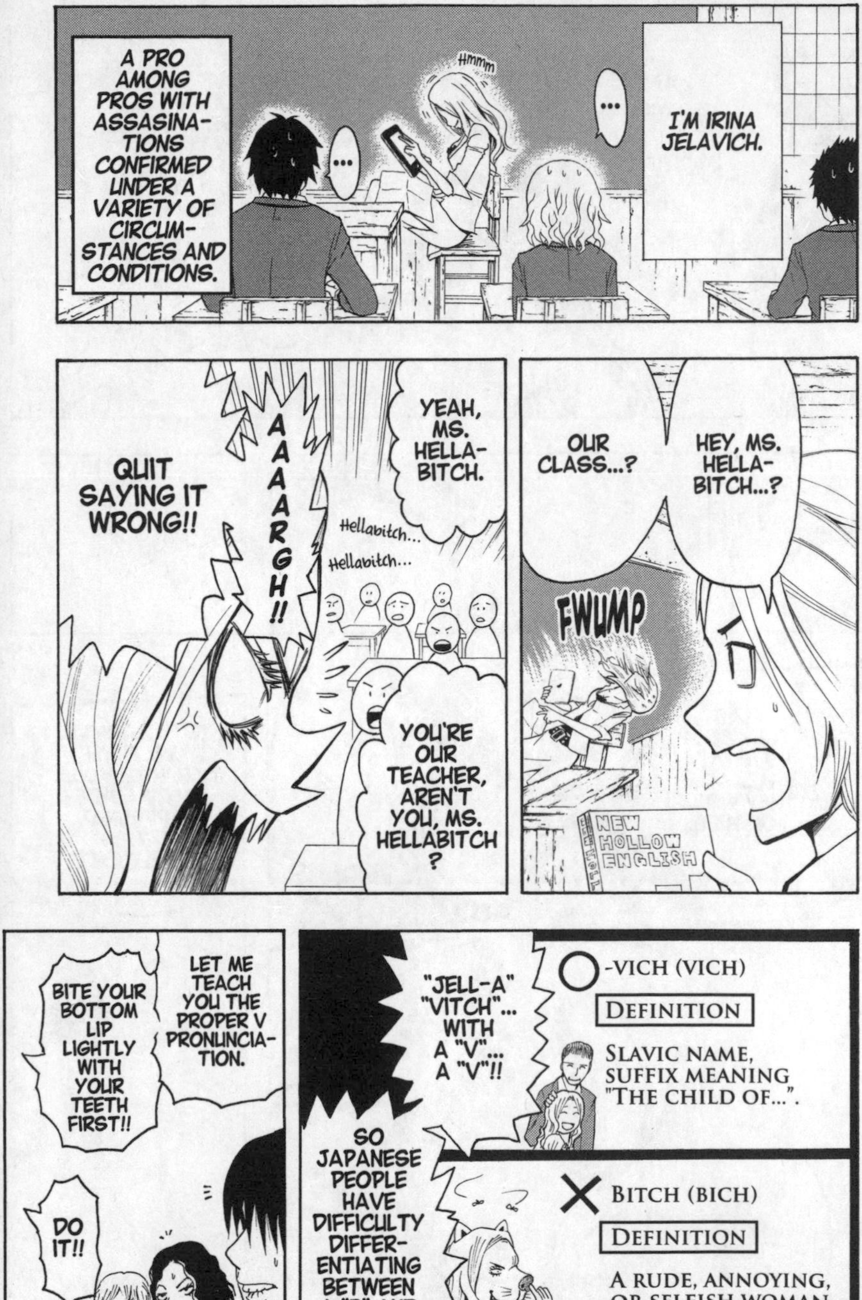
I'M IRINA JELAVICH.
...
Hmmm
...
A PRO AMONG PROS WITH ASSASINATIONS CONFIRMED UNDER A VARIETY OF CIRCUMSTANCES AND CONDITIONS.
HEY, MS. HELLA-BITCH...?
OUR CLASS...?
FWUMP
NEW HOLLOW ENGLISH
YEAH, MS. HELLA-BITCH.
AAAAARGH!!
QUIT SAYING IT WRONG!!
Hellabitch...
Hellabitch...
YOU'RE OUR TEACHER, AREN'T YOU, MS. HELLABITCH?
-VICH (VICH)
DEFINITION
SLAVIC NAME, SUFFIX MEANING "THE CHILD OF...".
"JELL-A" "VITCH"... WITH A "V"... A "V"!!
SO JAPANESE PEOPLE HAVE DIFFICULTY DIFFERENTIATING BETWEEN A "B" AND A "V"?
BITCH (BICH)
DEFINITION
A RUDE, ANNOYING, OR SELFISH WOMAN, OR A FEMALE DOG.
LET ME TEACH YOU THE PROPER V PRONUNCIATION.
BITE YOUR BOTTOM LIP LIGHTLY WITH YOUR TEETH FIRST!!
DO IT!!

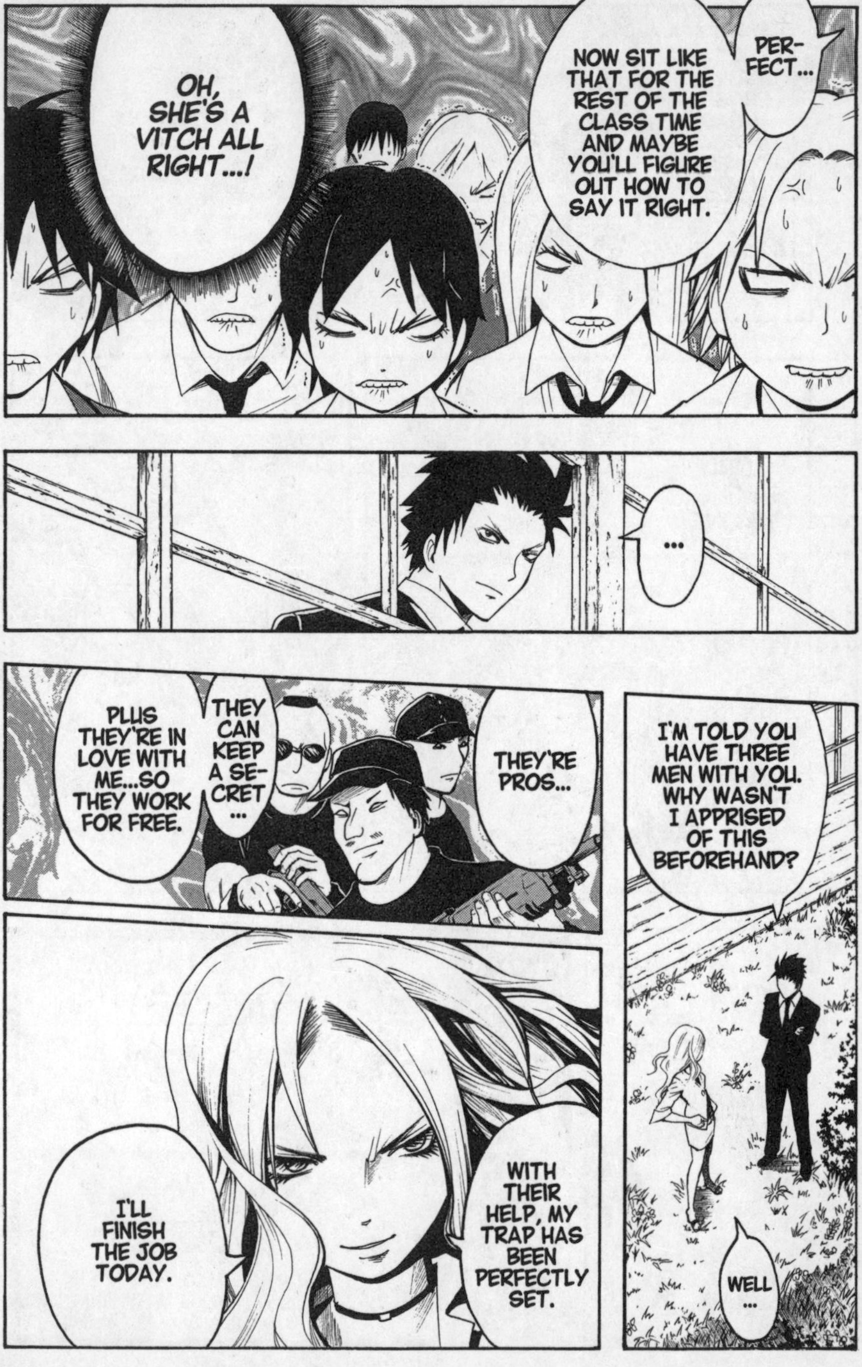
PER-FECT...
NOW SIT LIKE THAT FOR THE REST OF THE CLASS TIME AND MAYBE YOU'LL FIGURE OUT HOW TO SAY IT RIGHT.
OH, SHE'S A VITCH ALL RIGHT...!
...
I'M TOLD YOU HAVE THREE MEN WITH YOU. WHY WASN'T I APPRISED OF THIS BEFOREHAND?
WELL...
THEY'RE PROS...
THEY CAN KEEP A SE-CRET...
PLUS THEY'RE IN LOVE WITH ME...SO THEY WORK FOR FREE.
WITH THEIR HELP, MY TRAP HAS BEEN PERFECTLY SET.
I'LL FINISH THE JOB TODAY.

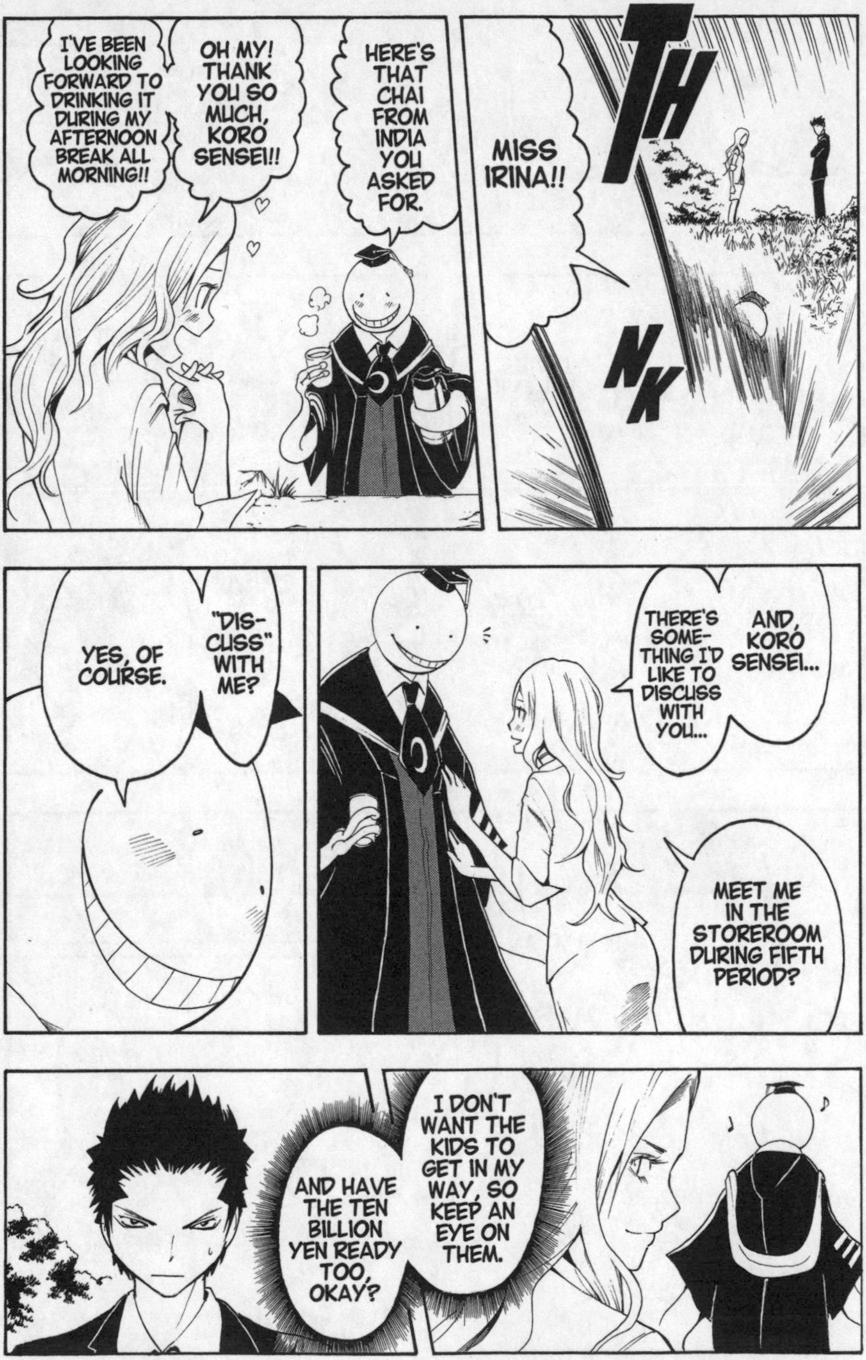
THNK
MISS IRINA!!
HERE'S THAT CHAI FROM INDIA YOU ASKED FOR.
OH MY! THANK YOU SO MUCH, KORO SENSEI!!
I'VE BEEN LOOKING FORWARD TO DRINKING IT DURING MY AFTERNOON BREAK ALL MORNING!!
AND, KORO SENSEI...
THERE'S SOME-THING I'D LIKE TO DISCUSS WITH YOU...
MEET ME IN THE STOREROOM DURING FIFTH PERIOD?
"DIS-CUSS" WITH ME?
YES, OF COURSE.
I DON'T WANT THE KIDS TO GET IN MY WAY, SO KEEP AN EYE ON THEM.
AND HAVE THE TEN BILLION YEN READY TOO, OKAY?

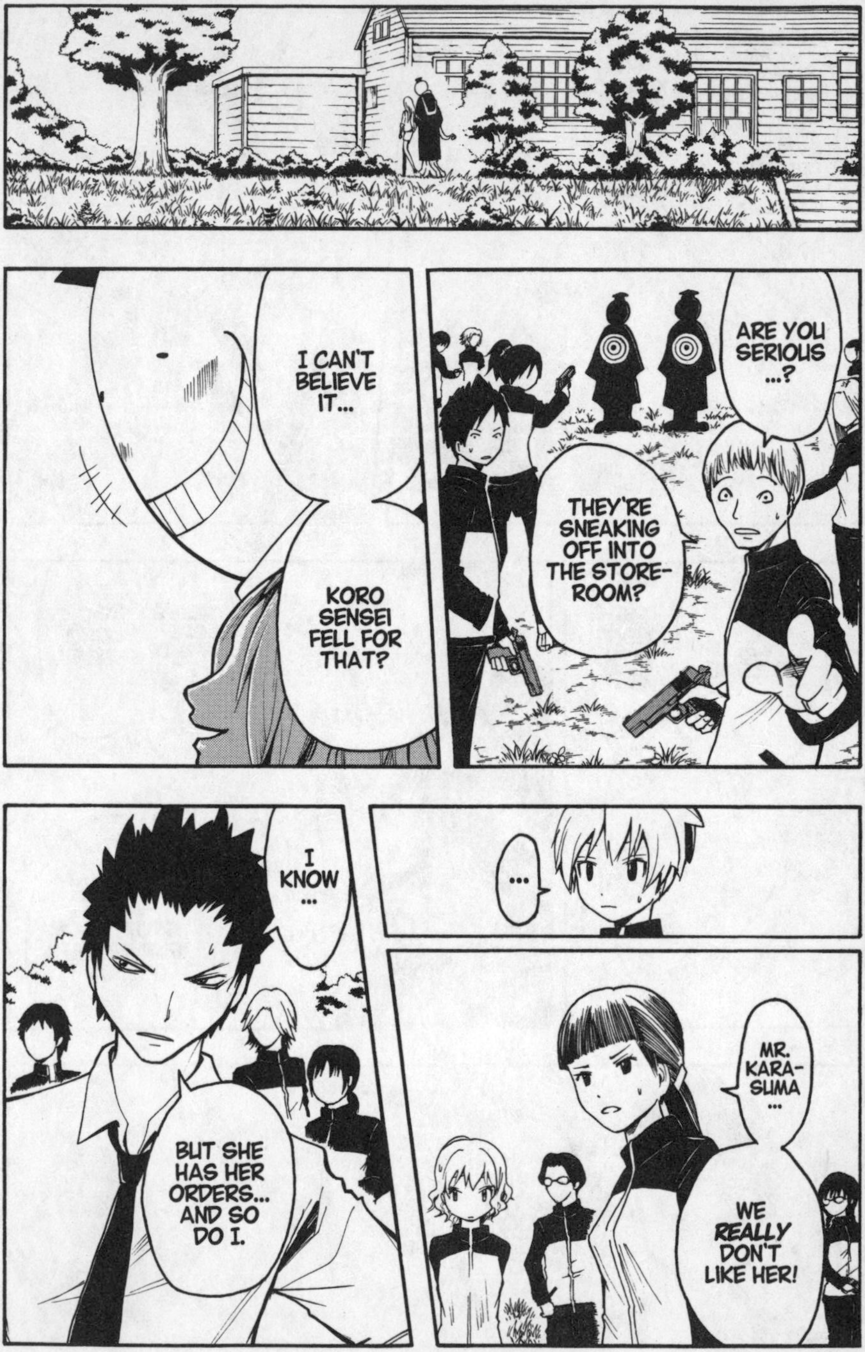
ARE YOU SERIOUS ...?
THEY'RE SNEAKING OFF INTO THE STORE-ROOM?
I CAN'T BELIEVE IT...
KORO SENSEI FELL FOR THAT?
...
MR. KARASUMA ...
WE REALLY DON'T LIKE HER!
I KNOW ...
BUT SHE HAS HER ORDERS... AND SO DO I.

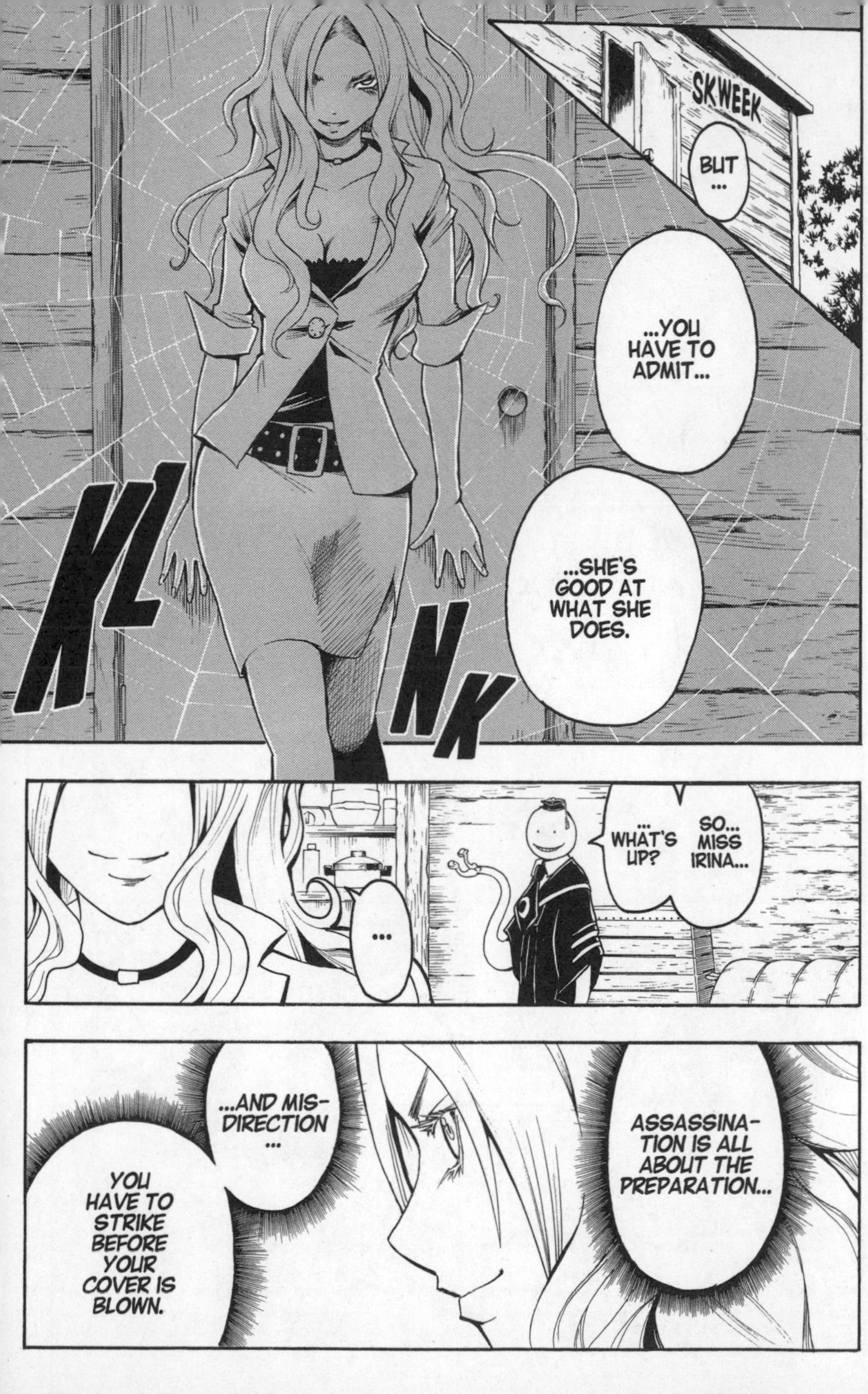
SKWEEK
BUT...
...YOU HAVE TO ADMIT...
...SHE'S GOOD AT WHAT SHE DOES.
KLNK
SO... MISS IRINA...
...WHAT'S UP?
...
ASSASSINATION IS ALL ABOUT THE PREPARATION...
...AND MISDIRECTION...
YOU HAVE TO STRIKE BEFORE YOUR COVER IS BLOWN.

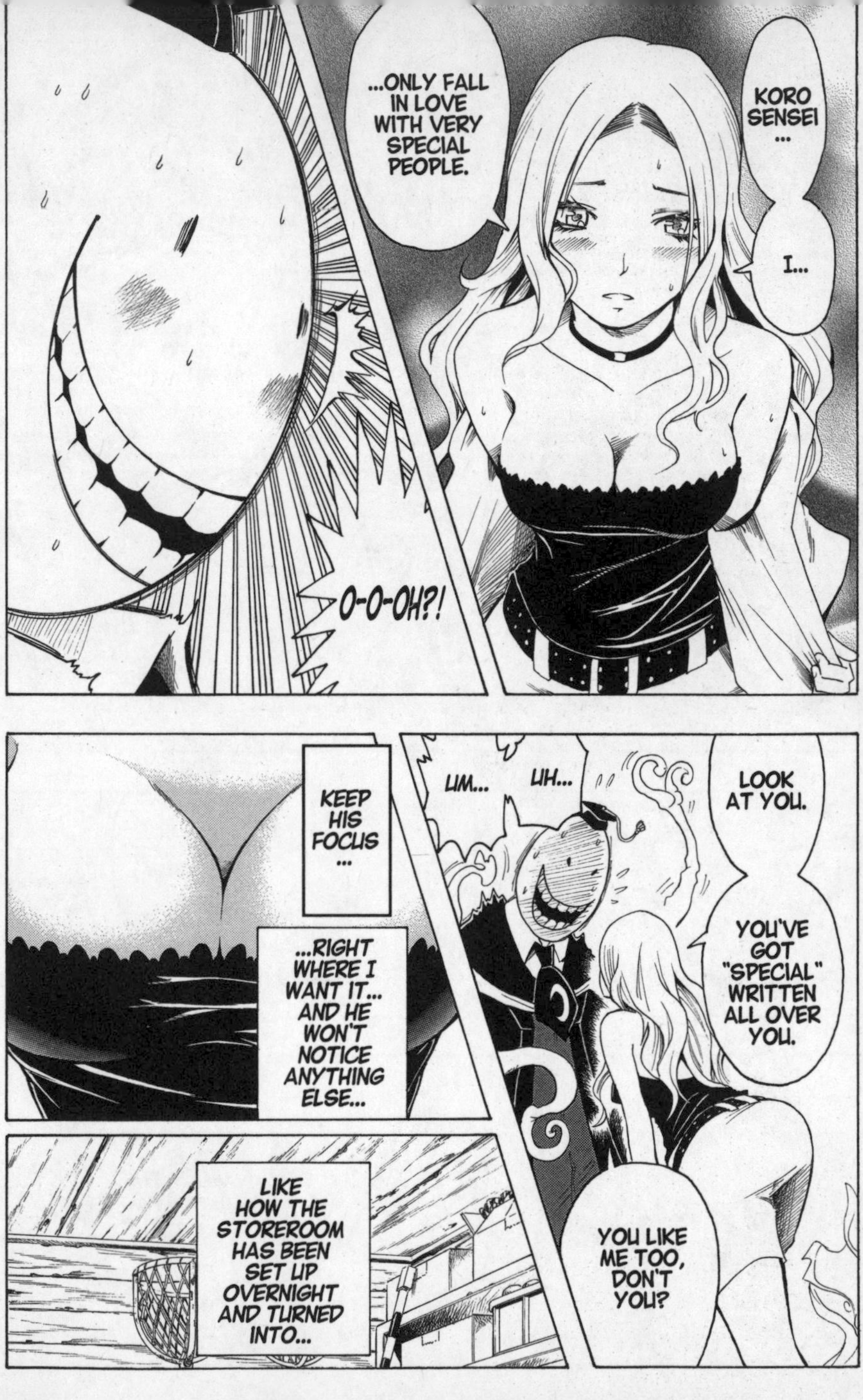
KORO SENSEI ...
I...
...ONLY FALL IN LOVE WITH VERY SPECIAL PEOPLE.
O-O-OH?!
LOOK AT YOU.
YOU'VE GOT "SPECIAL" WRITTEN ALL OVER YOU.
UH...
UM...
YOU LIKE ME TOO, DON'T YOU?
KEEP HIS FOCUS ...
...RIGHT WHERE I WANT IT... AND HE WON'T NOTICE ANYTHING ELSE...
LIKE HOW THE STOREROOM HAS BEEN SET UP OVERNIGHT AND TURNED INTO...

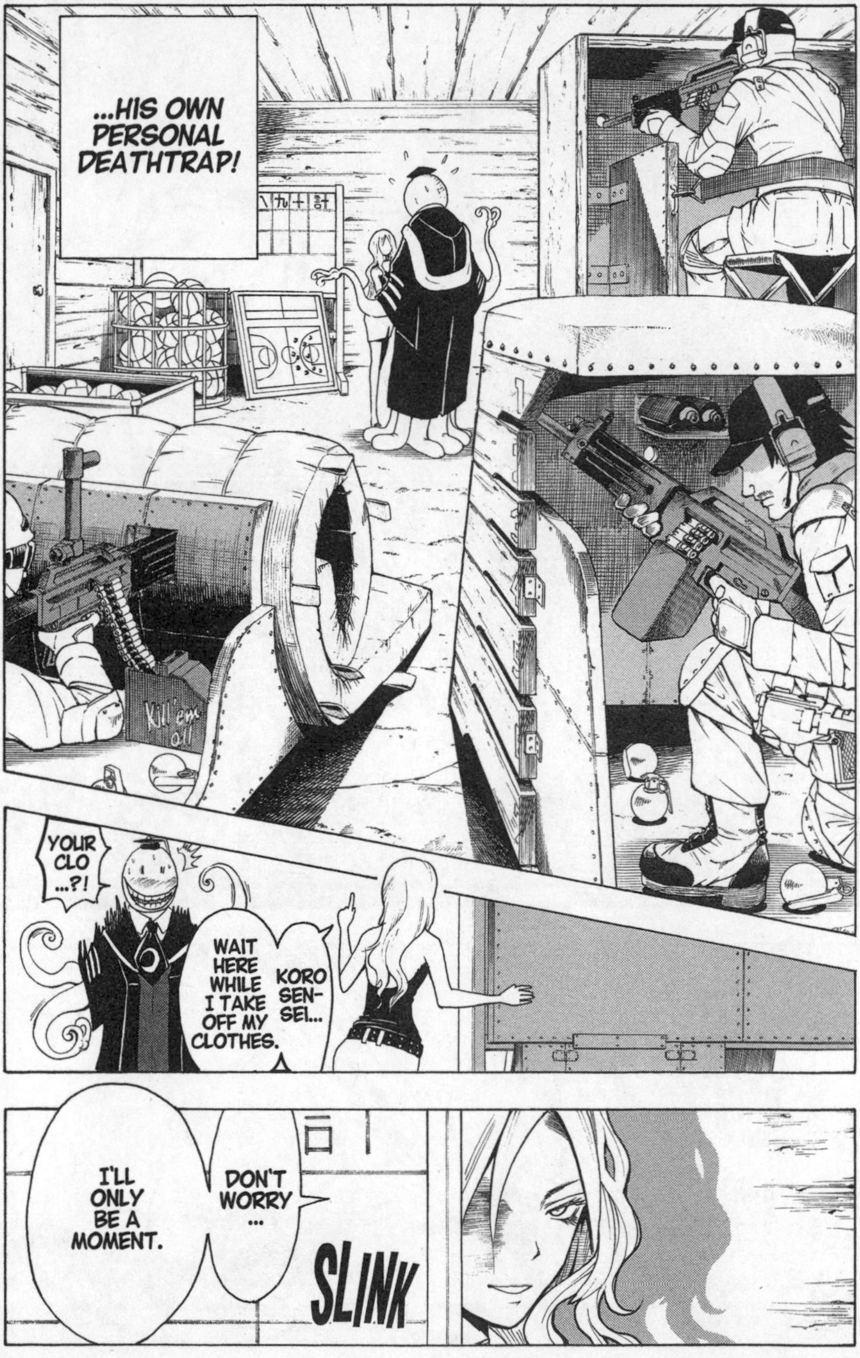
...HIS OWN PERSONAL DEATHTRAP!
Kill 'em all
KORO SEN-SEI...
WAIT HERE WHILE I TAKE OFF MY CLOTHES.
YOUR CLO ...?!
SLINK
DON'T WORRY ...
I'LL ONLY BE A MOMENT.

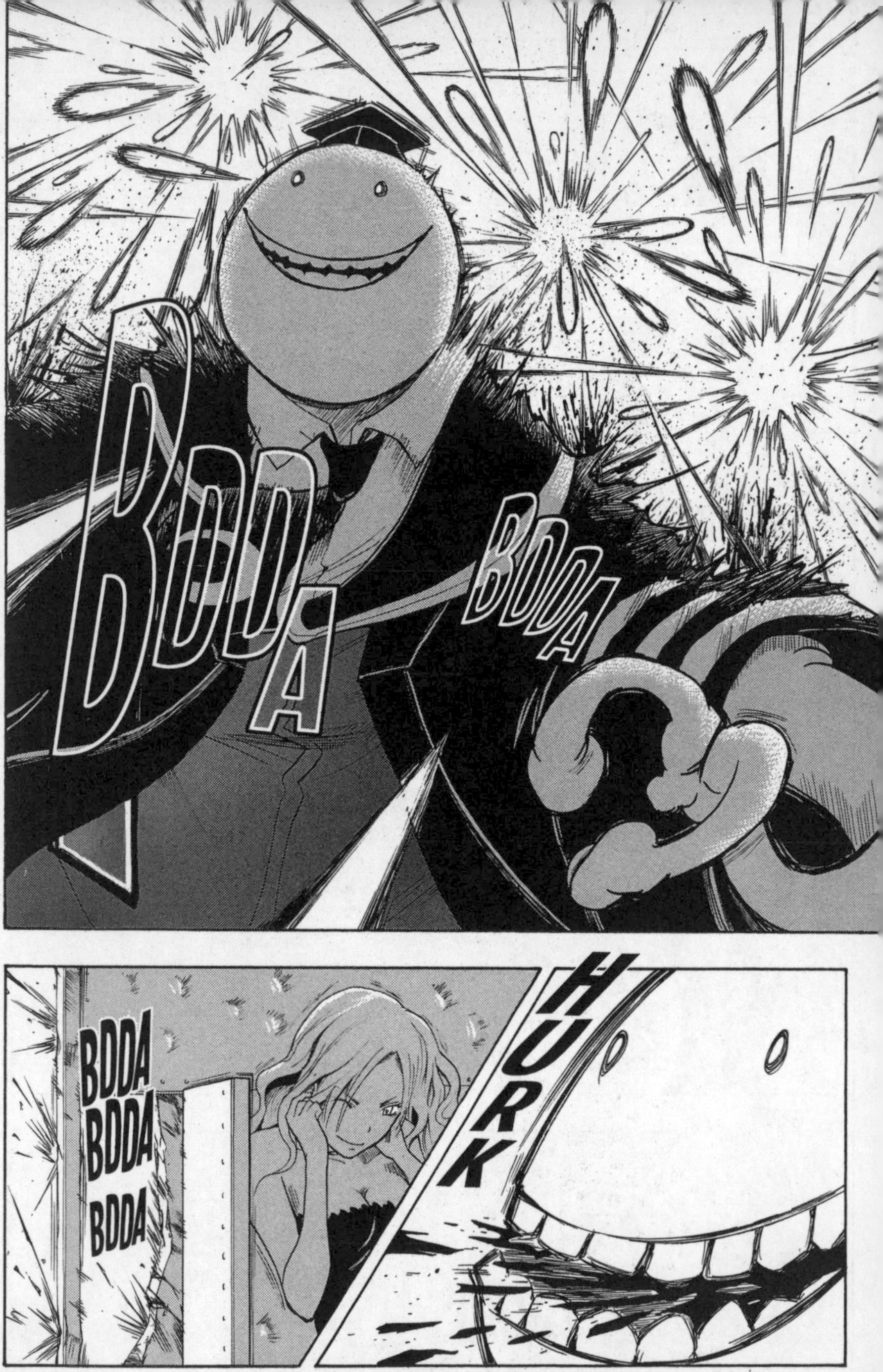
BDDA
BDDA
HURK
BDDA
BDDA
BDDA

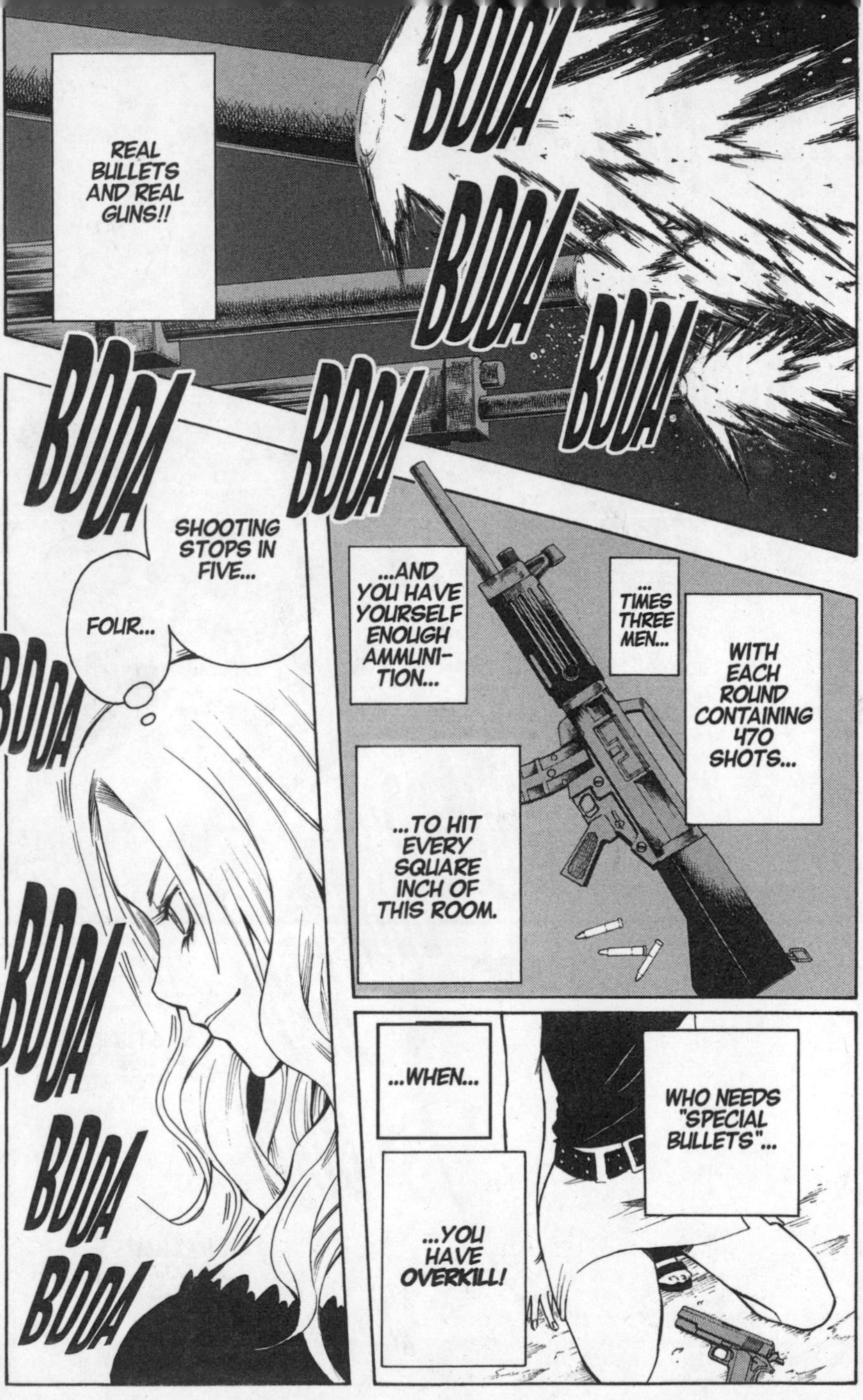
BDDA
BDDA
BDDA
BDDA
REAL BULLETS AND REAL GUNS!!
BDDA
WITH EACH ROUND CONTAINING 470 SHOTS...
... TIMES THREE MEN...
...AND YOU HAVE YOURSELF ENOUGH AMMUNITION...
...TO HIT EVERY SQUARE INCH OF THIS ROOM.
WHO NEEDS "SPECIAL BULLETS"...
...WHEN...
...YOU HAVE OVERKILL!
SHOOTING STOPS IN FIVE...
FOUR...
BDDA
BDDA
BDDA
BDDA

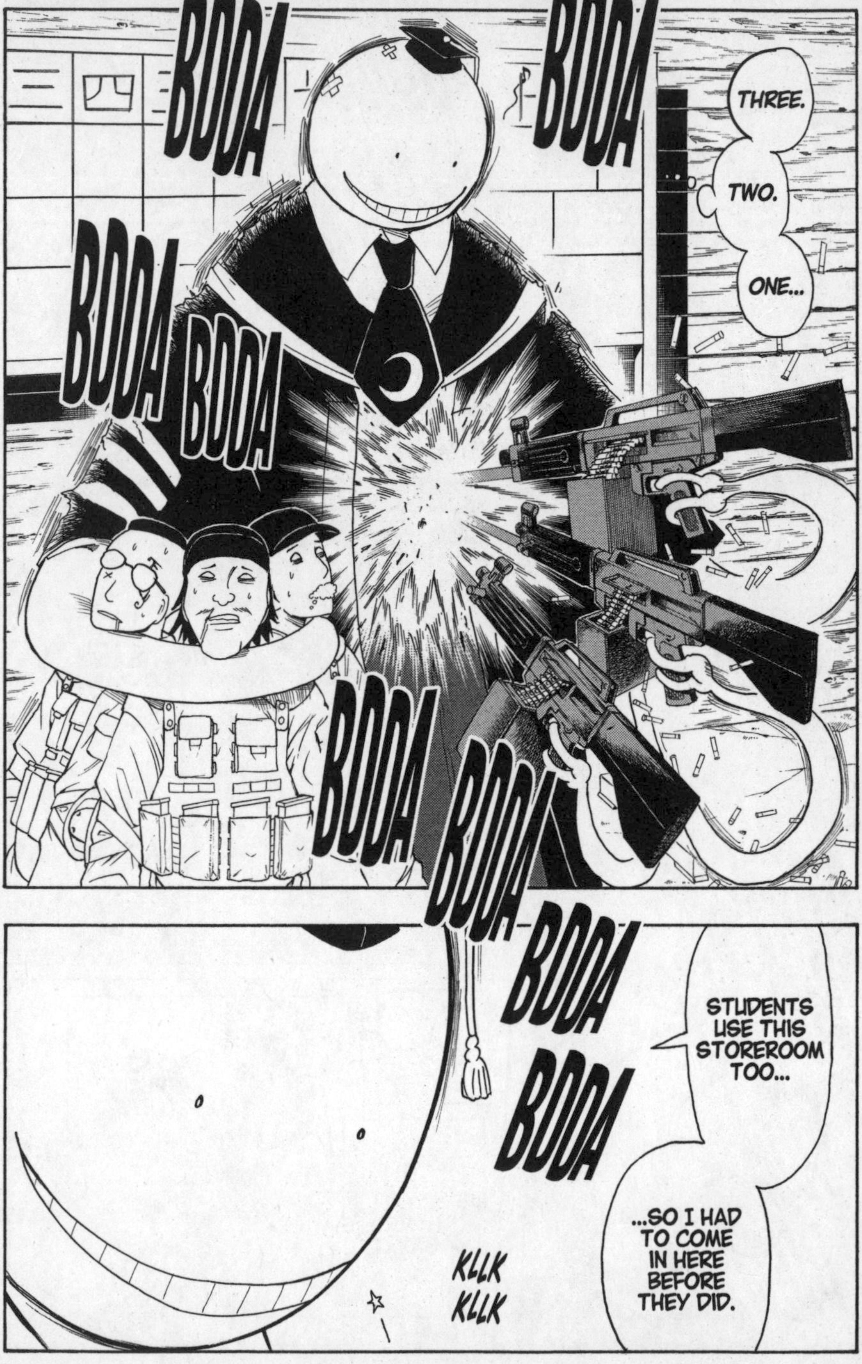
BDDA
THREE.
TWO.
ONE...
BDDA
BDDA
BDDA
BDDA
BDDA
BDDA
BDDA
STUDENTS USE THIS STOREROOM TOO...
...SO I HAD TO COME IN HERE BEFORE THEY DID.
KLLK KLLK

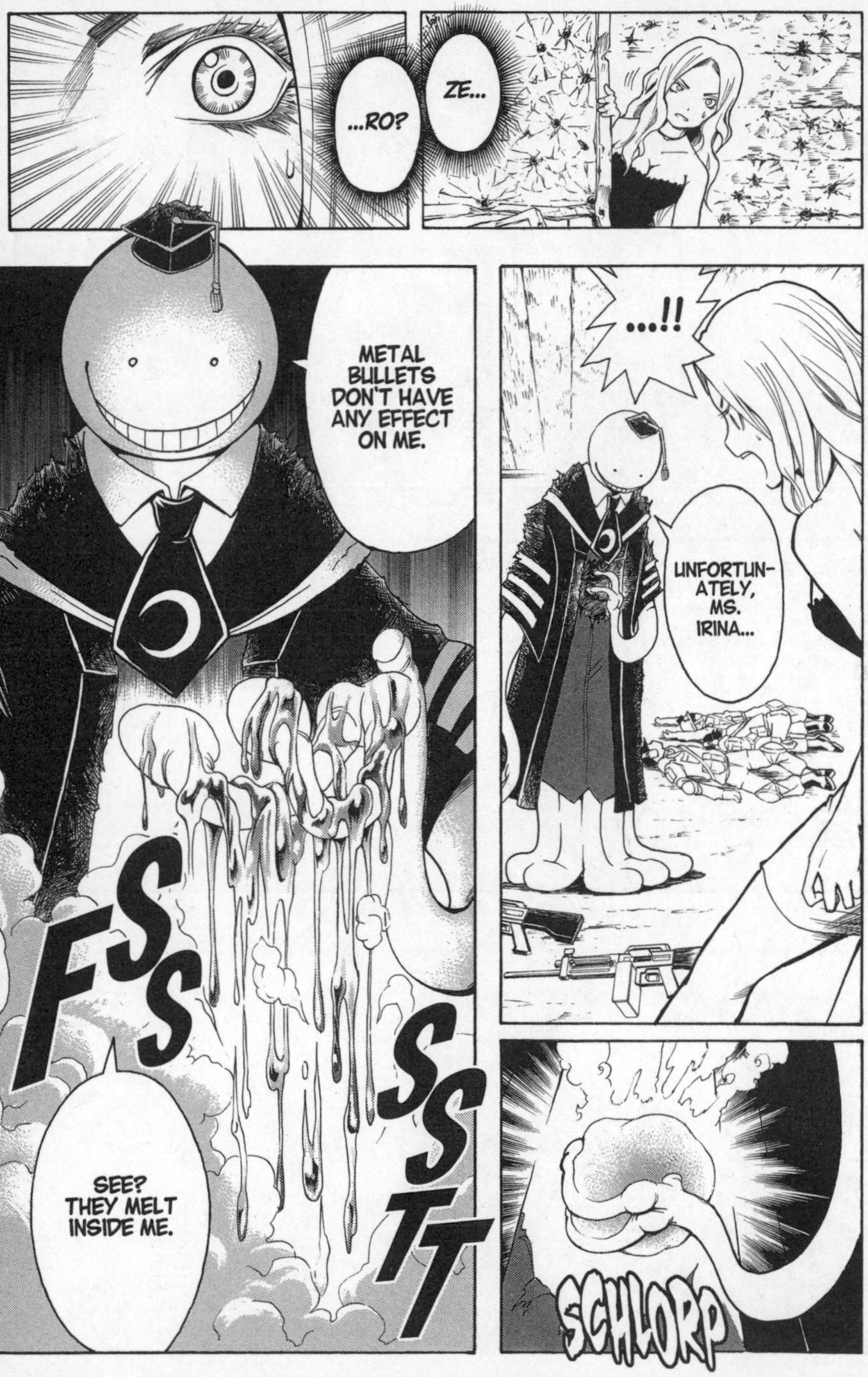
ZE...
...RO?
...!!
UNFORTUNATELY, MS. IRINA...
SCHLORP
METAL BULLETS DON'T HAVE ANY EFFECT ON ME.
FSSSSTT
SEE? THEY MELT INSIDE ME.

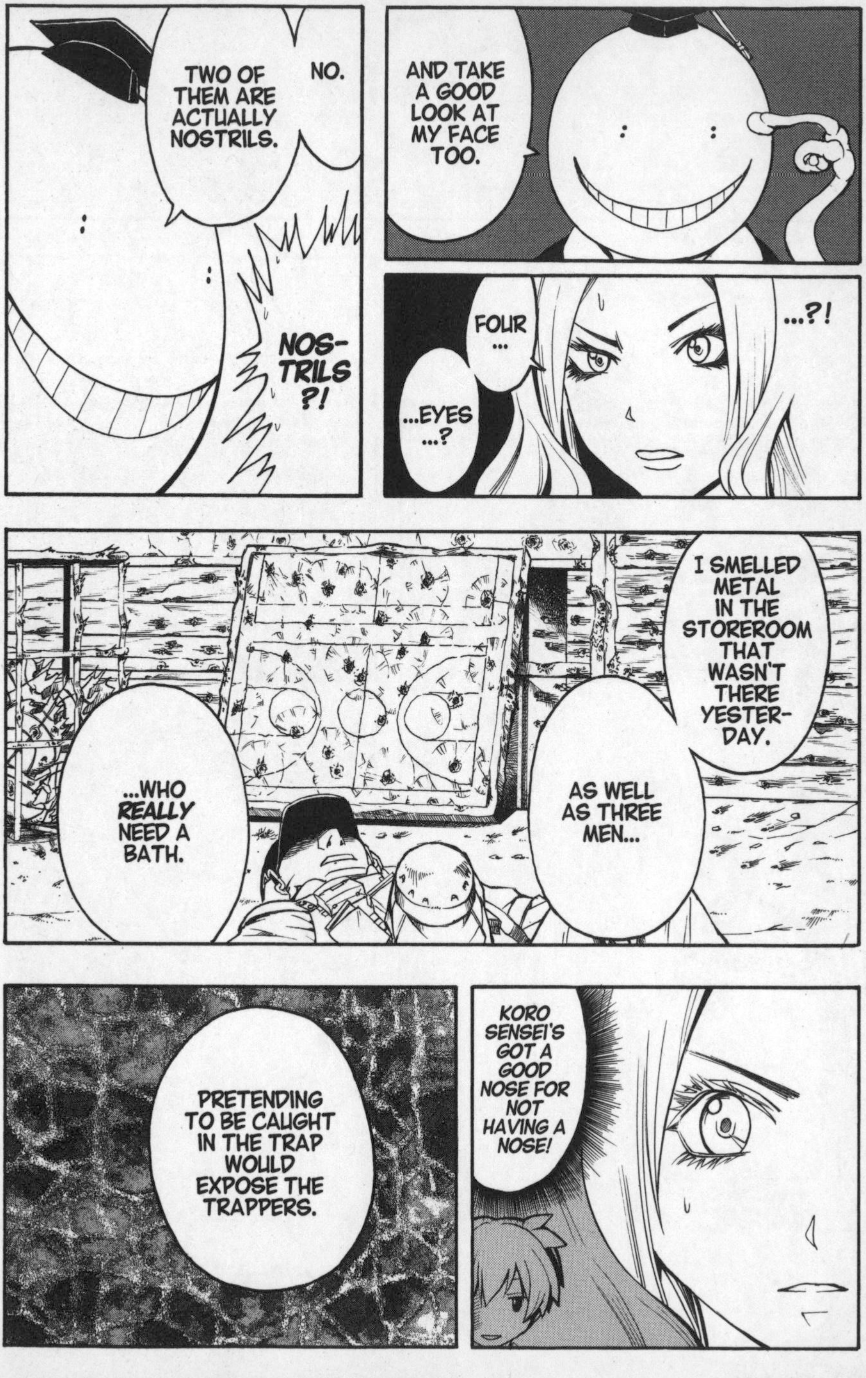
AND TAKE A GOOD LOOK AT MY FACE TOO.
...?!
FOUR ...
...EYES ...?
NO.
TWO OF THEM ARE ACTUALLY NOSTRILS.
NOS-TRILS ?!
I SMELLED METAL IN THE STOREROOM THAT WASN'T THERE YESTER-DAY.
AS WELL AS THREE MEN...
...WHO *REALLY* NEED A BATH.
KORO SENSEI'S GOT A GOOD NOSE FOR NOT HAVING A NOSE!
PRETENDING TO BE CAUGHT IN THE TRAP WOULD EXPOSE THE TRAPPERS.

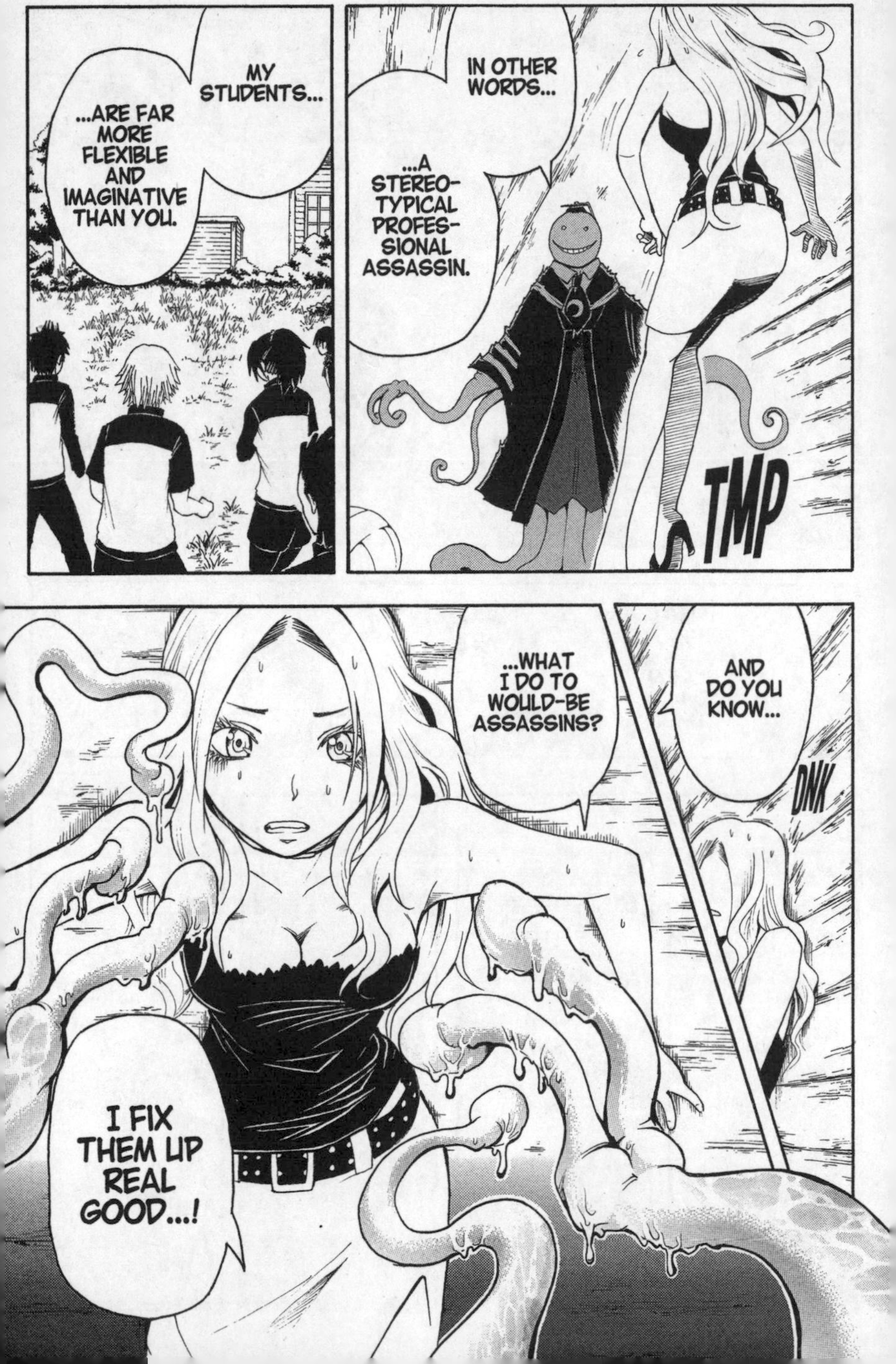
IN OTHER WORDS...
...A STEREOTYPICAL PROFESSIONAL ASSASSIN.
TMP
MY STUDENTS...
...ARE FAR MORE FLEXIBLE AND IMAGINATIVE THAN YOU.
AND DO YOU KNOW...
DNK
...WHAT I DO TO WOULD-BE ASSASSINS?
I FIX THEM UP REAL GOOD...!

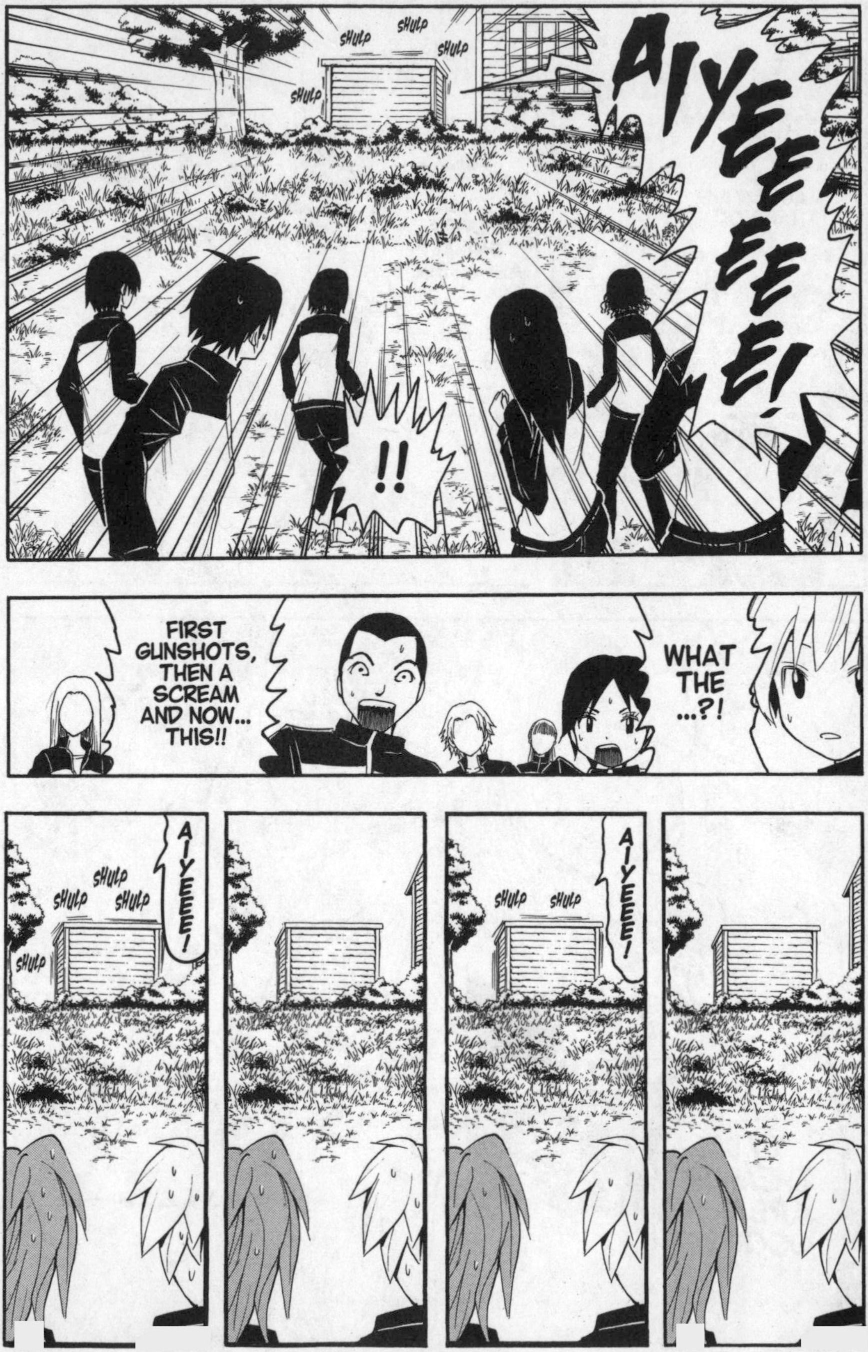
AIYEEEEE!
SHULP
SHULP
SHULP
SHULP
!!
WHAT THE ...?!
FIRST GUNSHOTS, THEN A SCREAM AND NOW... THIS!!
AIYEEEE!
SHULP
SHULP
AIYEEEE!
SHULP
SHULP
SHULP
SHULP

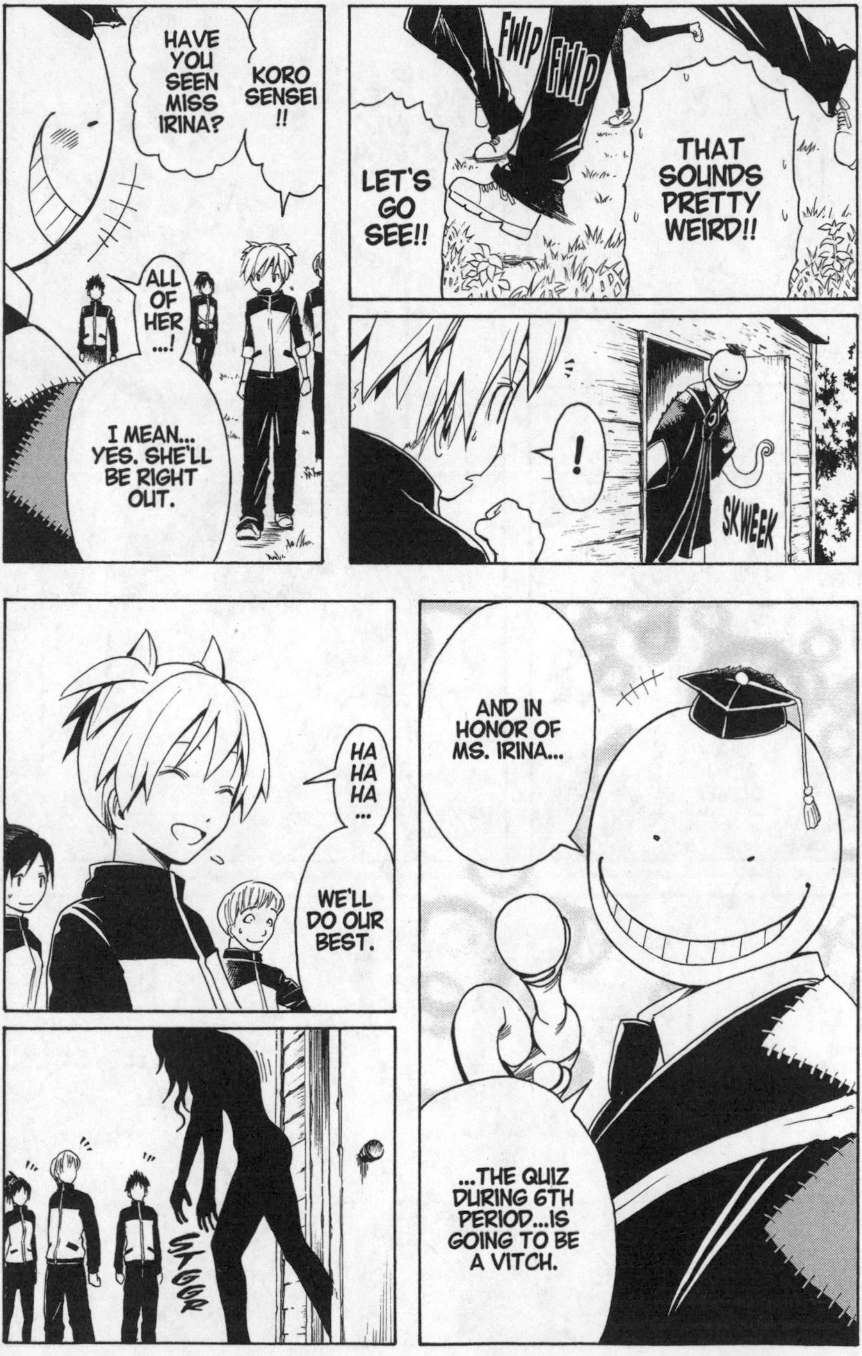
FWIP FWIP
THAT SOUNDS PRETTY WEIRD!!
LET'S GO SEE!!
!
SKWEEK
KORO SENSEI!!
HAVE YOU SEEN MISS IRINA?
ALL OF HER...!
I MEAN... YES. SHE'LL BE RIGHT OUT.
AND IN HONOR OF MS. IRINA...
...THE QUIZ DURING 6TH PERIOD...IS GOING TO BE A VITCH.
HA HA HA...
WE'LL DO OUR BEST.
STGGR

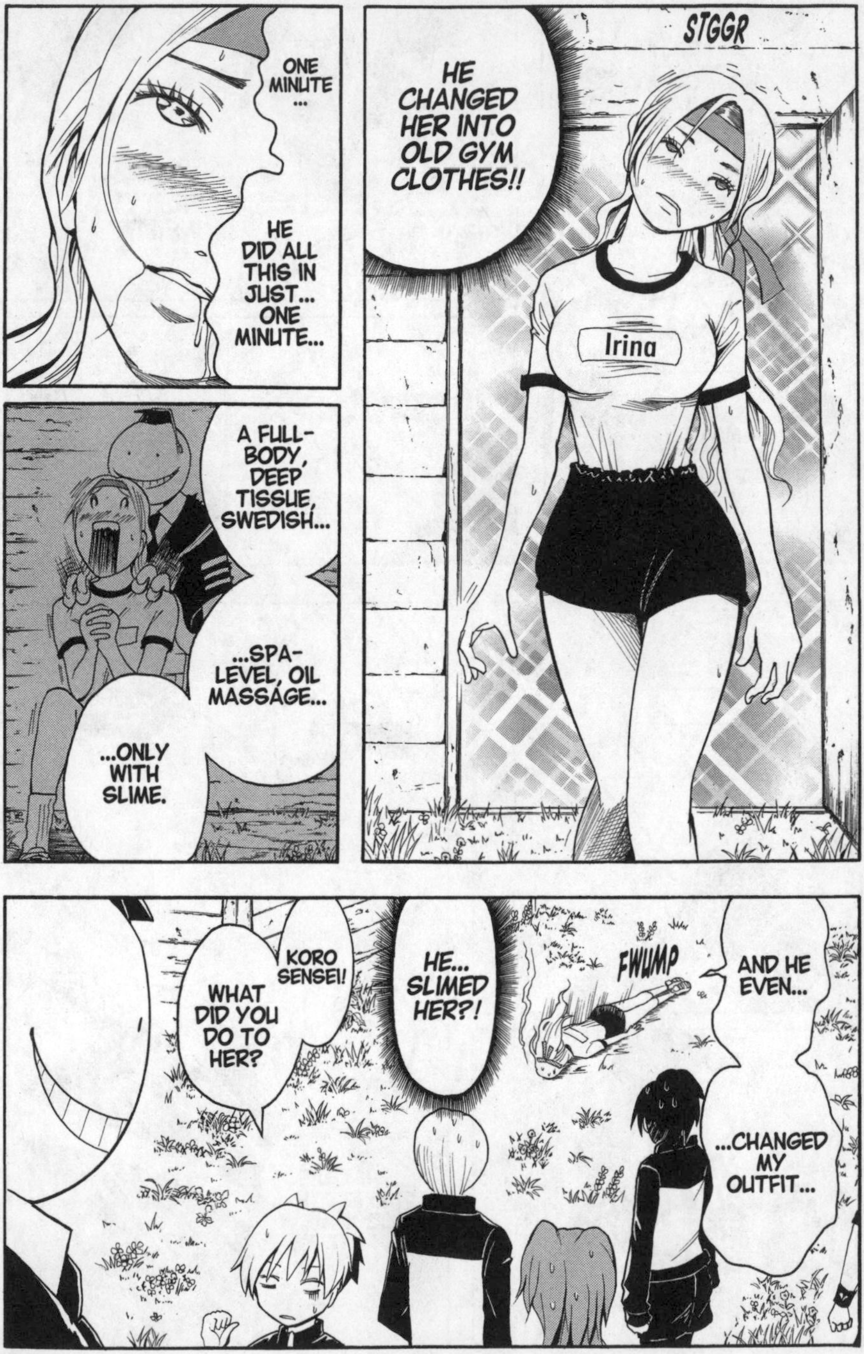
STGGR
HE CHANGED HER INTO OLD GYM CLOTHES!!
ONE MINUTE...
HE DID ALL THIS IN JUST... ONE MINUTE...
A FULL-BODY, DEEP TISSUE, SWEDISH...
...SPA-LEVEL, OIL MASSAGE...
...ONLY WITH SLIME.
AND HE EVEN...
FWUMP
HE... SLIMED HER?!
KORO SENSEI!
WHAT DID YOU DO TO HER?
...CHANGED MY OUTFIT...
Irina

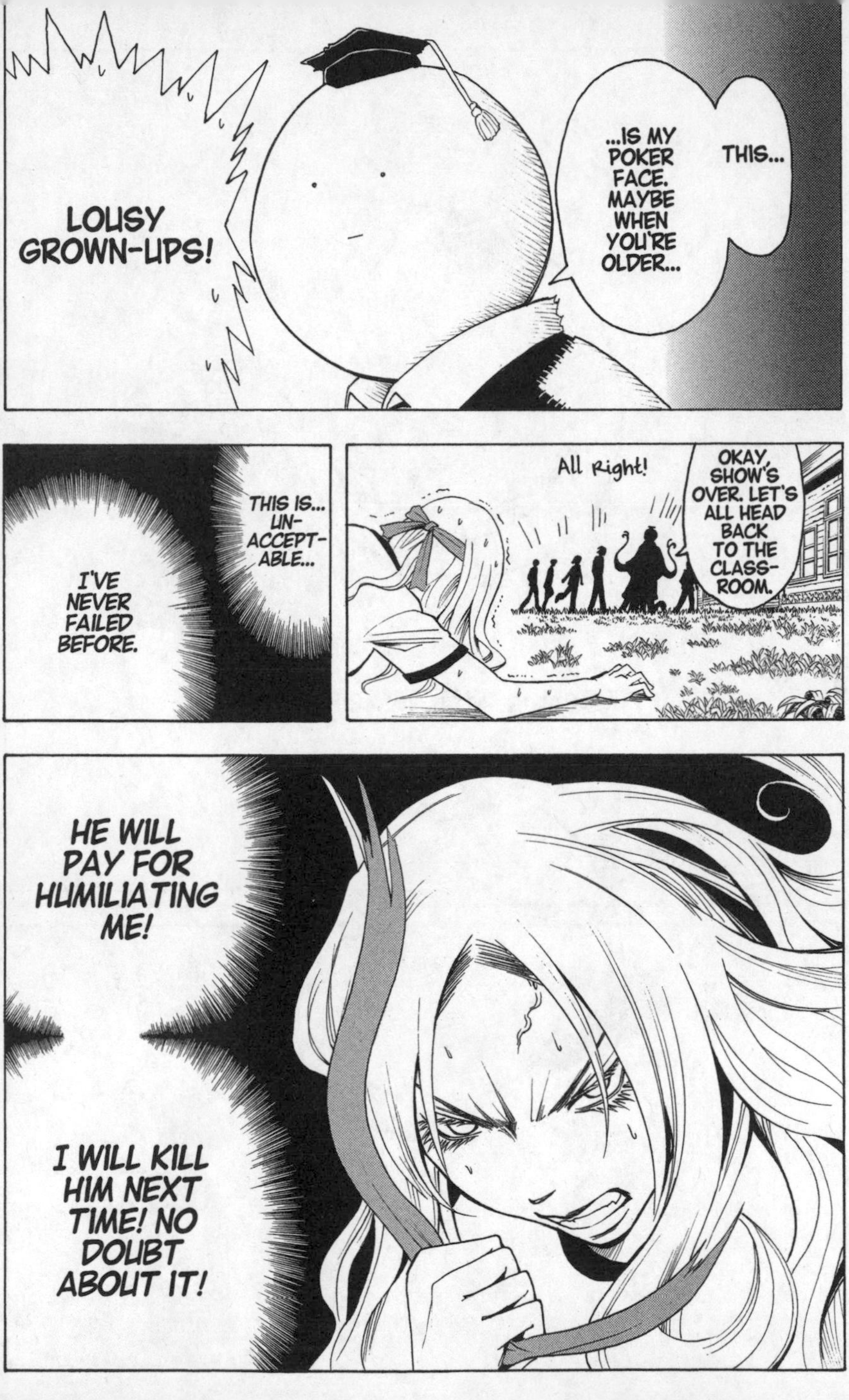
THIS...
...IS MY POKER FACE. MAYBE WHEN YOU'RE OLDER...
LOUSY GROWN-UPS!
OKAY, SHOW'S OVER. LET'S ALL HEAD BACK TO THE CLASS-ROOM.
All Right!
THIS IS... UN-ACCEPT-ABLE...
I'VE NEVER FAILED BEFORE.
HE WILL PAY FOR HUMILIATING ME!
I WILL KILL HIM NEXT TIME! NO DOUBT ABOUT IT!

Using his nose.

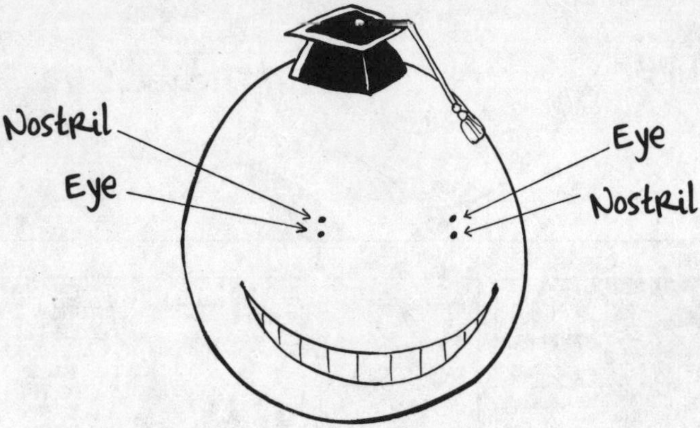
Nostril
Eye
Eye
Nostril

Listening with his ears.

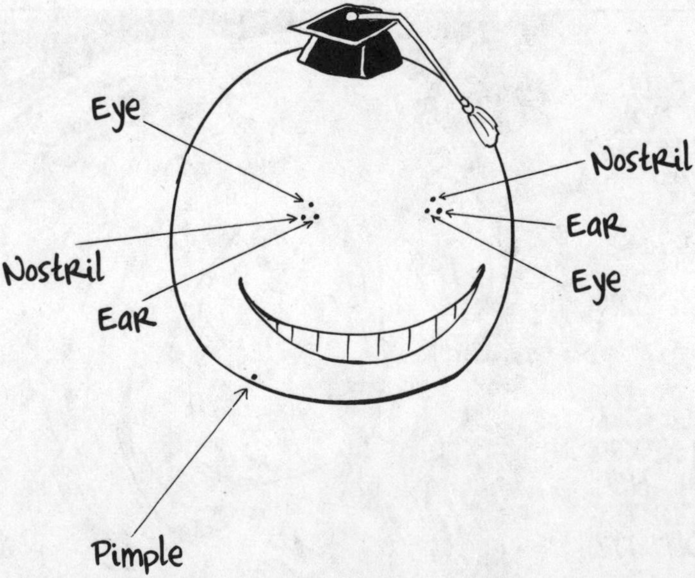
Eye
Nostril
Nostril
Ear
Ear
Eye
Pimple

Class 10 Time to Send in the Pros

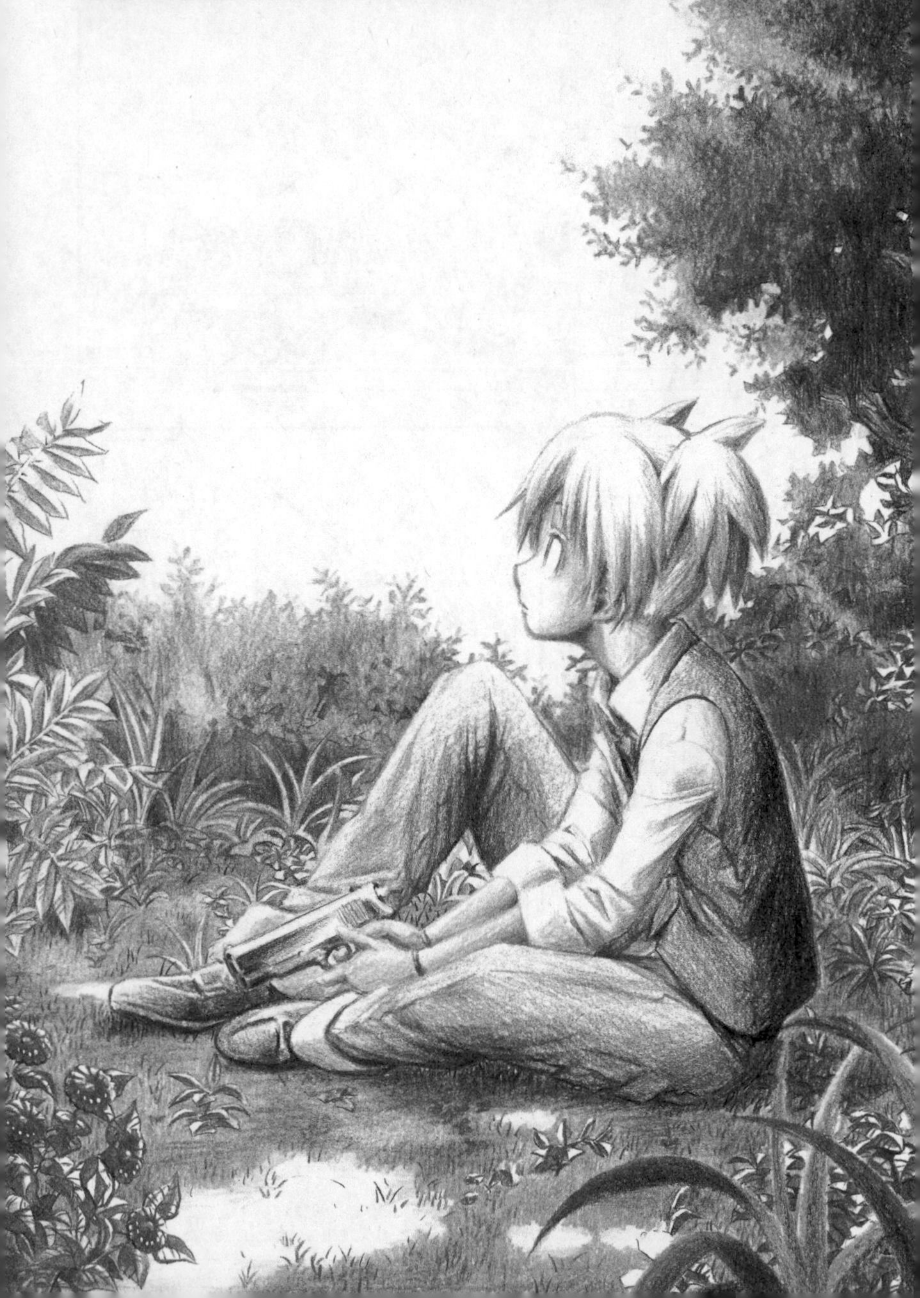

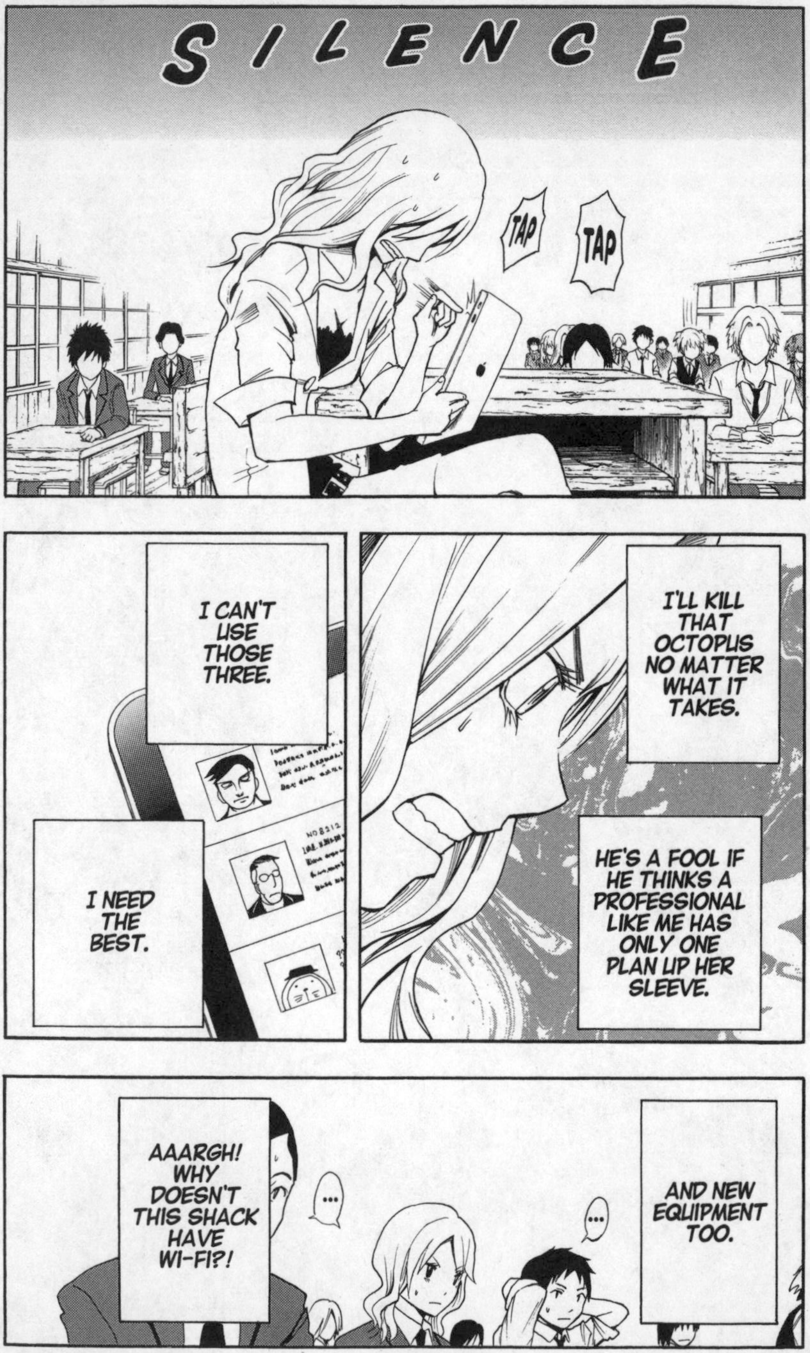
SILENCE
TAP
TAP
I'LL KILL THAT OCTOPUS NO MATTER WHAT IT TAKES.
HE'S A FOOL IF HE THINKS A PROFESSIONAL LIKE ME HAS ONLY ONE PLAN UP HER SLEEVE.
I CAN'T USE THOSE THREE.
I NEED THE BEST.
AND NEW EQUIPMENT TOO.
...
...
AARGH! WHY DOESN'T THIS SHACK HAVE WI-FI?!

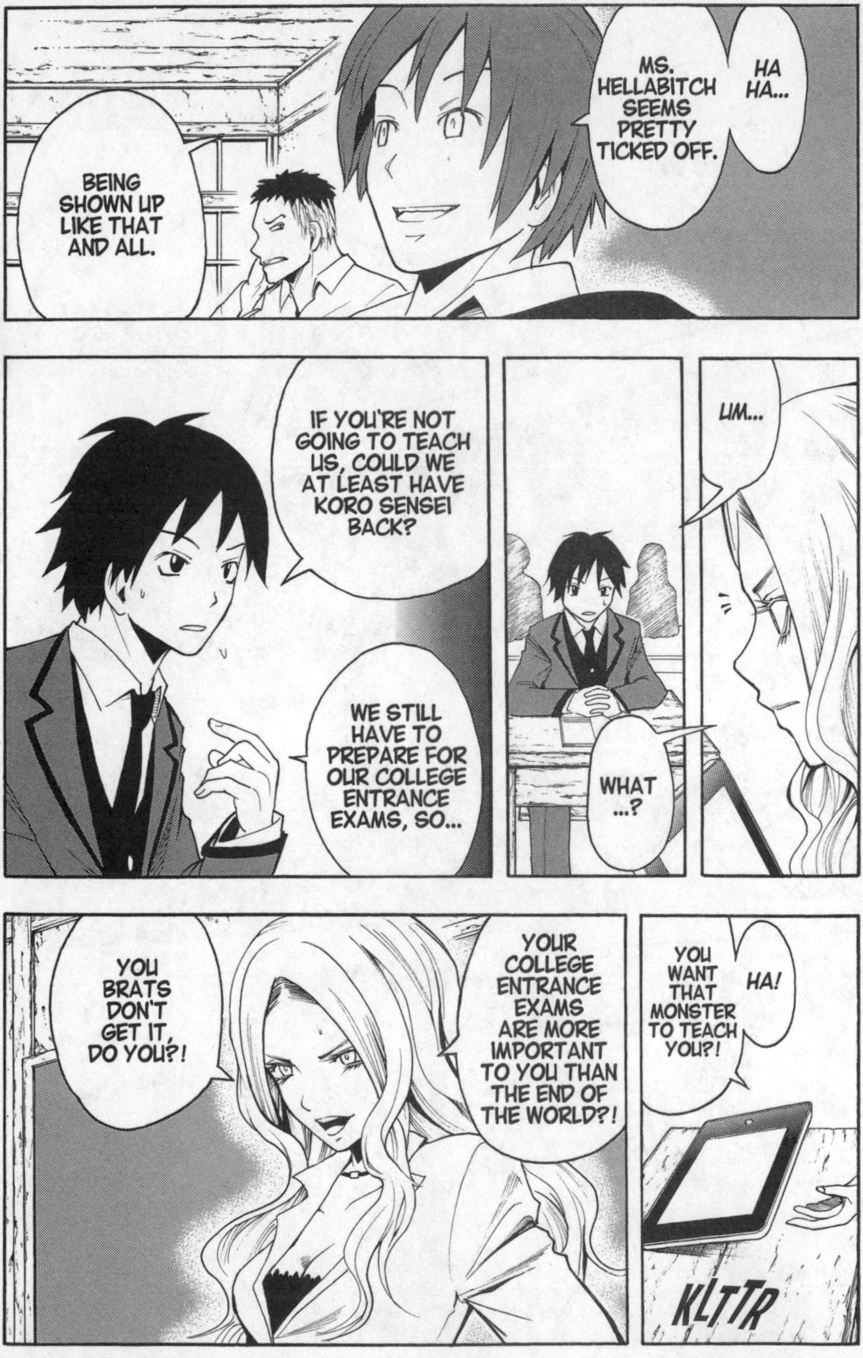
HA HA...
MS. HELLABITCH SEEMS PRETTY TICKED OFF.
BEING SHOWN UP LIKE THAT AND ALL.
UM...
WHAT ...?
IF YOU'RE NOT GOING TO TEACH US, COULD WE AT LEAST HAVE KORO SENSEI BACK?
WE STILL HAVE TO PREPARE FOR OUR COLLEGE ENTRANCE EXAMS, SO...
HA!
YOU WANT THAT MONSTER TO TEACH YOU?!
KLTTR
YOUR COLLEGE ENTRANCE EXAMS ARE MORE IMPORTANT TO YOU THAN THE END OF THE WORLD?!
YOU BRATS DON'T GET IT, DO YOU?!

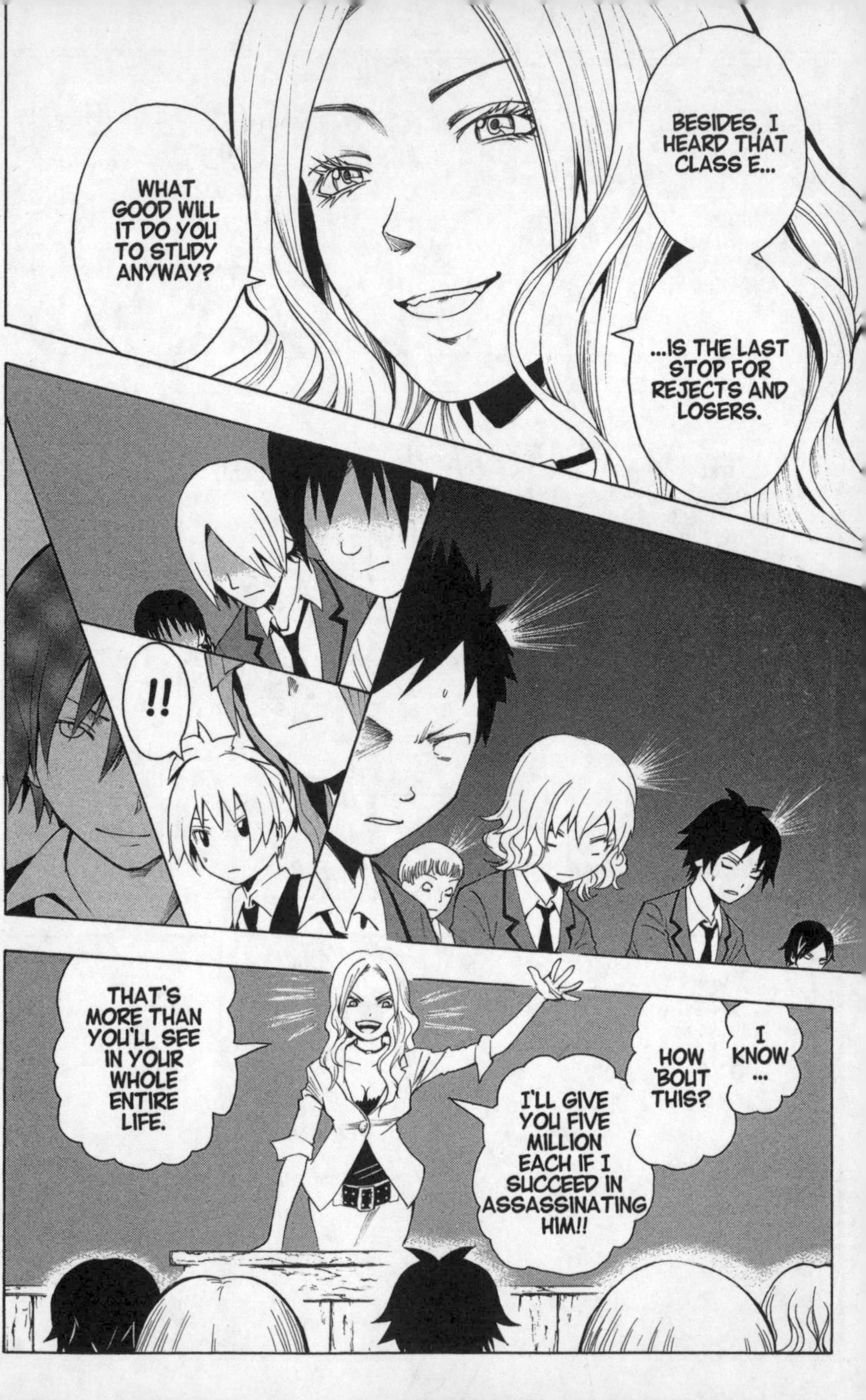
BESIDES, I HEARD THAT CLASS E...
...IS THE LAST STOP FOR REJECTS AND LOSERS.
WHAT GOOD WILL IT DO YOU TO STUDY ANYWAY?
!!
I KNOW...
HOW 'BOUT THIS?
I'LL GIVE YOU FIVE MILLION EACH IF I SUCCEED IN ASSASSINATING HIM!!
THAT'S MORE THAN YOU'LL SEE IN YOUR WHOLE ENTIRE LIFE.

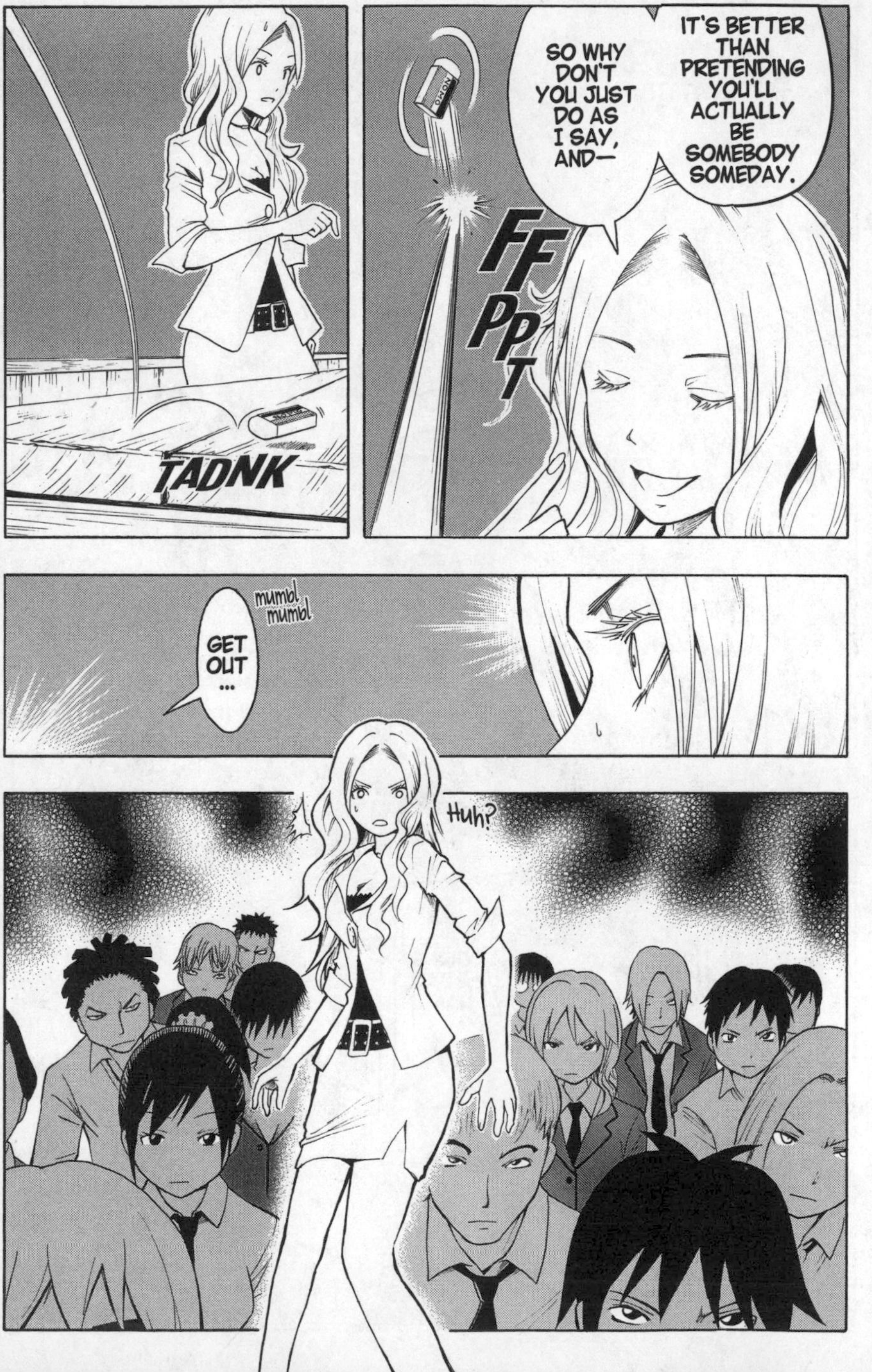
IT'S BETTER THAN PRETENDING YOU'LL ACTUALLY BE SOMEBODY SOMEDAY.
SO WHY DON'T YOU JUST DO AS I SAY, AND—
FFPPT
TADNK
mumbl mumbl
GET OUT ...
Huh?

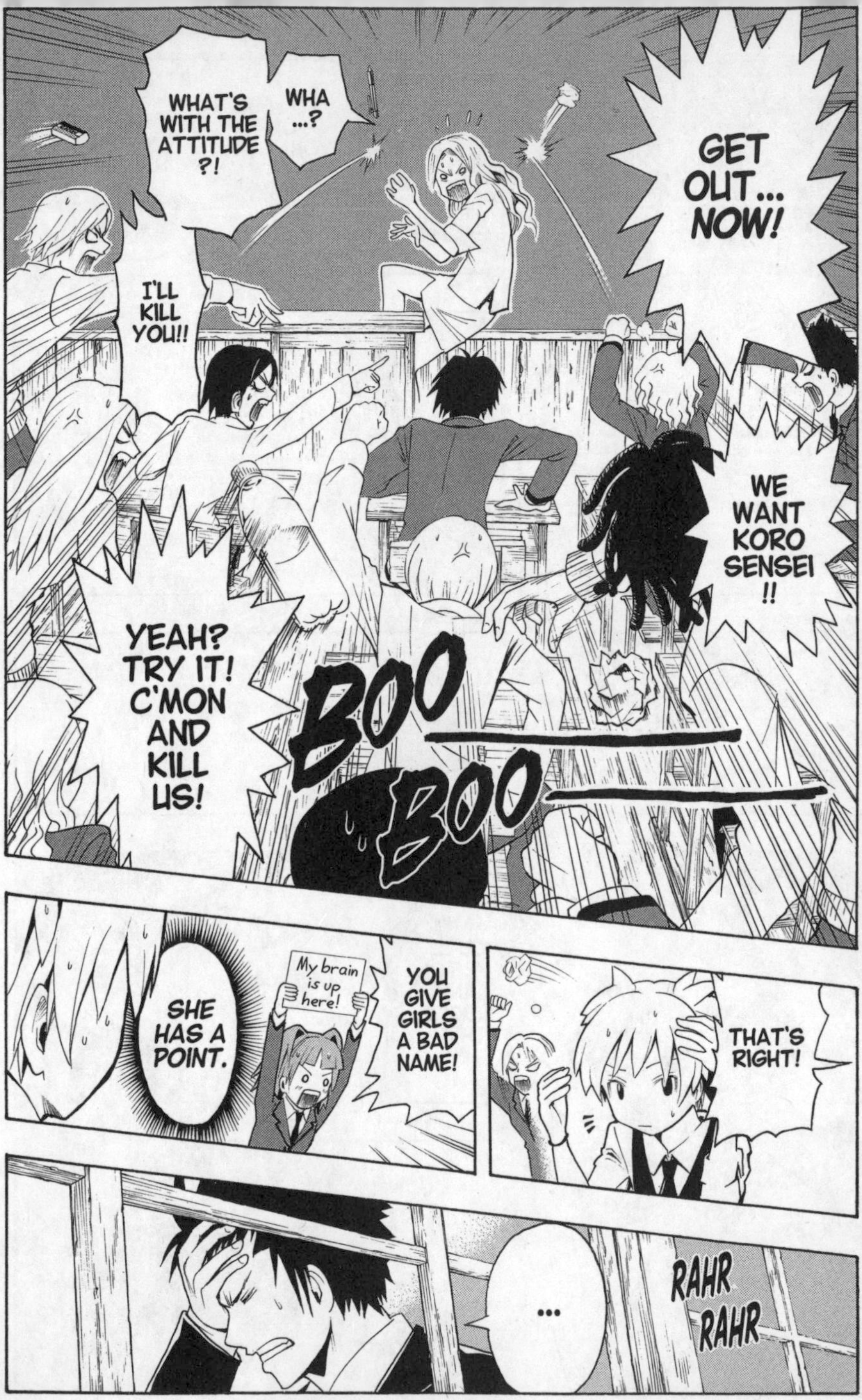
GET OUT... NOW!
WHA ...?
WHAT'S WITH THE ATTITUDE ?!
WE WANT KORO SENSEI !!
I'LL KILL YOU!!
YEAH? TRY IT! C'MON AND KILL US!
BOO BOO
THAT'S RIGHT!
YOU GIVE GIRLS A BAD NAME!
My brain is up here!
SHE HAS A POINT.
RAHR RAHR
...

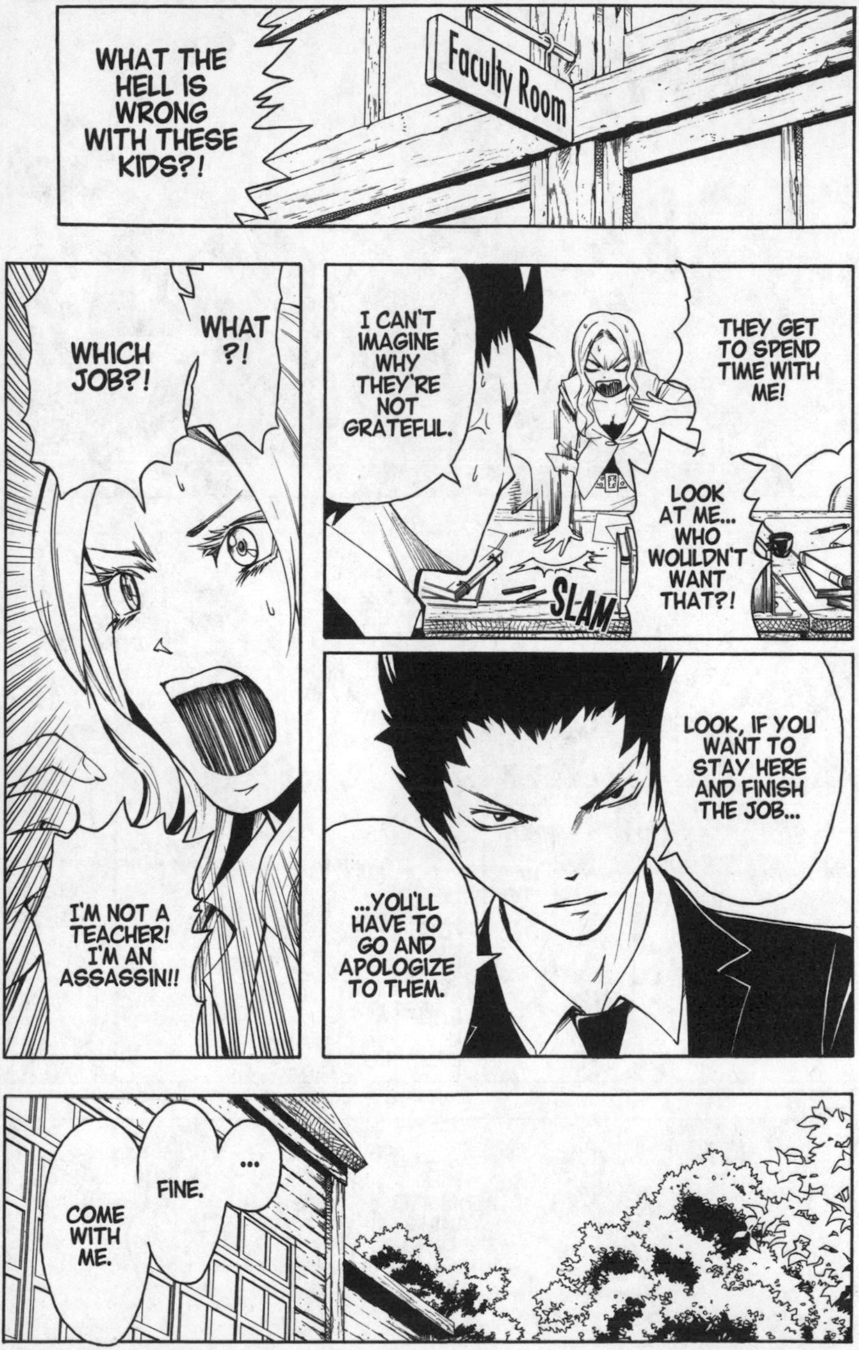
Faculty Room
WHAT THE HELL IS WRONG WITH THESE KIDS?!
THEY GET TO SPEND TIME WITH ME!
I CAN'T IMAGINE WHY THEY'RE NOT GRATEFUL.
LOOK AT ME... WHO WOULDN'T WANT THAT?!
SLAM
LOOK, IF YOU WANT TO STAY HERE AND FINISH THE JOB...
...YOU'LL HAVE TO GO AND APOLOGIZE TO THEM.
WHAT?!
WHICH JOB?!
I'M NOT A TEACHER! I'M AN ASSASSIN!!
...
FINE.
COME WITH ME.

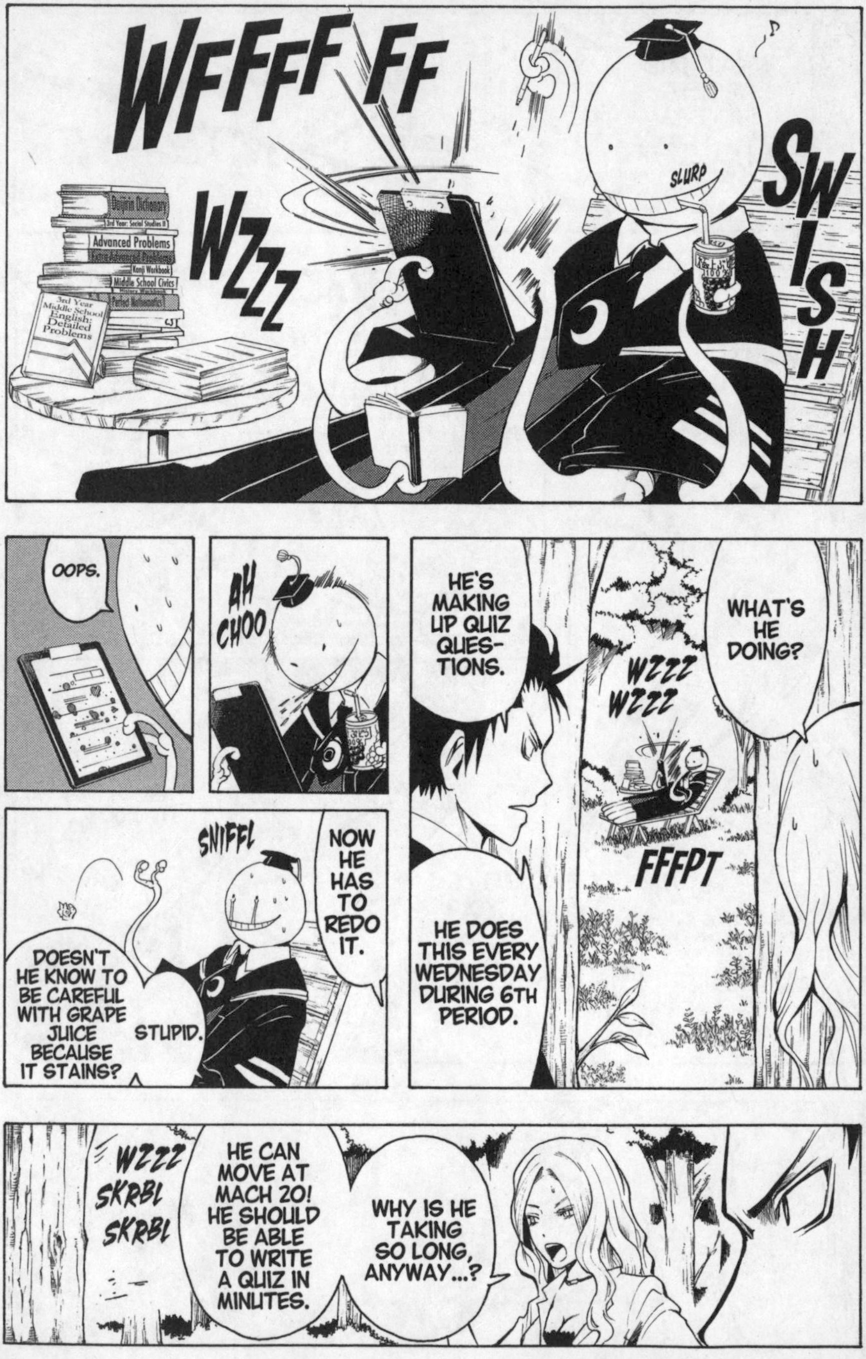
SWISH
SLURP
WFFFF FF
WZZZ
Daijirin Dictionary
3rd Year: Social Studies II
Advanced Problems
Extra Advanced Problems
Kanji Workbook
Middle School Civics
Perfect Mathematics
3rd Year Middle School English: Detailed Problems
WHAT'S HE DOING?
HE'S MAKING UP QUIZ QUES-TIONS.
WZZZ WZZZ
FFFPT
HE DOES THIS EVERY WEDNESDAY DURING 6TH PERIOD.
AH CHOO
OOPS.
NOW HE HAS TO REDO IT.
SNIFFL
DOESN'T HE KNOW TO BE CAREFUL WITH GRAPE JUICE BECAUSE IT STAINS?
STUPID.
WHY IS HE TAKING SO LONG, ANYWAY...?
HE CAN MOVE AT MACH 20! HE SHOULD BE ABLE TO WRITE A QUIZ IN MINUTES.
WZZZ
SKRBL SKRBL

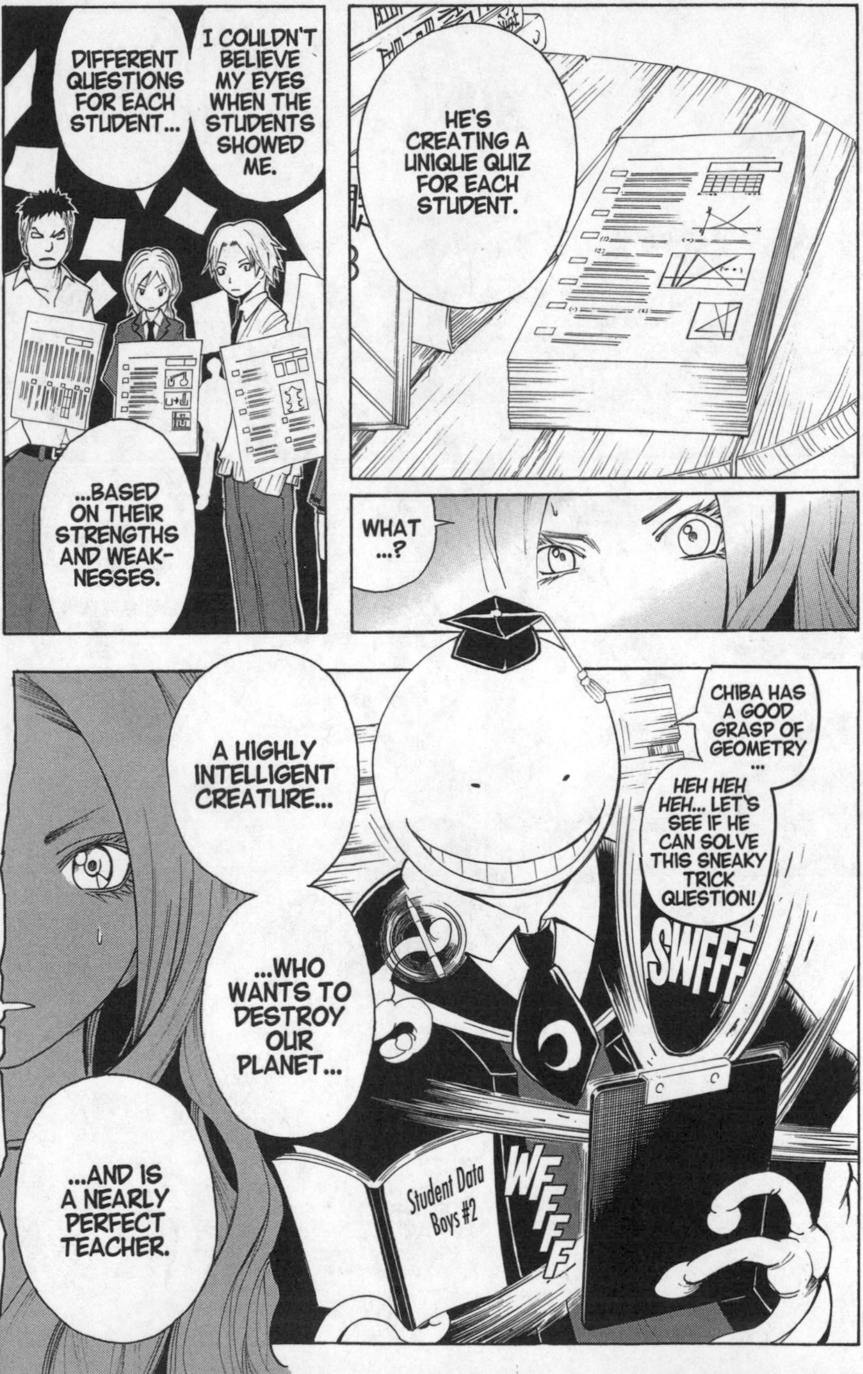
HE'S CREATING A UNIQUE QUIZ FOR EACH STUDENT.
WHAT ...?
I COULDN'T BELIEVE MY EYES WHEN THE STUDENTS SHOWED ME.
DIFFERENT QUESTIONS FOR EACH STUDENT...
...BASED ON THEIR STRENGTHS AND WEAK-NESSES.
CHIBA HAS A GOOD GRASP OF GEOMETRY ...
HEH HEH HEH... LET'S SEE IF HE CAN SOLVE THIS SNEAKY TRICK QUESTION!
SWFFF
A HIGHLY INTELLIGENT CREATURE...
...WHO WANTS TO DESTROY OUR PLANET...
WFFFF
Student Data Boys #2
...AND IS A NEARLY PERFECT TEACHER.

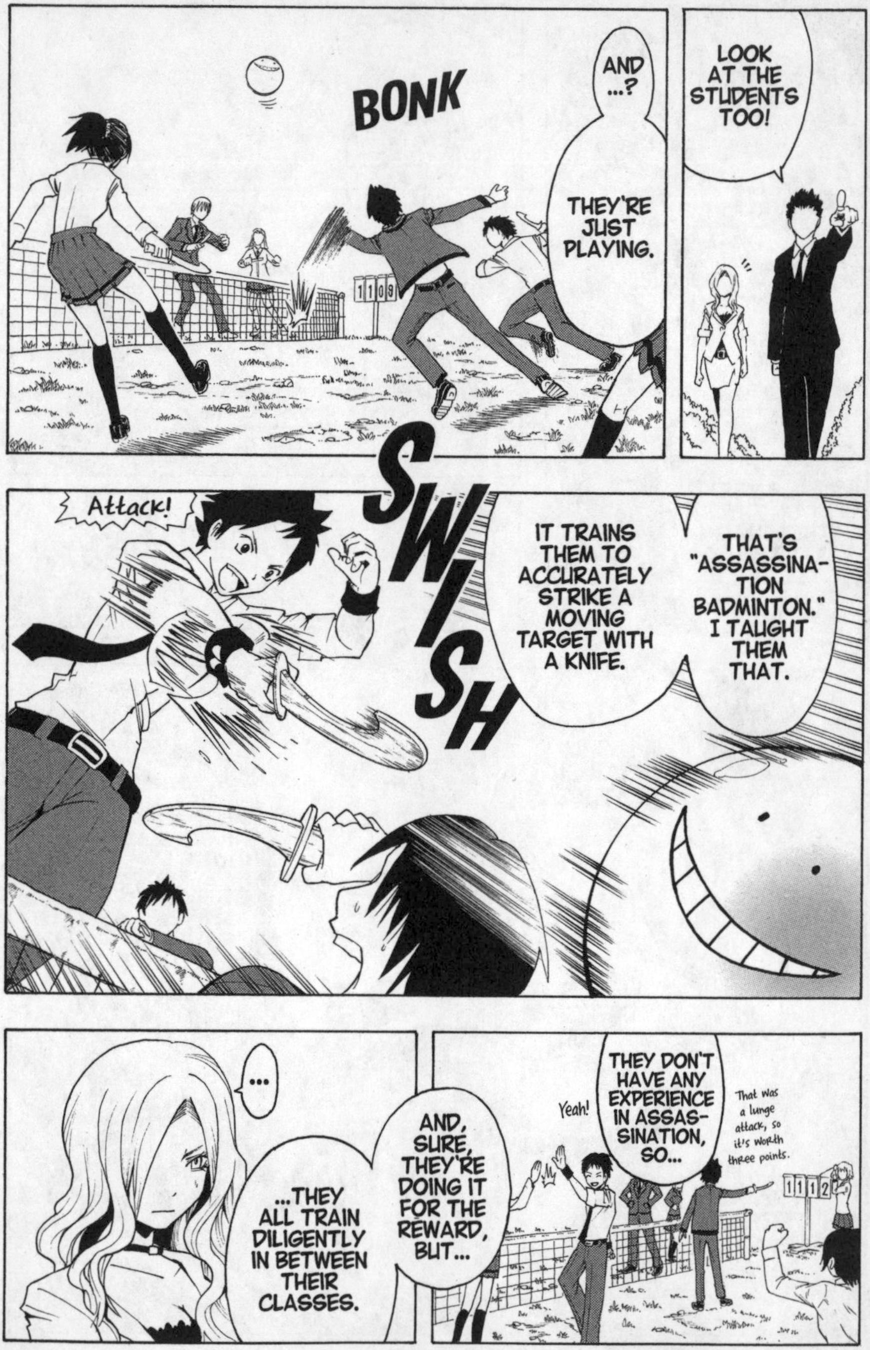
LOOK AT THE STUDENTS TOO!
AND ...?
THEY'RE JUST PLAYING.
BONK
SWISH
THAT'S "ASSASSINATION BADMINTON." I TAUGHT THEM THAT.
IT TRAINS THEM TO ACCURATELY STRIKE A MOVING TARGET WITH A KNIFE.
Attack!
THEY DON'T HAVE ANY EXPERIENCE IN ASSASSINATION, SO...
That was a lunge attack, so it's worth three points.
Yeah!
AND, SURE, THEY'RE DOING IT FOR THE REWARD, BUT...
...THEY ALL TRAIN DILIGENTLY IN BETWEEN THEIR CLASSES.
...

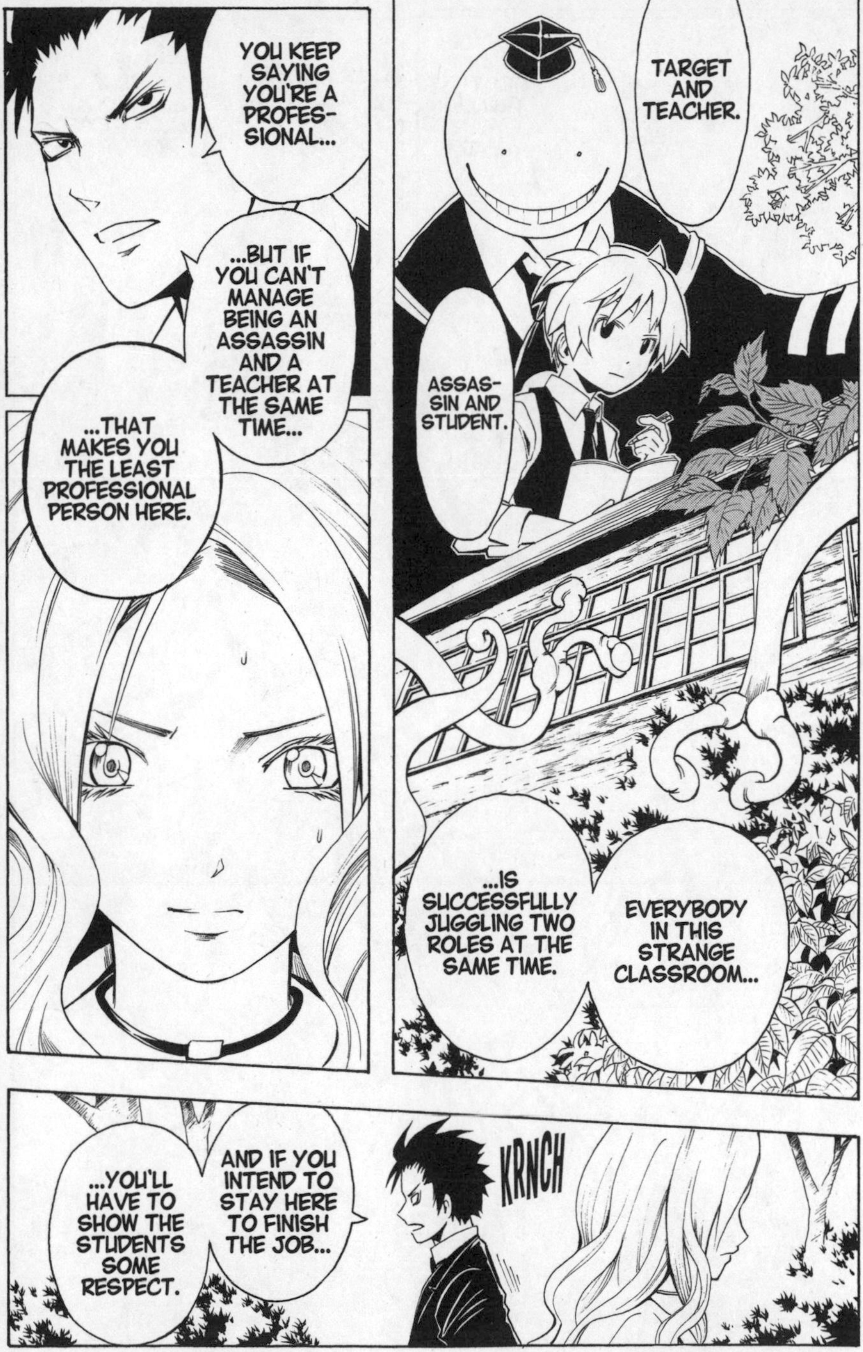
TARGET AND TEACHER.
ASSAS-SIN AND STUDENT.
EVERYBODY IN THIS STRANGE CLASSROOM...
...IS SUCCESSFULLY JUGGLING TWO ROLES AT THE SAME TIME.
YOU KEEP SAYING YOU'RE A PROFES-SIONAL...
...BUT IF YOU CAN'T MANAGE BEING AN ASSASSIN AND A TEACHER AT THE SAME TIME...
...THAT MAKES YOU THE LEAST PROFESSIONAL PERSON HERE.
KRNCH
AND IF YOU INTEND TO STAY HERE TO FINISH THE JOB...
...YOU'LL HAVE TO SHOW THE STUDENTS SOME RESPECT.

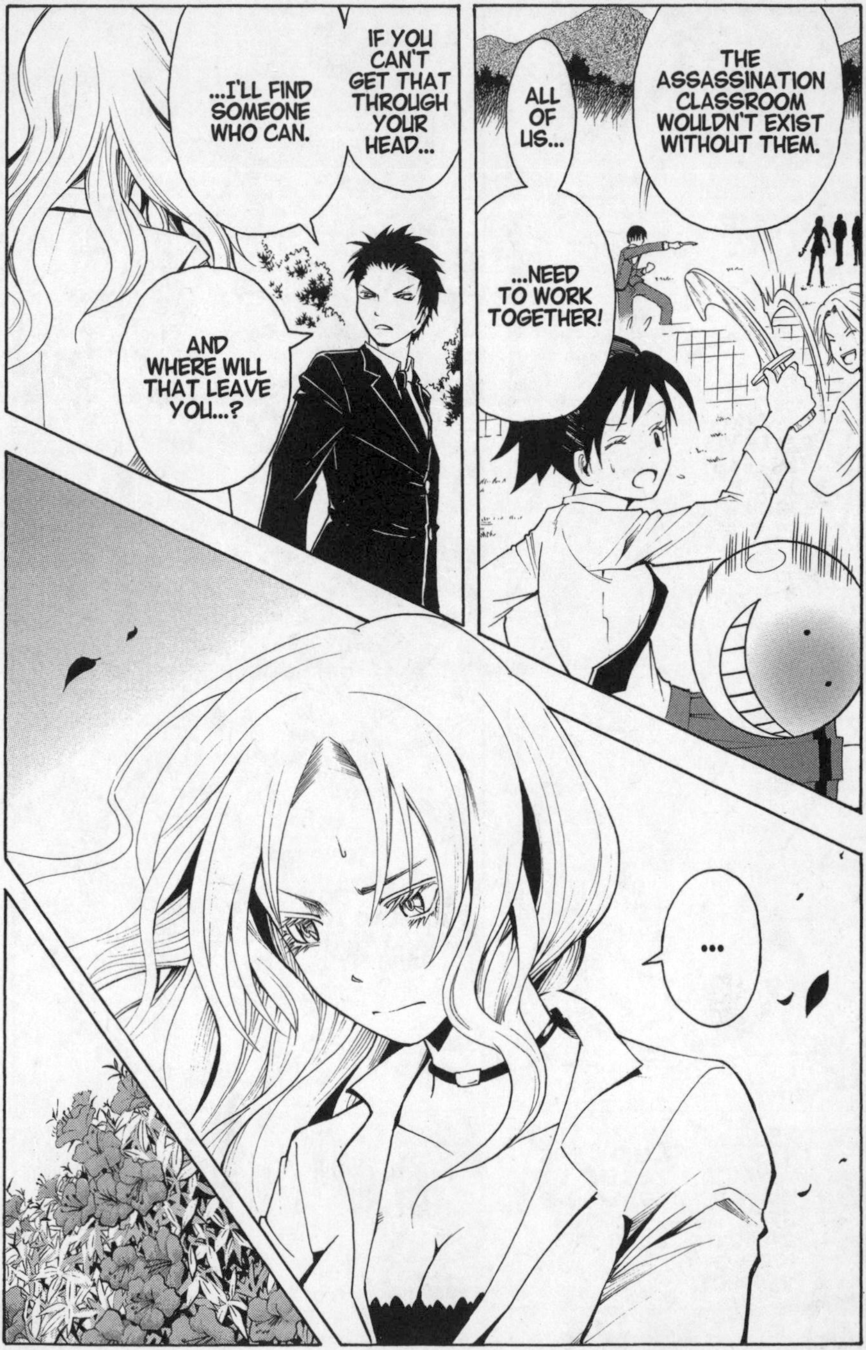
THE ASSASSINATION CLASSROOM WOULDN'T EXIST WITHOUT THEM.
ALL OF US...
...NEED TO WORK TOGETHER!
IF YOU CAN'T GET THAT THROUGH YOUR HEAD...
...I'LL FIND SOMEONE WHO CAN.
AND WHERE WILL THAT LEAVE YOU...?
...

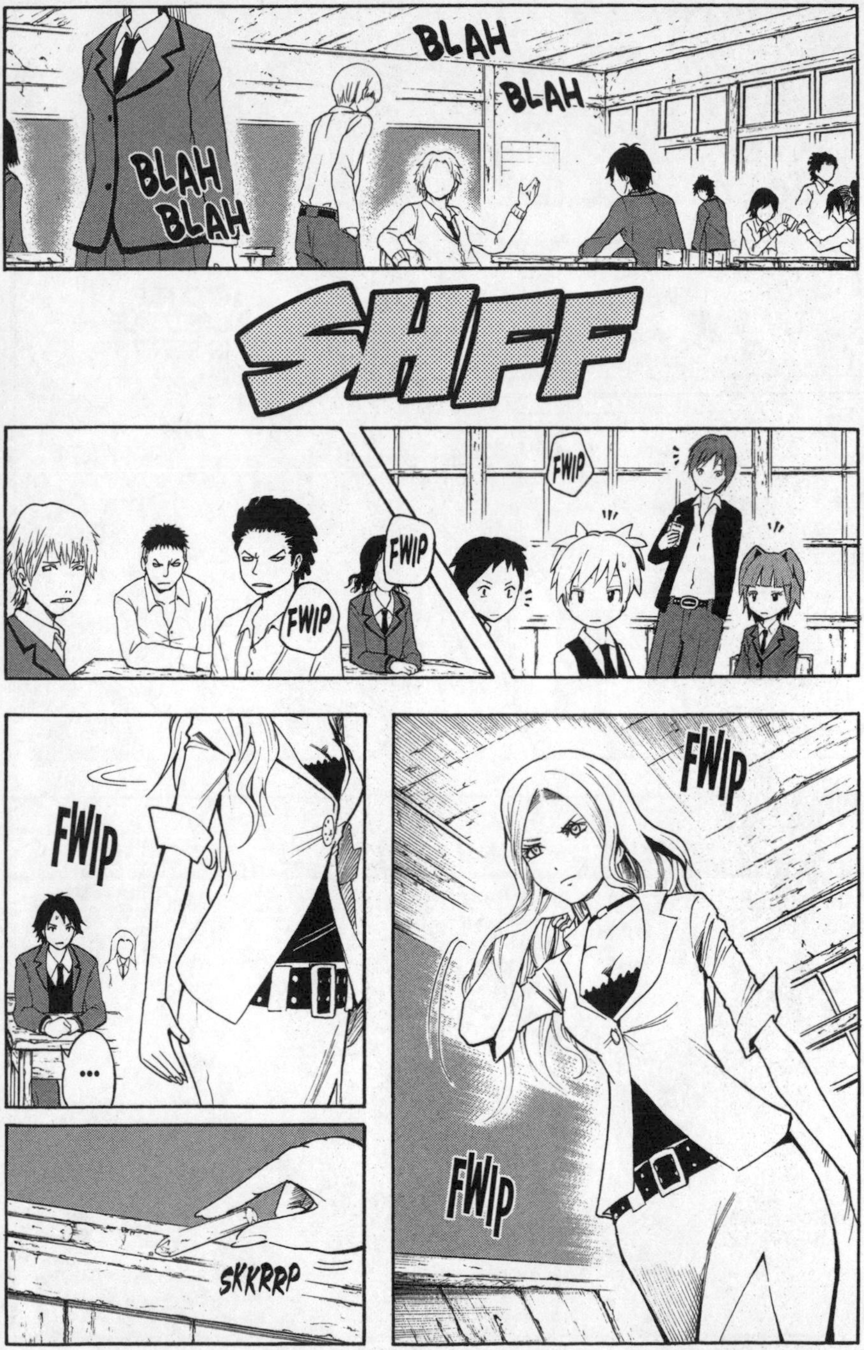
BLAH
BLAH
BLAH
BLAH
SHFF
FWIP
FWIP
FWIP
FWIP
FWIP
FWIP
...
SKKRRP

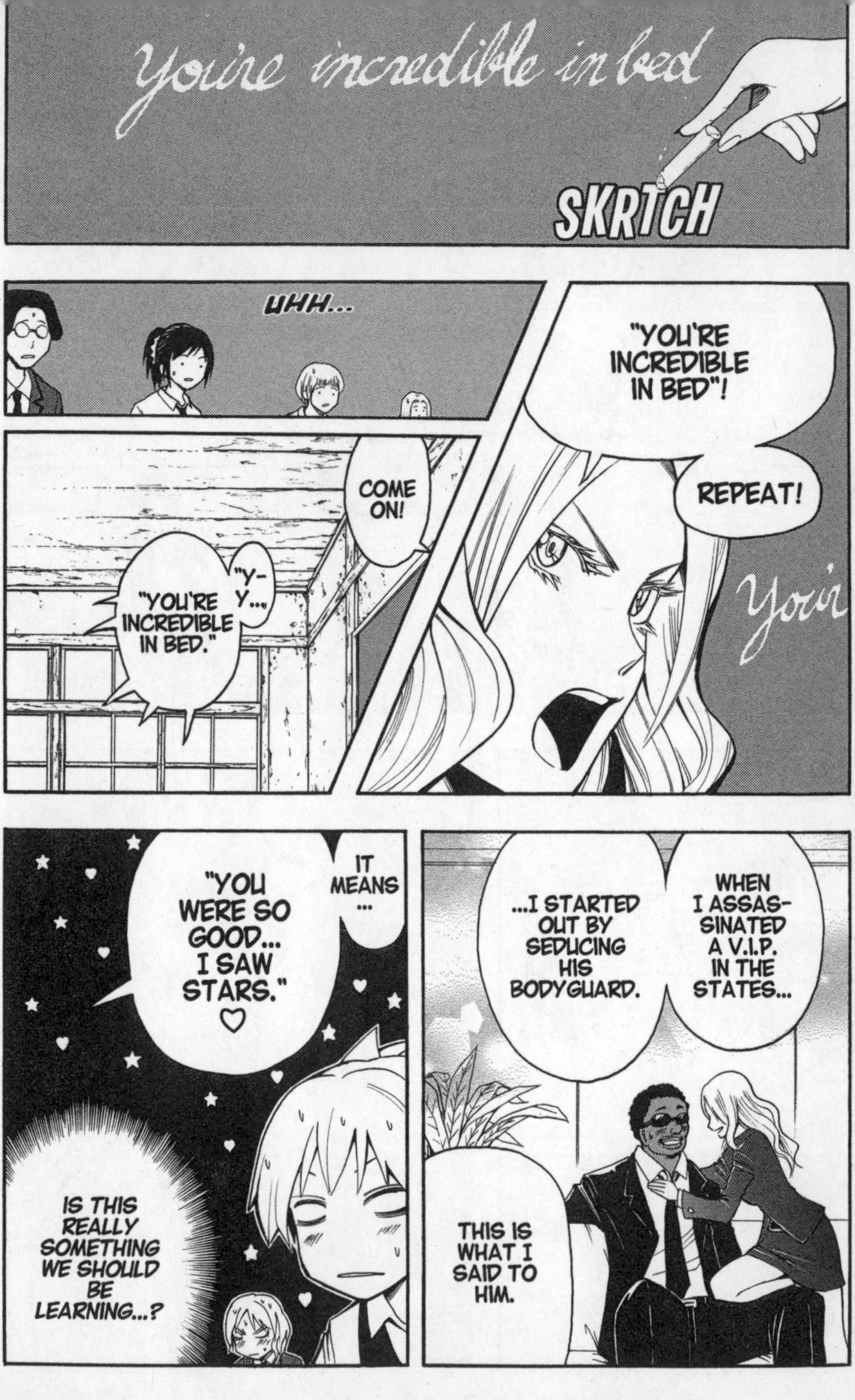
You're incredible in bed
SKRTCH
"YOU'RE INCREDIBLE IN BED"!
REPEAT!
You'r
UHH...
COME ON!
"Y-Y...
"YOU'RE INCREDIBLE IN BED."
WHEN I ASSASSINATED A V.I.P. IN THE STATES...
...I STARTED OUT BY SEDUCING HIS BODYGUARD.
THIS IS WHAT I SAID TO HIM.
IT MEANS...
"YOU WERE SO GOOD... I SAW STARS." ♡
IS THIS REALLY SOMETHING WE SHOULD BE LEARNING...?

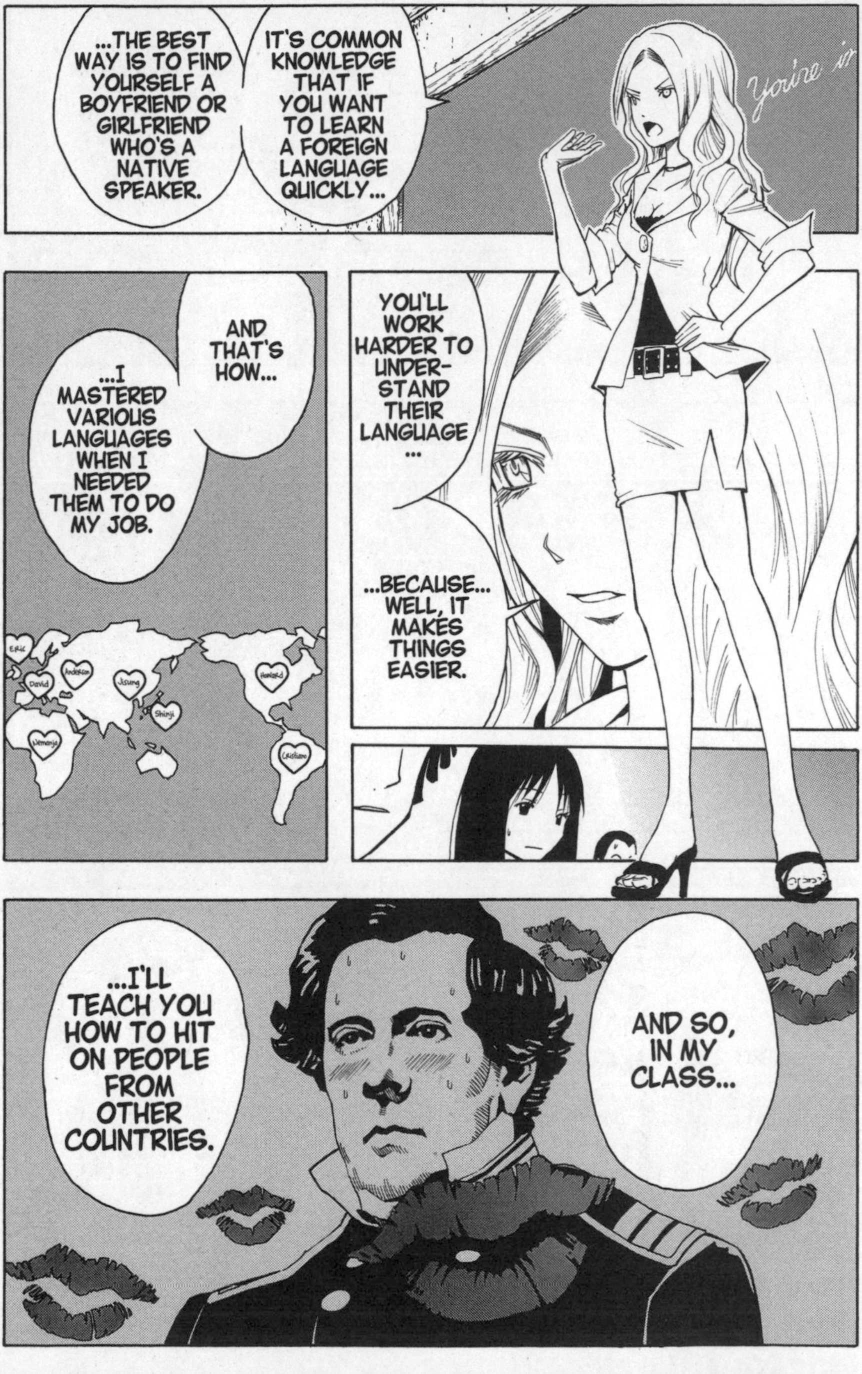
IT'S COMMON KNOWLEDGE THAT IF YOU WANT TO LEARN A FOREIGN LANGUAGE QUICKLY...
...THE BEST WAY IS TO FIND YOURSELF A BOYFRIEND OR GIRLFRIEND WHO'S A NATIVE SPEAKER.
You're in
YOU'LL WORK HARDER TO UNDER-STAND THEIR LANGUAGE...
...BECAUSE... WELL, IT MAKES THINGS EASIER.
AND THAT'S HOW...
...I MASTERED VARIOUS LANGUAGES WHEN I NEEDED THEM TO DO MY JOB.
Eric
David
Anderson
Jisung
Shinji
Howard
Nemanja
Cristiano
AND SO, IN MY CLASS...
...I'LL TEACH YOU HOW TO HIT ON PEOPLE FROM OTHER COUNTRIES.

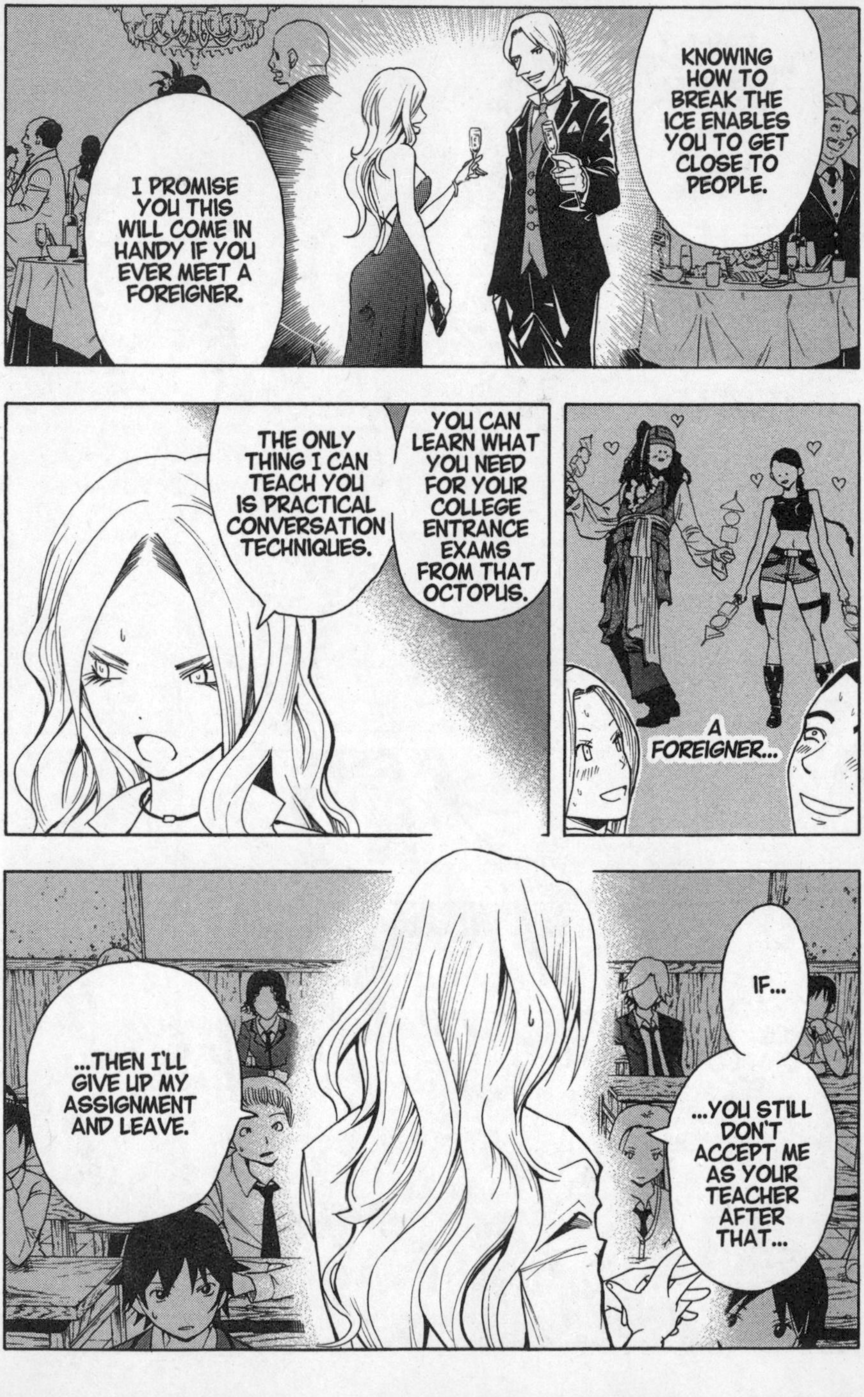
KNOWING HOW TO BREAK THE ICE ENABLES YOU TO GET CLOSE TO PEOPLE.
I PROMISE YOU THIS WILL COME IN HANDY IF YOU EVER MEET A FOREIGNER.
A FOREIGNER...
YOU CAN LEARN WHAT YOU NEED FOR YOUR COLLEGE ENTRANCE EXAMS FROM THAT OCTOPUS.
THE ONLY THING I CAN TEACH YOU IS PRACTICAL CONVERSATION TECHNIQUES.
IF...
...YOU STILL DON'T ACCEPT ME AS YOUR TEACHER AFTER THAT...
...THEN I'LL GIVE UP MY ASSIGNMENT AND LEAVE.

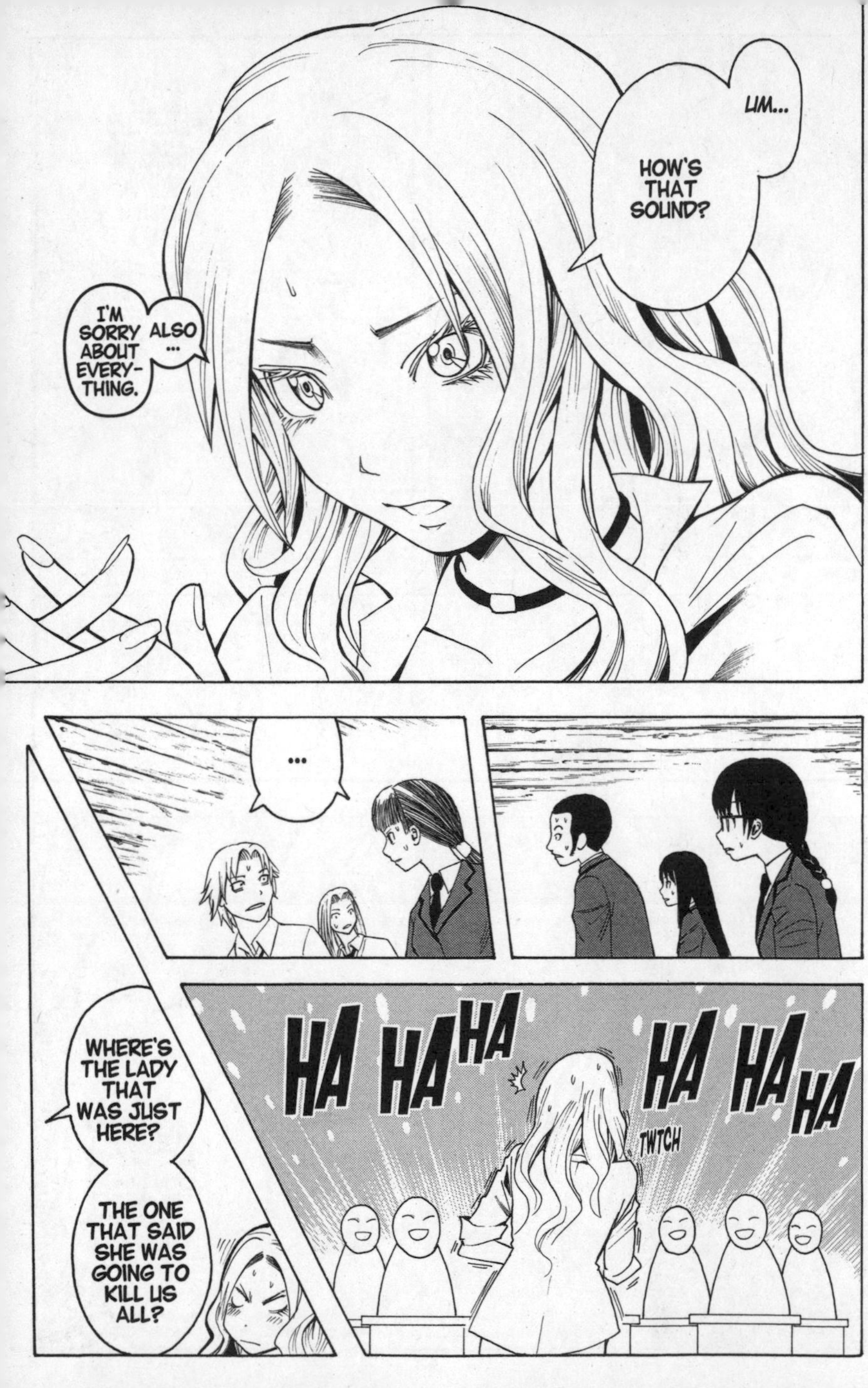
UM... HOW'S THAT SOUND?
ALSO ...
I'M SORRY ABOUT EVERYTHING.
...
HA HA HA HA HA
HA HA HA
TWTCH
WHERE'S THE LADY THAT WAS JUST HERE?
THE ONE THAT SAID SHE WAS GOING TO KILL US ALL?

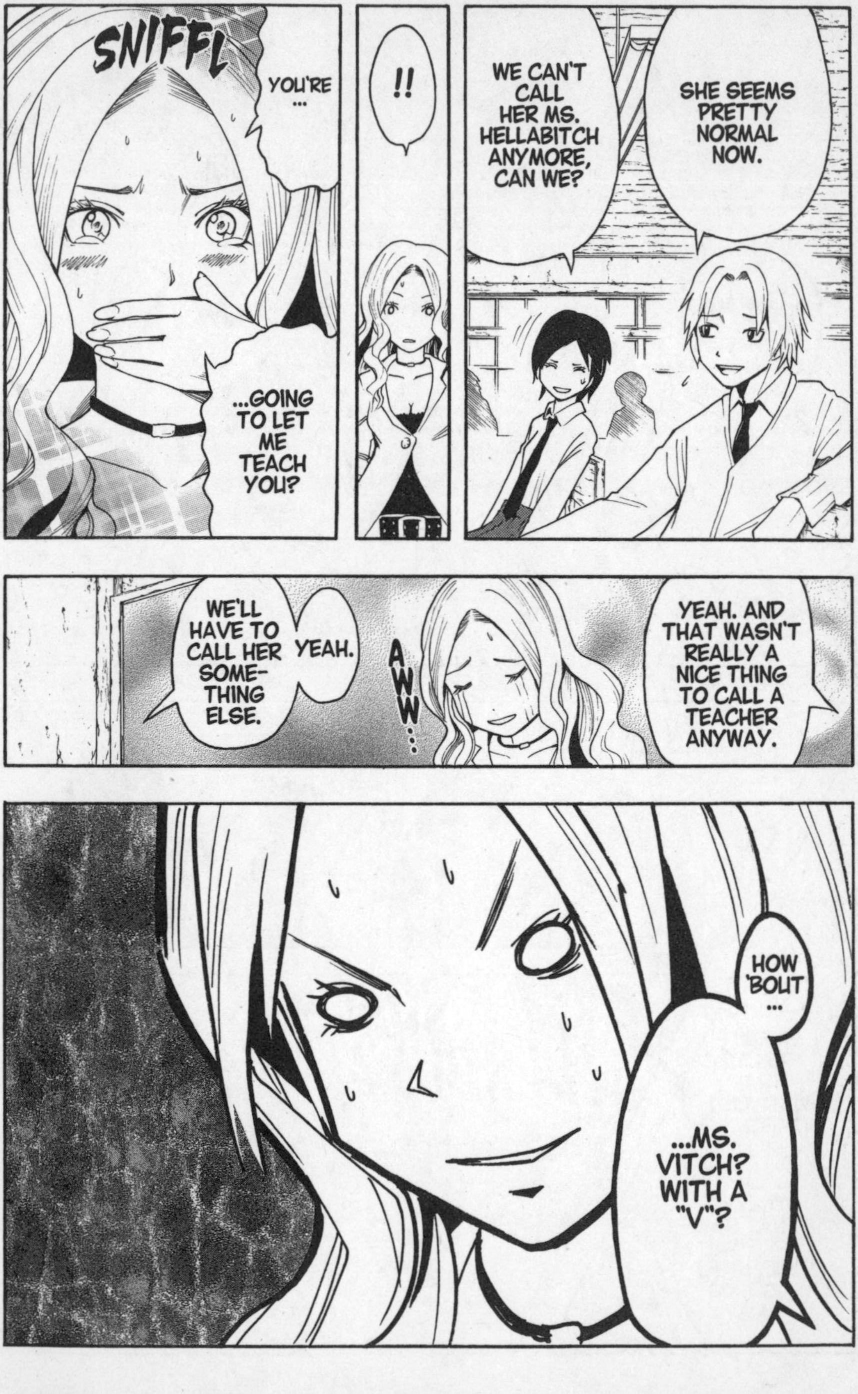
SHE SEEMS PRETTY NORMAL NOW.
WE CAN'T CALL HER MS. HELLABITCH ANYMORE, CAN WE?
!!
SNIFFL
YOU'RE ...
...GOING TO LET ME TEACH YOU?
YEAH. AND THAT WASN'T REALLY A NICE THING TO CALL A TEACHER ANYWAY.
YEAH.
WE'LL HAVE TO CALL HER SOME-THING ELSE.
AWW...
HOW 'BOUT ...
...MS. VITCH? WITH A "V"?

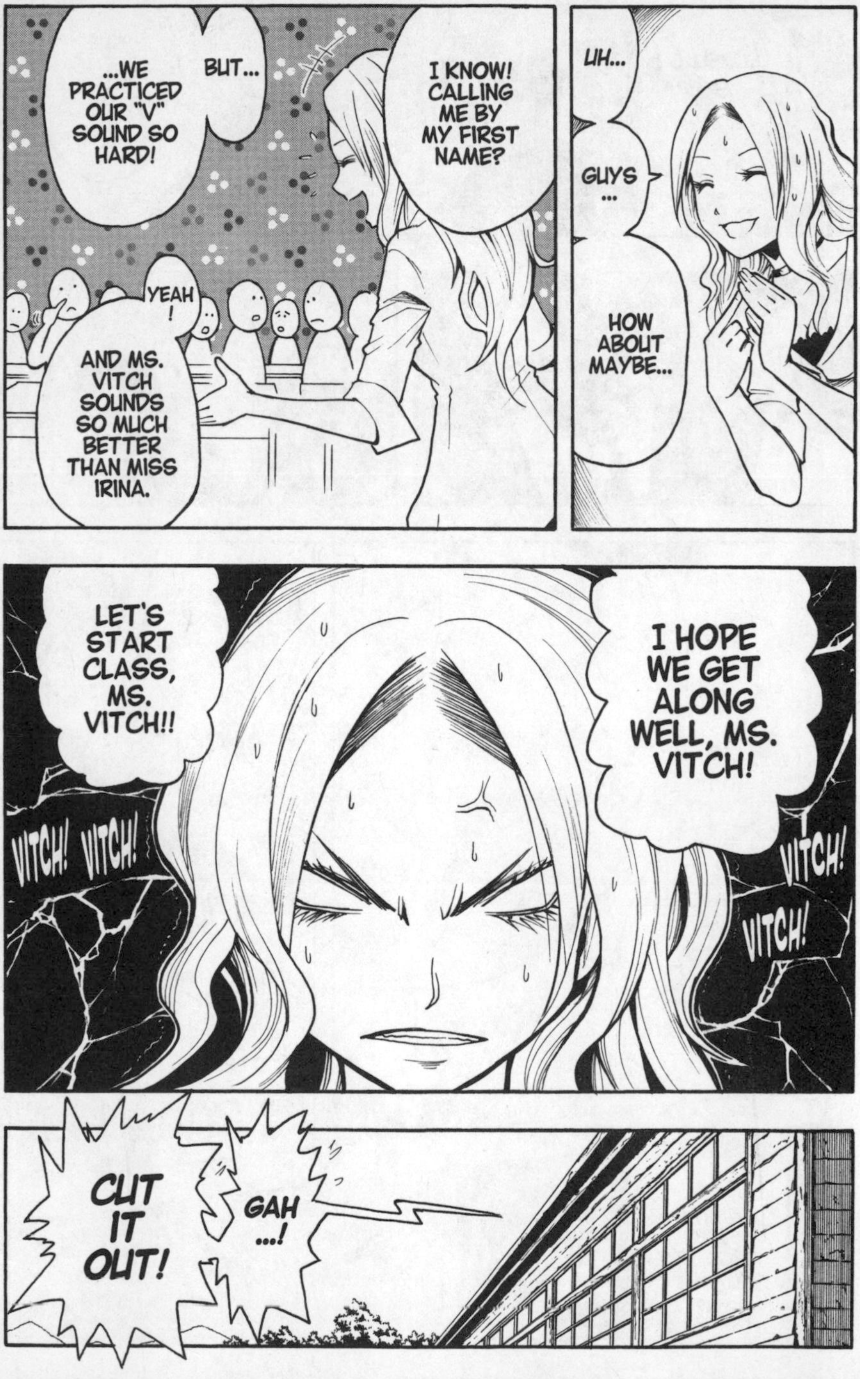
UH...
GUYS...
HOW ABOUT MAYBE...
I KNOW! CALLING ME BY MY FIRST NAME?
BUT...
...WE PRACTICED OUR "V" SOUND SO HARD!
YEAH!
AND MS. VITCH SOUNDS SO MUCH BETTER THAN MISS IRINA.
I HOPE WE GET ALONG WELL, MS. VITCH!
VITCH!
VITCH!
LET'S START CLASS, MS. VITCH!!
VITCH! VITCH!
GAH...!
CUT IT OUT!

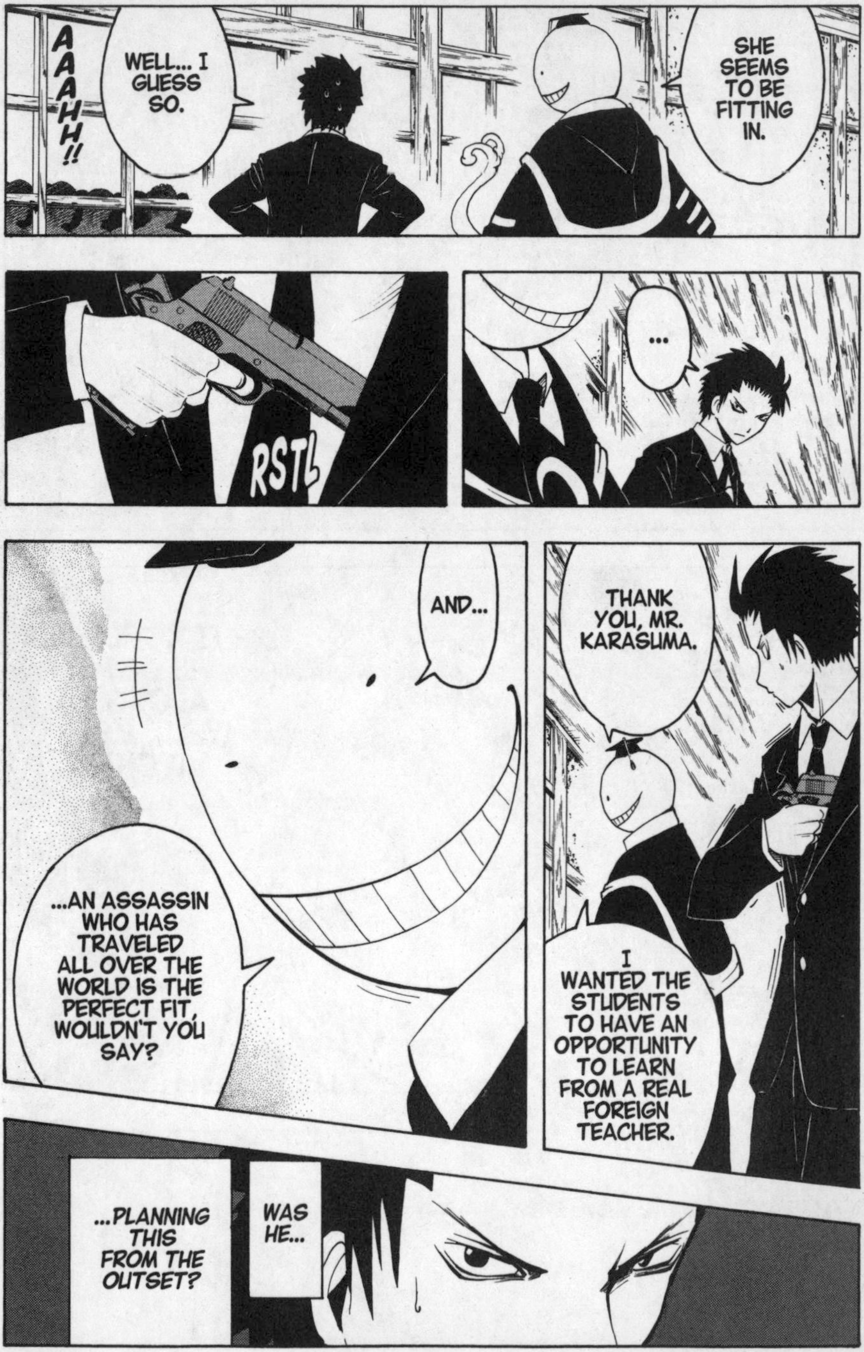
SHE SEEMS TO BE FITTING IN.
WELL... I GUESS SO.
AAAAHH!!
...
RSTL
THANK YOU, MR. KARASUMA.
I WANTED THE STUDENTS TO HAVE AN OPPORTUNITY TO LEARN FROM A REAL FOREIGN TEACHER.
AND...
...AN ASSASSIN WHO HAS TRAVELED ALL OVER THE WORLD IS THE PERFECT FIT, WOULDN'T YOU SAY?
WAS HE...
...PLANNING THIS FROM THE OUTSET?

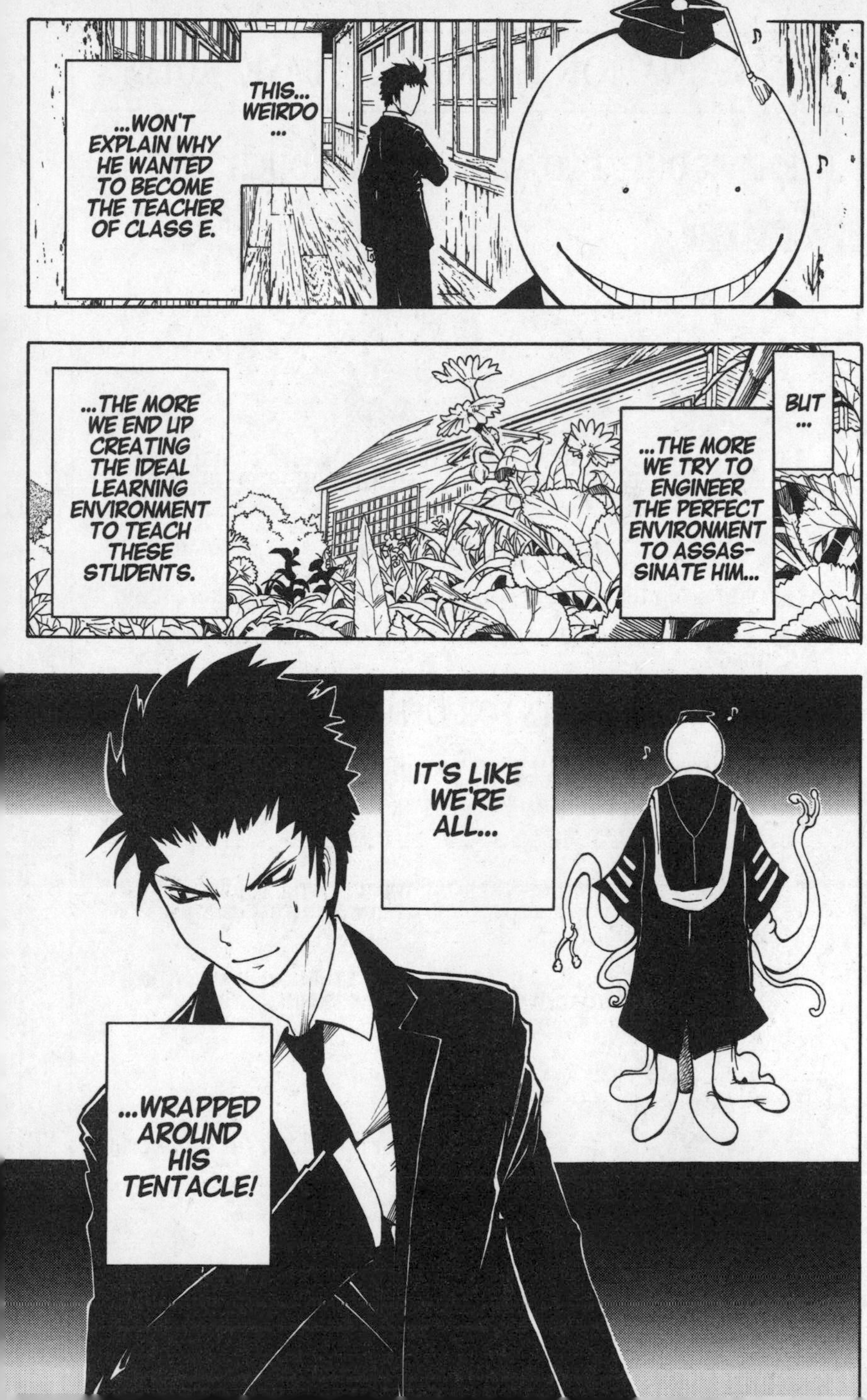
THIS... WEIRDO ...
...WON'T EXPLAIN WHY HE WANTED TO BECOME THE TEACHER OF CLASS E.
BUT ...
...THE MORE WE TRY TO ENGINEER THE PERFECT ENVIRONMENT TO ASSAS-SINATE HIM...
...THE MORE WE END UP CREATING THE IDEAL LEARNING ENVIRONMENT TO TEACH THESE STUDENTS.
IT'S LIKE WE'RE ALL...
...WRAPPED AROUND HIS TENTACLE!

Assassination Badminton Basic Rules

There are only two ways you may touch the ball.

The Slash, in which you strike the ball with the blade of the knife.

The Lunge, in which you strike the ball with the tip of the knife.

Rules for Offense

● One point if the ball falls into the opponent's field through a Slash.

● Three points if the ball falls into the opponent's field through a Lunge.

Rules for Defense

● You may only hit the ball three times using a Slash per turn.

● You may hit the ball as many times as you wish with a Lunge.

● The opposing team will get the ball if you touch the ball with anything but a Slash or a Lunge. You may hit the ball as many times as you wish with a Lunge.

● You need a lot of skill to successfully strike the moving ball with a Lunge, so it is regarded as a more advanced technique than a regular badminton Strike.

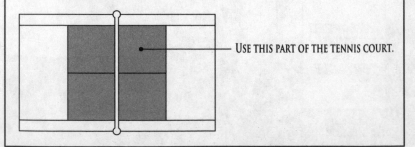

Use this part of the tennis court.

Class 11 Assembly Time

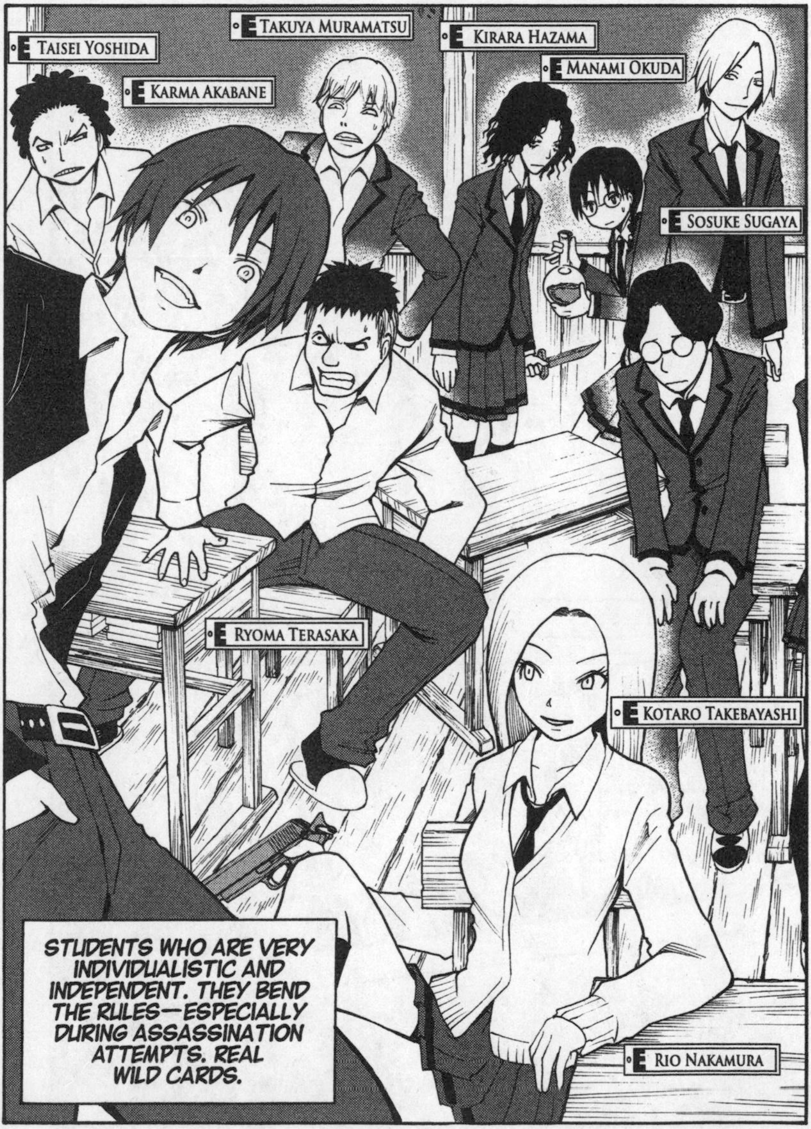
E Kirara Hazama
E Manami Okuda
E Takuya Muramatsu
E Karma Akabane
E Taisei Yoshida
E Sosuke Sugaya
E Ryoma Terasaka
E Kotaro Takebayashi
E Rio Nakamura
STUDENTS WHO ARE VERY INDIVIDUALISTIC AND INDEPENDENT. THEY BEND THE RULES—ESPECIALLY DURING ASSASSINATION ATTEMPTS. REAL WILD CARDS.

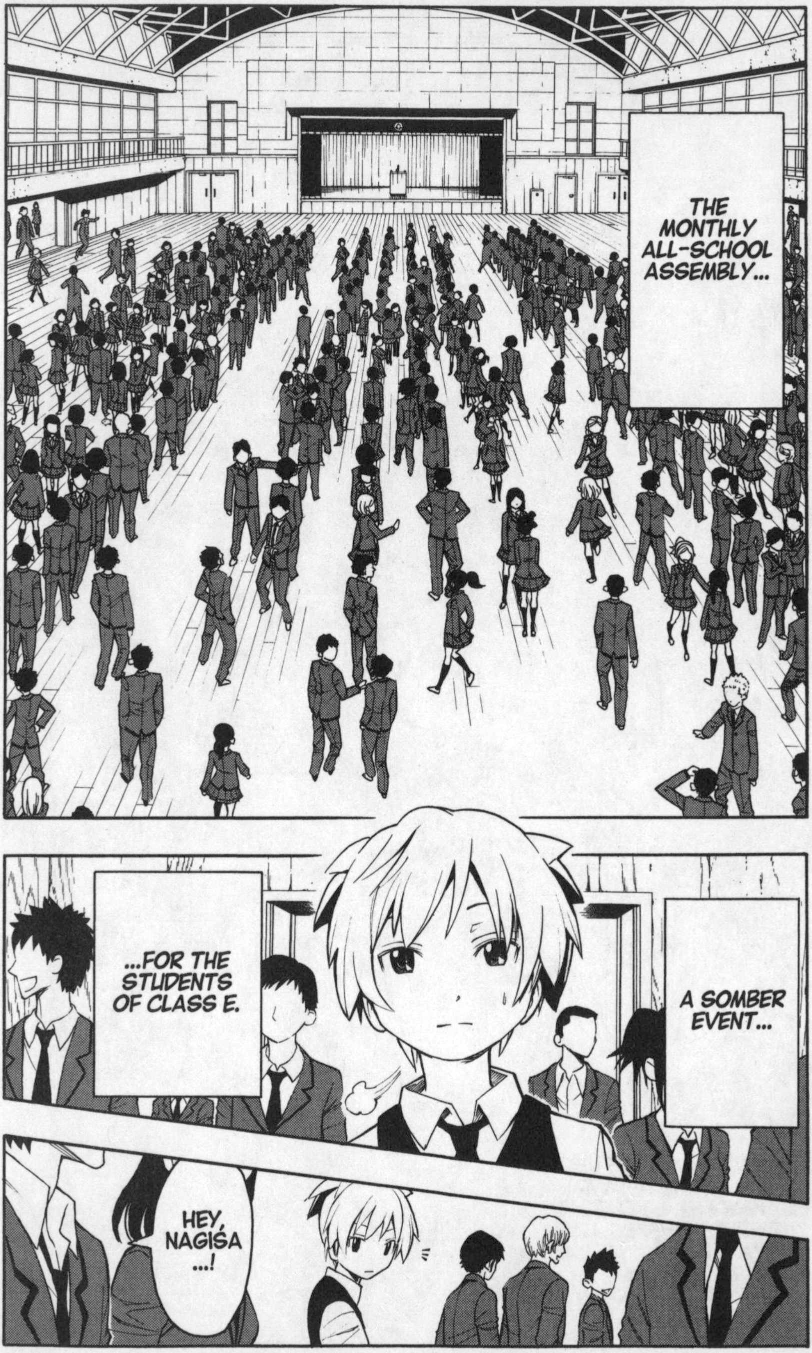
THE MONTHLY ALL-SCHOOL ASSEMBLY...
A SOMBER EVENT...
...FOR THE STUDENTS OF CLASS E.
HEY, NAGISA ...!

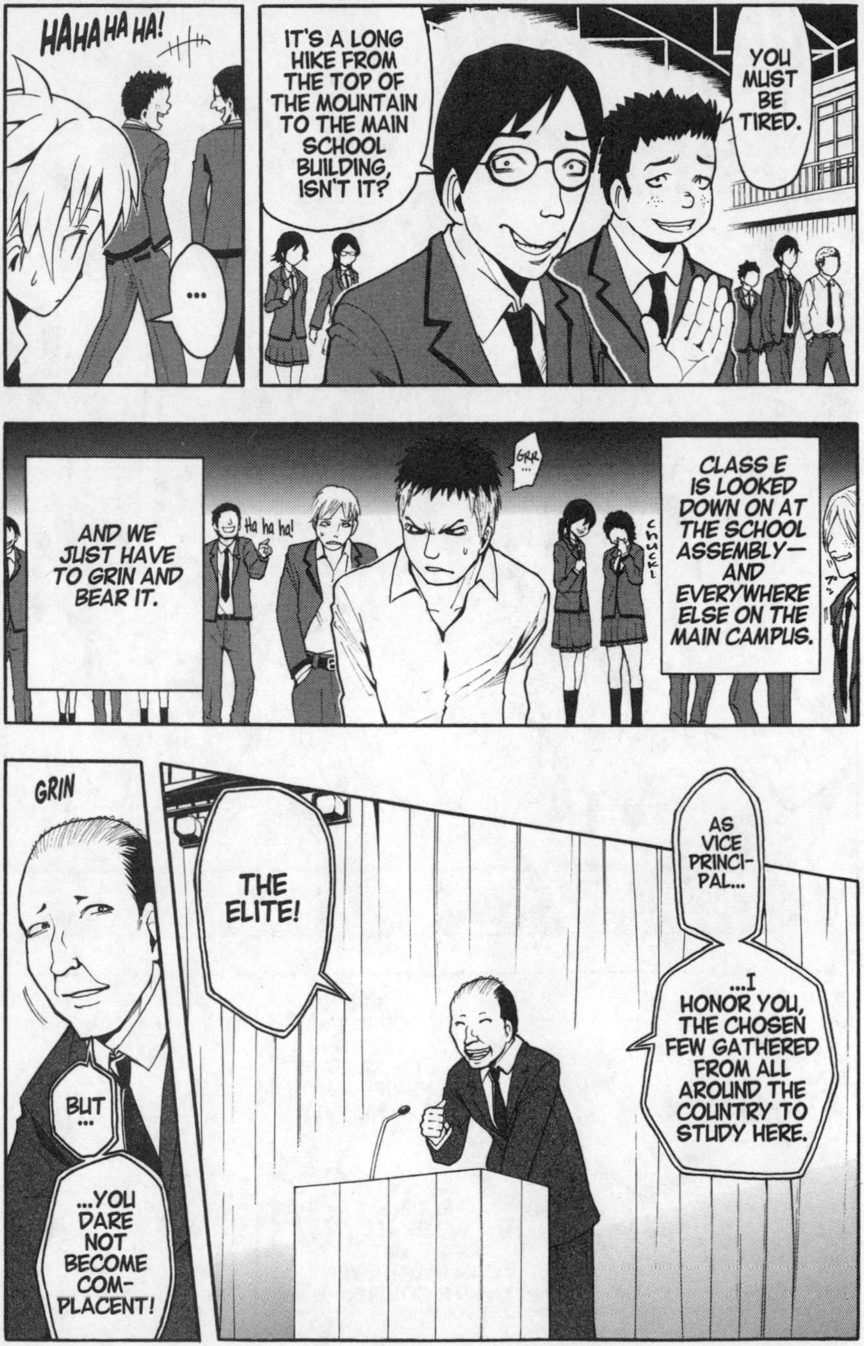
YOU MUST BE TIRED.
IT'S A LONG HIKE FROM THE TOP OF THE MOUNTAIN TO THE MAIN SCHOOL BUILDING, ISN'T IT?
HAHAHA HA HA!
...
CLASS E IS LOOKED DOWN ON AT THE SCHOOL ASSEMBLY—AND EVERYWHERE ELSE ON THE MAIN CAMPUS.
GRR...
CHUCKL
Ha ha ha!
AND WE JUST HAVE TO GRIN AND BEAR IT.
AS VICE PRINCI-PAL...
...I HONOR YOU, THE CHOSEN FEW GATHERED FROM ALL AROUND THE COUNTRY TO STUDY HERE.
THE ELITE!
GRIN
BUT...
...YOU DARE NOT BECOME COM-PLACENT!

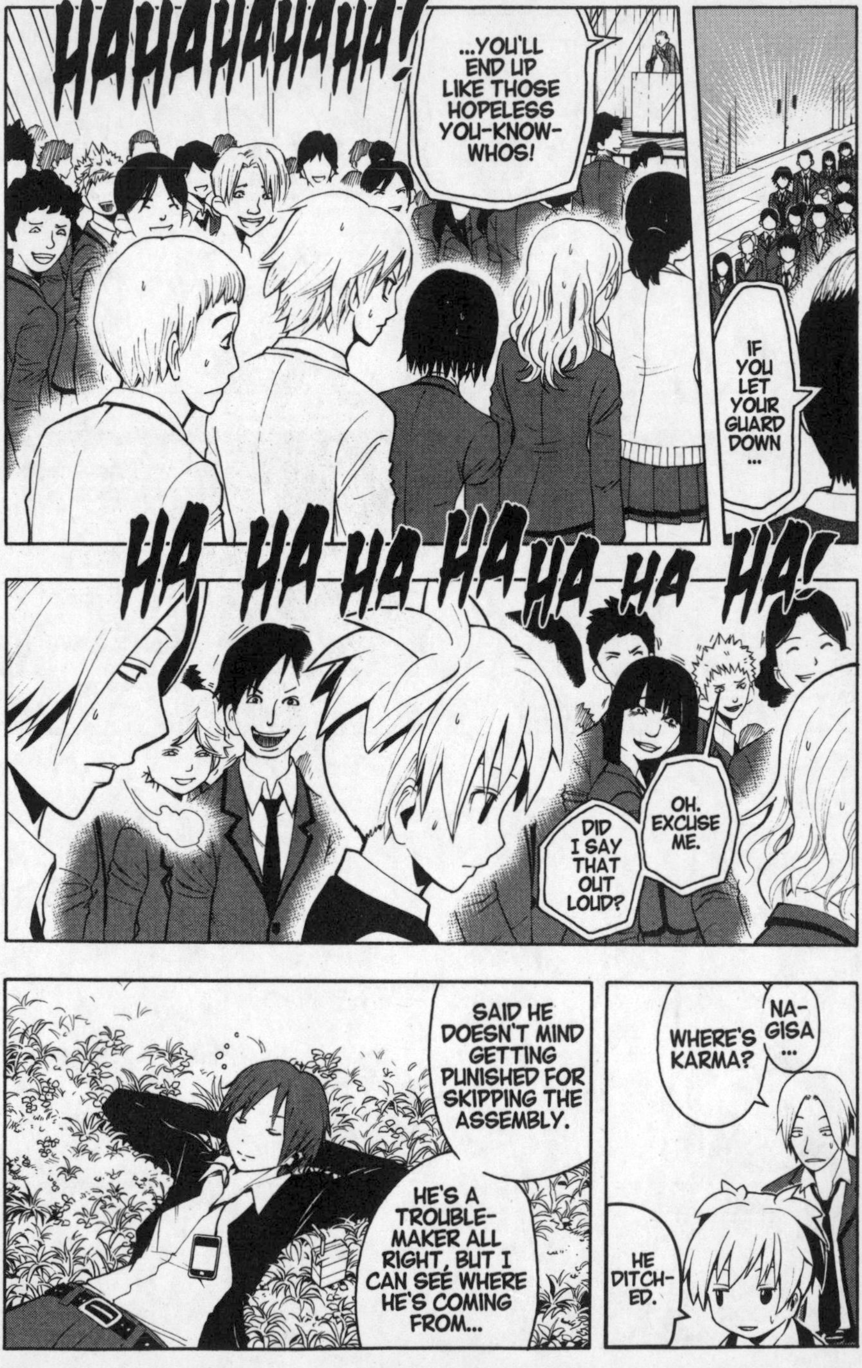
IF YOU LET YOUR GUARD DOWN...
...YOU'LL END UP LIKE THOSE HOPELESS YOU-KNOW-WHOS!
HAHAHAHAHAHA!
HA HA HA HA HA HA HA!
OH. EXCUSE ME.
DID I SAY THAT OUT LOUD?
NA-GISA...
WHERE'S KARMA?
HE DITCH-ED.
SAID HE DOESN'T MIND GETTING PUNISHED FOR SKIPPING THE ASSEMBLY.
HE'S A TROUBLE-MAKER ALL RIGHT, BUT I CAN SEE WHERE HE'S COMING FROM...

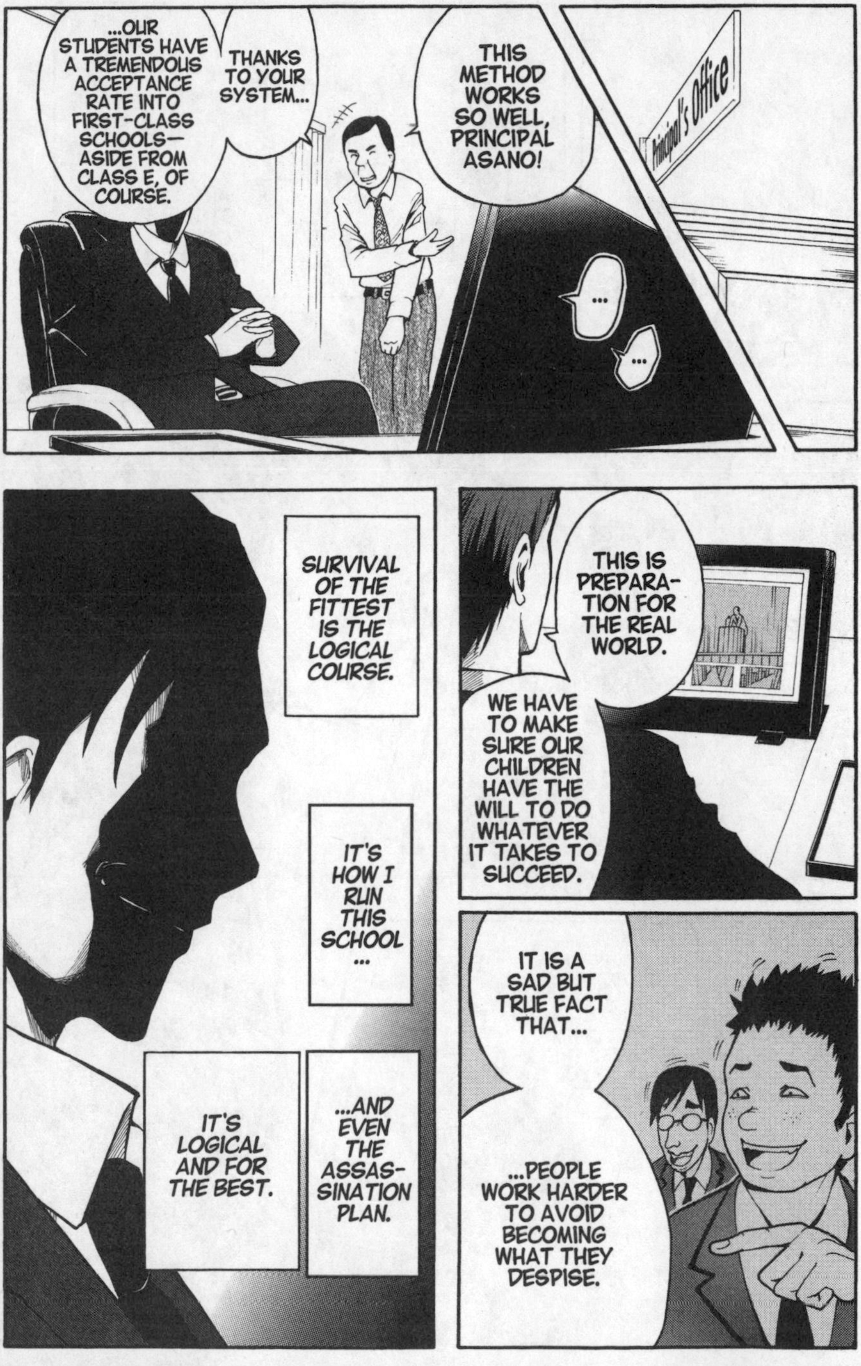
Principal's Office
THIS METHOD WORKS SO WELL, PRINCIPAL ASANO!
THANKS TO YOUR SYSTEM...
...OUR STUDENTS HAVE A TREMENDOUS ACCEPTANCE RATE INTO FIRST-CLASS SCHOOLS— ASIDE FROM CLASS E, OF COURSE.
...
...
THIS IS PREPARATION FOR THE REAL WORLD.
WE HAVE TO MAKE SURE OUR CHILDREN HAVE THE WILL TO DO WHATEVER IT TAKES TO SUCCEED.
IT IS A SAD BUT TRUE FACT THAT...
...PEOPLE WORK HARDER TO AVOID BECOMING WHAT THEY DESPISE.
SURVIVAL OF THE FITTEST IS THE LOGICAL COURSE.
IT'S HOW I RUN THIS SCHOOL...
...AND EVEN THE ASSASSINATION PLAN.
IT'S LOGICAL AND FOR THE BEST.

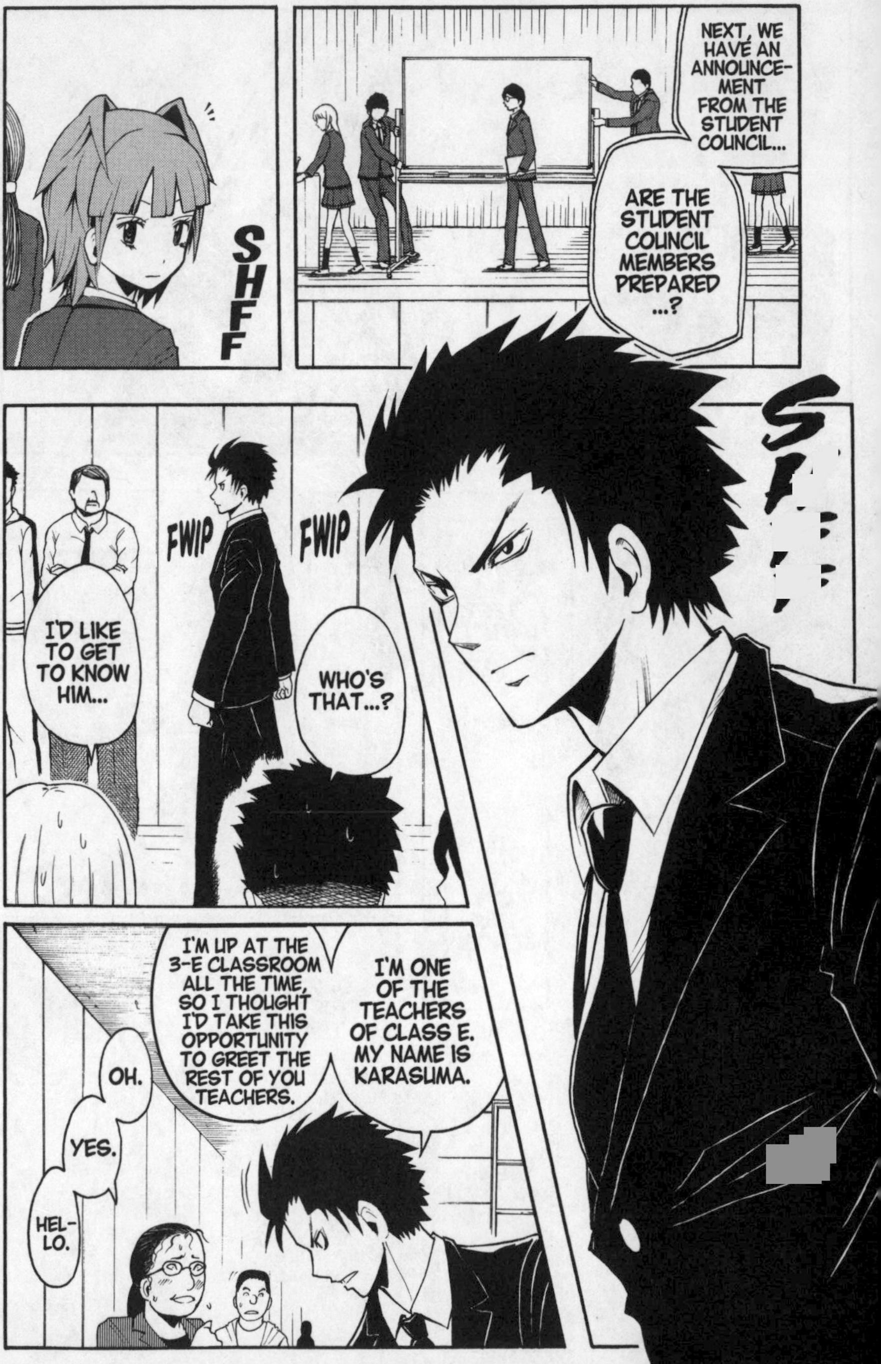
NEXT, WE HAVE AN ANNOUNCEMENT FROM THE STUDENT COUNCIL...
ARE THE STUDENT COUNCIL MEMBERS PREPARED ...?
SHFF
FWIP
FWIP
WHO'S THAT...?
I'D LIKE TO GET TO KNOW HIM...
I'M ONE OF THE TEACHERS OF CLASS E. MY NAME IS KARASUMA.
I'M UP AT THE 3-E CLASSROOM ALL THE TIME, SO I THOUGHT I'D TAKE THIS OPPORTUNITY TO GREET THE REST OF YOU TEACHERS.
OH.
YES.
HEL-LO.

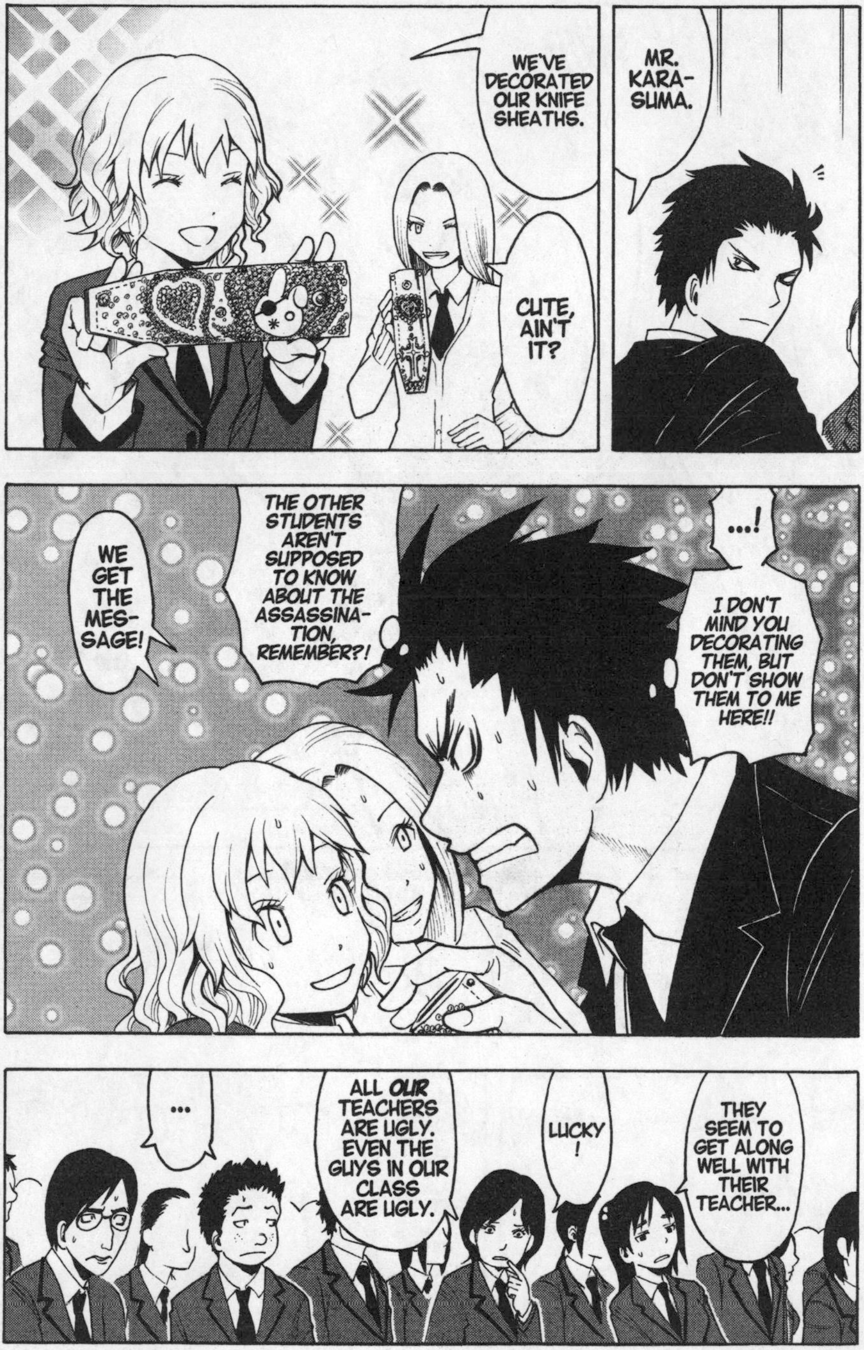
MR. KARA-SUMA.
WE'VE DECORATED OUR KNIFE SHEATHS.
CUTE, AIN'T IT?
...!
I DON'T MIND YOU DECORATING THEM, BUT DON'T SHOW THEM TO ME HERE!!
THE OTHER STUDENTS AREN'T SUPPOSED TO KNOW ABOUT THE ASSASSINA-TION, REMEMBER?!
WE GET THE MES-SAGE!
THEY SEEM TO GET ALONG WELL WITH THEIR TEACHER...
LUCKY!
ALL *OUR* TEACHERS ARE UGLY. EVEN THE GUYS IN OUR CLASS ARE UGLY.
...

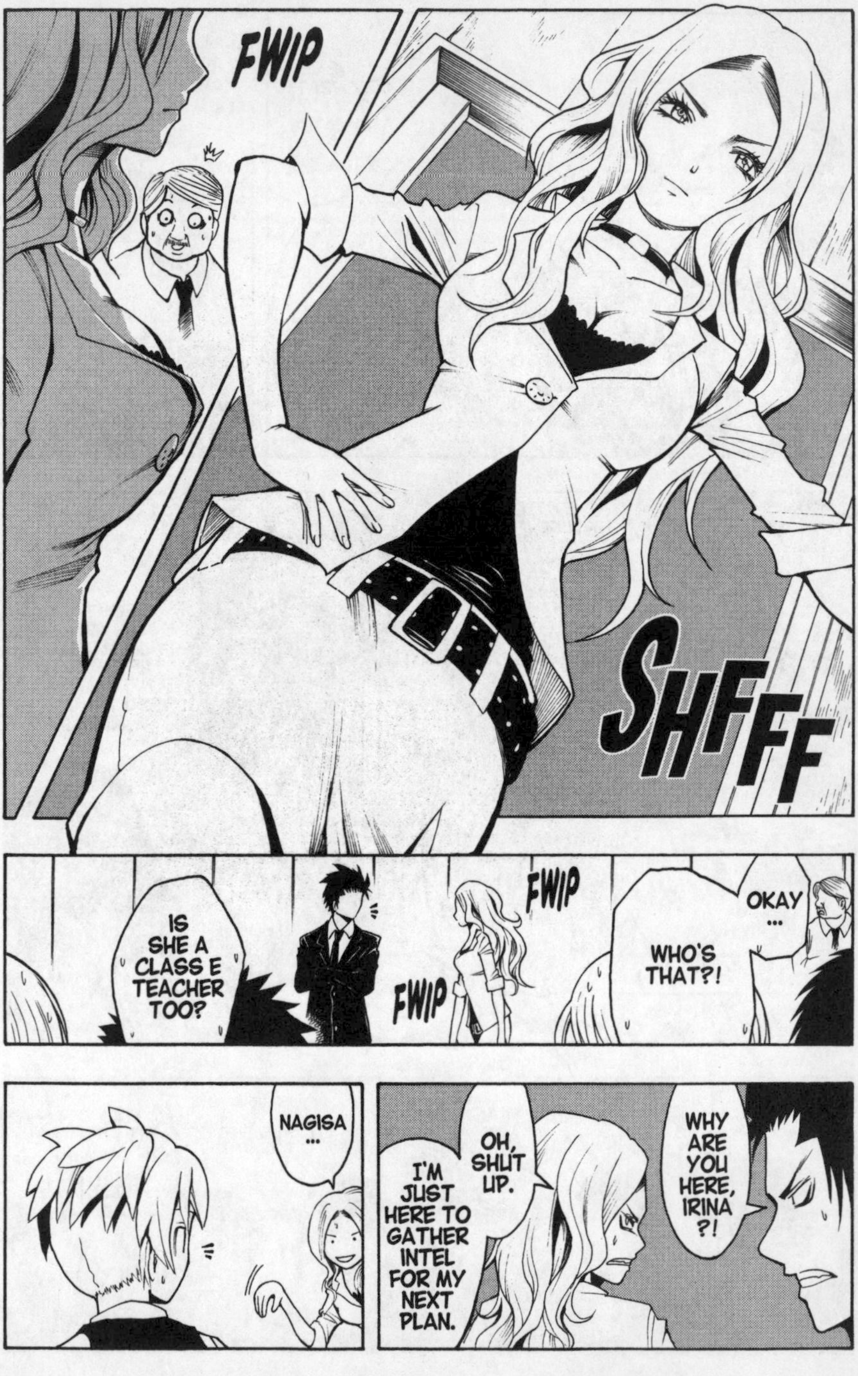
FWIP
SHFFF
OKAY...
WHO'S THAT?!
FWIP
FWIP
IS SHE A CLASS E TEACHER TOO?
WHY ARE YOU HERE, IRINA?!
OH, SHUT UP.
I'M JUST HERE TO GATHER INTEL FOR MY NEXT PLAN.
NAGISA...

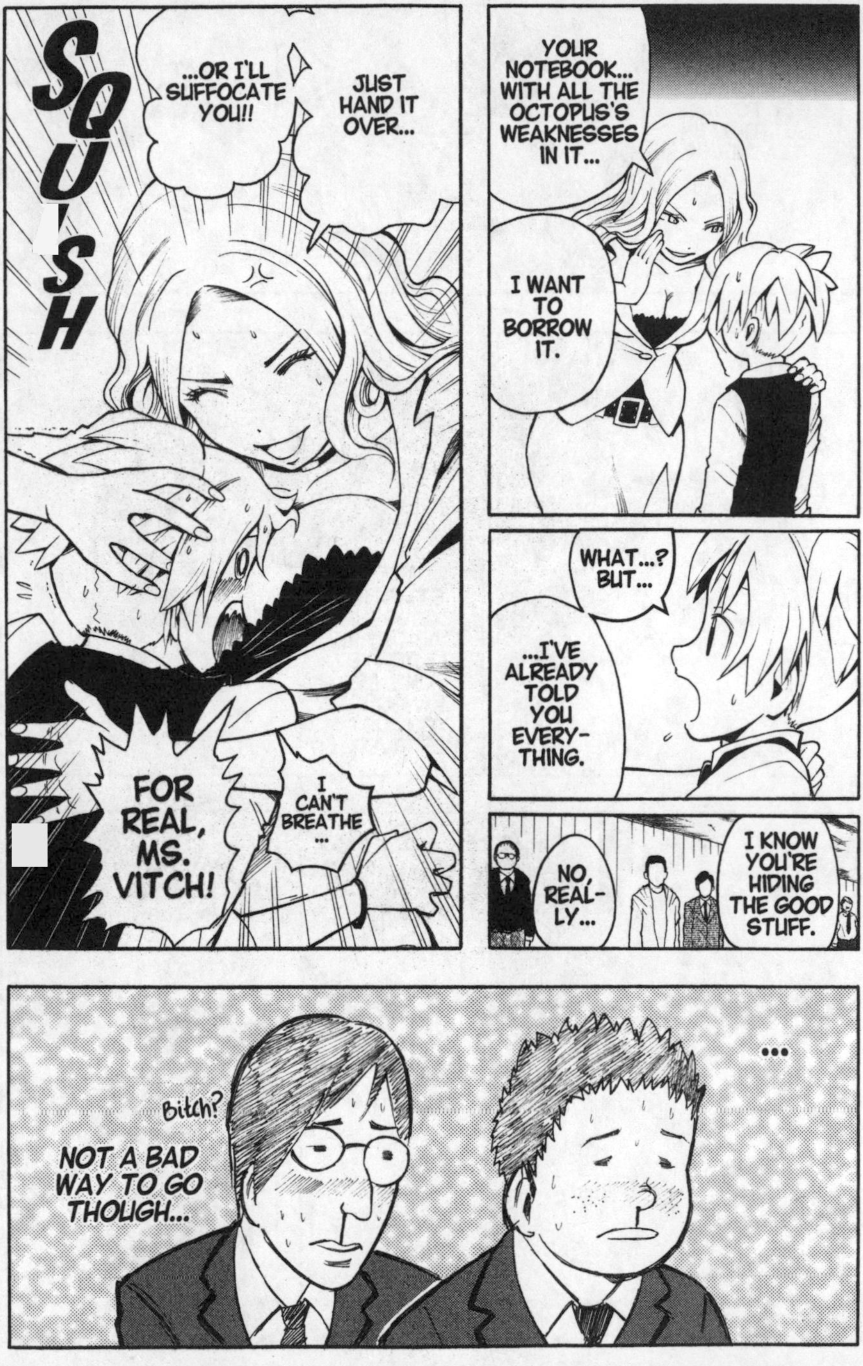
YOUR NOTEBOOK... WITH ALL THE OCTOPUS'S WEAKNESSES IN IT...
I WANT TO BORROW IT.
WHAT...? BUT...
...I'VE ALREADY TOLD YOU EVERYTHING.
I KNOW YOU'RE HIDING THE GOOD STUFF.
NO, REALLY...
JUST HAND IT OVER...
...OR I'LL SUFFOCATE YOU!!
SQUISH
I CAN'T BREATHE...
FOR REAL, MS. VITCH!
...
Bitch?
NOT A BAD WAY TO GO THOUGH...

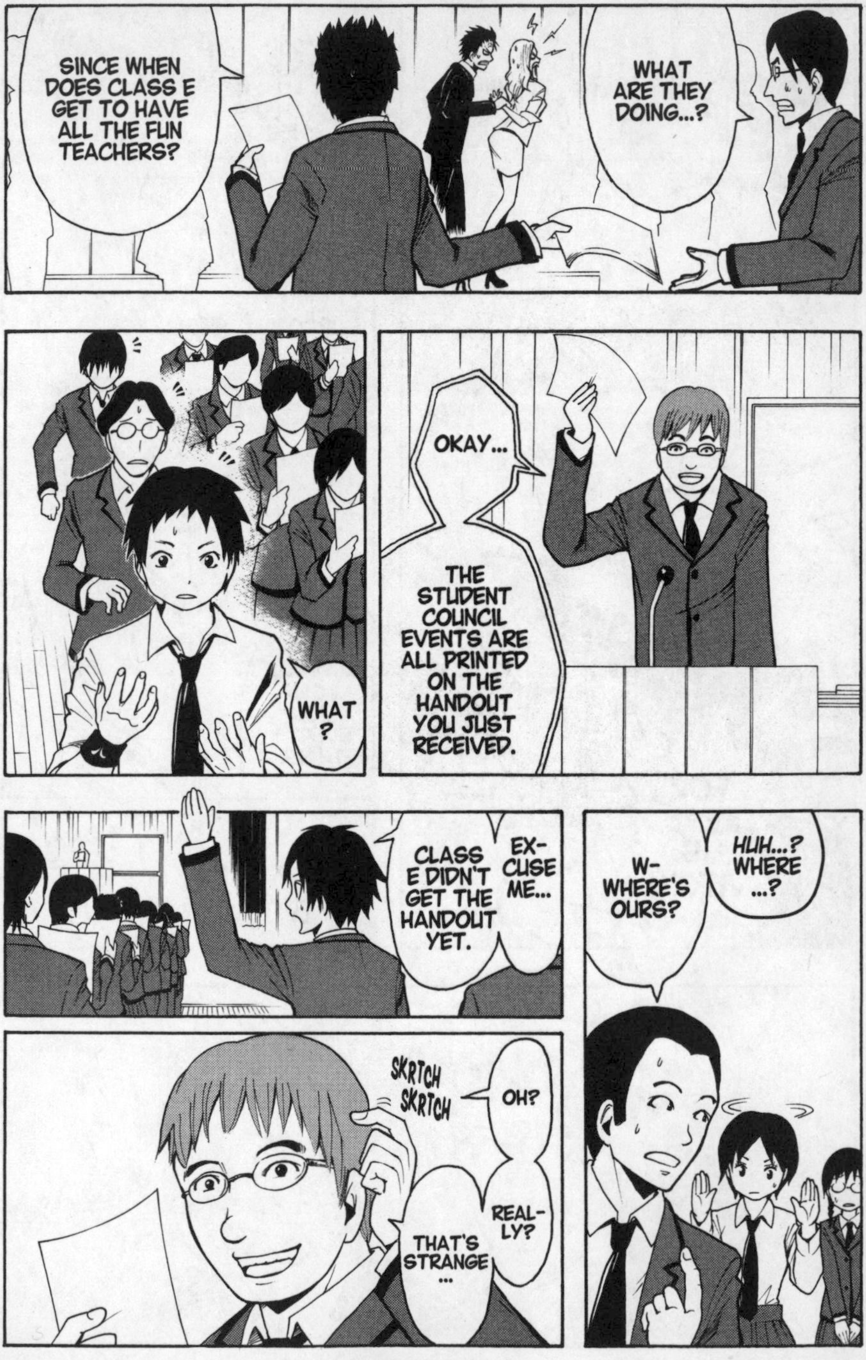
WHAT ARE THEY DOING...?
SINCE WHEN DOES CLASS E GET TO HAVE ALL THE FUN TEACHERS?
OKAY...
THE STUDENT COUNCIL EVENTS ARE ALL PRINTED ON THE HANDOUT YOU JUST RECEIVED.
WHAT?
HUH...? WHERE ...?
W-WHERE'S OURS?
EX-CUSE ME...
CLASS E DIDN'T GET THE HANDOUT YET.
OH?
SKRTCH SKRTCH
REAL-LY?
THAT'S STRANGE ...

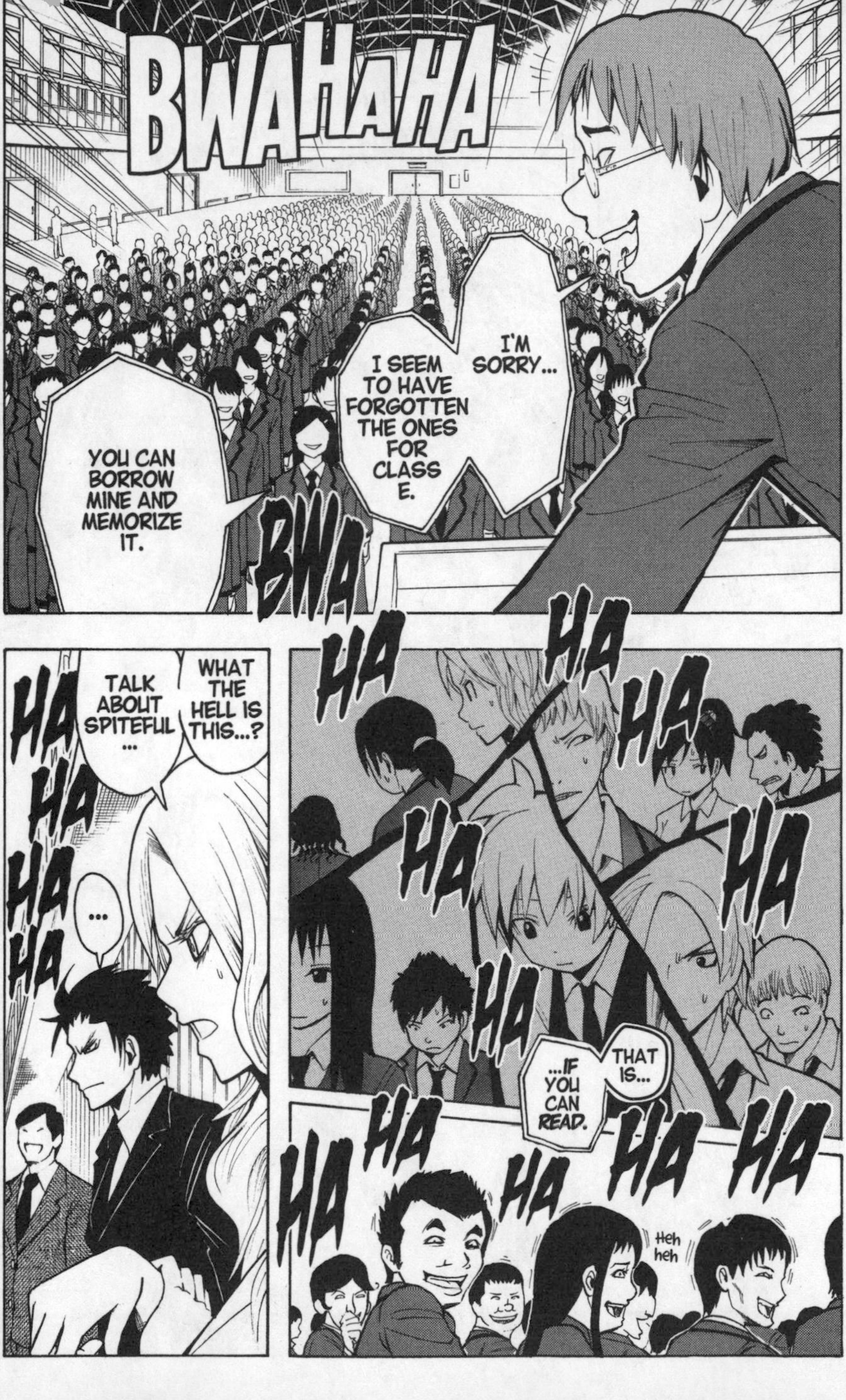
BWAHAHAHA
I'M SORRY...
I SEEM TO HAVE FORGOTTEN THE ONES FOR CLASS E.
YOU CAN BORROW MINE AND MEMORIZE IT.
BWA
HA HA HA HA HA HA
THAT IS...
...IF YOU CAN READ.
HA HA HA HA HA HA
Heh heh
WHAT THE HELL IS THIS...?
TALK ABOUT SPITEFUL...
...
HA HA HA HA

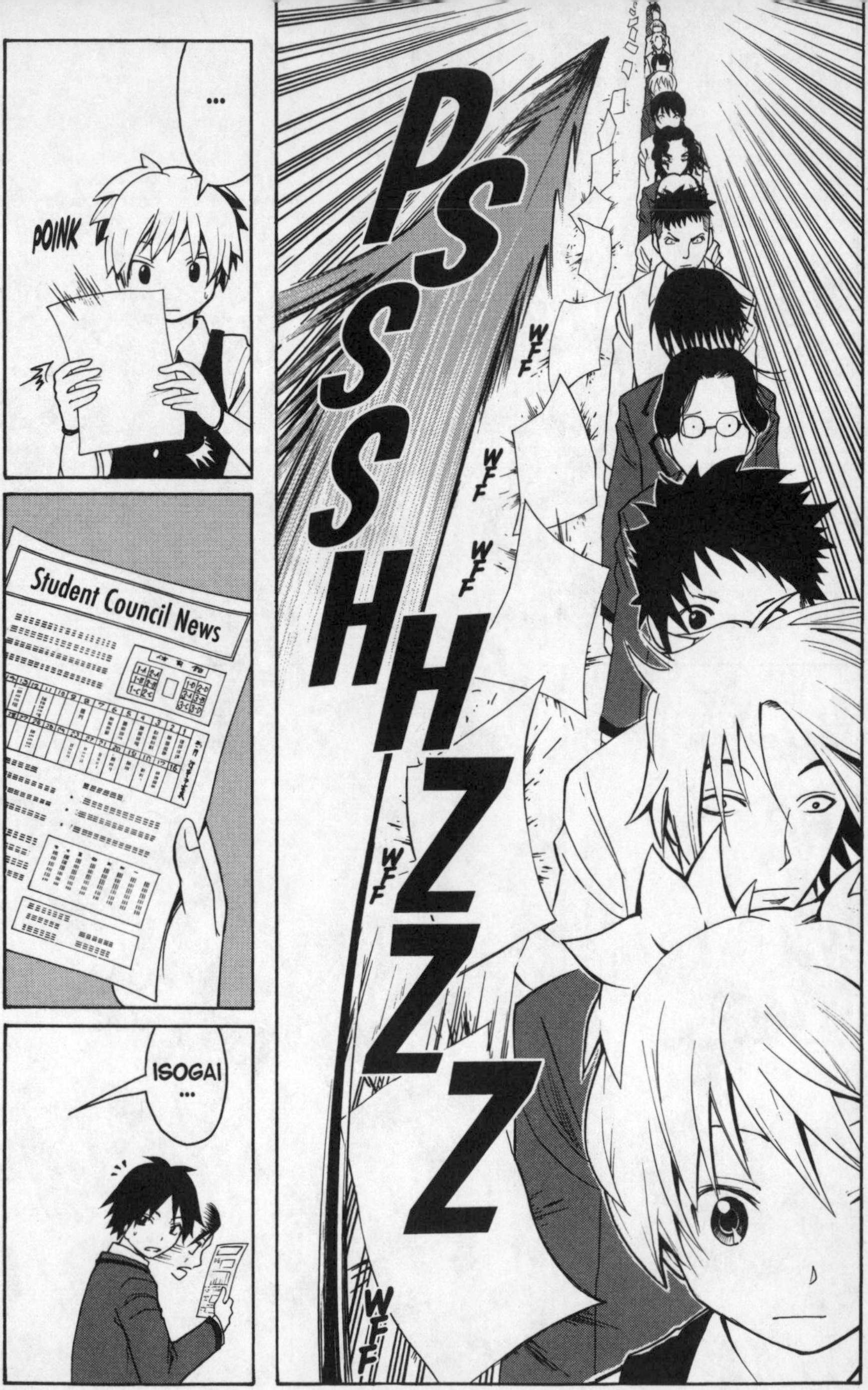
PSSSHHZZZ
WFF
WFF
WFF
WFF
WFF
...
POINK
Student Council News
ISOGAI ...

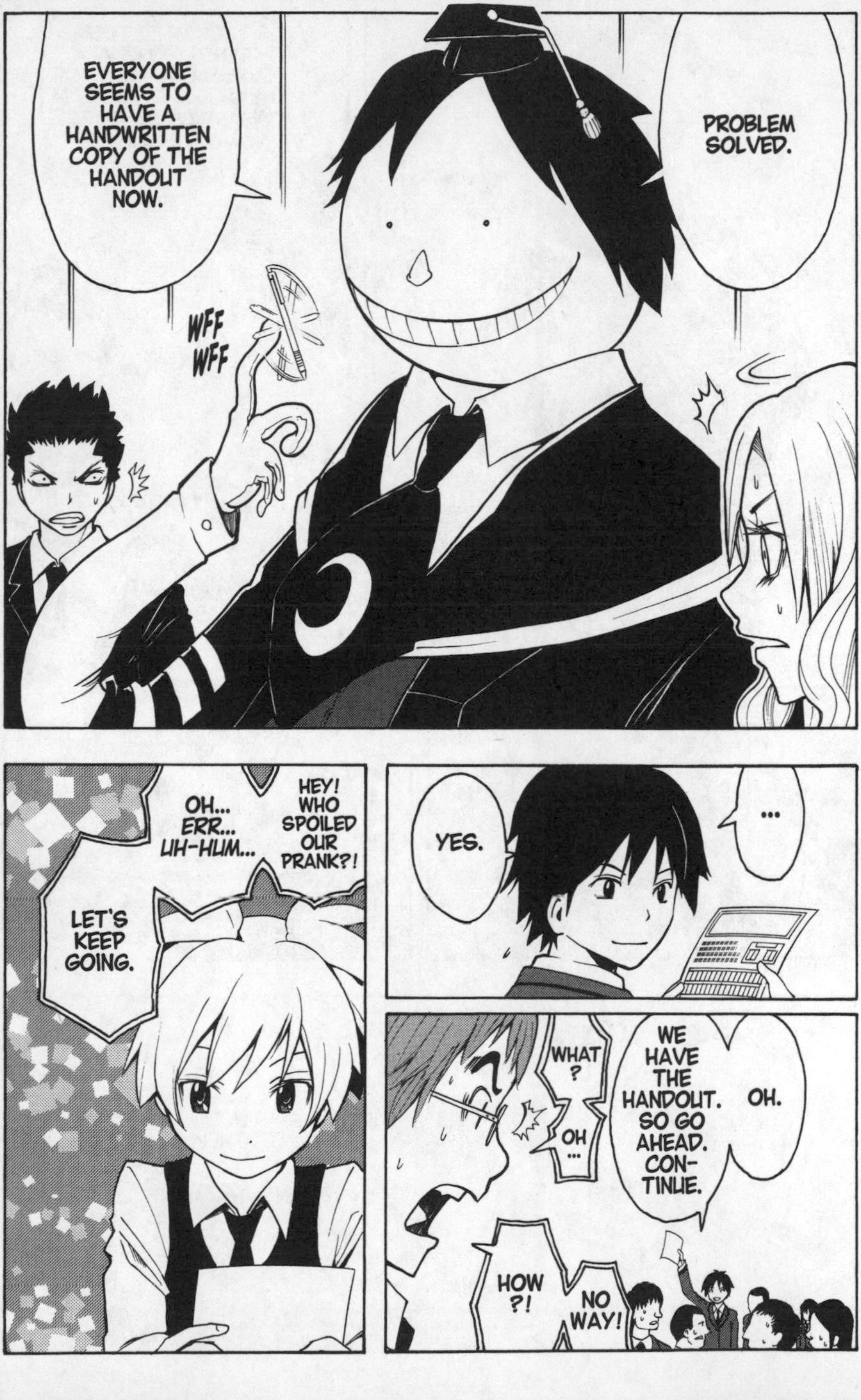
PROBLEM SOLVED.
EVERYONE SEEMS TO HAVE A HANDWRITTEN COPY OF THE HANDOUT NOW.
WFF WFF
...
YES.
OH.
WE HAVE THE HANDOUT. SO GO AHEAD. CON-TINUE.
WHAT?
OH...
NO WAY!
HOW?!
HEY! WHO SPOILED OUR PRANK?!
OH... ERR... UH-HUM...
LET'S KEEP GOING.

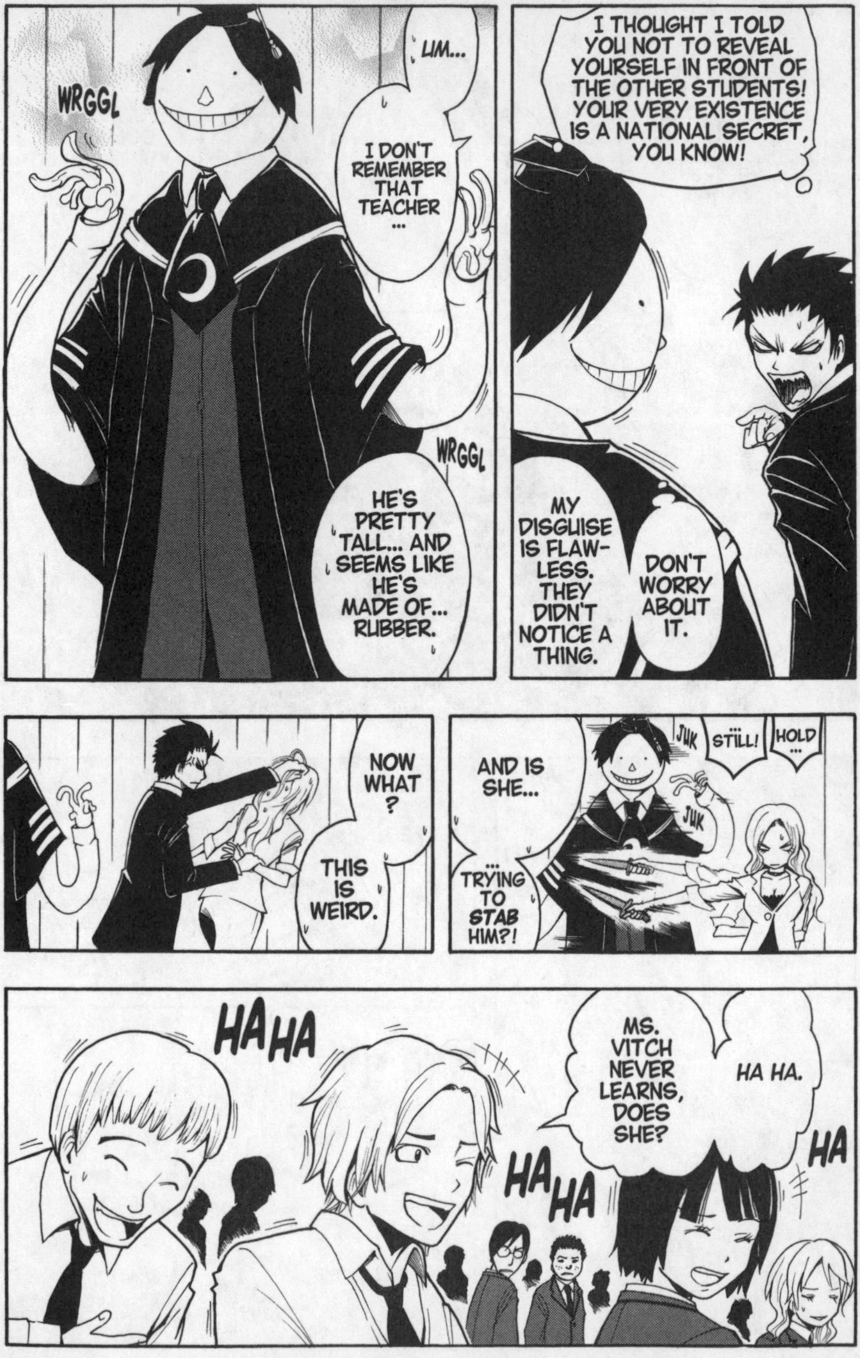
I THOUGHT I TOLD YOU NOT TO REVEAL YOURSELF IN FRONT OF THE OTHER STUDENTS! YOUR VERY EXISTENCE IS A NATIONAL SECRET, YOU KNOW!
DON'T WORRY ABOUT IT.
MY DISGUISE IS FLAWLESS. THEY DIDN'T NOTICE A THING.
UM...
WRGGL
I DON'T REMEMBER THAT TEACHER ...
WRGGL
HE'S PRETTY TALL... AND SEEMS LIKE HE'S MADE OF... RUBBER.
HOLD...
STILL!
JUK
JUK
AND IS SHE...
...TRYING TO STAB HIM?!
NOW WHAT?
THIS IS WEIRD.
HA
HA HA.
MS. VITCH NEVER LEARNS, DOES SHE?
HA HA
HA HA

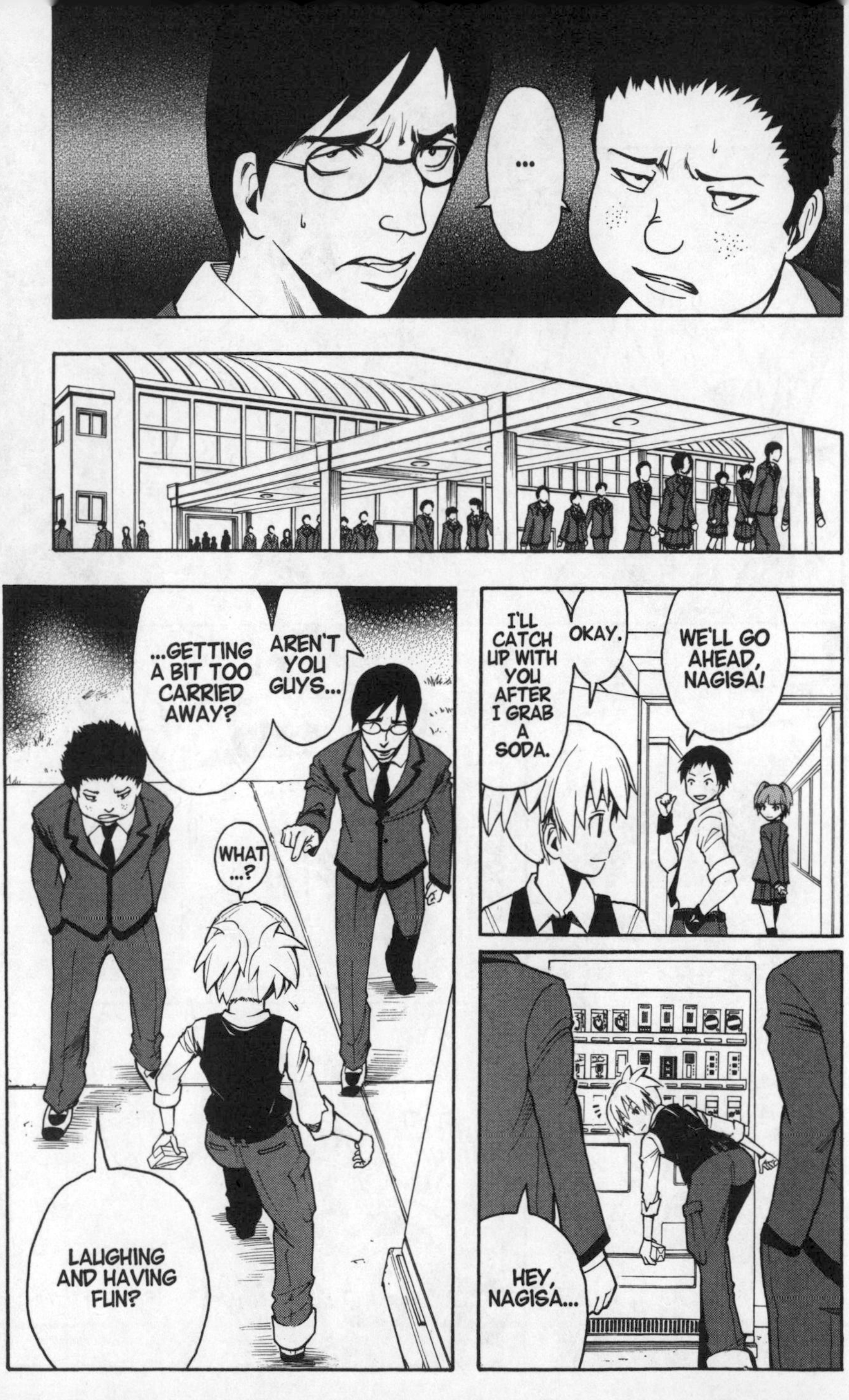
...
WE'LL GO AHEAD, NAGISA!
OKAY.
I'LL CATCH UP WITH YOU AFTER I GRAB A SODA.
HEY, NAGISA...
AREN'T YOU GUYS...
...GETTING A BIT TOO CARRIED AWAY?
WHAT ...?
LAUGHING AND HAVING FUN?

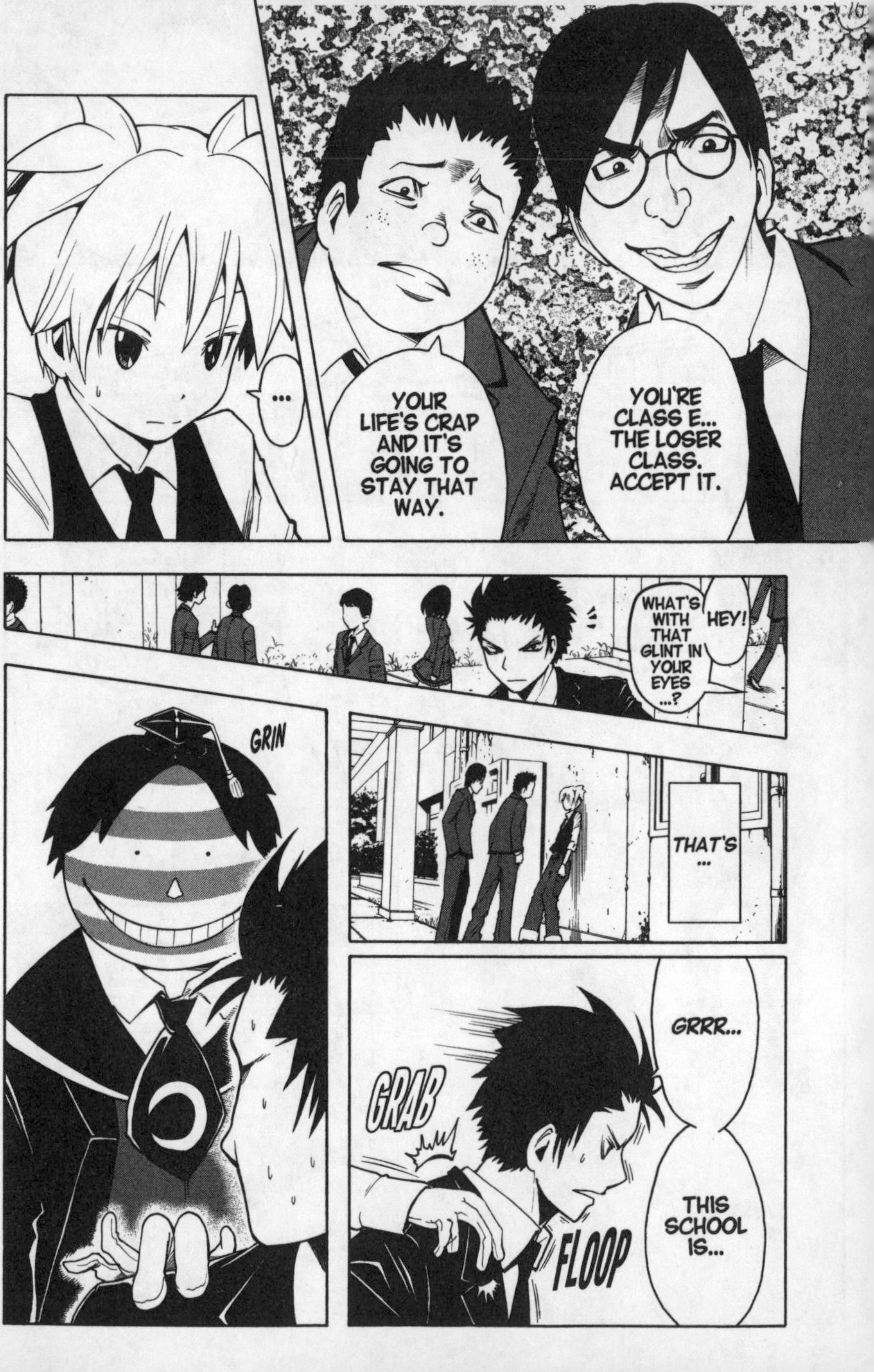
YOU'RE CLASS E... THE LOSER CLASS. ACCEPT IT.
YOUR LIFE'S CRAP AND IT'S GOING TO STAY THAT WAY.
...
HEY!
WHAT'S WITH THAT GLINT IN YOUR EYES ...?
THAT'S ...
GRRR...
THIS SCHOOL IS...
GRAB
FLOOP
GRIN

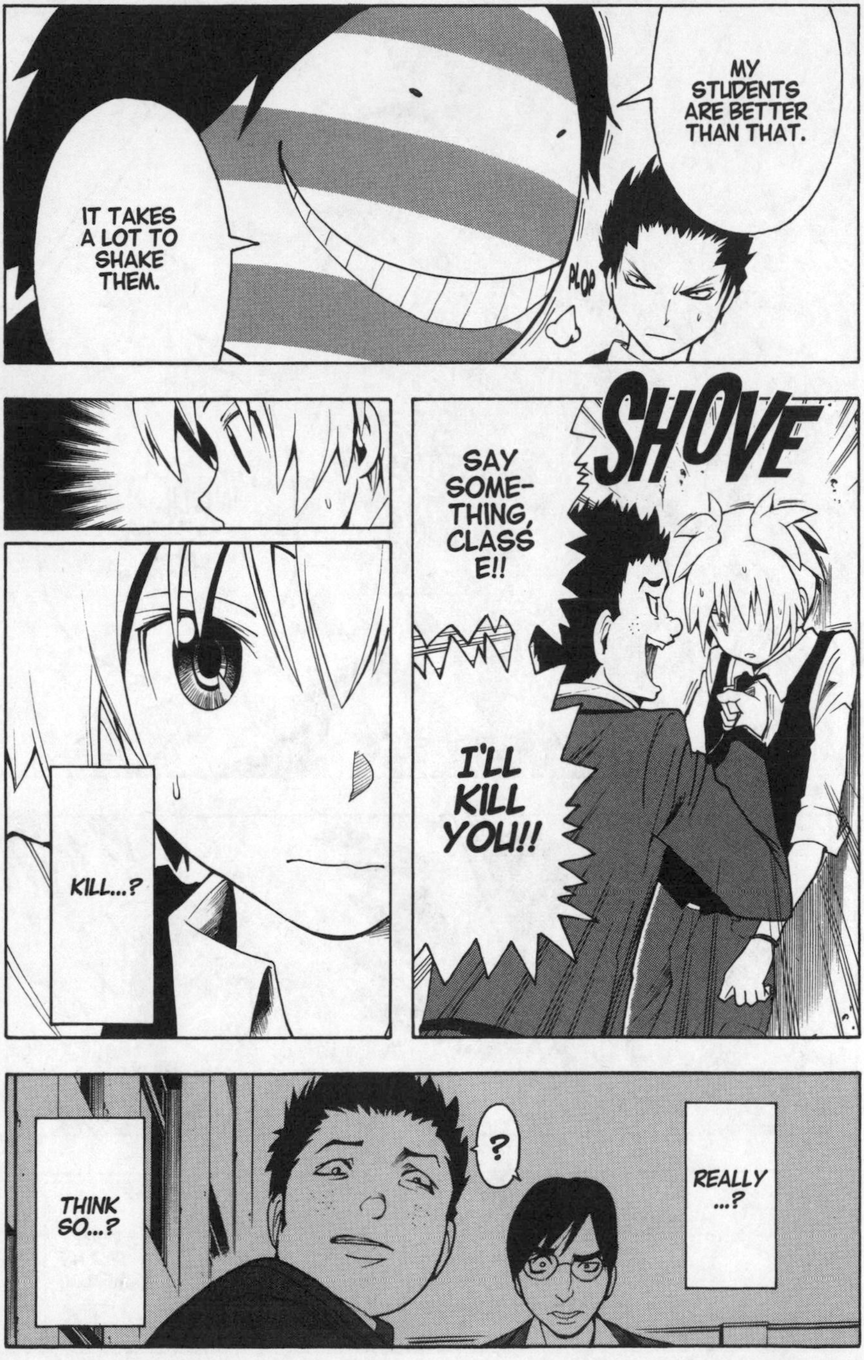
MY STUDENTS ARE BETTER THAN THAT.
PLOP
IT TAKES A LOT TO SHAKE THEM.
SHOVE
SAY SOME-THING, CLASS E!!
I'LL KILL YOU!!
KILL...?
REALLY ...?
?
THINK SO...?

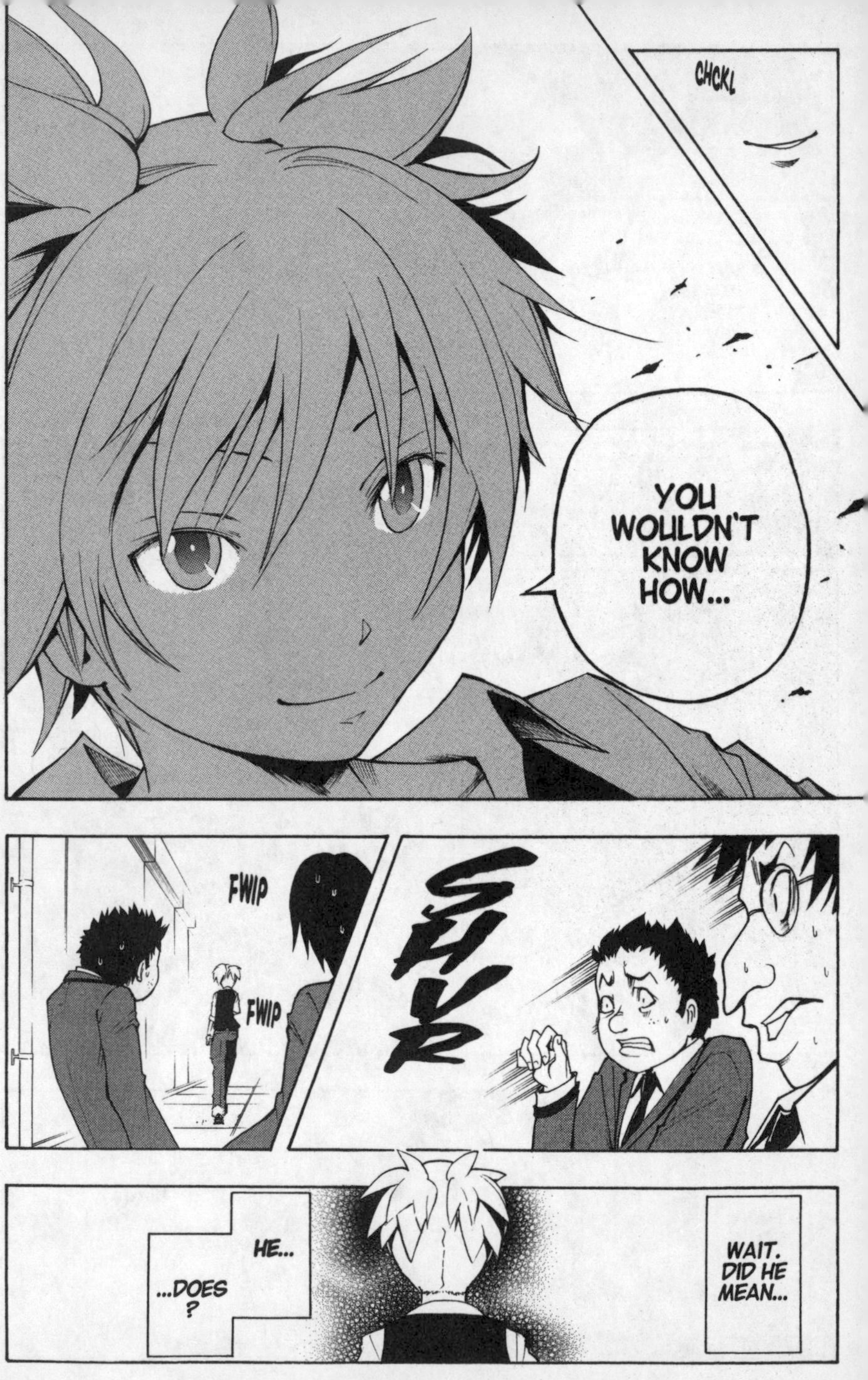
CHCKL
YOU WOULDN'T KNOW HOW...
FWIP
FWIP
WAIT. DID HE MEAN...
HE...
...DOES ?

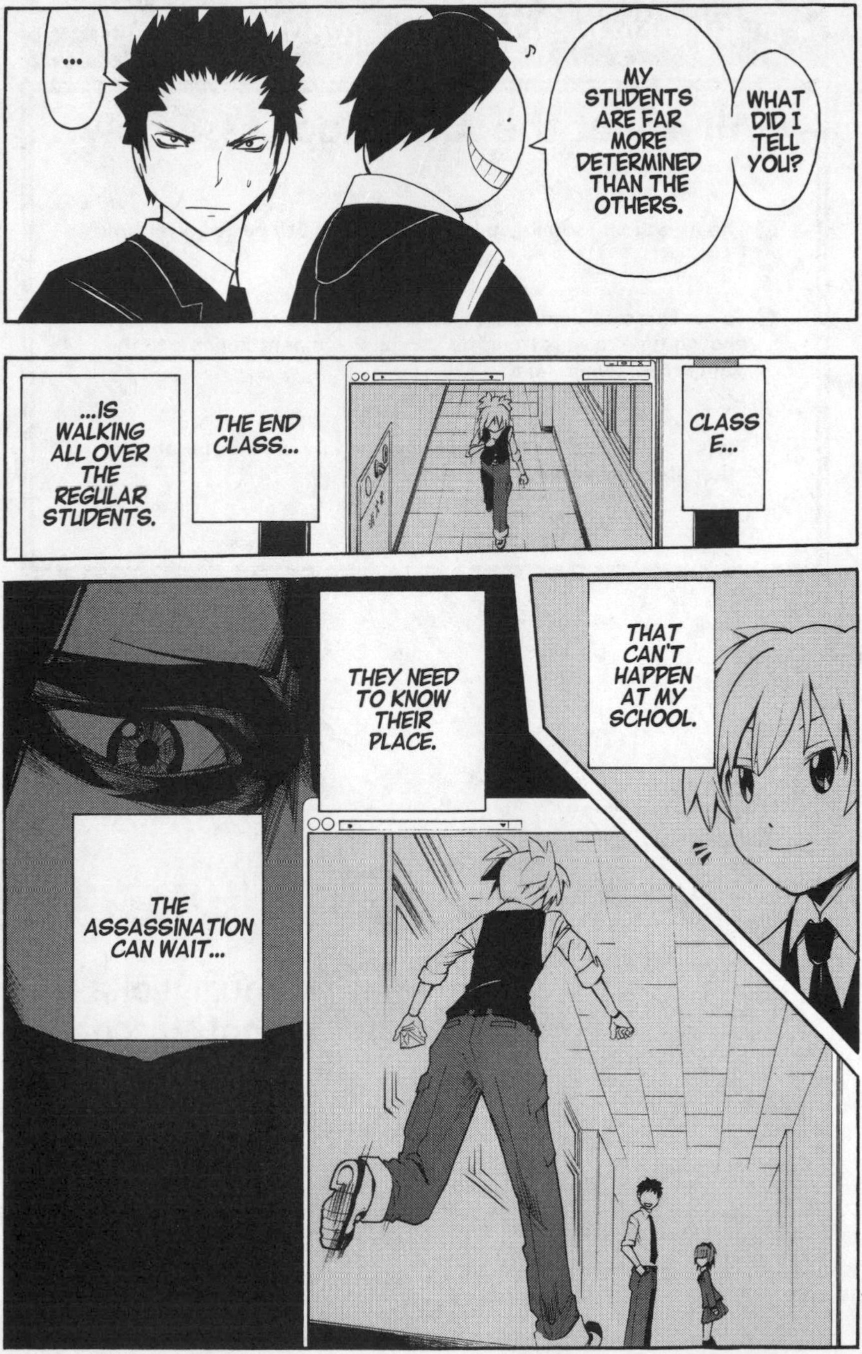
WHAT DID I TELL YOU?
MY STUDENTS ARE FAR MORE DETERMINED THAN THE OTHERS.
...
CLASS E...
THE END CLASS...
...IS WALKING ALL OVER THE REGULAR STUDENTS.
THAT CAN'T HAPPEN AT MY SCHOOL.
THEY NEED TO KNOW THEIR PLACE.
THE ASSASSINATION CAN WAIT...

All About the All-School Assembly

- The All-School Assembly takes place during 5th period after lunch.
- To get there on time, Class E students have to skip lunch to have enough time to walk from the Special Placement Building to the Main School Gymnasium.
- Class E students are expected to be lined up in place before the other students arrive.

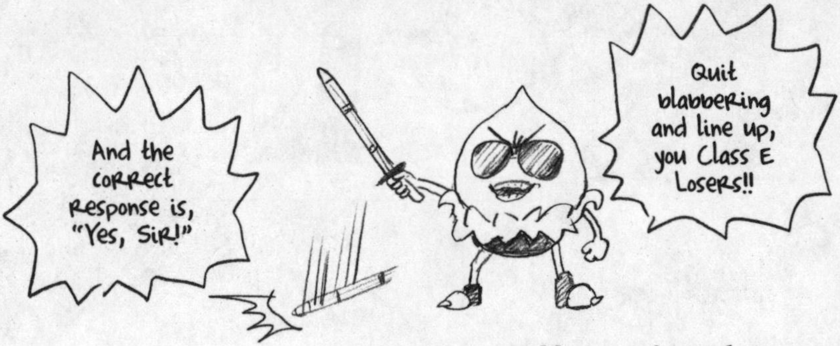
Quit blabbering and line up, you Class E Losers!!
And the correct response is, "Yes, Sir!"

Kunugigaoka School Mascot Kunudon

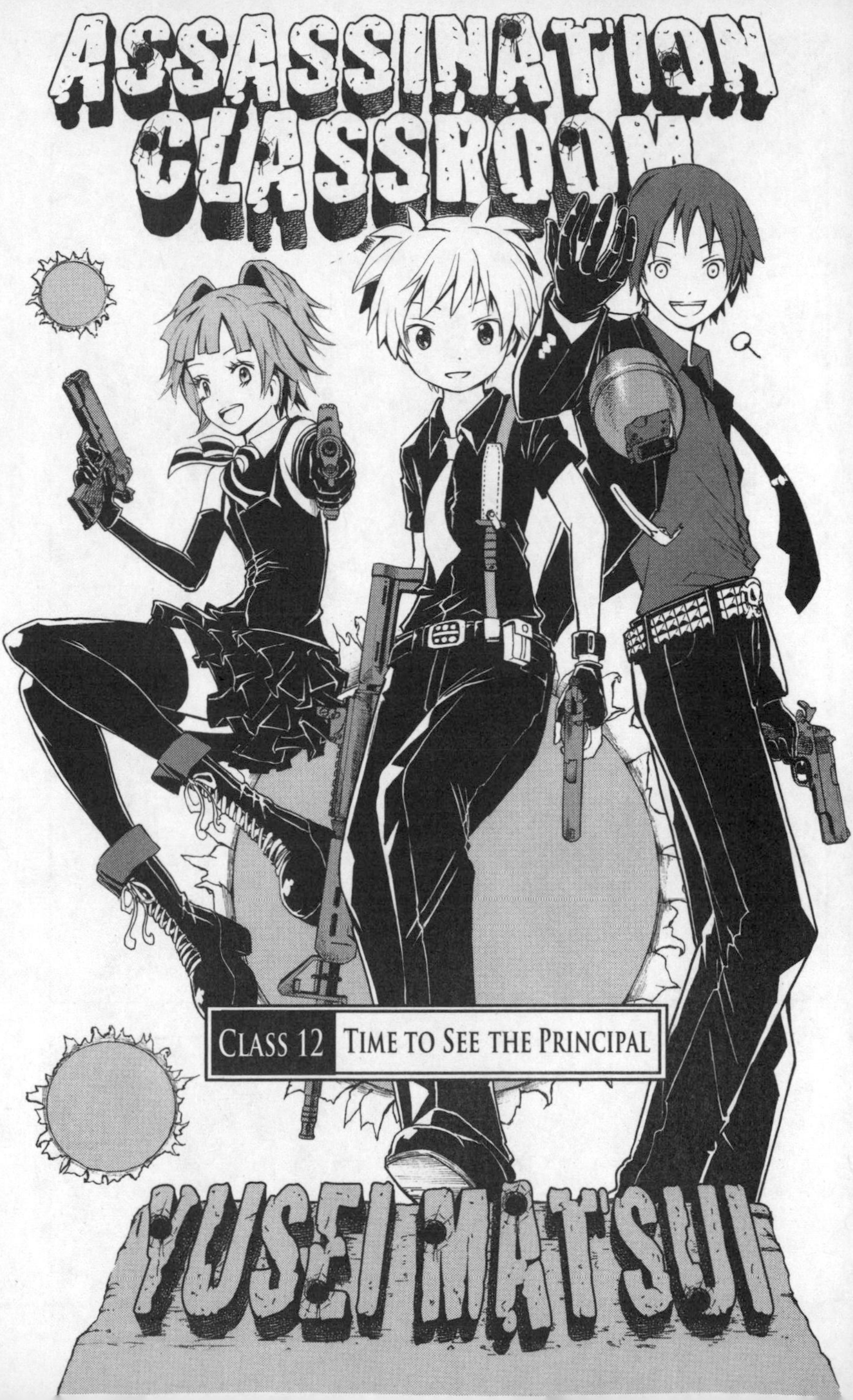
ASSASSINATION CLASSROOM
CLASS 12 TIME TO SEE THE PRINCIPAL
YUSEI MATSUI

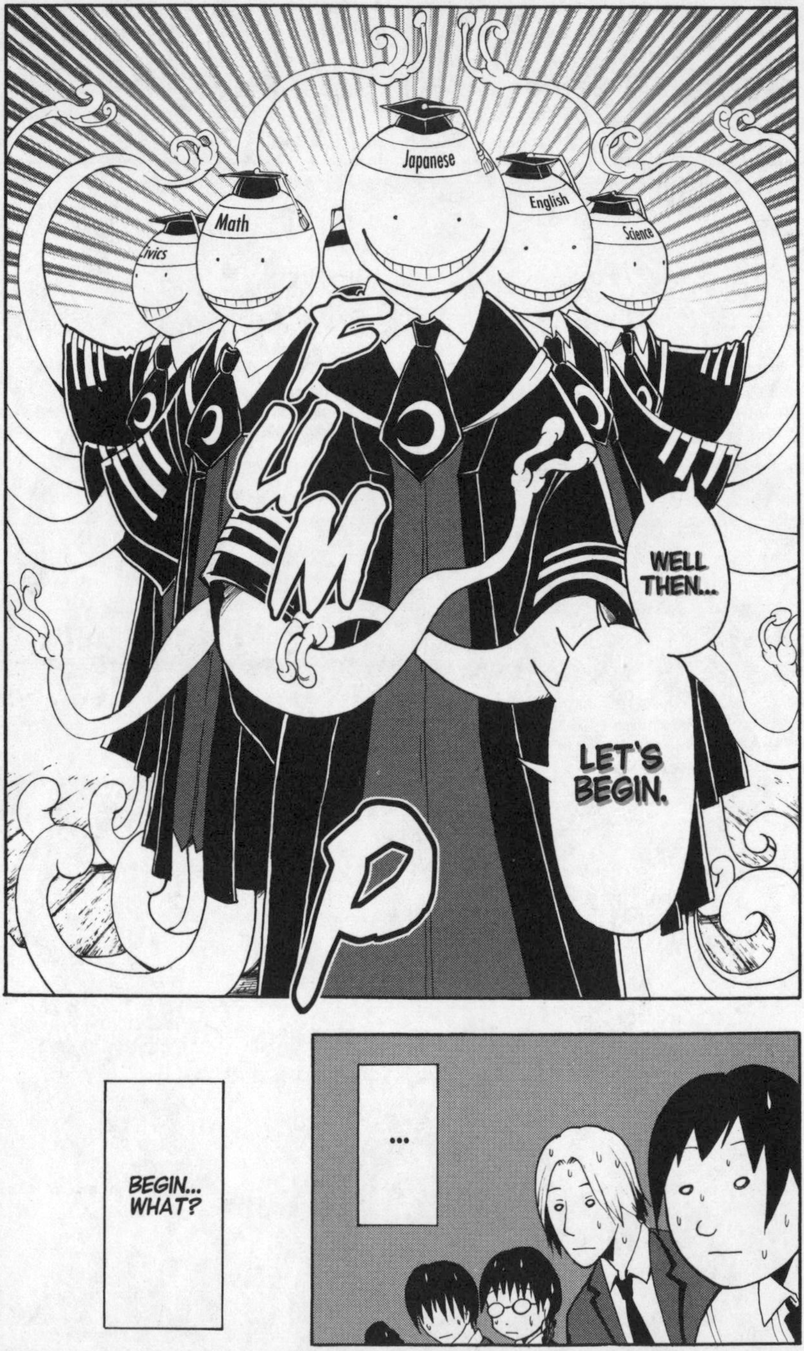
Japanese
English
Science
Math
Civics
WELL THEN...
LET'S BEGIN.
...
BEGIN... WHAT?

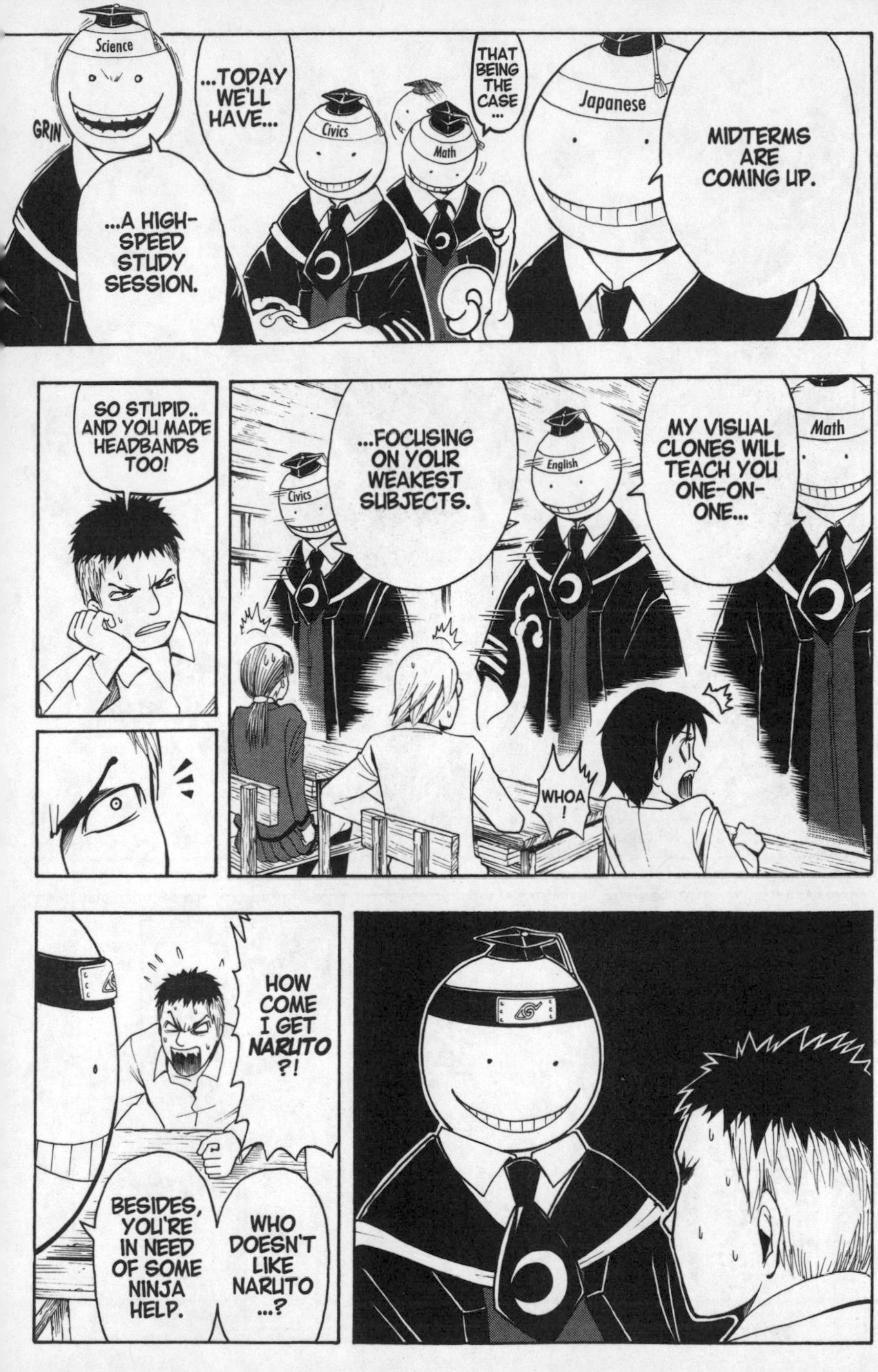
Japanese
MIDTERMS ARE COMING UP.
Math
THAT BEING THE CASE...
Civics
...TODAY WE'LL HAVE...
Science
GRIN
...A HIGH-SPEED STUDY SESSION.
Math
MY VISUAL CLONES WILL TEACH YOU ONE-ON-ONE...
English
...FOCUSING ON YOUR WEAKEST SUBJECTS.
Civics
WHOA!
SO STUPID.. AND YOU MADE HEADBANDS TOO!
HOW COME I GET NARUTO?!
WHO DOESN'T LIKE NARUTO...?
BESIDES, YOU'RE IN NEED OF SOME NINJA HELP.

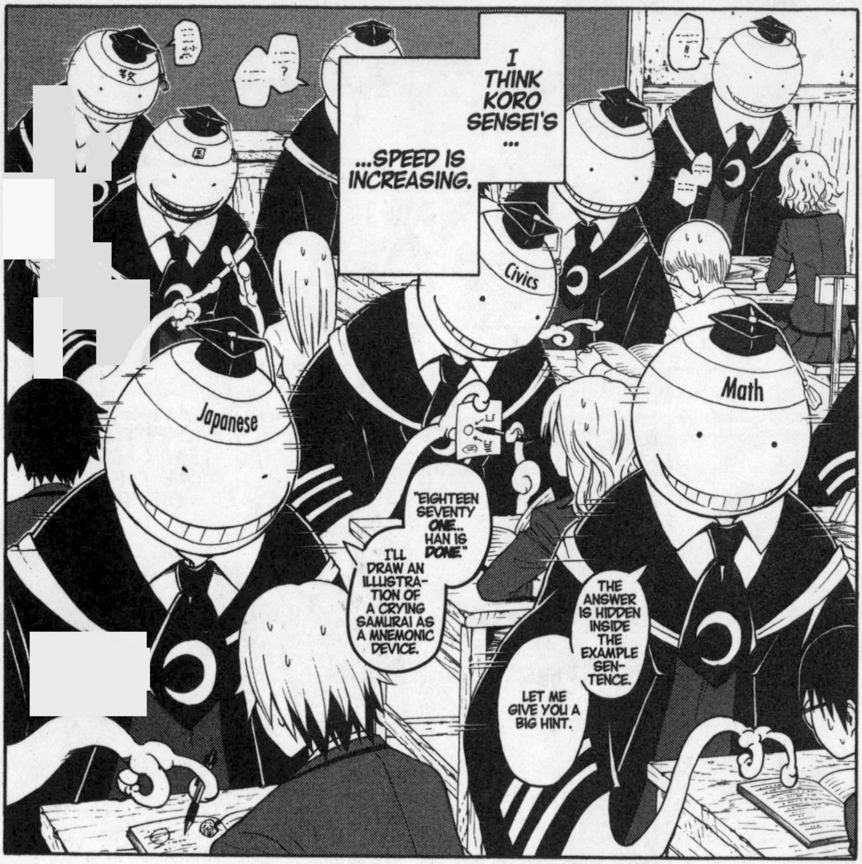
I THINK KORO SENSEI'S...
...SPEED IS INCREASING.
Civics
Math
Japanese
THE ANSWER IS HIDDEN INSIDE THE EXAMPLE SENTENCE.
LET ME GIVE YOU A BIG HINT.
"EIGHTEEN SEVENTY ONE... HAN IS DONE."
I'LL DRAW AN ILLUSTRATION OF A CRYING SAMURAI AS A MNEMONIC DEVICE.

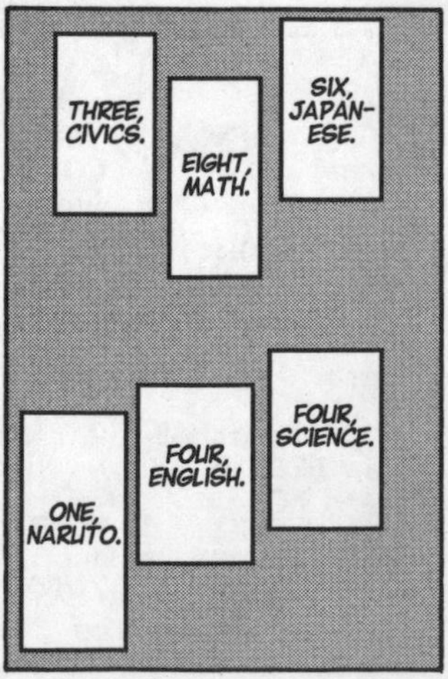
SIX, JAPANESE.
EIGHT, MATH.
THREE, CIVICS.
FOUR, SCIENCE.
FOUR, ENGLISH.
ONE, NARUTO.

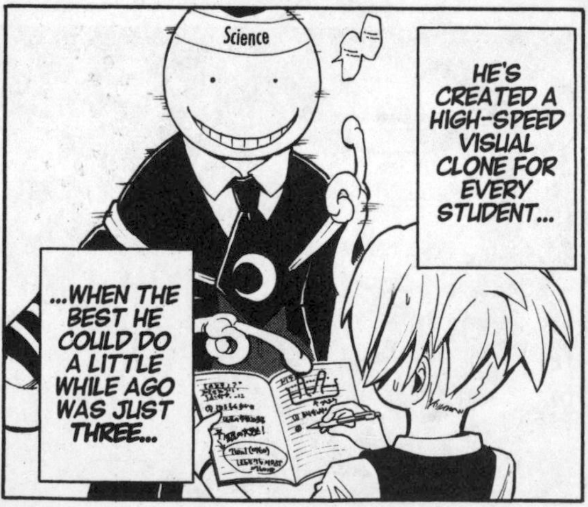
Science
HE'S CREATED A HIGH-SPEED VISUAL CLONE FOR EVERY STUDENT...
...WHEN THE BEST HE COULD DO A LITTLE WHILE AGO WAS JUST THREE...

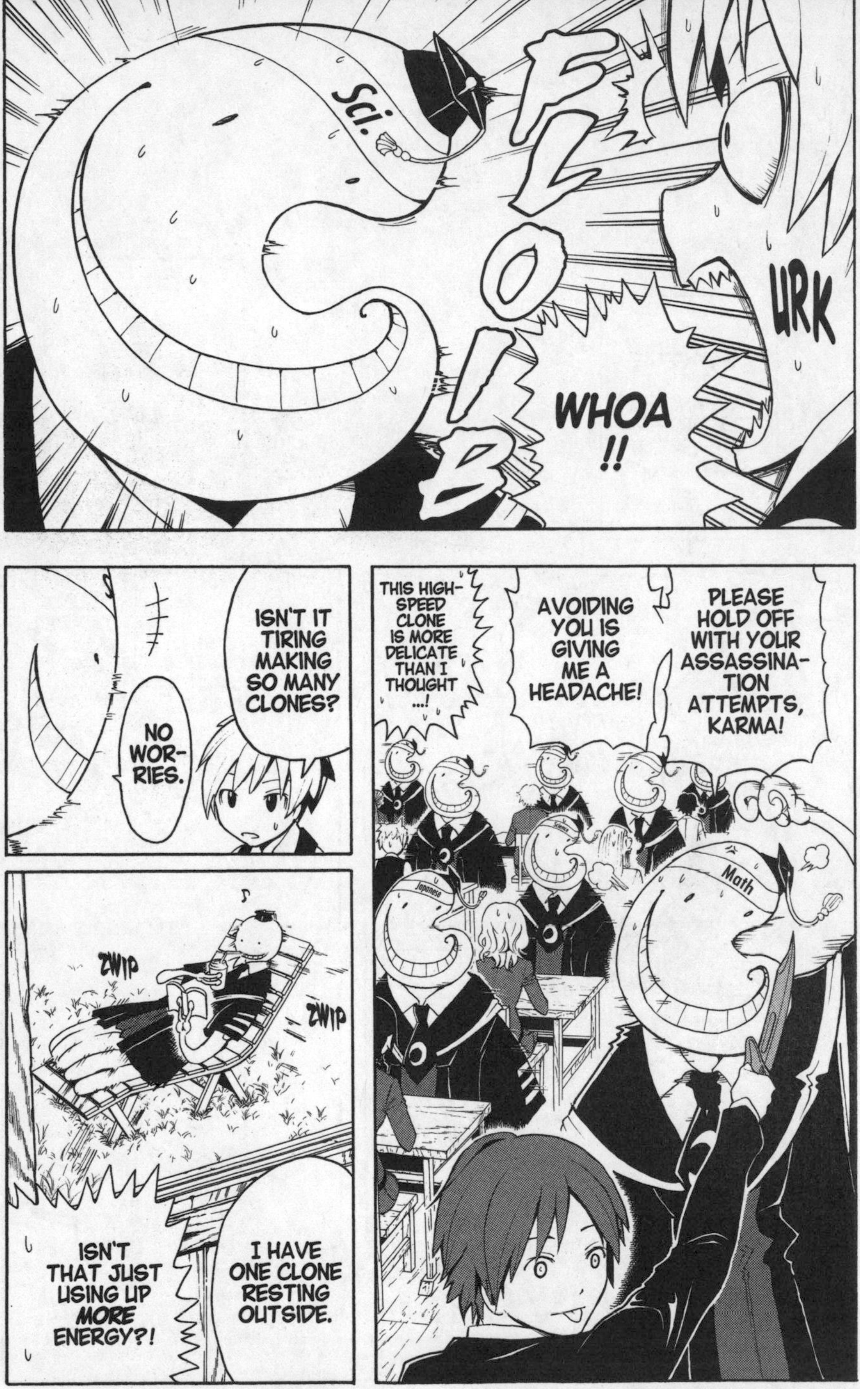
URK
WHOA !!
Sci.
PLEASE HOLD OFF WITH YOUR ASSASSINATION ATTEMPTS, KARMA!
AVOIDING YOU IS GIVING ME A HEADACHE!
THIS HIGH-SPEED CLONE IS MORE DELICATE THAN I THOUGHT ...!
Math
Japanese
ISN'T IT TIRING MAKING SO MANY CLONES?
NO WORRIES.
ZWIP
ZWIP
I HAVE ONE CLONE RESTING OUTSIDE.
ISN'T THAT JUST USING UP *MORE* ENERGY?!

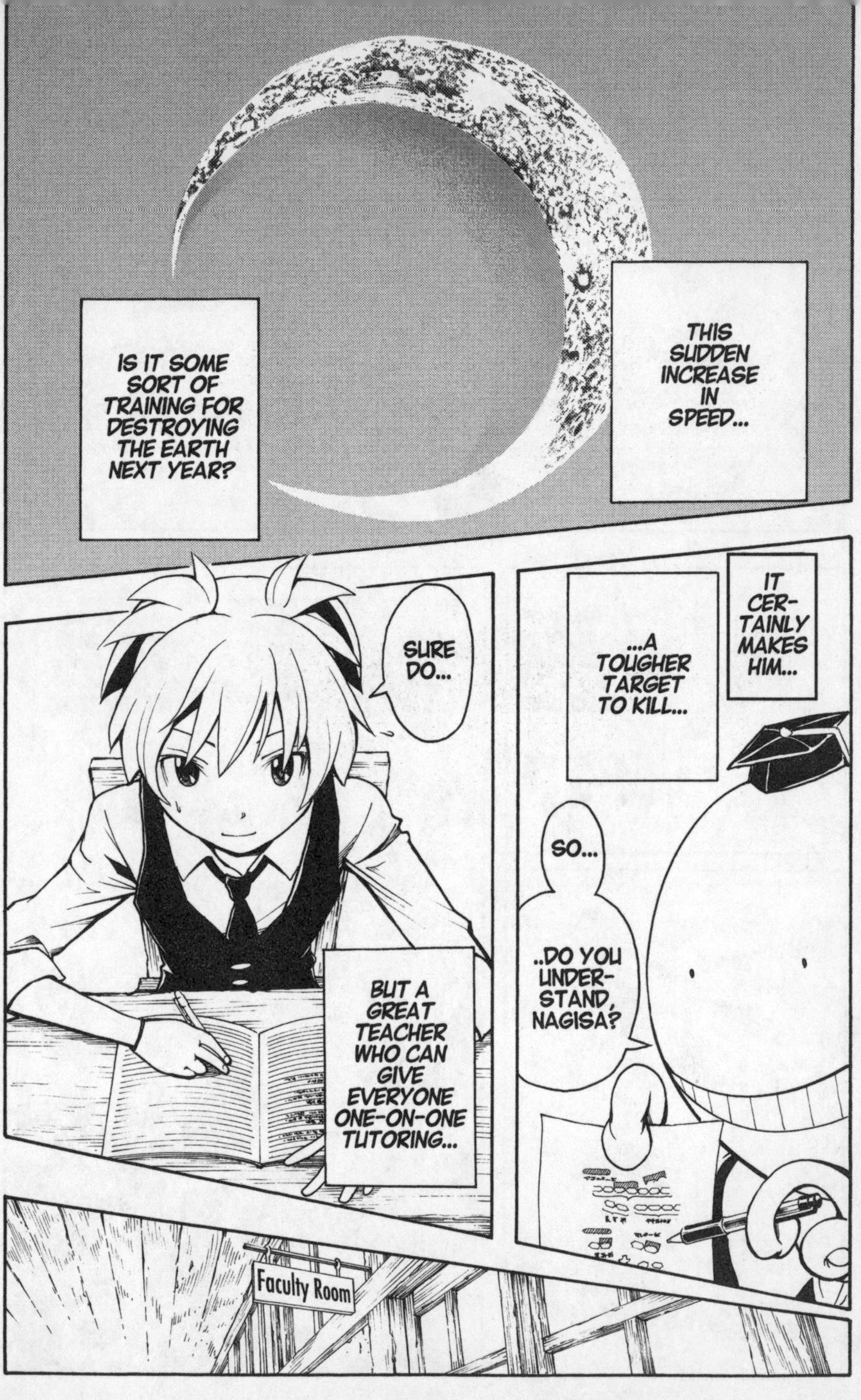
THIS SUDDEN INCREASE IN SPEED...
IS IT SOME SORT OF TRAINING FOR DESTROYING THE EARTH NEXT YEAR?
IT CER-TAINLY MAKES HIM...
...A TOUGHER TARGET TO KILL...
SO...
..DO YOU UNDER-STAND, NAGISA?
SURE DO...
BUT A GREAT TEACHER WHO CAN GIVE EVERYONE ONE-ON-ONE TUTORING...
Faculty Room

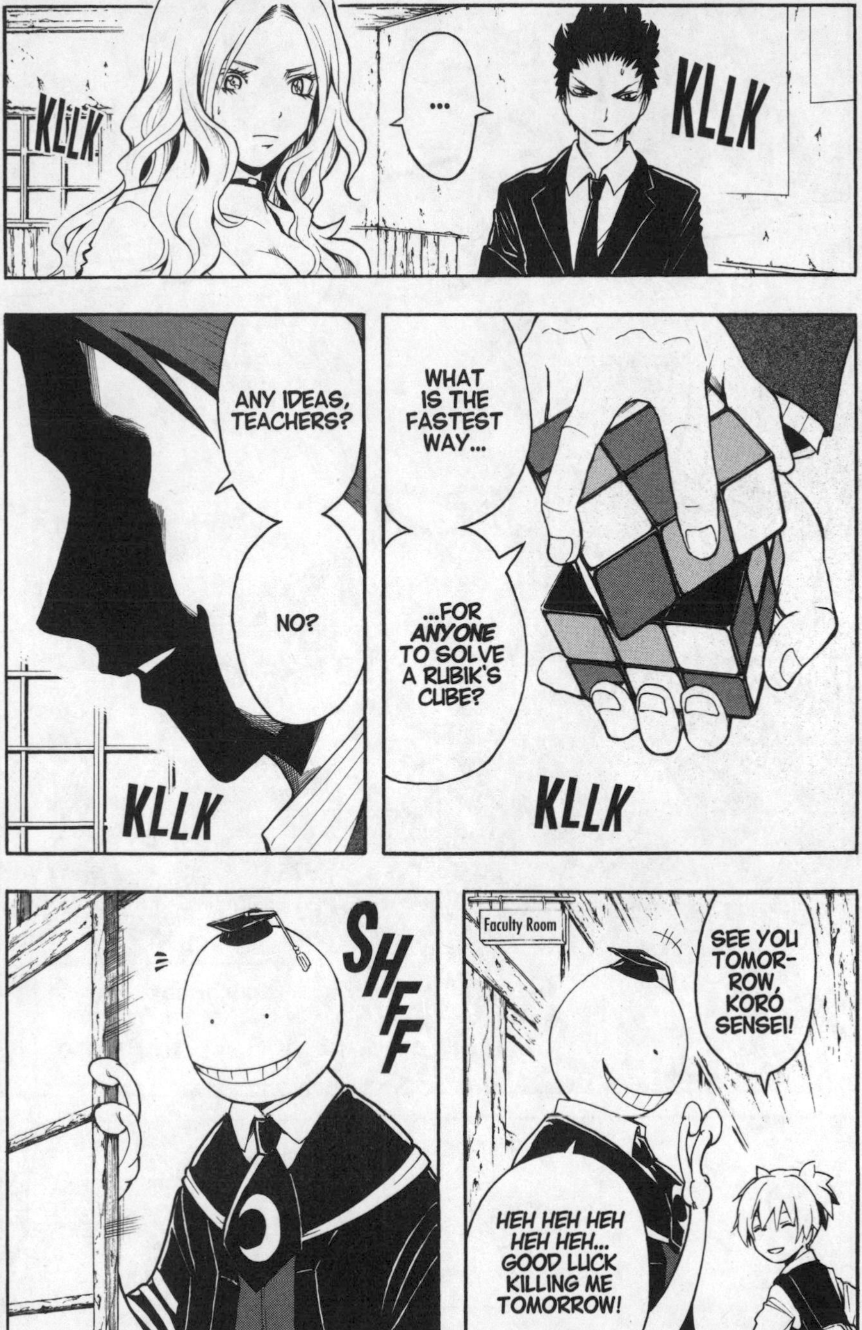
KLLK
...
KLLK
WHAT IS THE FASTEST WAY...
...FOR *ANYONE* TO SOLVE A RUBIK'S CUBE?
KLLK
ANY IDEAS, TEACHERS?
NO?
KLLK
Faculty Room
SEE YOU TOMOR-ROW, KORO SENSEI!
HEH HEH HEH HEH HEH... GOOD LUCK KILLING ME TOMORROW!
SHFF

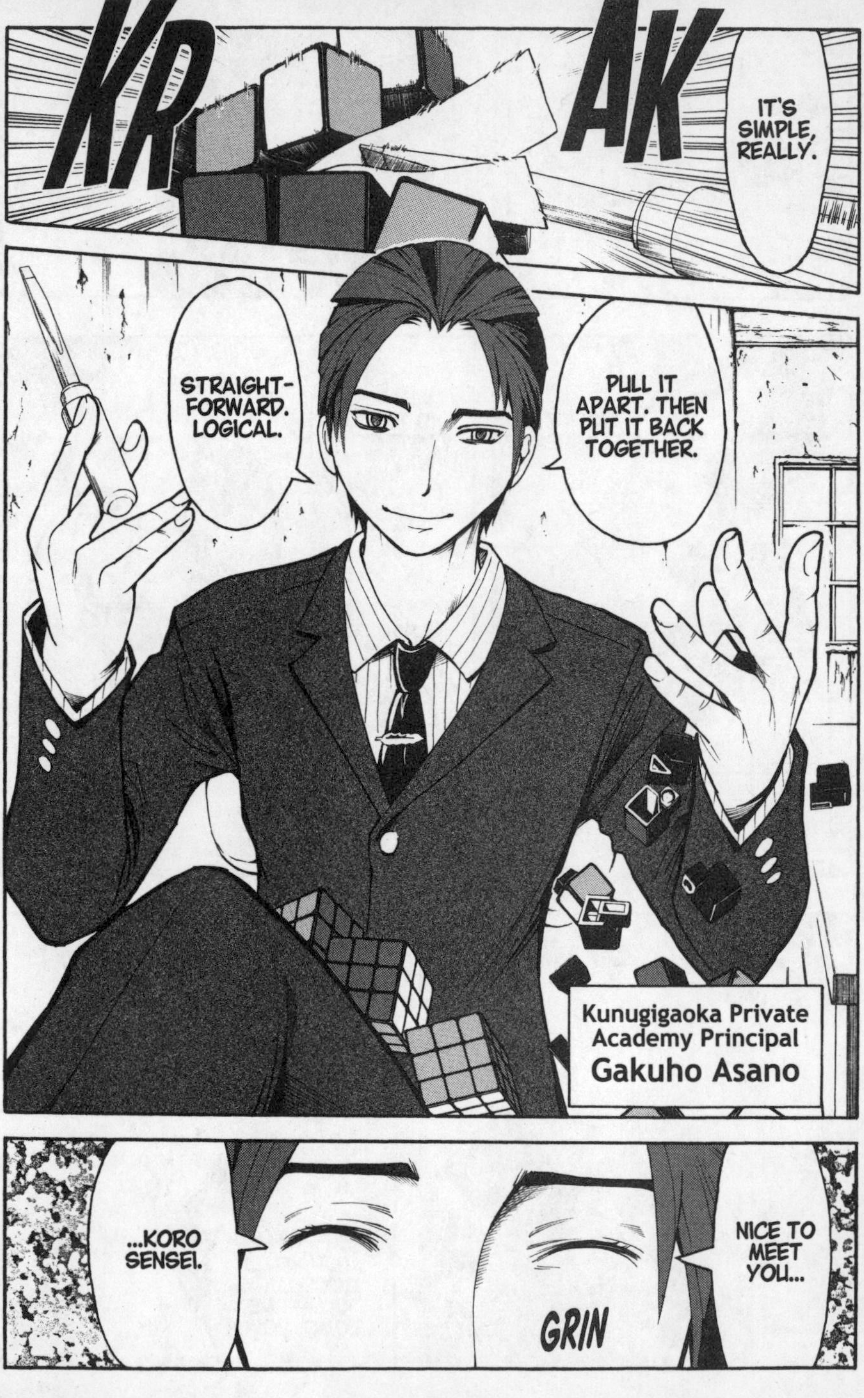
IT'S SIMPLE, REALLY.
KRAK
PULL IT APART. THEN PUT IT BACK TOGETHER.
STRAIGHT-FORWARD. LOGICAL.
Kunugigaoka Private Academy Principal
Gakuho Asano
NICE TO MEET YOU...
...KORO SENSEI.
GRIN

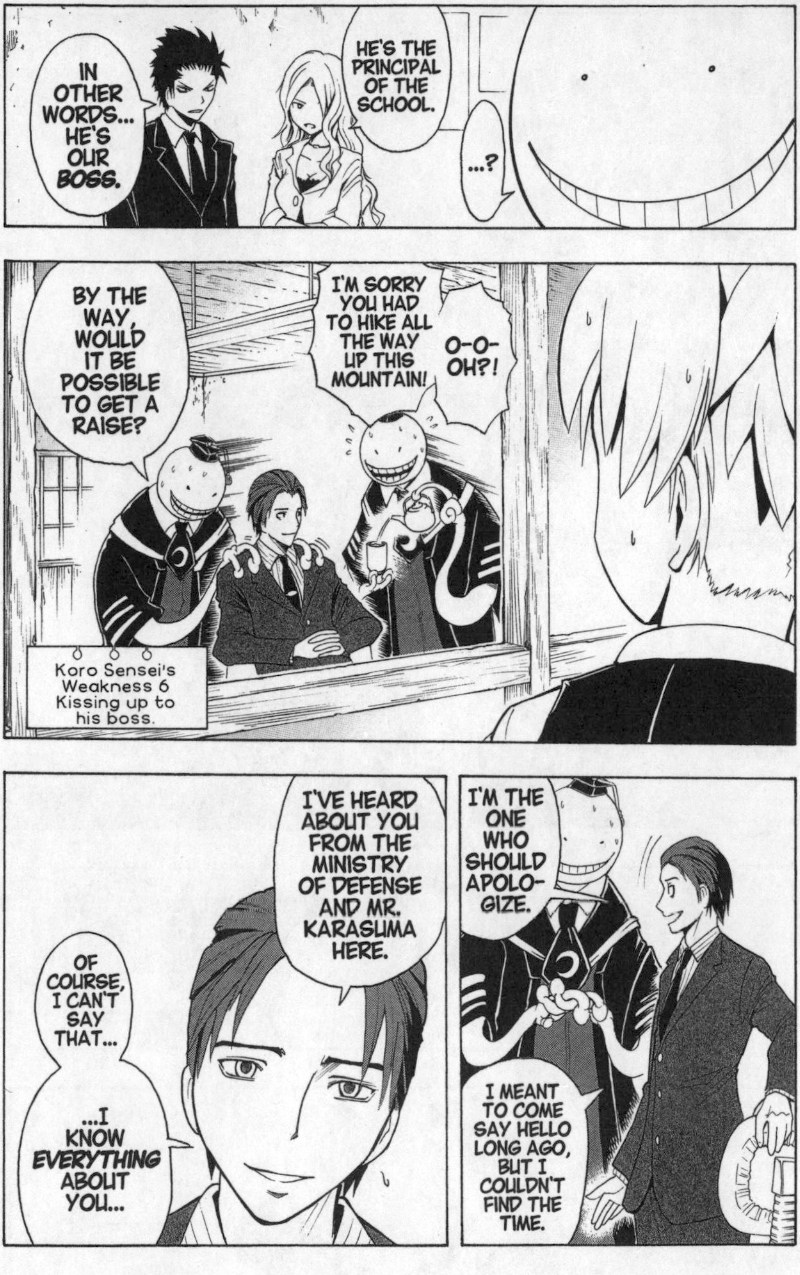
HE'S THE PRINCIPAL OF THE SCHOOL.
...?
IN OTHER WORDS... HE'S OUR BOSS.
O-O-OH?!
I'M SORRY YOU HAD TO HIKE ALL THE WAY UP THIS MOUNTAIN!
BY THE WAY, WOULD IT BE POSSIBLE TO GET A RAISE?
Koro Sensei's Weakness 6 Kissing up to his boss.
I'M THE ONE WHO SHOULD APOLOGIZE.
I MEANT TO COME SAY HELLO LONG AGO, BUT I COULDN'T FIND THE TIME.
I'VE HEARD ABOUT YOU FROM THE MINISTRY OF DEFENSE AND MR. KARASUMA HERE.
OF COURSE, I CAN'T SAY THAT...
...I KNOW EVERYTHING ABOUT YOU...

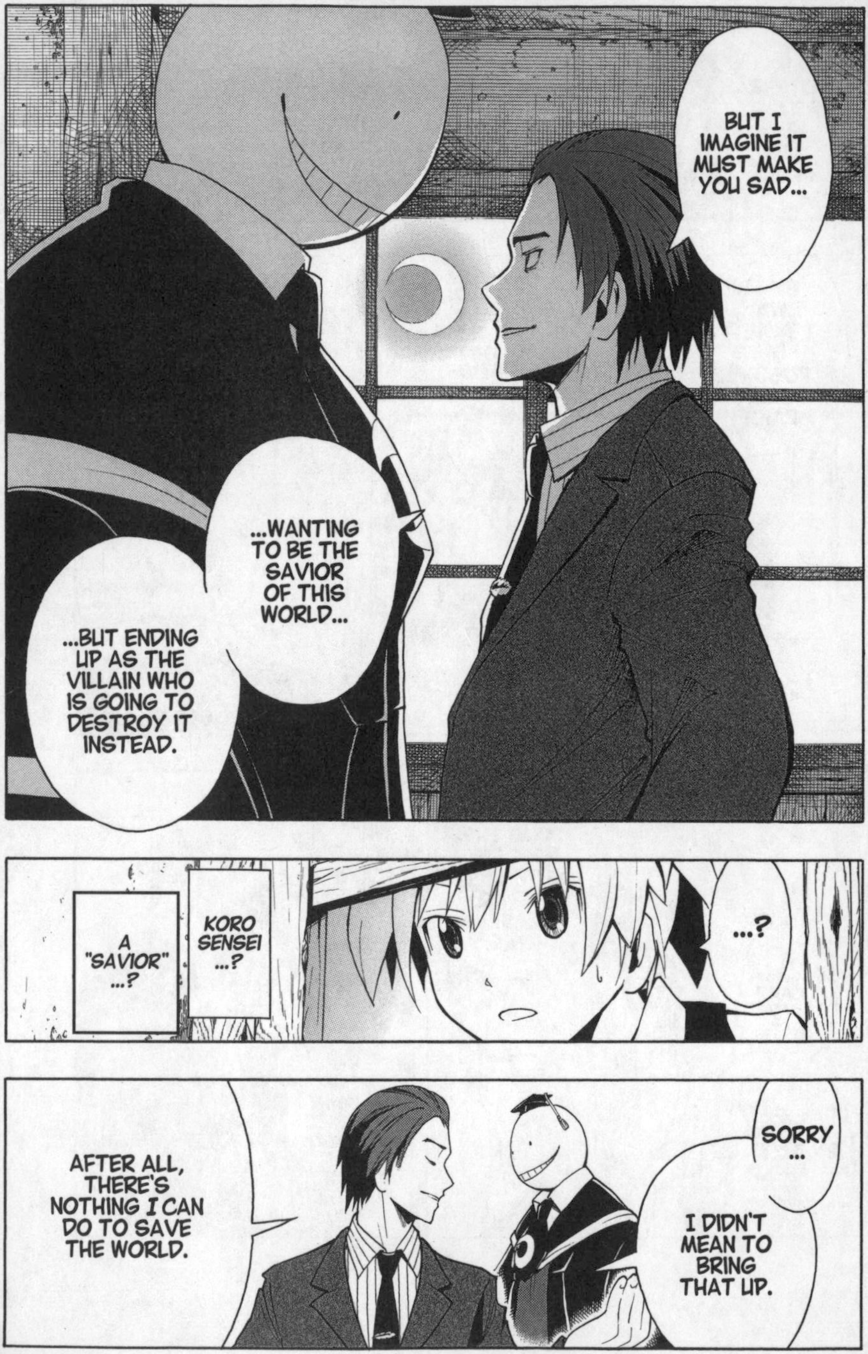
BUT I IMAGINE IT MUST MAKE YOU SAD...
...WANTING TO BE THE SAVIOR OF THIS WORLD...
...BUT ENDING UP AS THE VILLAIN WHO IS GOING TO DESTROY IT INSTEAD.
...?
KORO SENSEI ...?
A "SAVIOR" ...?
SORRY ...
I DIDN'T MEAN TO BRING THAT UP.
AFTER ALL, THERE'S NOTHING *I* CAN DO TO SAVE THE WORLD.

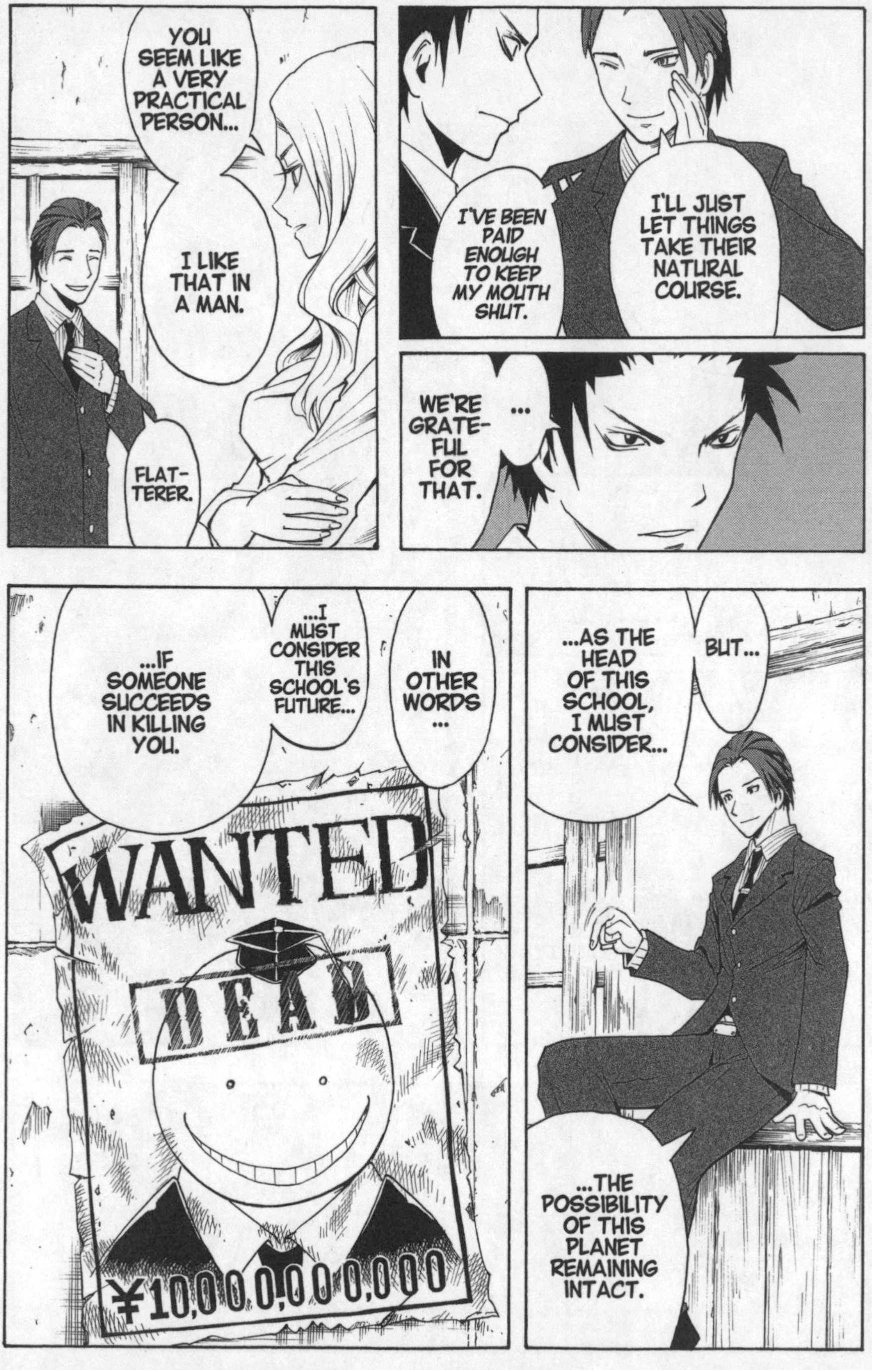
I'LL JUST LET THINGS TAKE THEIR NATURAL COURSE.
I'VE BEEN PAID ENOUGH TO KEEP MY MOUTH SHUT.
...
WE'RE GRATE-FUL FOR THAT.
YOU SEEM LIKE A VERY PRACTICAL PERSON...
I LIKE THAT IN A MAN.
FLAT-TERER.
BUT...
...AS THE HEAD OF THIS SCHOOL, I MUST CONSIDER...
...THE POSSIBILITY OF THIS PLANET REMAINING INTACT.
IN OTHER WORDS...
...I MUST CONSIDER THIS SCHOOL'S FUTURE...
...IF SOMEONE SUCCEEDS IN KILLING YOU.
WANTED
DEAD
¥10,000,000,000

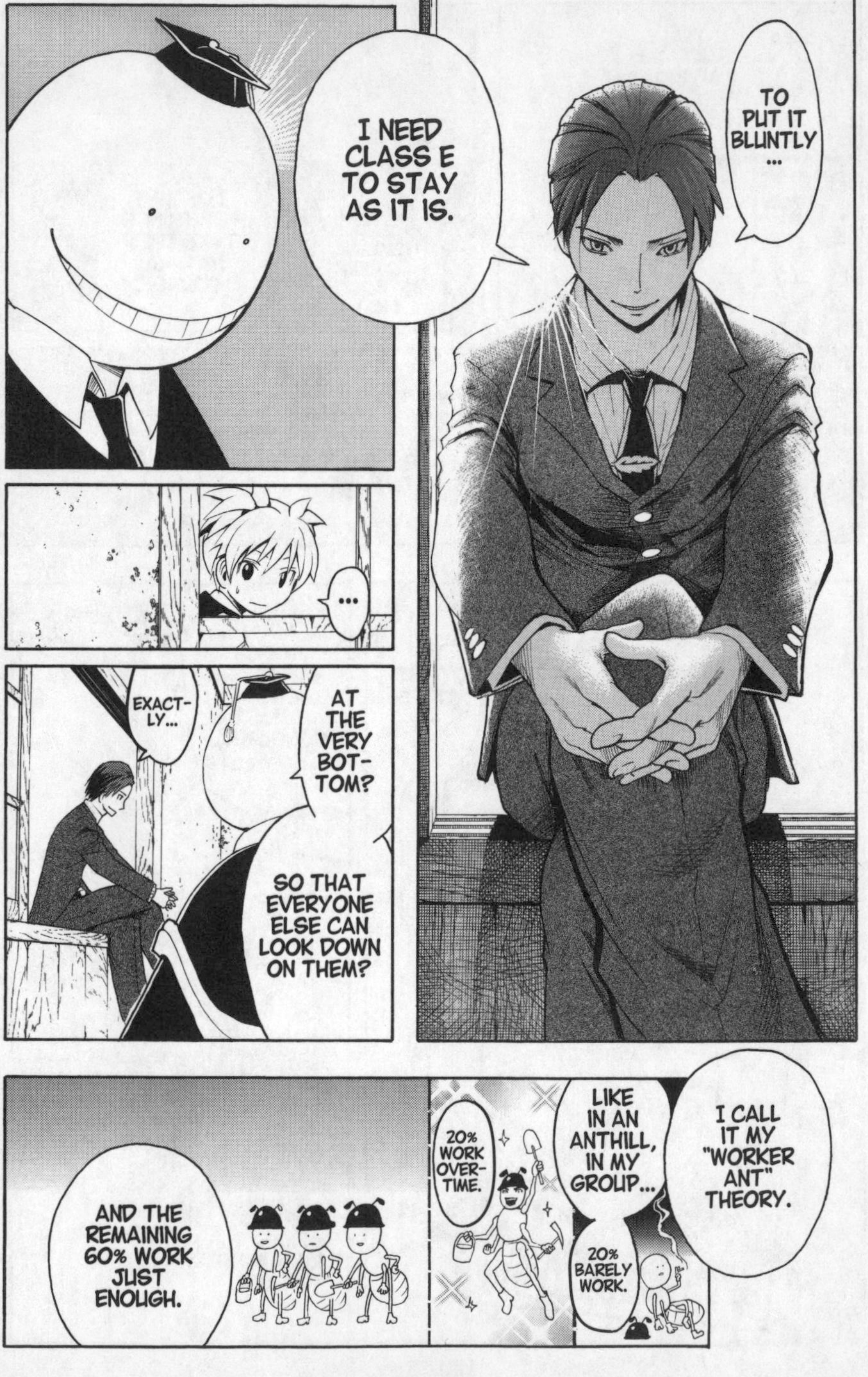
TO PUT IT BLUNTLY...
I NEED CLASS E TO STAY AS IT IS.
...
AT THE VERY BOTTOM?
EXACTLY...
SO THAT EVERYONE ELSE CAN LOOK DOWN ON THEM?
I CALL IT MY "WORKER ANT" THEORY.
LIKE IN AN ANTHILL, IN MY GROUP...
20% WORK OVERTIME.
20% BARELY WORK.
AND THE REMAINING 60% WORK JUST ENOUGH.

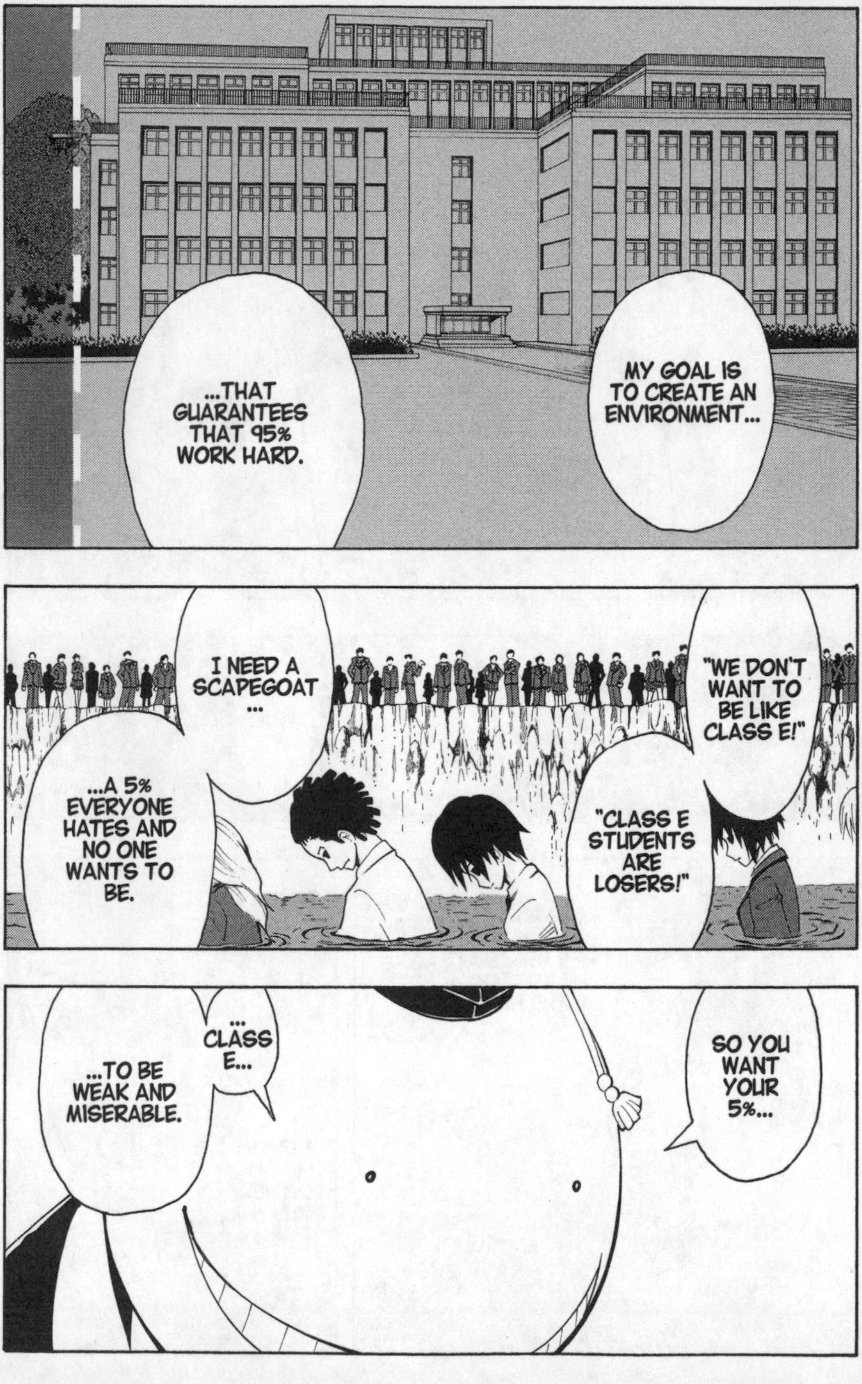
MY GOAL IS TO CREATE AN ENVIRONMENT...
...THAT GUARANTEES THAT 95% WORK HARD.
"WE DON'T WANT TO BE LIKE CLASS E!"
"CLASS E STUDENTS ARE LOSERS!"
I NEED A SCAPEGOAT ...
...A 5% EVERYONE HATES AND NO ONE WANTS TO BE.
SO YOU WANT YOUR 5%...
... CLASS E...
...TO BE WEAK AND MISERABLE.

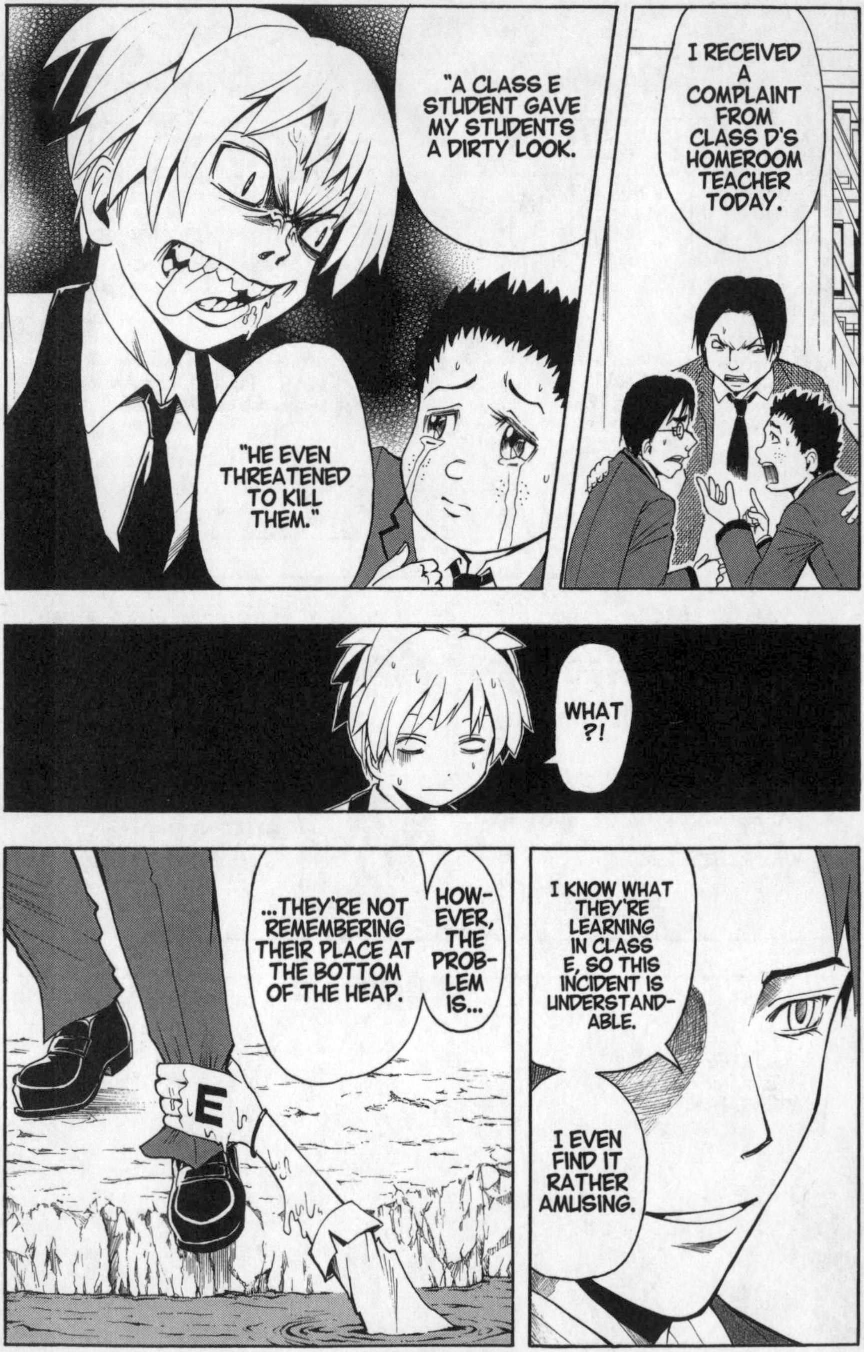
I RECEIVED A COMPLAINT FROM CLASS D'S HOMEROOM TEACHER TODAY.
"A CLASS E STUDENT GAVE MY STUDENTS A DIRTY LOOK.
"HE EVEN THREATENED TO KILL THEM."
WHAT ?!
I KNOW WHAT THEY'RE LEARNING IN CLASS E, SO THIS INCIDENT IS UNDERSTANDABLE.
I EVEN FIND IT RATHER AMUSING.
HOW-EVER, THE PROB-LEM IS...
...THEY'RE NOT REMEMBERING THEIR PLACE AT THE BOTTOM OF THE HEAP.
E

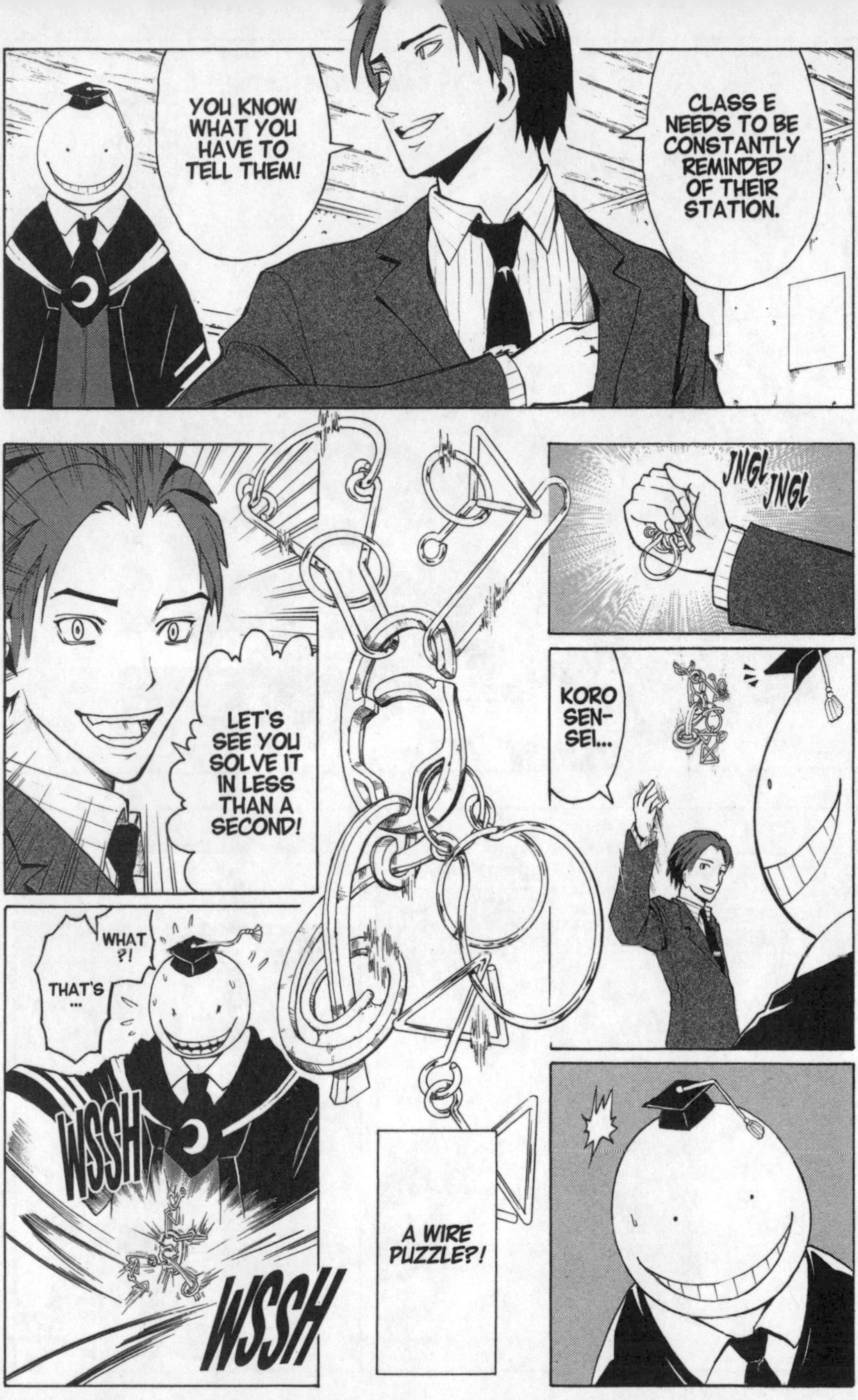
CLASS E NEEDS TO BE CONSTANTLY REMINDED OF THEIR STATION.
YOU KNOW WHAT YOU HAVE TO TELL THEM!
JNGL JNGL
KORO SENSEI...
LET'S SEE YOU SOLVE IT IN LESS THAN A SECOND!
A WIRE PUZZLE?!
WSSH
WSSH
WHAT ?!
THAT'S ...

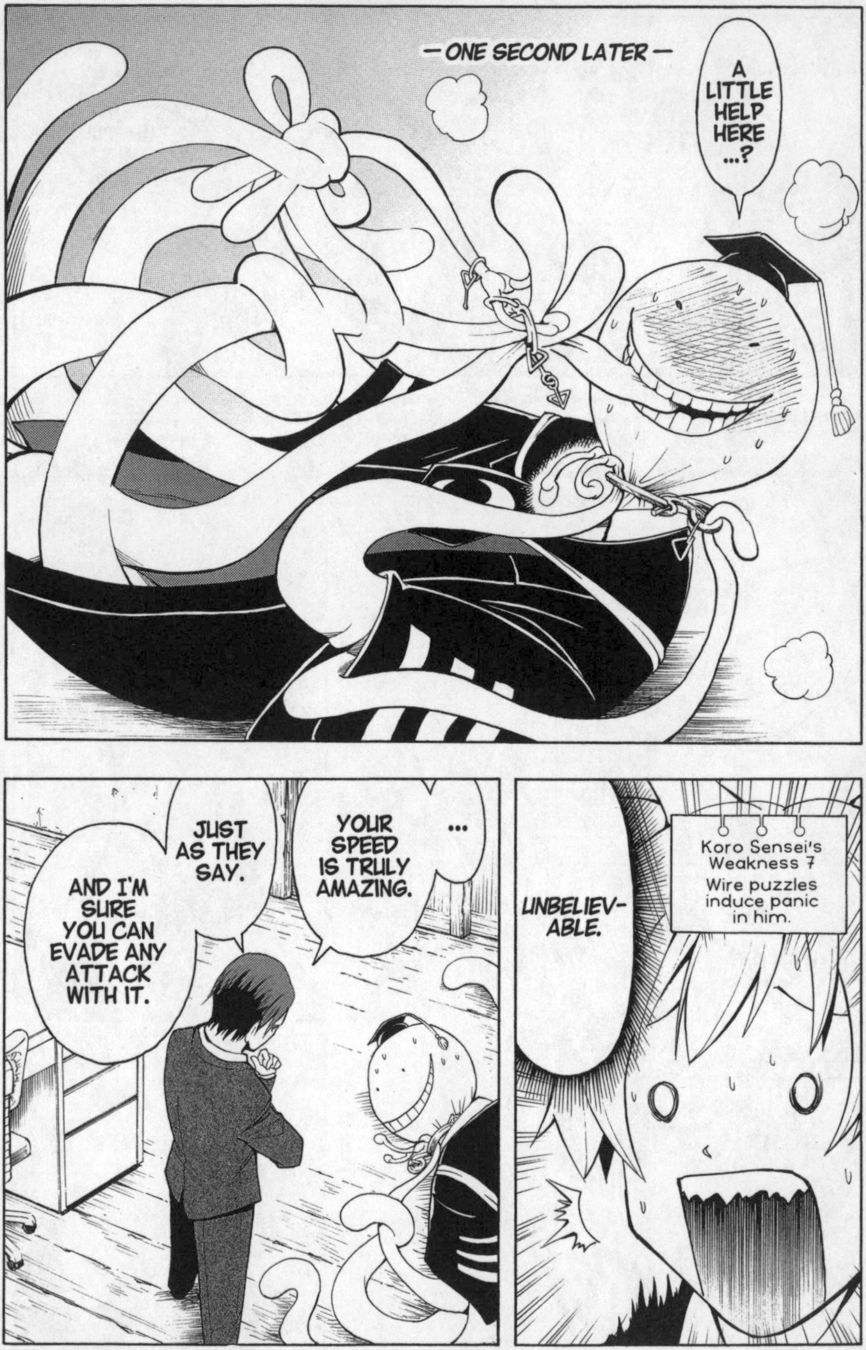
—ONE SECOND LATER—
A LITTLE HELP HERE...?
Koro Sensei's Weakness 7 Wire puzzles induce panic in him.
UNBELIEV-ABLE.
...
YOUR SPEED IS TRULY AMAZING.
JUST AS THEY SAY.
AND I'M SURE YOU CAN EVADE ANY ATTACK WITH IT.

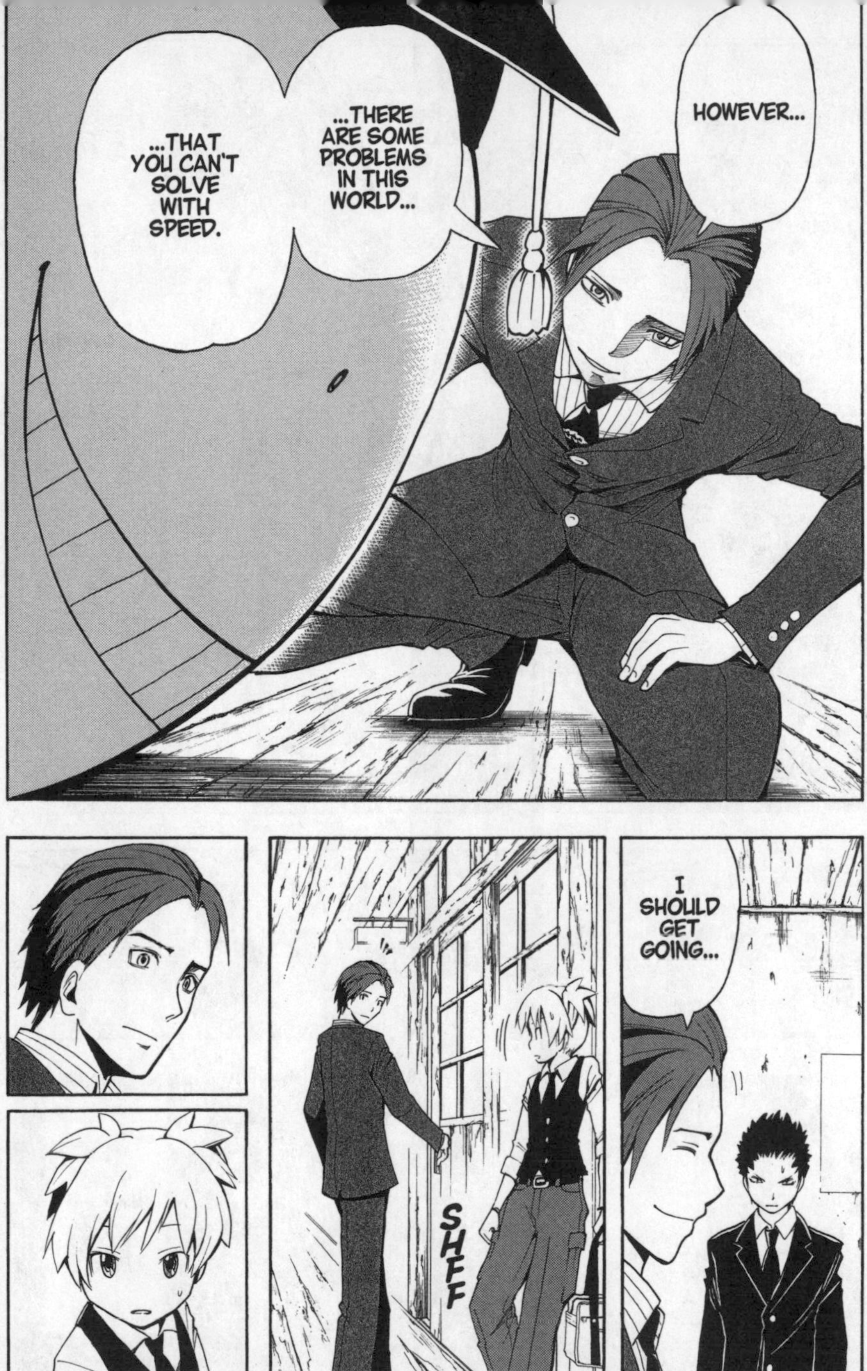
HOWEVER...
...THERE ARE SOME PROBLEMS IN THIS WORLD...
...THAT YOU CAN'T SOLVE WITH SPEED.
I SHOULD GET GOING...
SHFF

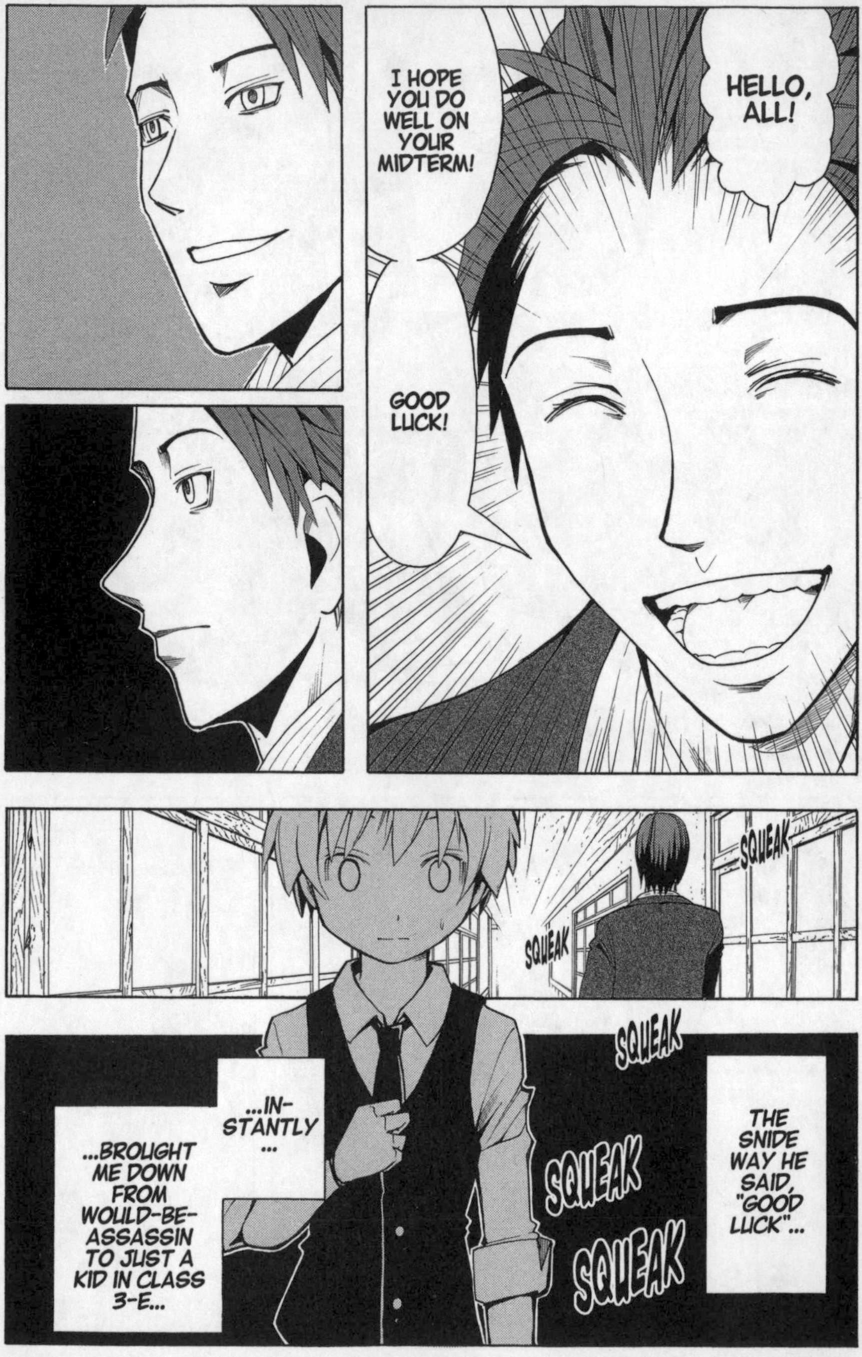
HELLO, ALL!
I HOPE YOU DO WELL ON YOUR MIDTERM!
GOOD LUCK!
SQUEAK
SQUEAK
THE SNIDE WAY HE SAID, "GOOD LUCK"...
SQUEAK
SQUEAK
SQUEAK
...IN-STANTLY...
...BROUGHT ME DOWN FROM WOULD-BE-ASSASSIN TO JUST A KID IN CLASS 3-E...

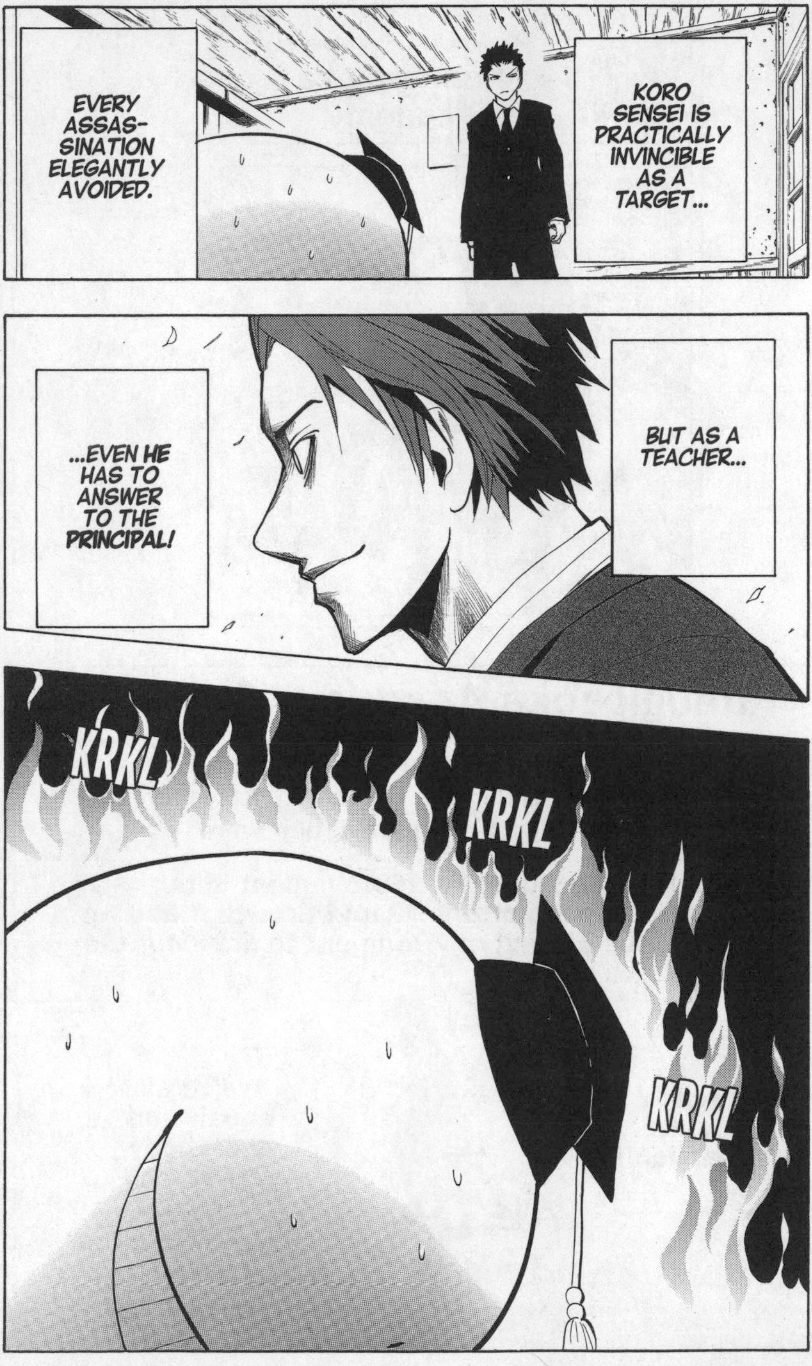
KORO SENSEI IS PRACTICALLY INVINCIBLE AS A TARGET...
EVERY ASSAS-SINATION ELEGANTLY AVOIDED.
BUT AS A TEACHER...
...EVEN HE HAS TO ANSWER TO THE PRINCIPAL!
KRKL
KRKL
KRKL

-Grow to Your Full Potential-
Kunugigaoka Academy

Kunugigaoka Junior High
student body:
570 students

Kunugigaoka High School
student body:
600 students

Kunugigaoka Academy Guide

Kunugigaoka Junior High (Deviation Score: 66)
Kunugigaoka High School (Deviation Score: 71)

You can clearly see student's improvement in our numbers. Our school motto is "Rapid Growth," and we have created the perfect environment to draw out the potential of each student.

This school will ignite your passion!!

We're all equals and everybody gets along!!

Kunugigaoka
School Mascot
Kunudon

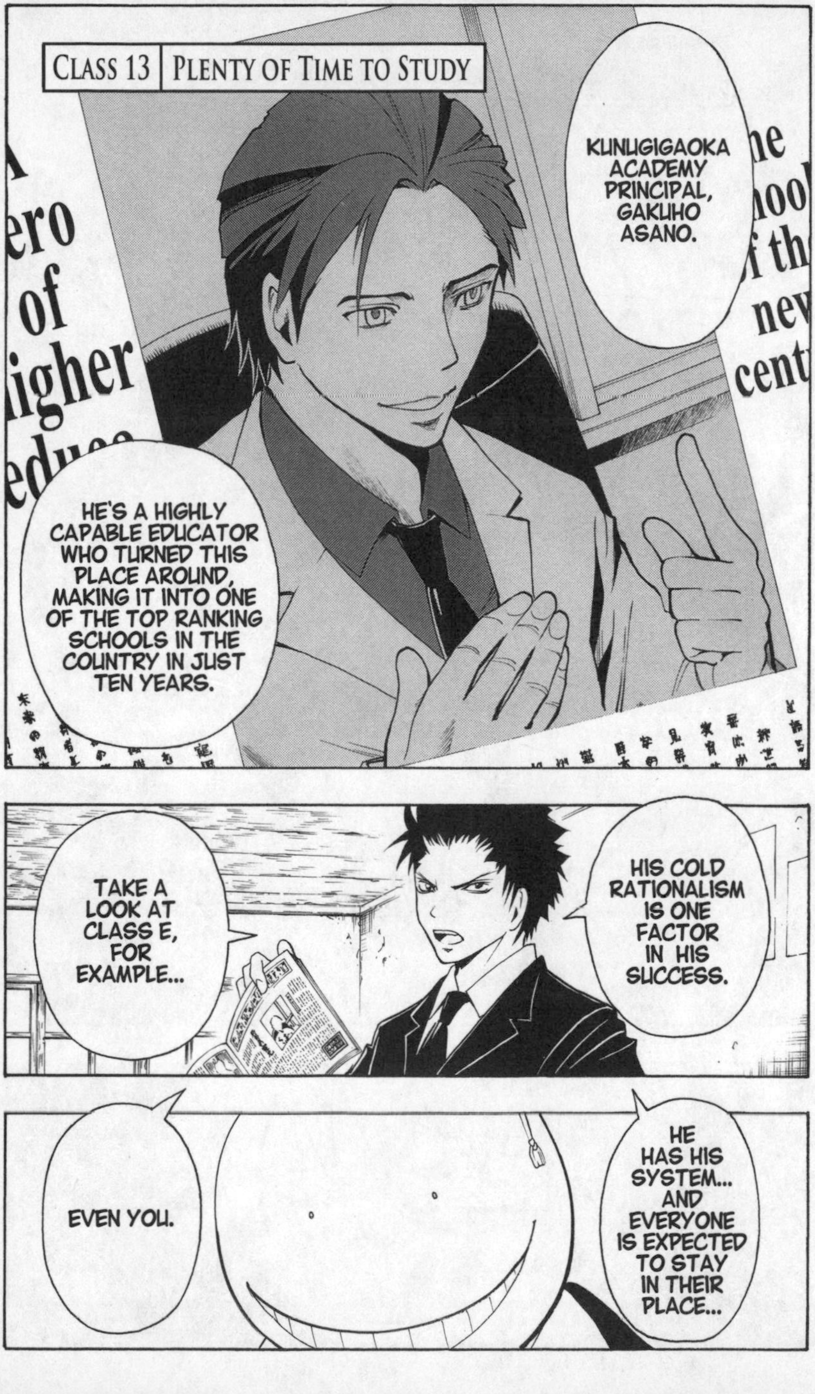
CLASS 13 PLENTY OF TIME TO STUDY
KUNUGIGAOKA ACADEMY PRINCIPAL, GAKUHO ASANO.
HE'S A HIGHLY CAPABLE EDUCATOR WHO TURNED THIS PLACE AROUND, MAKING IT INTO ONE OF THE TOP RANKING SCHOOLS IN THE COUNTRY IN JUST TEN YEARS.
HIS COLD RATIONALISM IS ONE FACTOR IN HIS SUCCESS.
TAKE A LOOK AT CLASS E, FOR EXAMPLE...
HE HAS HIS SYSTEM... AND EVERYONE IS EXPECTED TO STAY IN THEIR PLACE...
EVEN YOU.

CLASS 13 PLENTY OF TIME TO STUDY

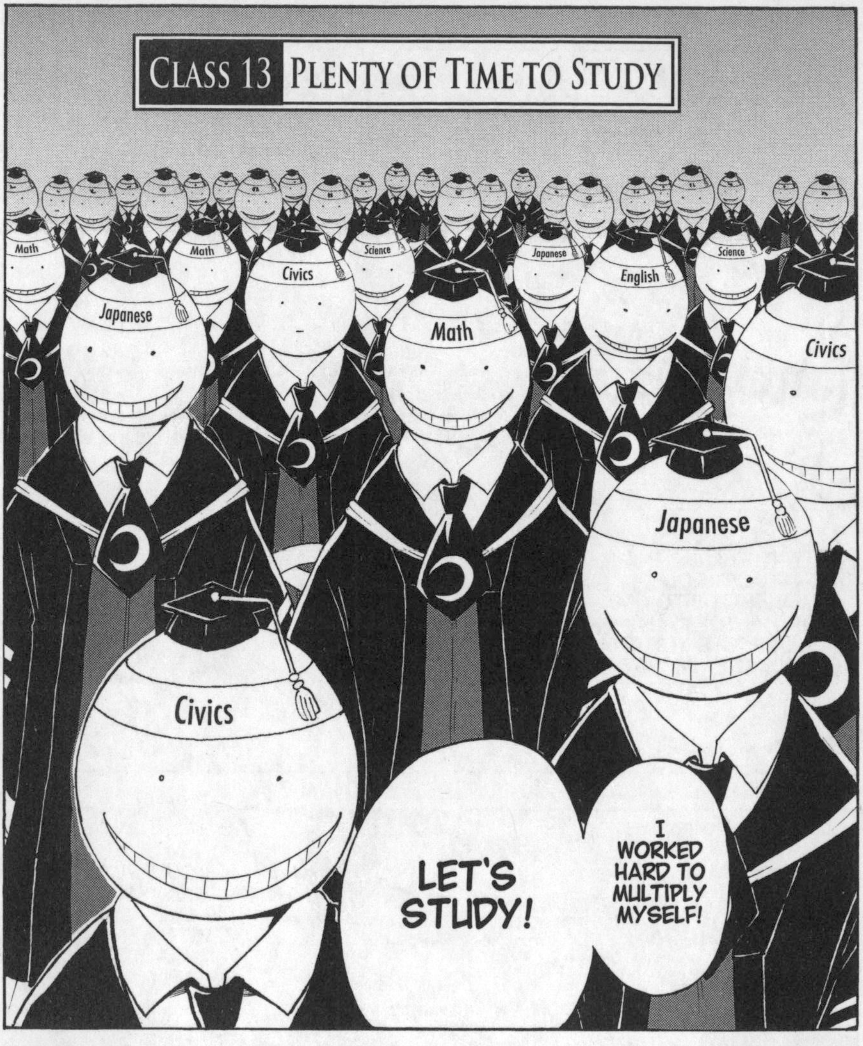
Math
Math
Science
Civics
Japanese
Math
Japanese
English
Science
Civics
Japanese
Civics
I WORKED HARD TO MULTIPLY MYSELF!
LET'S STUDY!

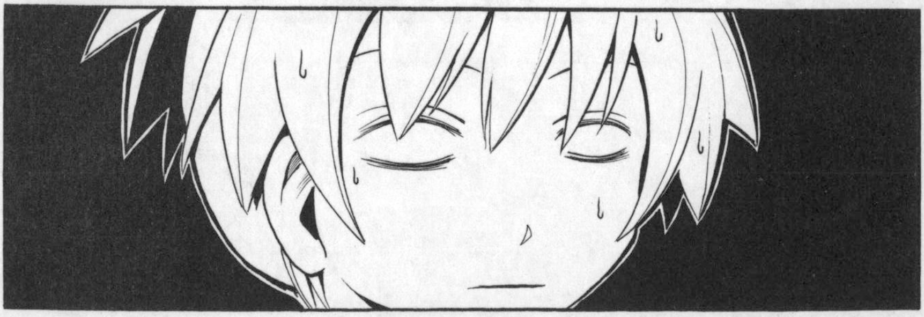

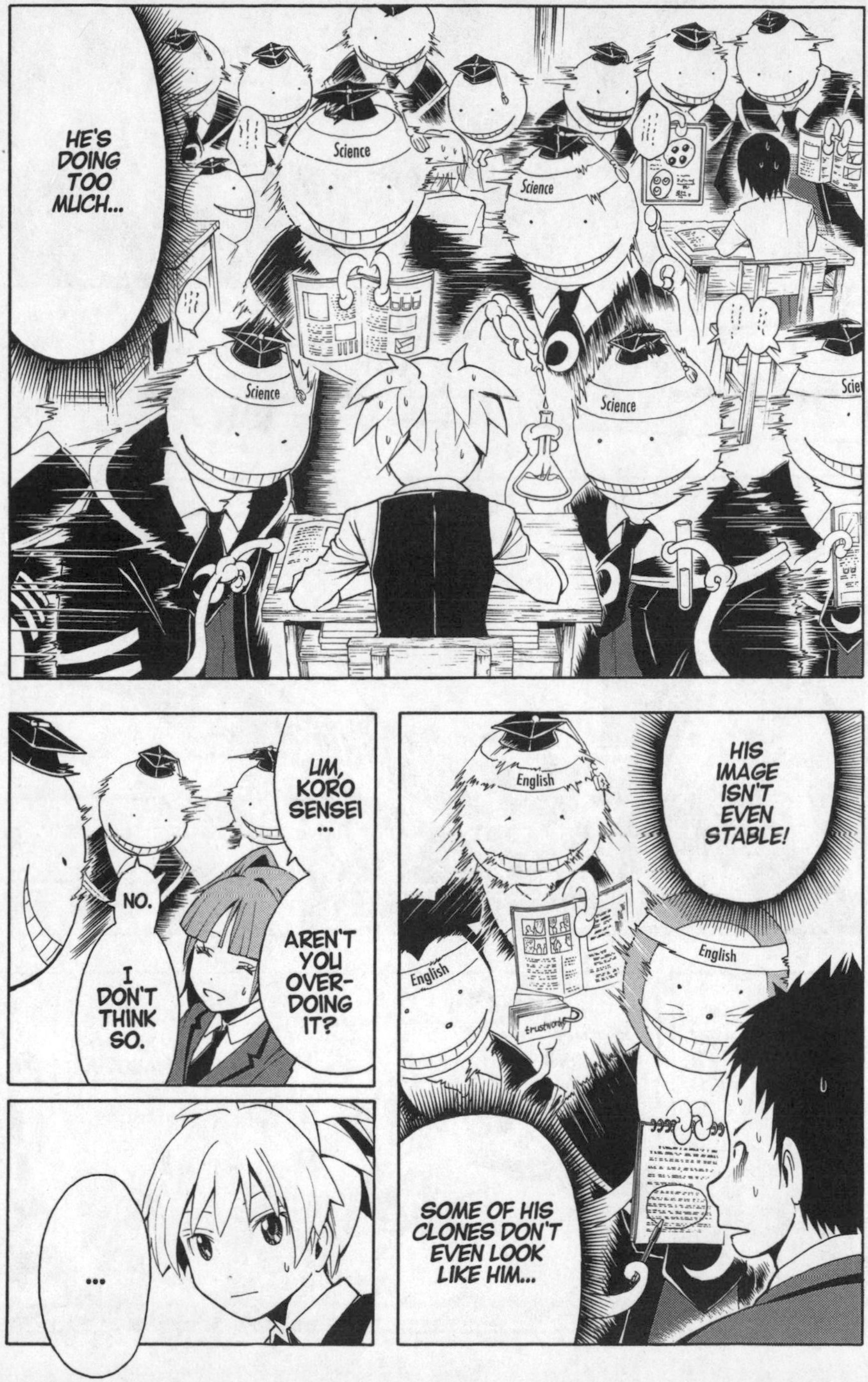
HE'S DOING TOO MUCH...
Science
Science
Science
Science
HIS IMAGE ISN'T EVEN STABLE!
English
English
English
SOME OF HIS CLONES DON'T EVEN LOOK LIKE HIM...
UM, KORO SENSEI ...
AREN'T YOU OVER-DOING IT?
NO.
I DON'T THINK SO.
...

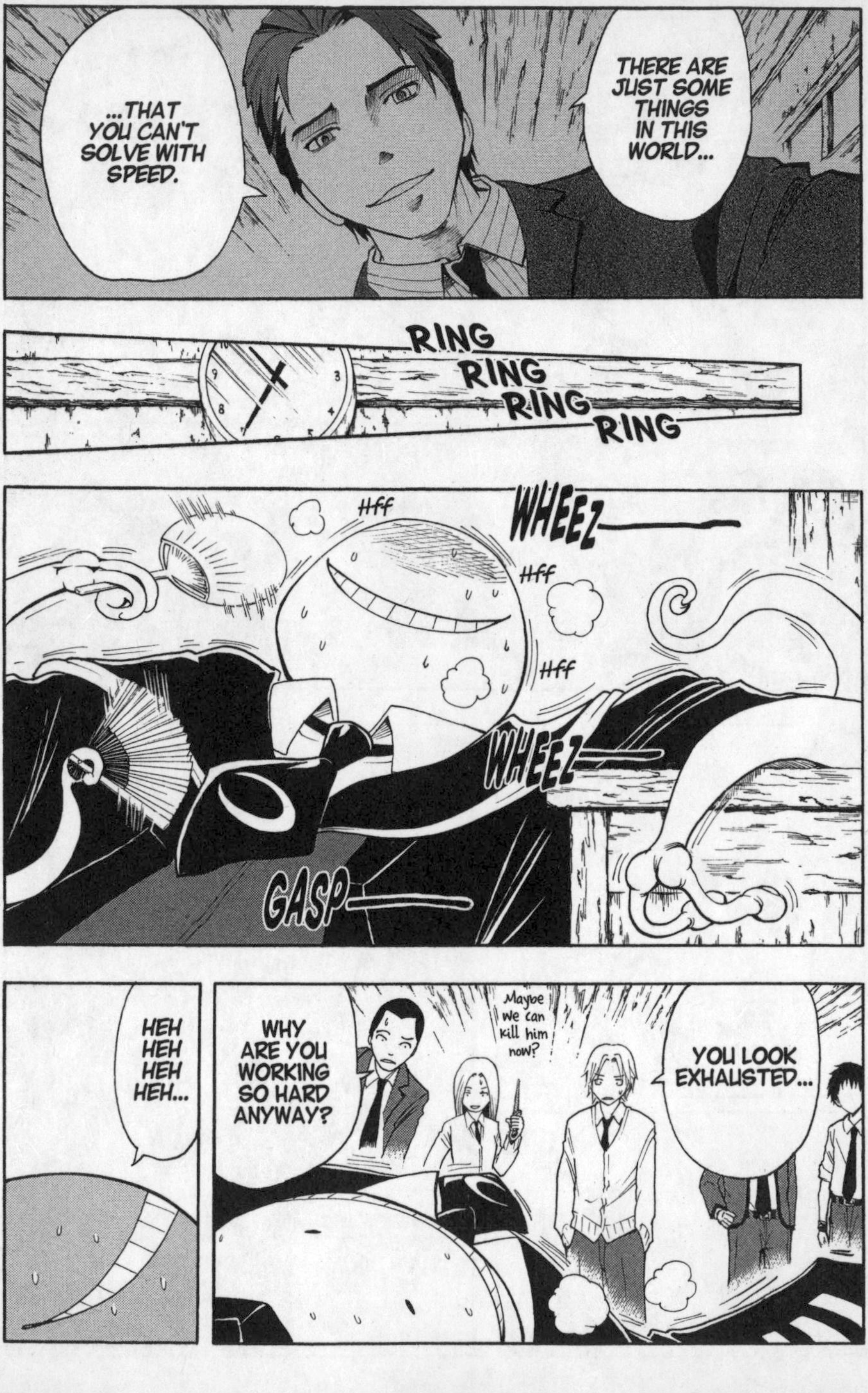
THERE ARE JUST SOME THINGS IN THIS WORLD...
...THAT YOU CAN'T SOLVE WITH SPEED.
RING
RING
RING
RING
WHEEZ—
Hff
Hff
Hff
WHEEZ—
GASP—
YOU LOOK EXHAUSTED...
Maybe we can kill him now?
WHY ARE YOU WORKING SO HARD ANYWAY?
HEH HEH HEH HEH...

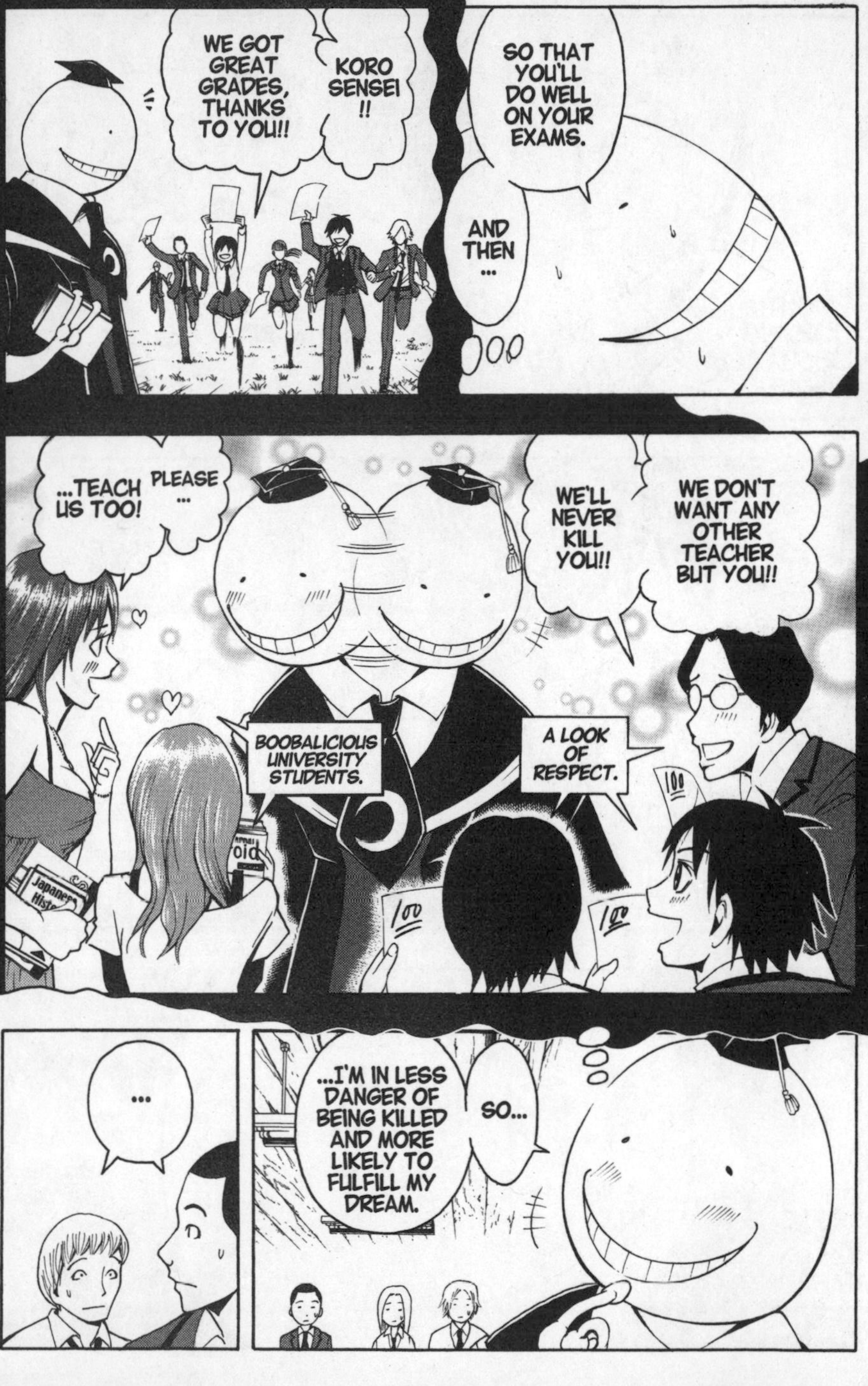
SO THAT YOU'LL DO WELL ON YOUR EXAMS.
AND THEN ...
KORO SENSEI !!
WE GOT GREAT GRADES, THANKS TO YOU!!
WE DON'T WANT ANY OTHER TEACHER BUT YOU!!
WE'LL NEVER KILL YOU!!
PLEASE ...
...TEACH US TOO!
A LOOK OF RESPECT.
BOOBALICIOUS UNIVERSITY STUDENTS.
SO...
...I'M IN LESS DANGER OF BEING KILLED AND MORE LIKELY TO FULFILL MY DREAM.
...

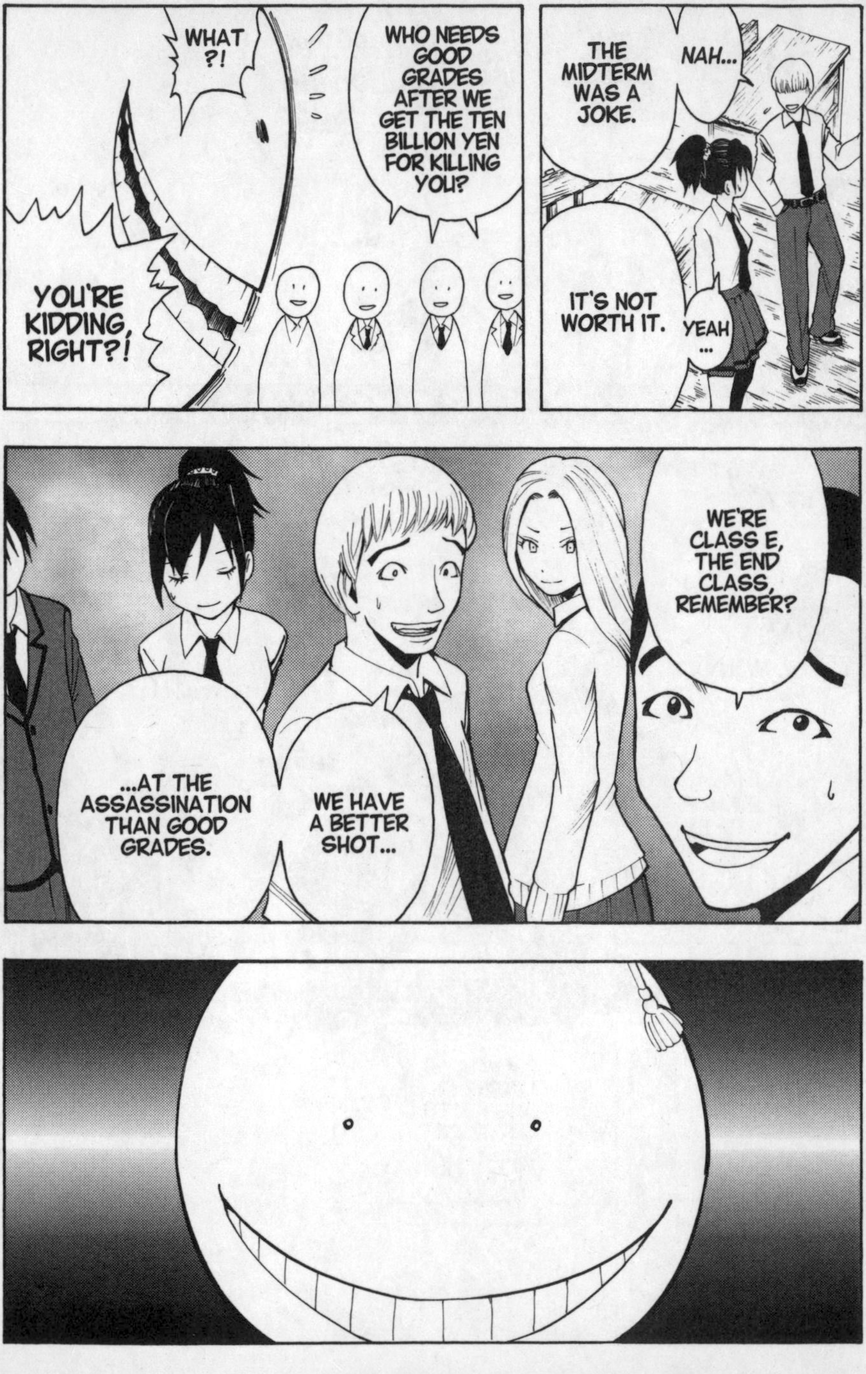
NAH...
THE MIDTERM WAS A JOKE.
IT'S NOT WORTH IT.
YEAH...
WHO NEEDS GOOD GRADES AFTER WE GET THE TEN BILLION YEN FOR KILLING YOU?
WHAT?!
YOU'RE KIDDING, RIGHT?!
WE'RE CLASS E, THE END CLASS, REMEMBER?
WE HAVE A BETTER SHOT...
...AT THE ASSASSINATION THAN GOOD GRADES.

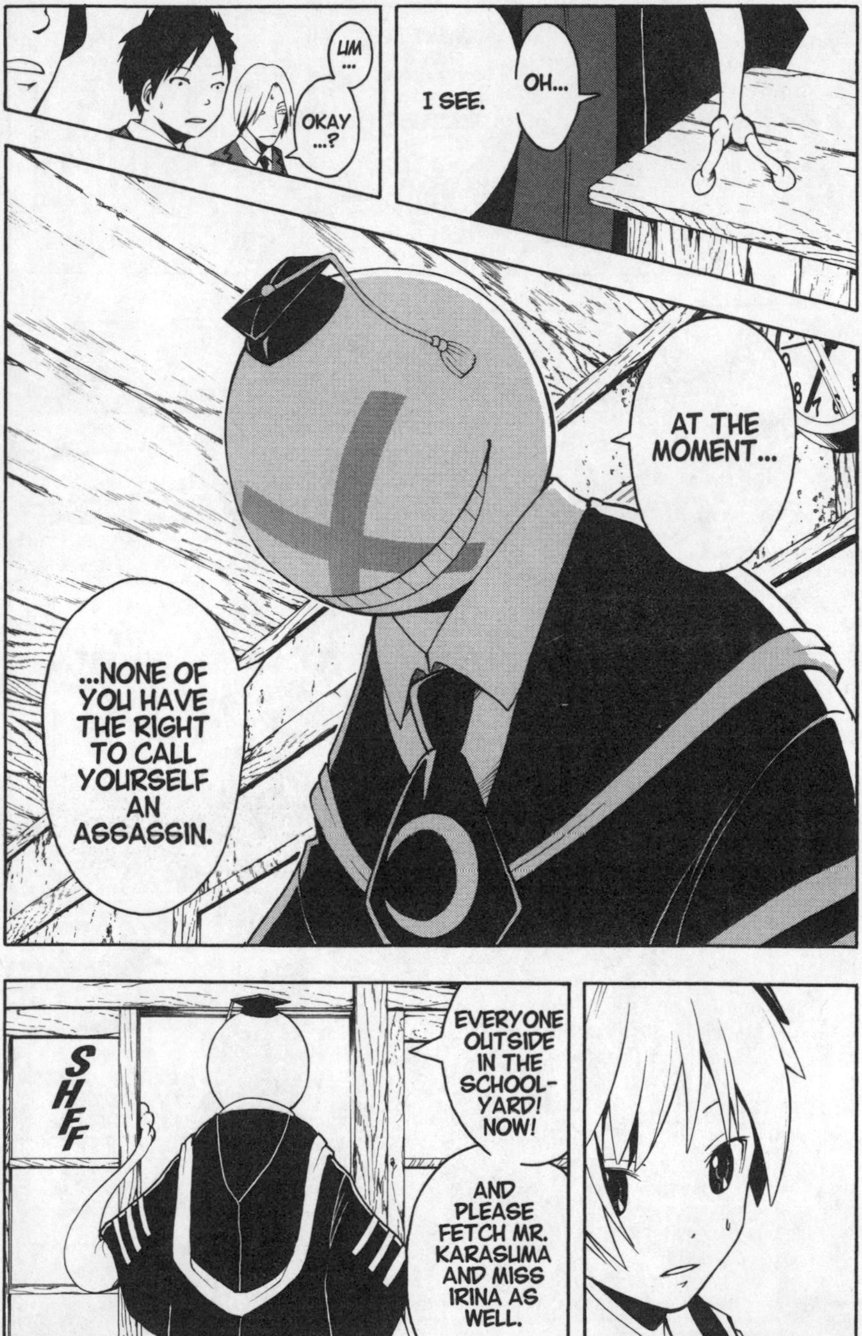
OH...
I SEE.
UM...
OKAY...?
AT THE MOMENT...
...NONE OF YOU HAVE THE RIGHT TO CALL YOURSELF AN ASSASSIN.
EVERYONE OUTSIDE IN THE SCHOOL-YARD! NOW!
AND PLEASE FETCH MR. KARASUMA AND MISS IRINA AS WELL.
SHFF

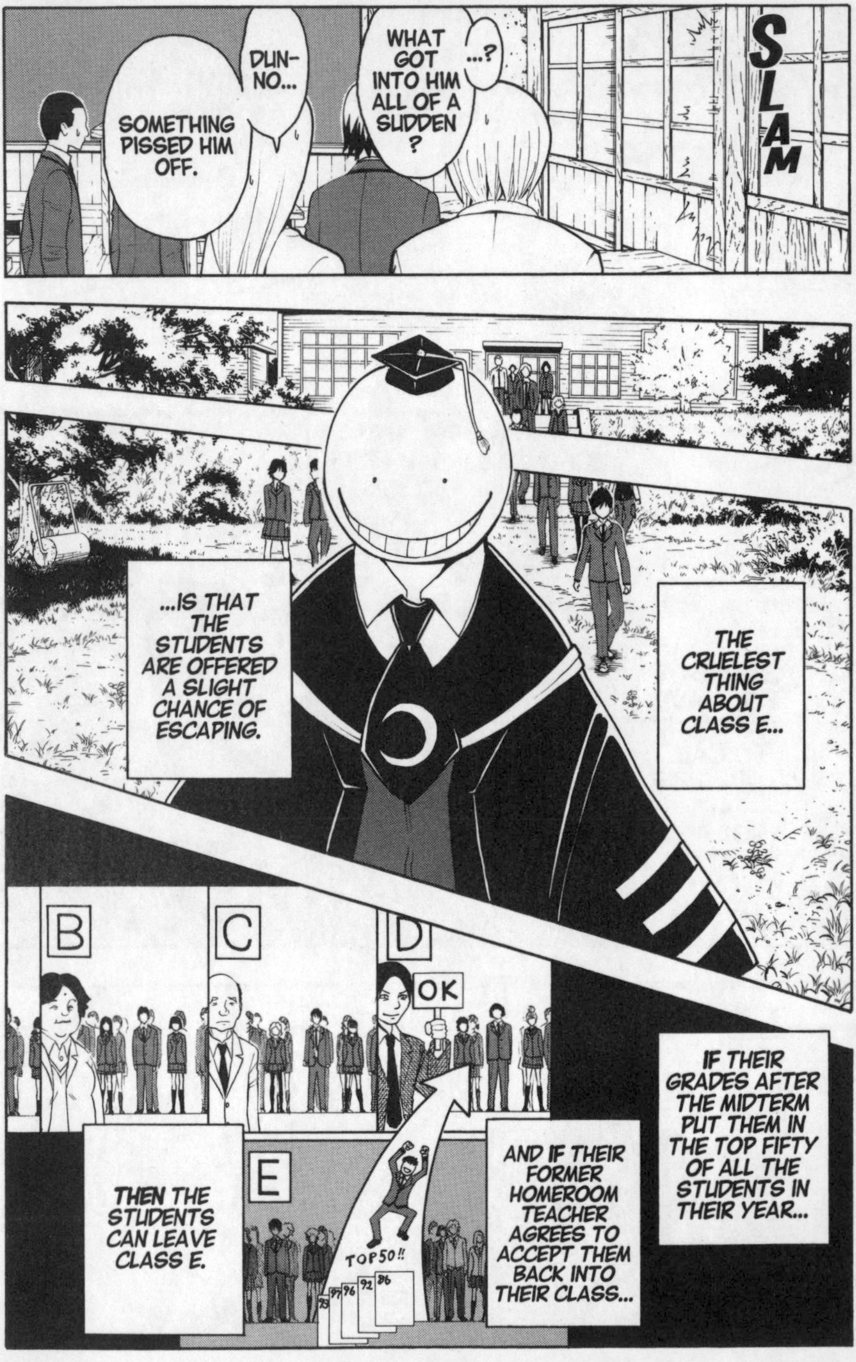
SLAM
...?
WHAT GOT INTO HIM ALL OF A SUDDEN?
DUN-NO...
SOMETHING PISSED HIM OFF.
THE CRUELEST THING ABOUT CLASS E...
...IS THAT THE STUDENTS ARE OFFERED A SLIGHT CHANCE OF ESCAPING.
IF THEIR GRADES AFTER THE MIDTERM PUT THEM IN THE TOP FIFTY OF ALL THE STUDENTS IN THEIR YEAR...
AND IF THEIR FORMER HOMEROOM TEACHER AGREES TO ACCEPT THEM BACK INTO THEIR CLASS...
THEN THE STUDENTS CAN LEAVE CLASS E.
D
OK
C
B
E
TOP50!!

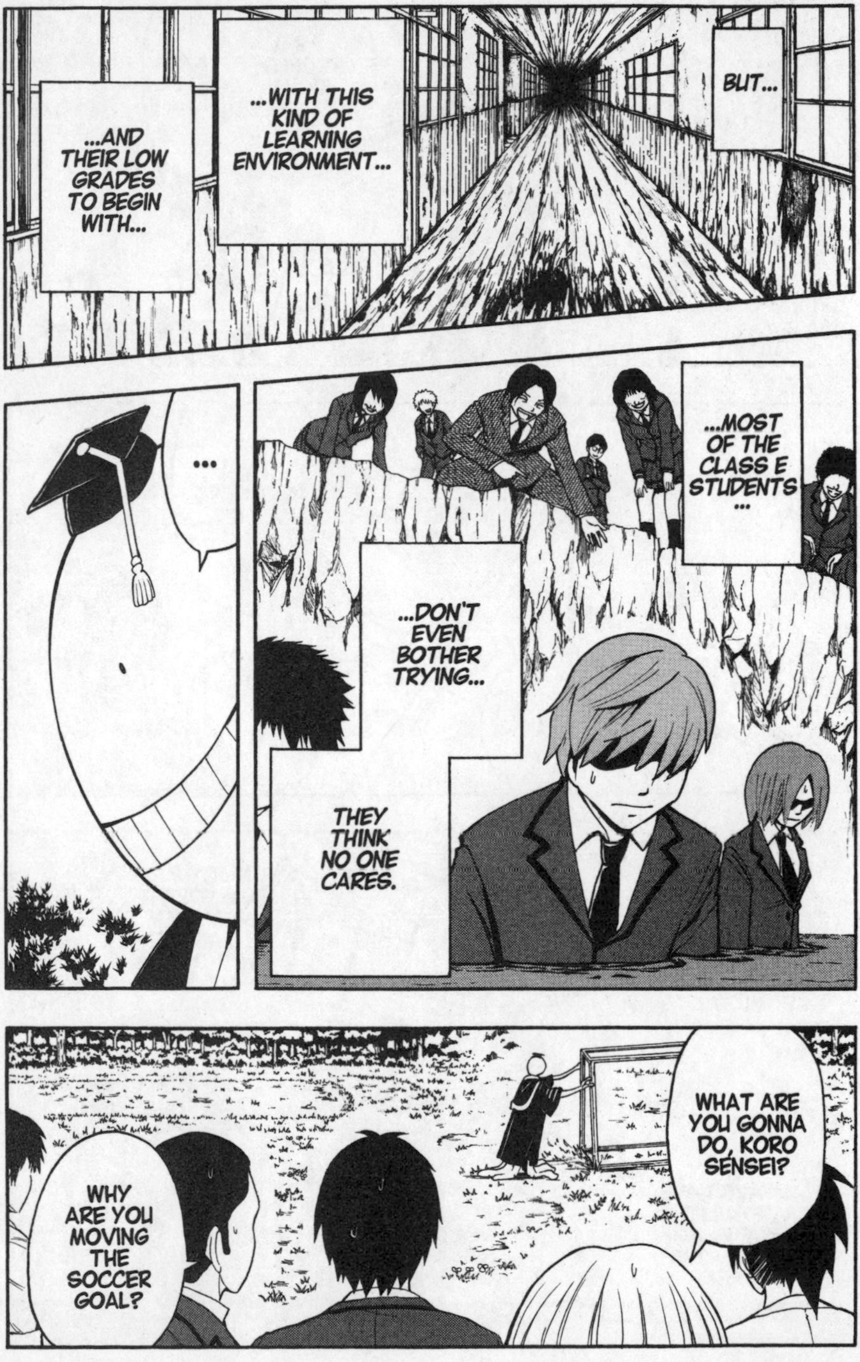
...AND THEIR LOW GRADES TO BEGIN WITH...
...WITH THIS KIND OF LEARNING ENVIRONMENT...
BUT...
...MOST OF THE CLASS E STUDENTS ...
...DON'T EVEN BOTHER TRYING...
THEY THINK NO ONE CARES.
...
WHAT ARE YOU GONNA DO, KORO SENSEI?
WHY ARE YOU MOVING THE SOCCER GOAL?

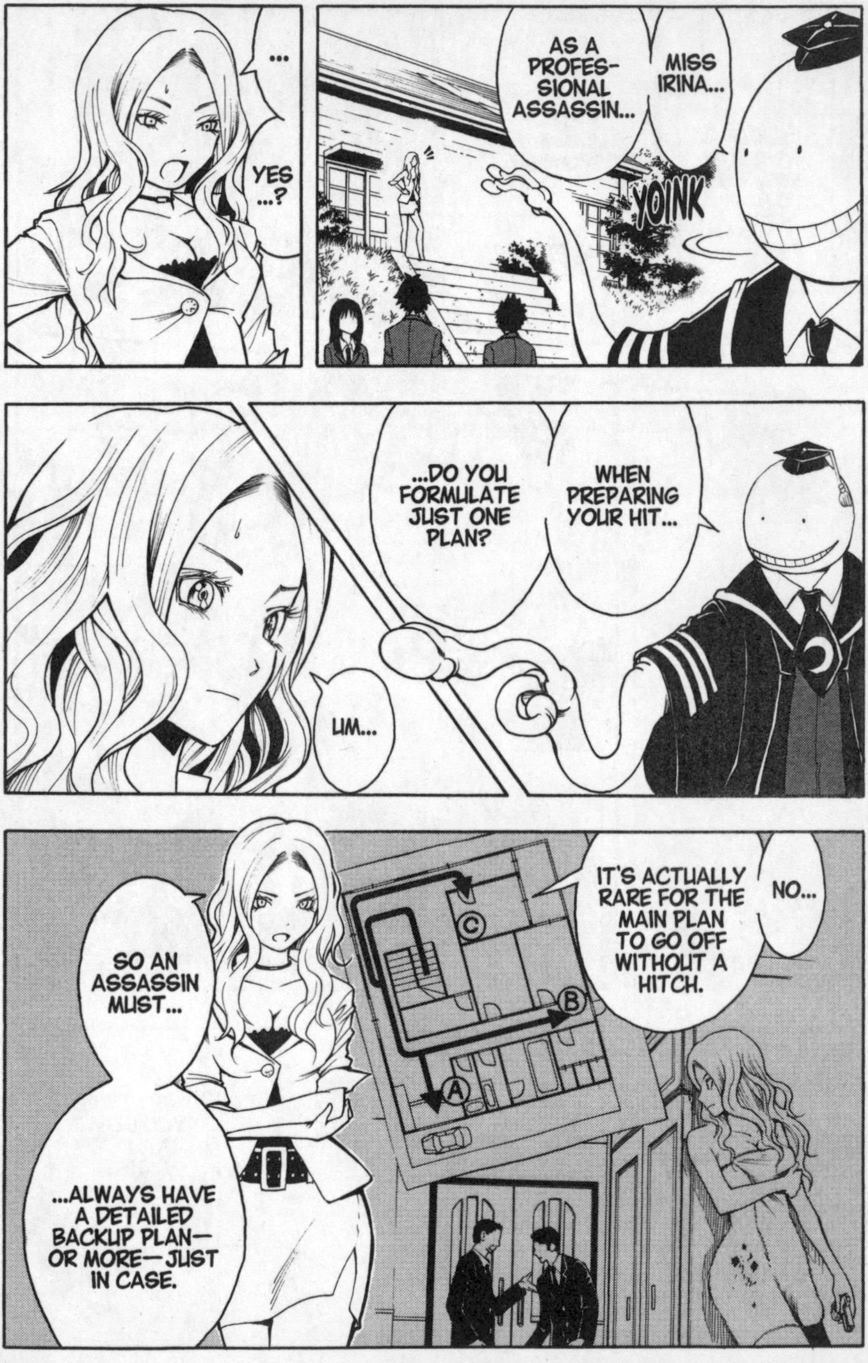
MISS IRINA...
AS A PROFES-SIONAL ASSASSIN...
YOINK
...
YES ...?
WHEN PREPARING YOUR HIT...
...DO YOU FORMULATE JUST ONE PLAN?
UM...
NO...
IT'S ACTUALLY RARE FOR THE MAIN PLAN TO GO OFF WITHOUT A HITCH.
SO AN ASSASSIN MUST...
...ALWAYS HAVE A DETAILED BACKUP PLAN—OR MORE—JUST IN CASE.

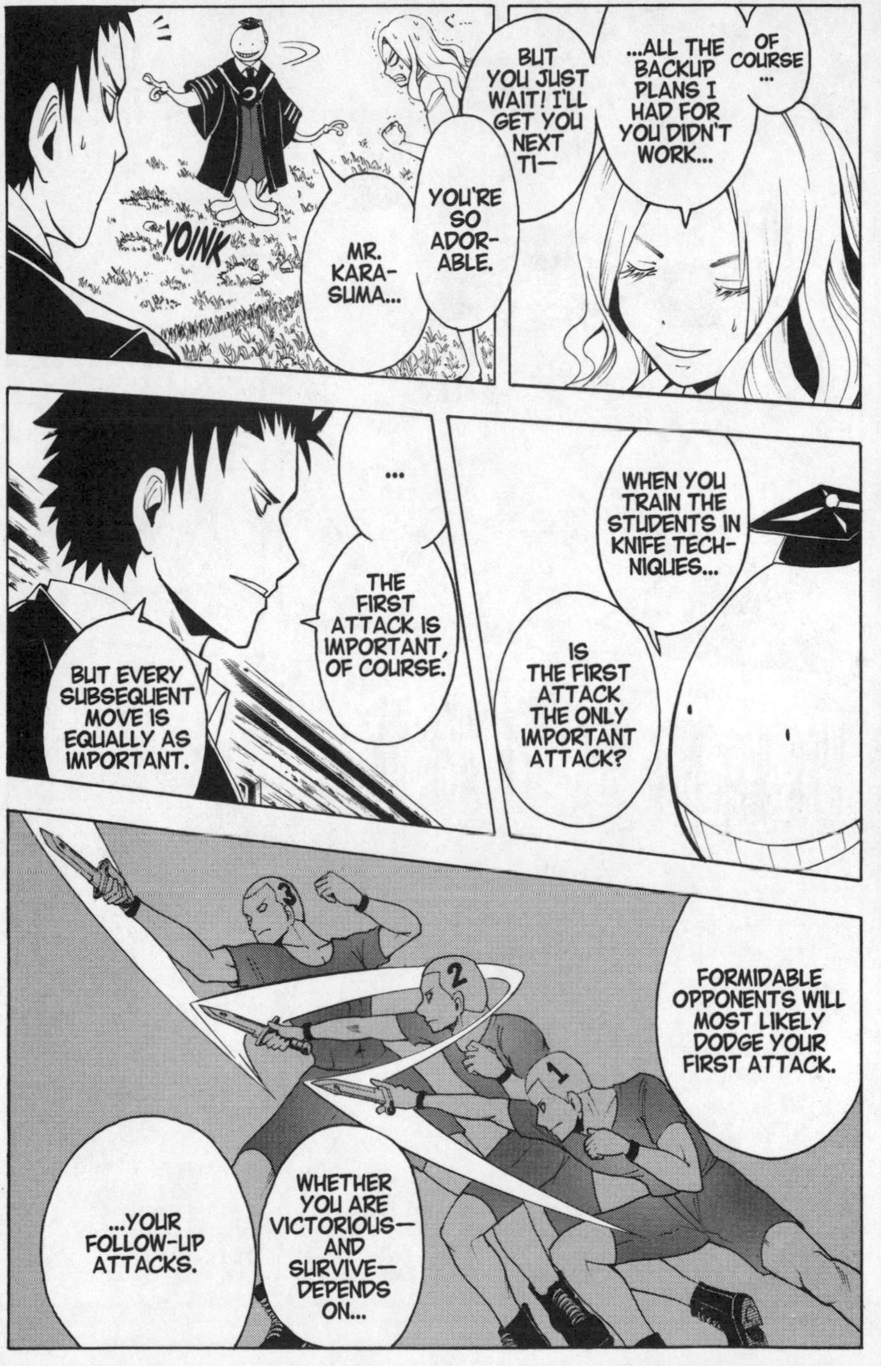
OF COURSE...
...ALL THE BACKUP PLANS I HAD FOR YOU DIDN'T WORK...
BUT YOU JUST WAIT! I'LL GET YOU NEXT TI—
YOU'RE SO ADORABLE.
MR. KARASUMA...
YOINK
WHEN YOU TRAIN THE STUDENTS IN KNIFE TECHNIQUES...
IS THE FIRST ATTACK THE ONLY IMPORTANT ATTACK?
...
THE FIRST ATTACK IS IMPORTANT, OF COURSE.
BUT EVERY SUBSEQUENT MOVE IS EQUALLY AS IMPORTANT.
FORMIDABLE OPPONENTS WILL MOST LIKELY DODGE YOUR FIRST ATTACK.
WHETHER YOU ARE VICTORIOUS—AND SURVIVE—DEPENDS ON...
...YOUR FOLLOW-UP ATTACKS.

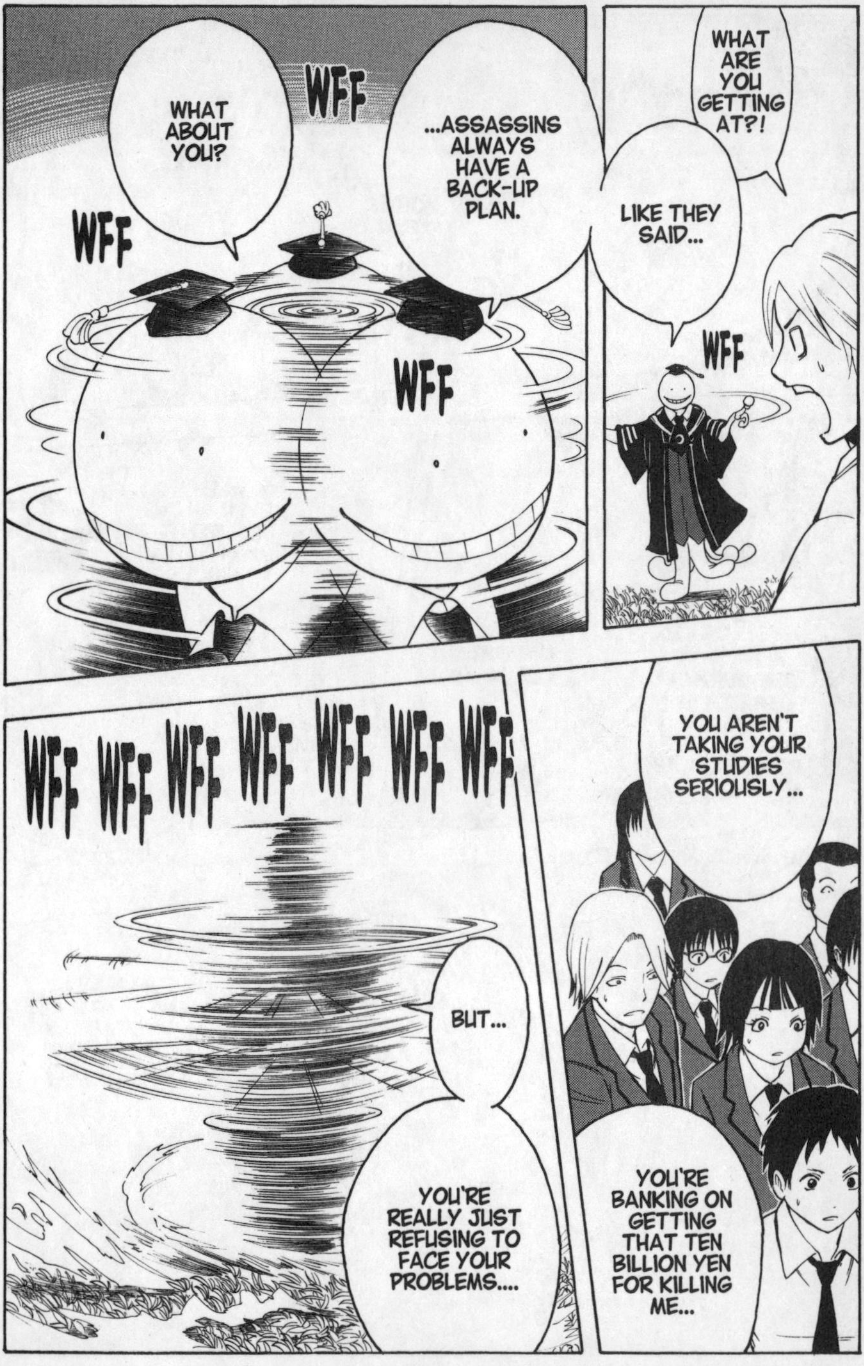
WHAT ARE YOU GETTING AT?!
LIKE THEY SAID...
WFF
...ASSASSINS ALWAYS HAVE A BACK-UP PLAN.
WFF
WHAT ABOUT YOU?
WFF
WFF
YOU AREN'T TAKING YOUR STUDIES SERIOUSLY...
YOU'RE BANKING ON GETTING THAT TEN BILLION YEN FOR KILLING ME...
WFF WFF WFF WFF WFF WFF WFF
BUT...
YOU'RE REALLY JUST REFUSING TO FACE YOUR PROBLEMS....

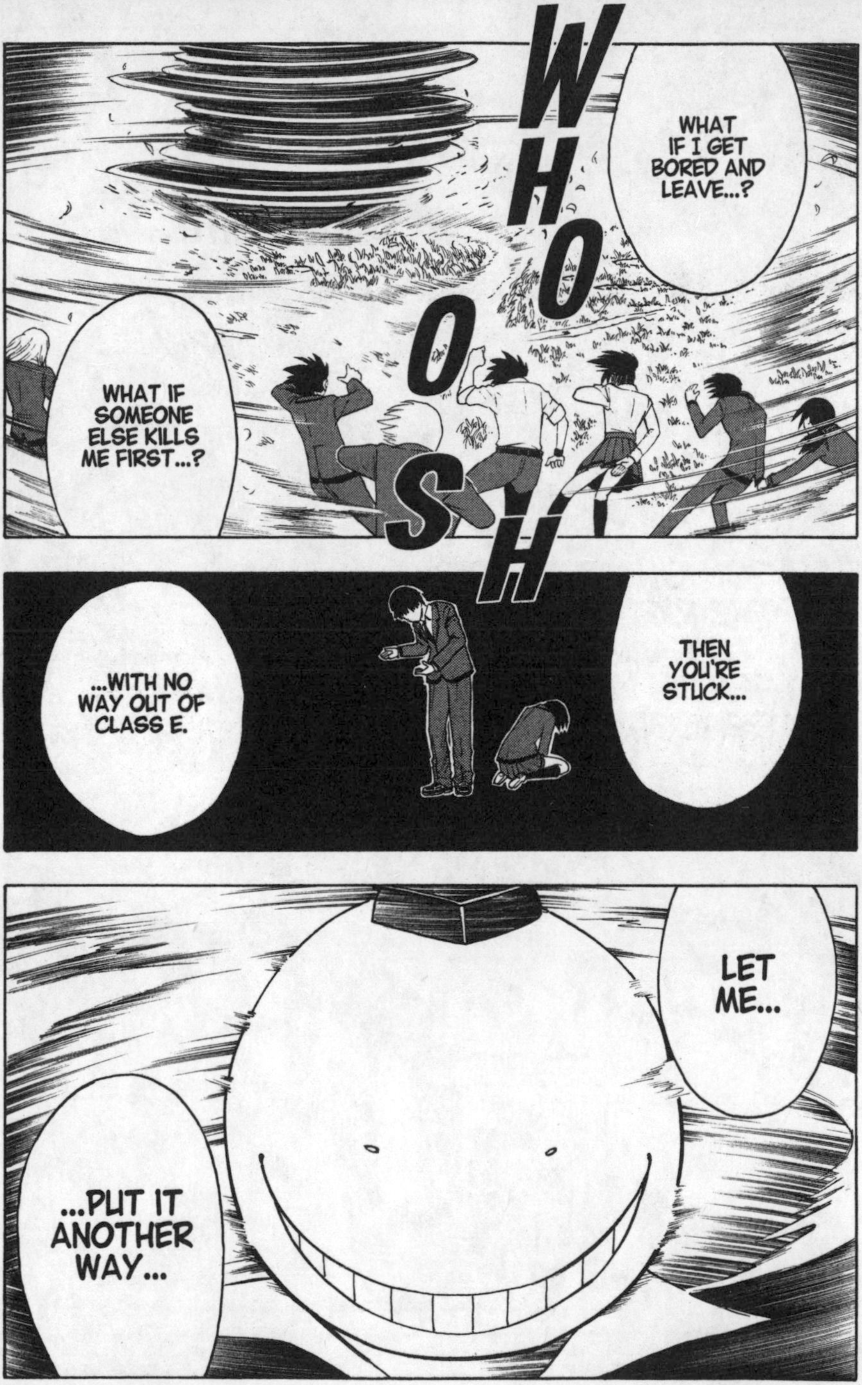
WHAT IF I GET BORED AND LEAVE...?
WHOOSH
WHAT IF SOMEONE ELSE KILLS ME FIRST...?
THEN YOU'RE STUCK...
...WITH NO WAY OUT OF CLASS E.
LET ME...
...PUT IT ANOTHER WAY...

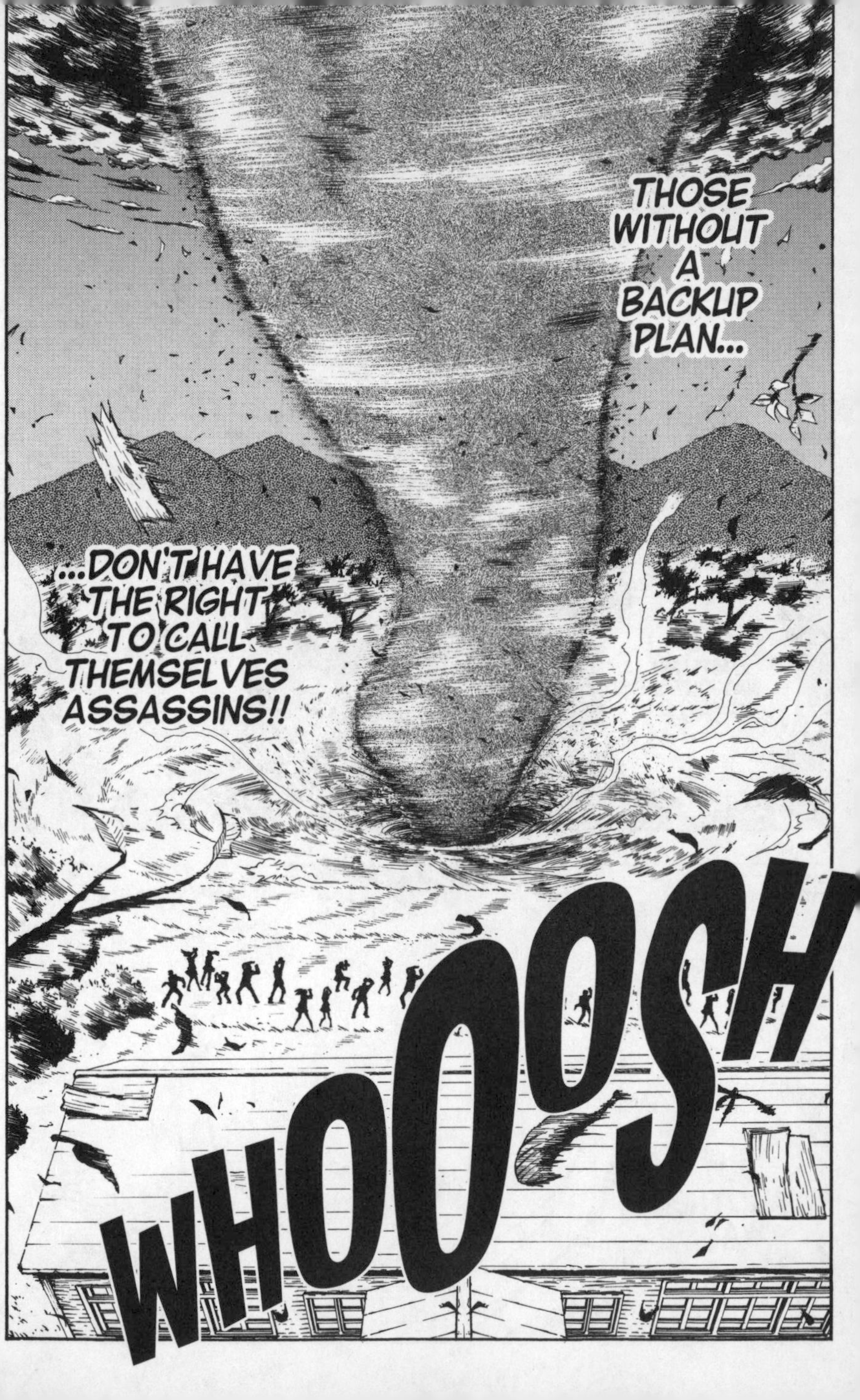
THOSE WITHOUT A BACKUP PLAN...
...DON'T HAVE THE RIGHT TO CALL THEMSELVES ASSASSINS!!
WHOOOOSH

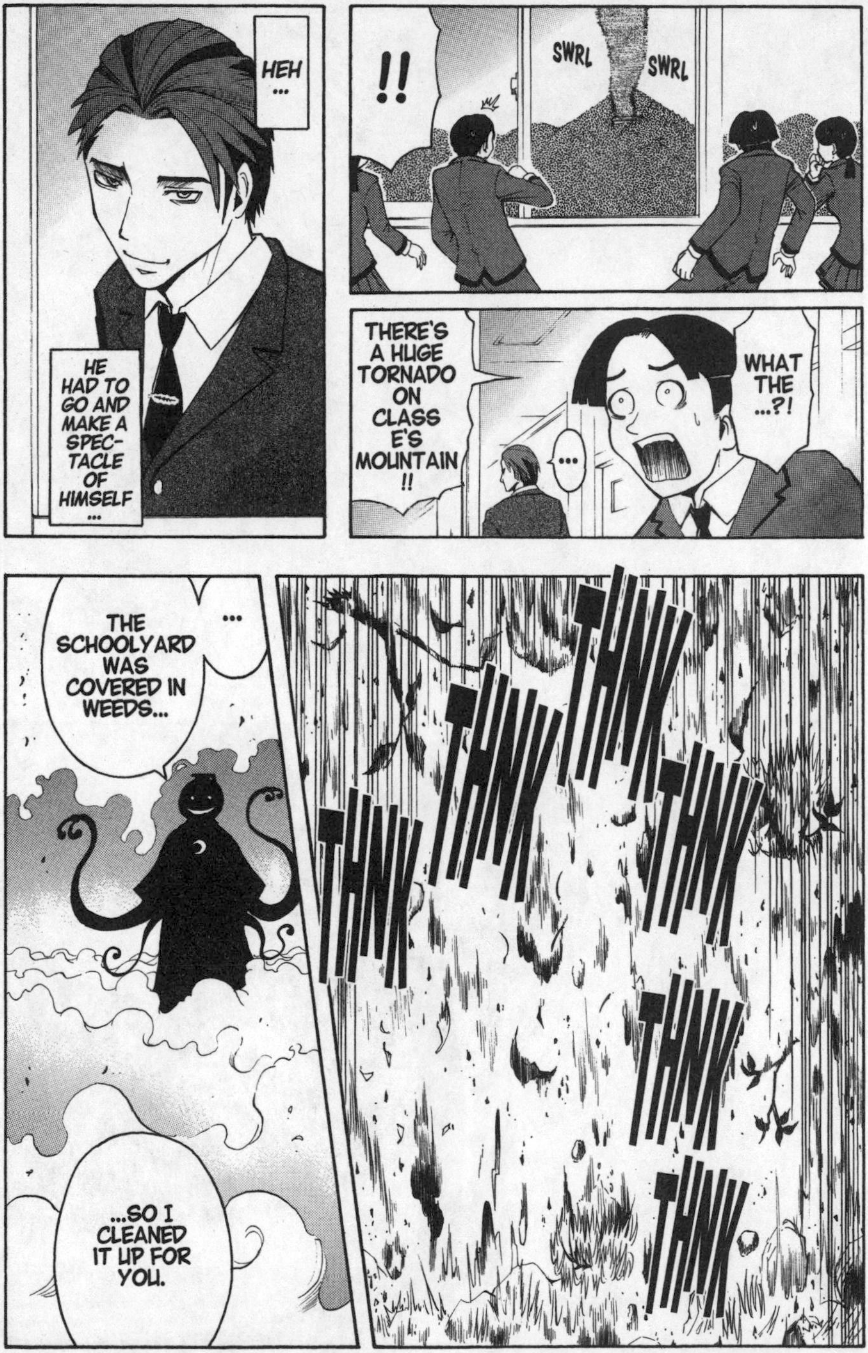
SWRL
SWRL
!!
WHAT THE ...?!
THERE'S A HUGE TORNADO ON CLASS E'S MOUNTAIN !!
...
HEH ...
HE HAD TO GO AND MAKE A SPEC-TACLE OF HIMSELF ...
THNK THNK THNK THNK THNK THNK
...
THE SCHOOLYARD WAS COVERED IN WEEDS...
...SO I CLEANED IT UP FOR YOU.

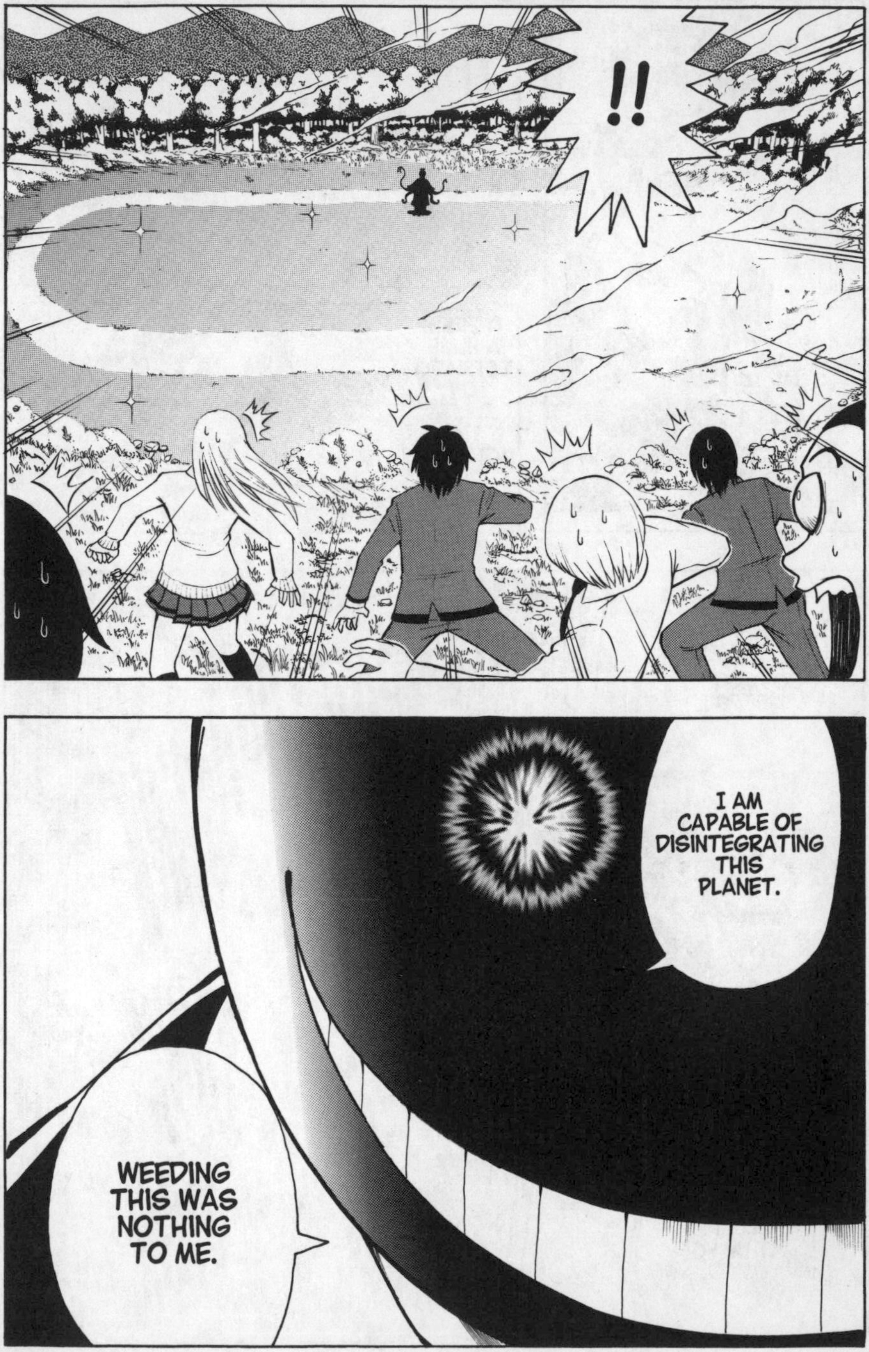
!!
I AM CAPABLE OF DISINTEGRATING THIS PLANET.
WEEDING THIS WAS NOTHING TO ME.

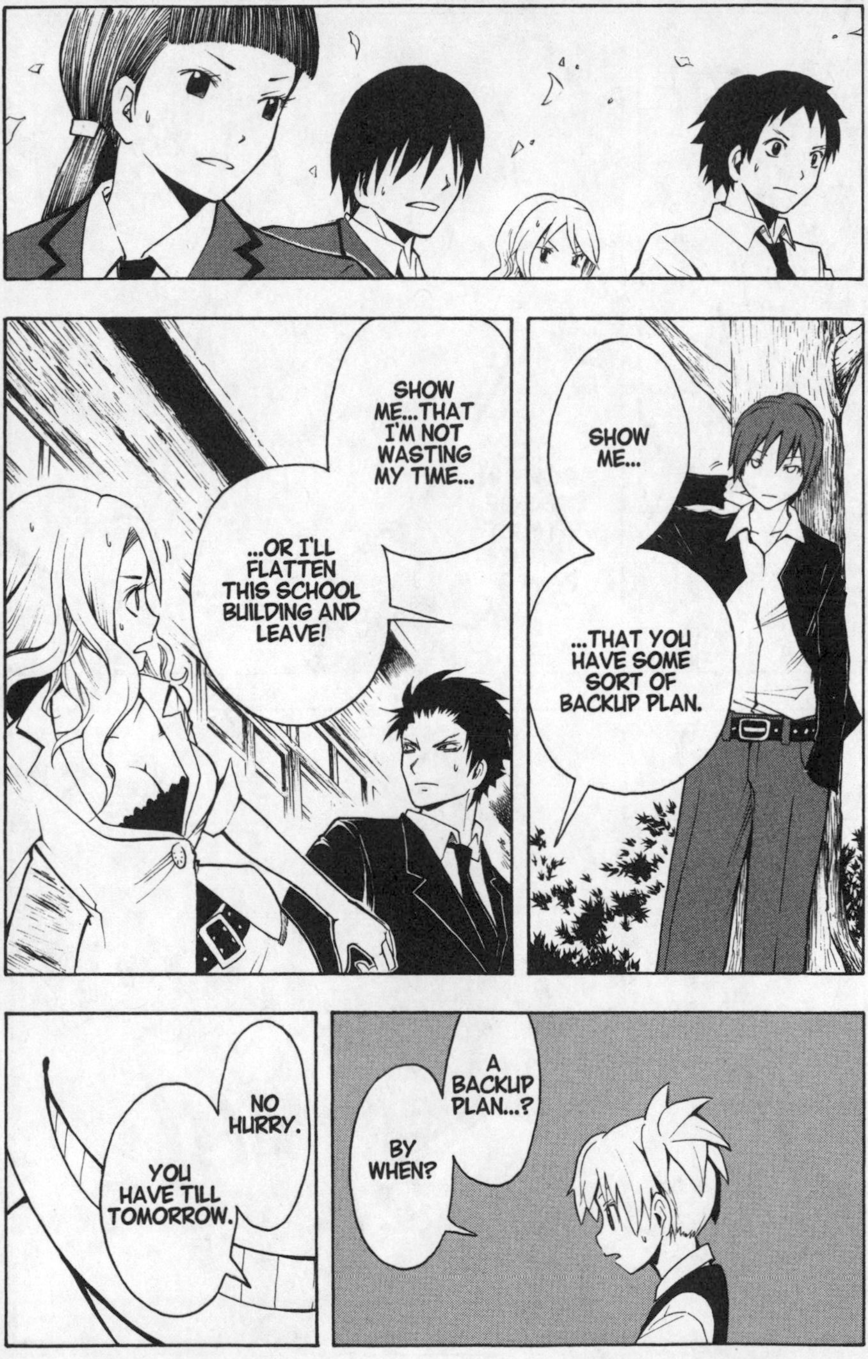
SHOW ME...
...THAT YOU HAVE SOME SORT OF BACKUP PLAN.
SHOW ME...THAT I'M NOT WASTING MY TIME...
...OR I'LL FLATTEN THIS SCHOOL BUILDING AND LEAVE!
A BACKUP PLAN...?
BY WHEN?
NO HURRY.
YOU HAVE TILL TOMORROW.

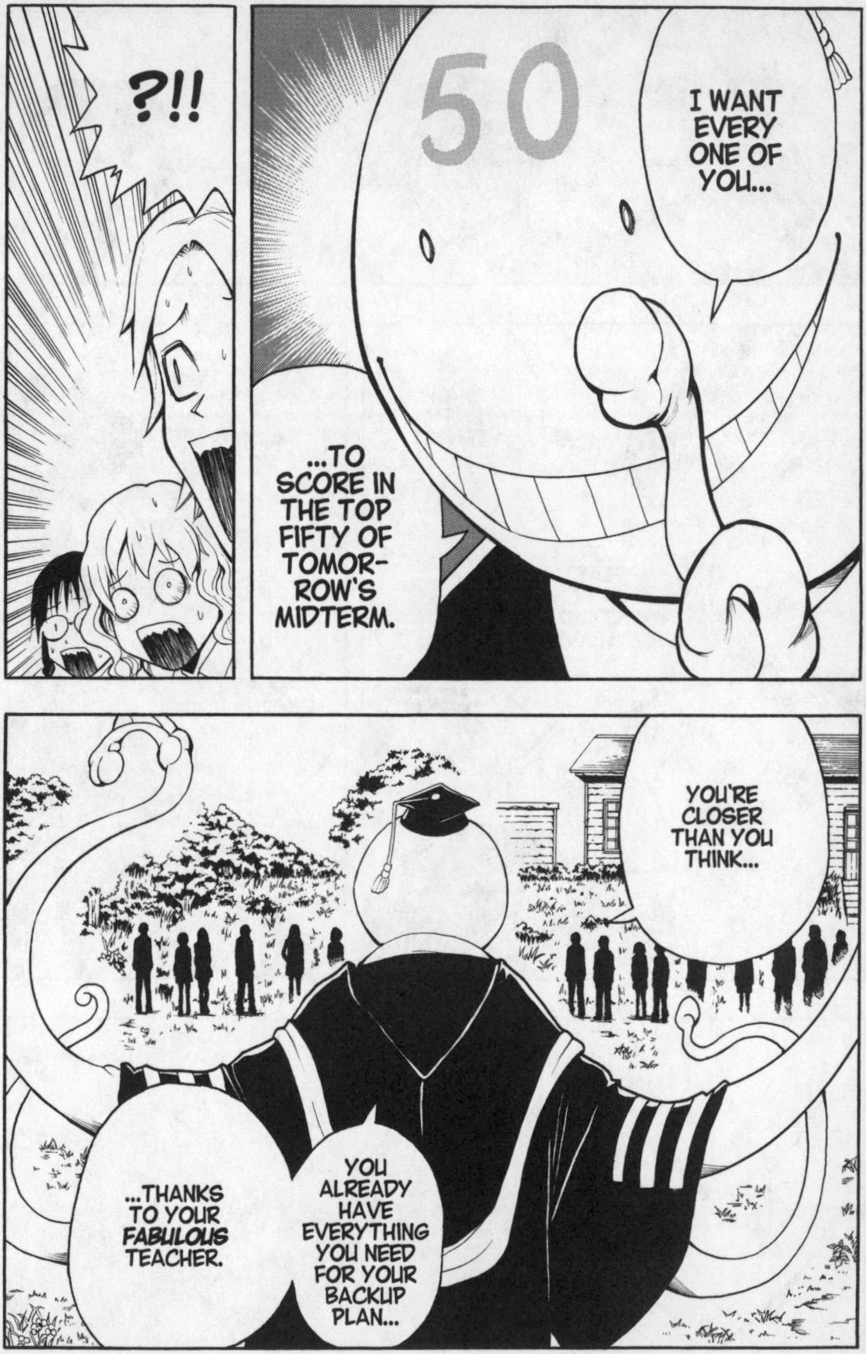
50
I WANT EVERY ONE OF YOU...
...TO SCORE IN THE TOP FIFTY OF TOMOR-ROW'S MIDTERM.
?!!
YOU'RE CLOSER THAN YOU THINK...
YOU ALREADY HAVE EVERYTHING YOU NEED FOR YOUR BACKUP PLAN...
...THANKS TO YOUR **FABULOUS** TEACHER.

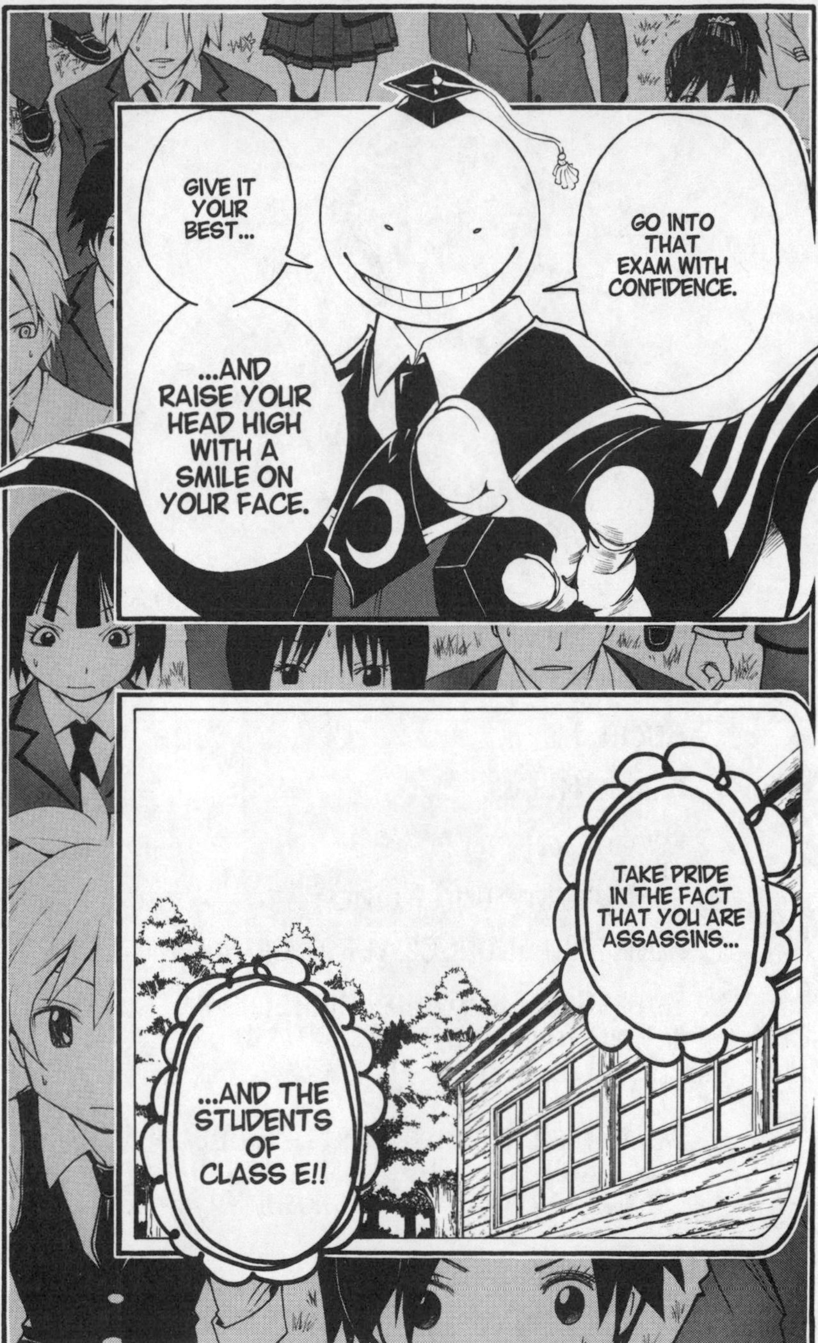
GO INTO THAT EXAM WITH CONFIDENCE.
GIVE IT YOUR BEST...
...AND RAISE YOUR HEAD HIGH WITH A SMILE ON YOUR FACE.
TAKE PRIDE IN THE FACT THAT YOU ARE ASSASSINS...
...AND THE STUDENTS OF CLASS E!!

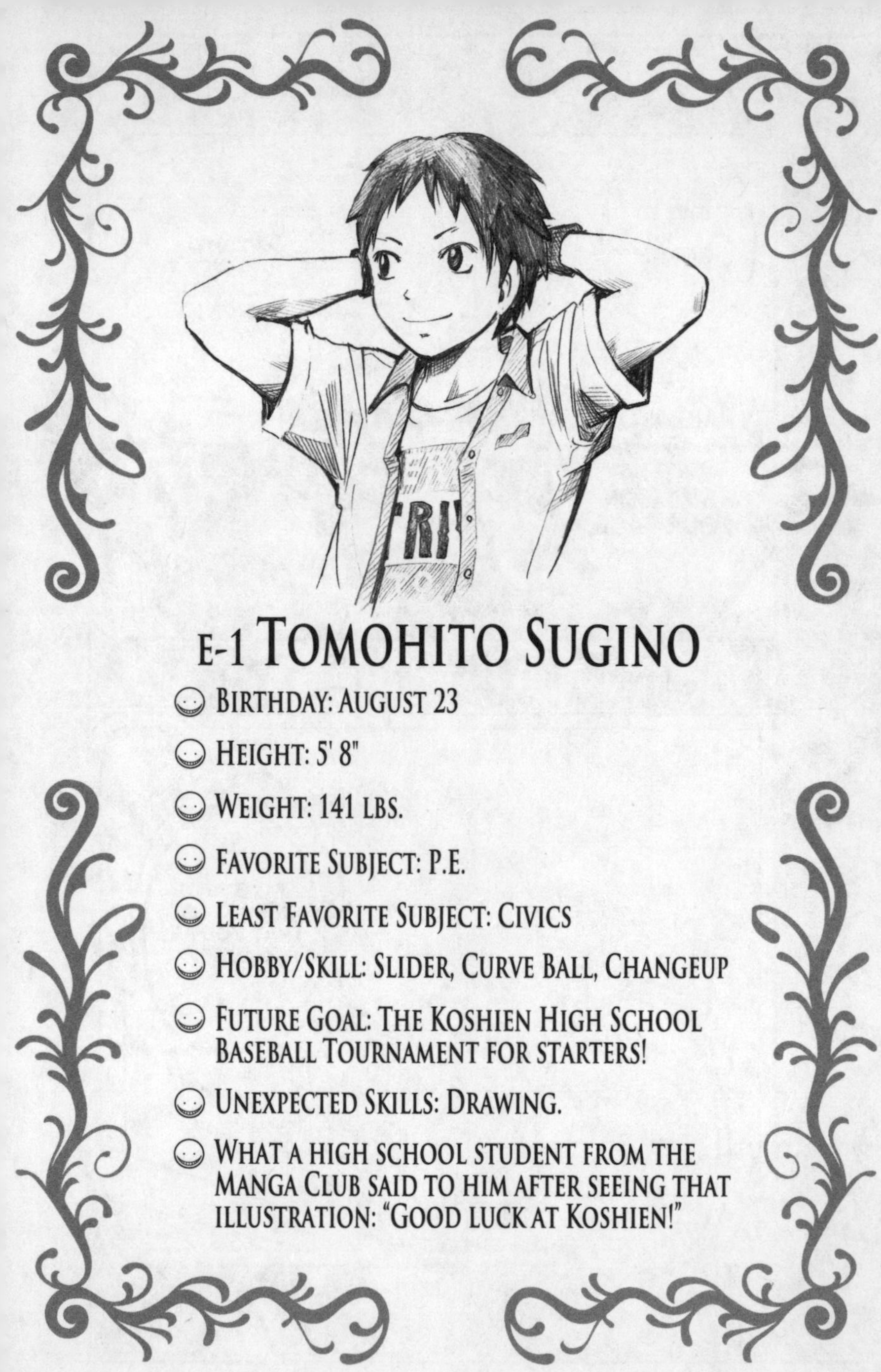
TRI

E-1 TOMOHITO SUGINO

- BIRTHDAY: AUGUST 23
- HEIGHT: 5' 8"
- WEIGHT: 141 LBS.
- FAVORITE SUBJECT: P.E.
- LEAST FAVORITE SUBJECT: CIVICS
- HOBBY/SKILL: SLIDER, CURVE BALL, CHANGEUP
- FUTURE GOAL: THE KOSHIEN HIGH SCHOOL BASEBALL TOURNAMENT FOR STARTERS!
- UNEXPECTED SKILLS: DRAWING.
- WHAT A HIGH SCHOOL STUDENT FROM THE MANGA CLUB SAID TO HIM AFTER SEEING THAT ILLUSTRATION: "GOOD LUCK AT KOSHIEN!"

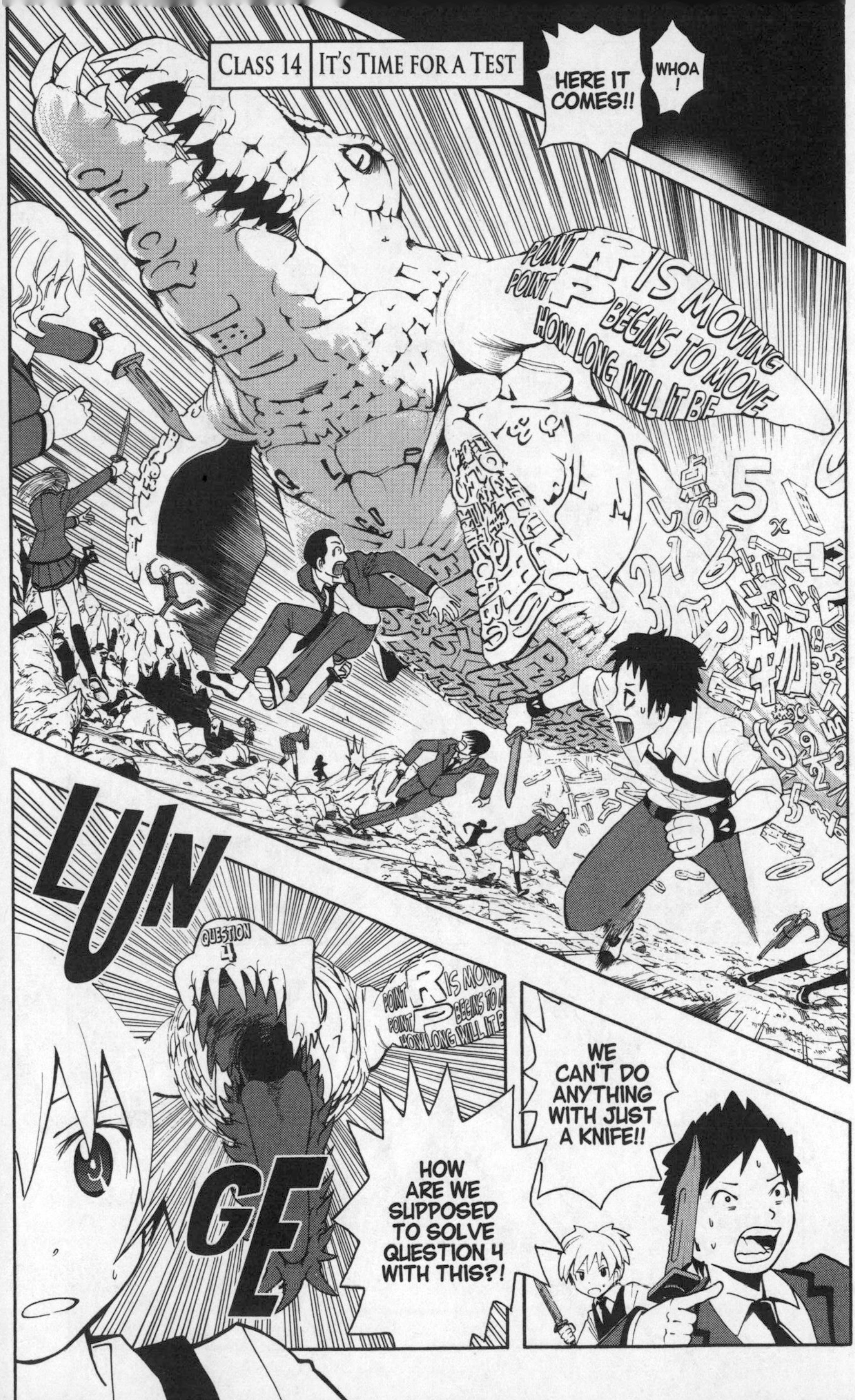
Class 14 It's Time for a Test
WHOA!
HERE IT COMES!!
POINT R IS MOVING
POINT P BEGINS TO MOVE
HOW LONG WILL IT BE
WE CAN'T DO ANYTHING WITH JUST A KNIFE!!
HOW ARE WE SUPPOSED TO SOLVE QUESTION 4 WITH THIS?!
LUNGE
QUESTION 4

Class 14 It's Time for a Test

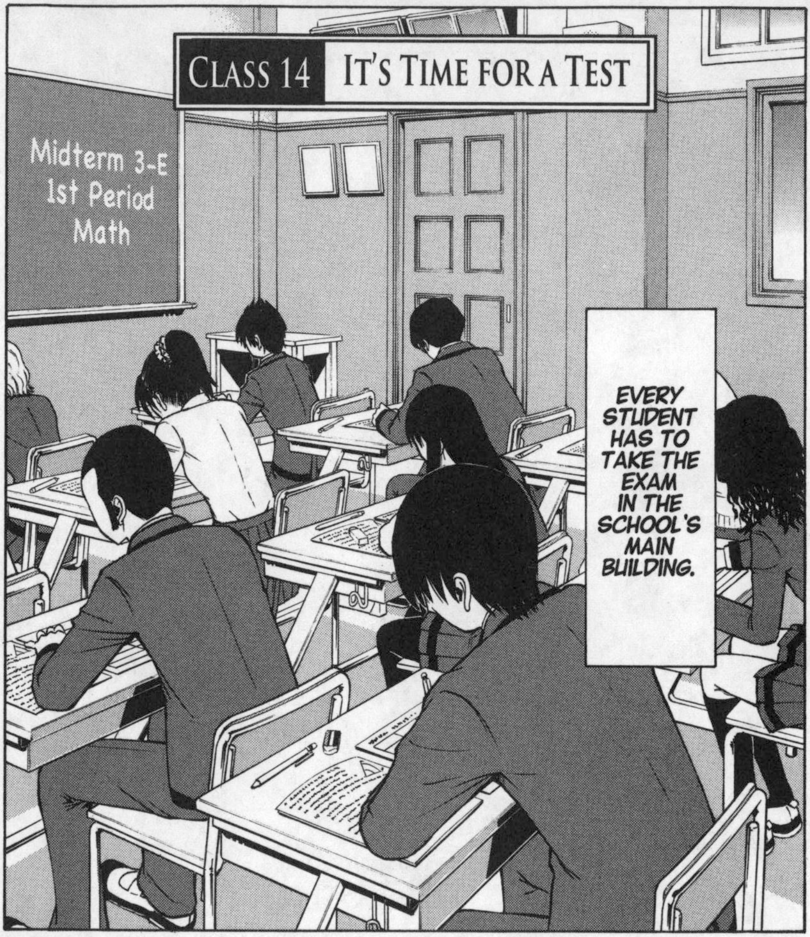
EVERY STUDENT HAS TO TAKE THE EXAM IN THE SCHOOL'S MAIN BUILDING.
Midterm 3-E 1st Period Math

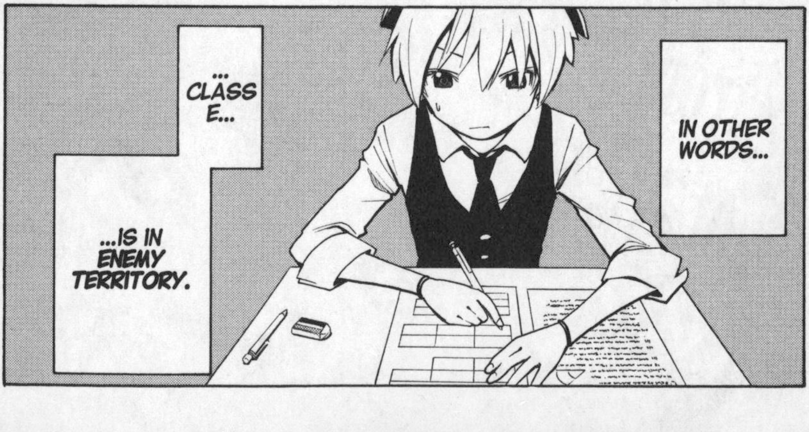
IN OTHER WORDS...
...CLASS E...
...IS IN ENEMY TERRITORY.

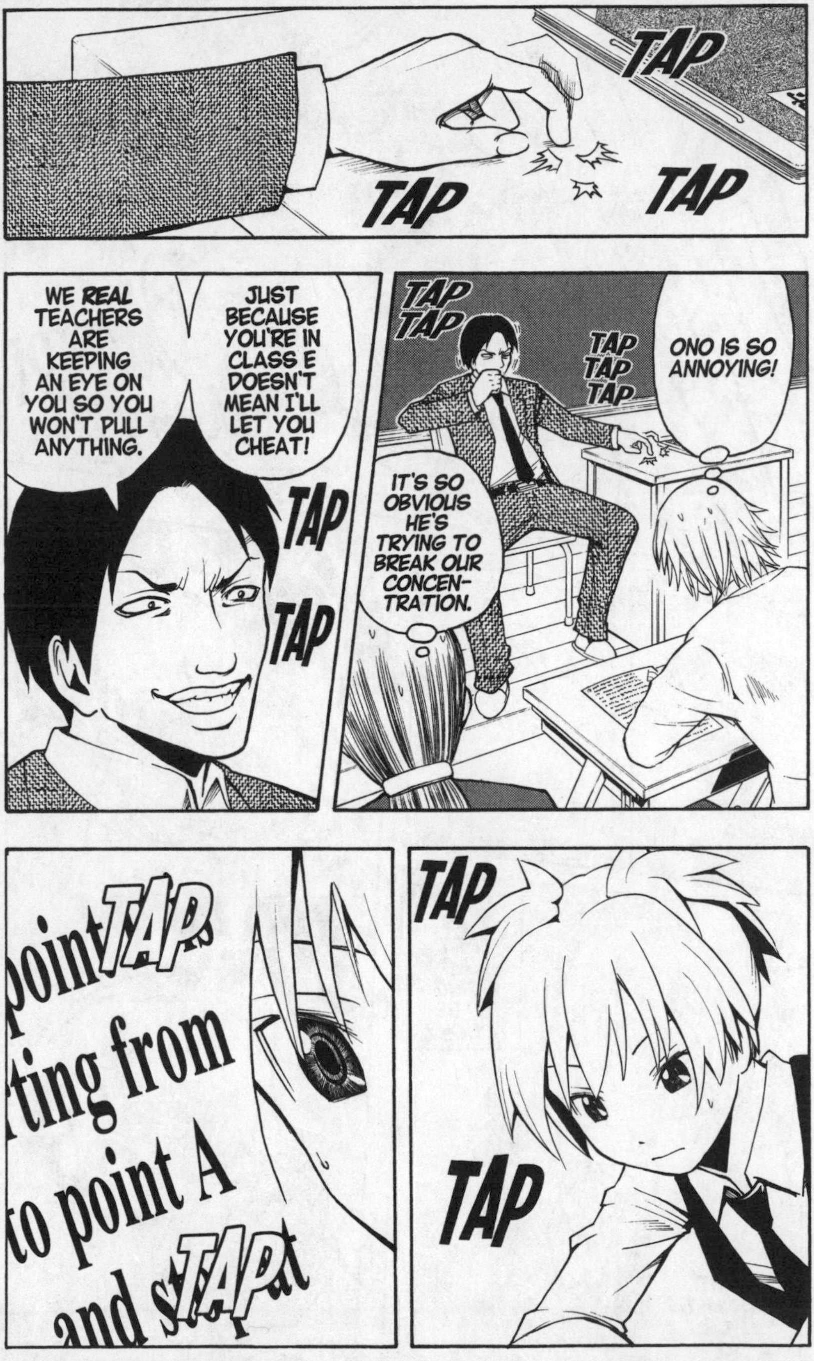
TAP
TAP
TAP
TAP TAP
TAP TAP TAP
ONO IS SO ANNOYING!
IT'S SO OBVIOUS HE'S TRYING TO BREAK OUR CONCENTRATION.
JUST BECAUSE YOU'RE IN CLASS E DOESN'T MEAN I'LL LET YOU CHEAT!
WE *REAL* TEACHERS ARE KEEPING AN EYE ON YOU SO YOU WON'T PULL ANYTHING.
TAP
TAP
TAP
TAP
TAP
point
ting from
to point A
and s
TAP

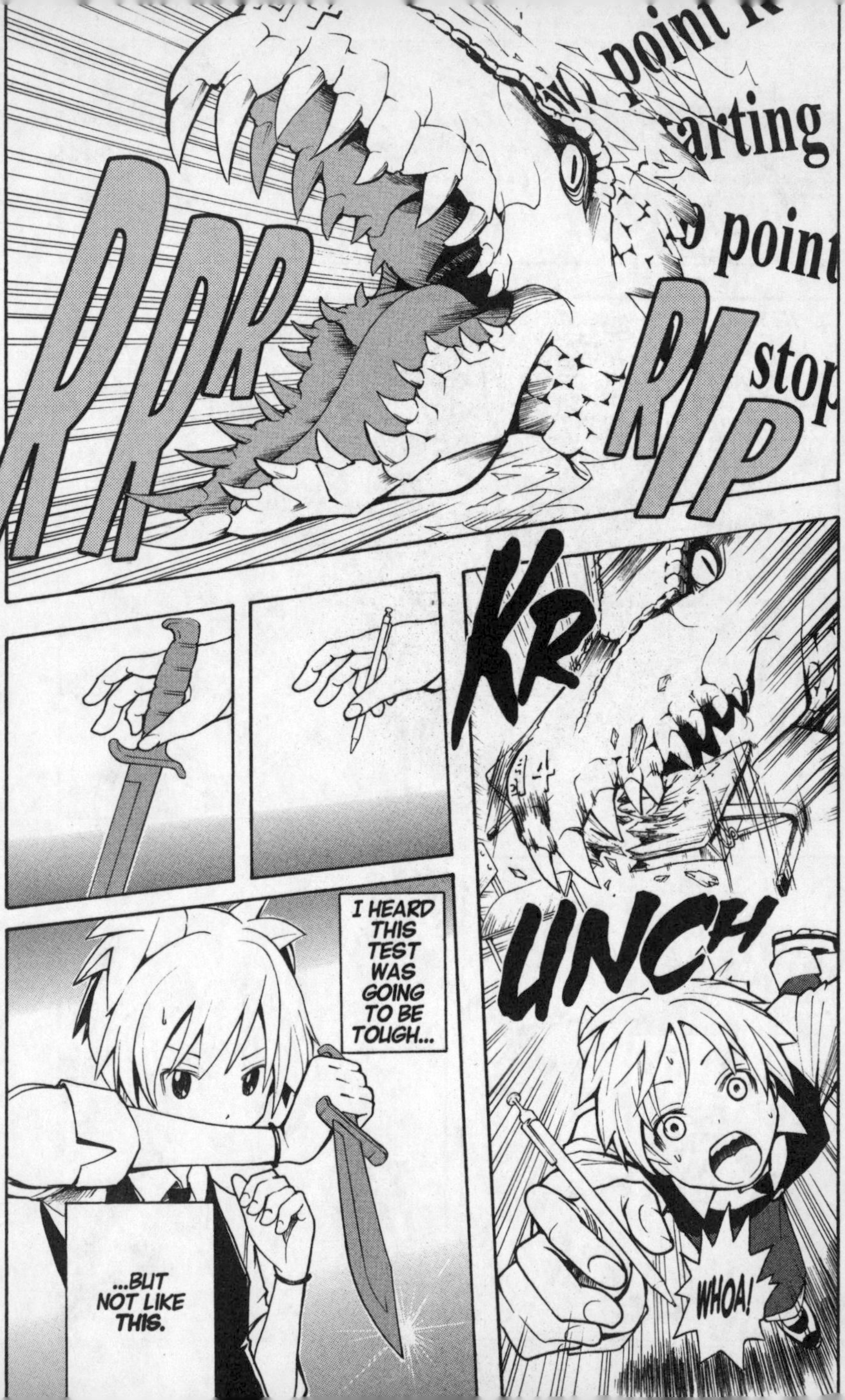
point
arting
point
stop
RIP
RRRR
KR
UNCH
WHOA!
I HEARD THIS TEST WAS GOING TO BE TOUGH...
...BUT NOT LIKE THIS.

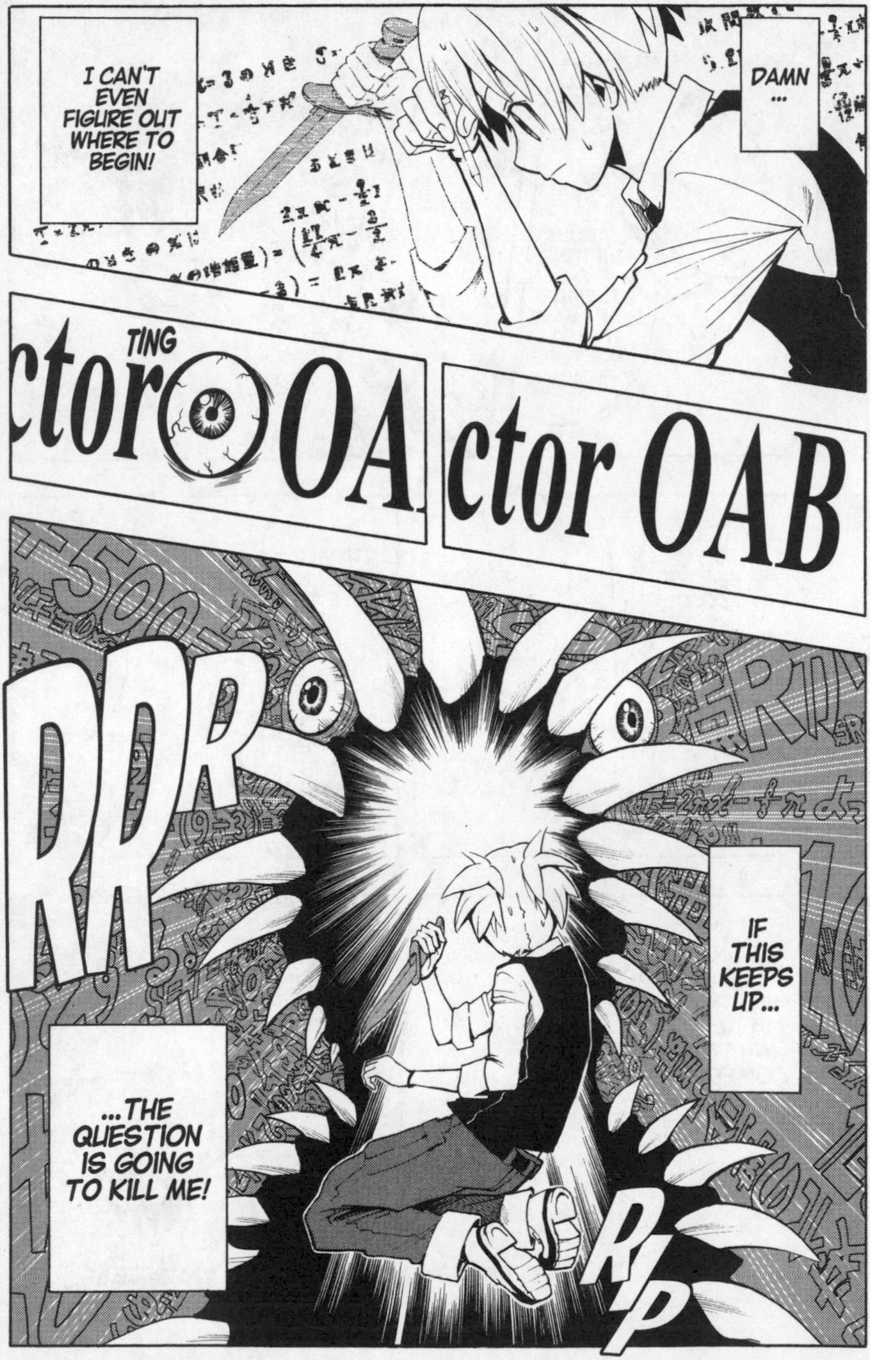
DAMN ...
I CAN'T EVEN FIGURE OUT WHERE TO BEGIN!
ctor OAB
TING
ctor OA
RRR
IF THIS KEEPS UP...
...THE QUESTION IS GOING TO KILL ME!
RIP

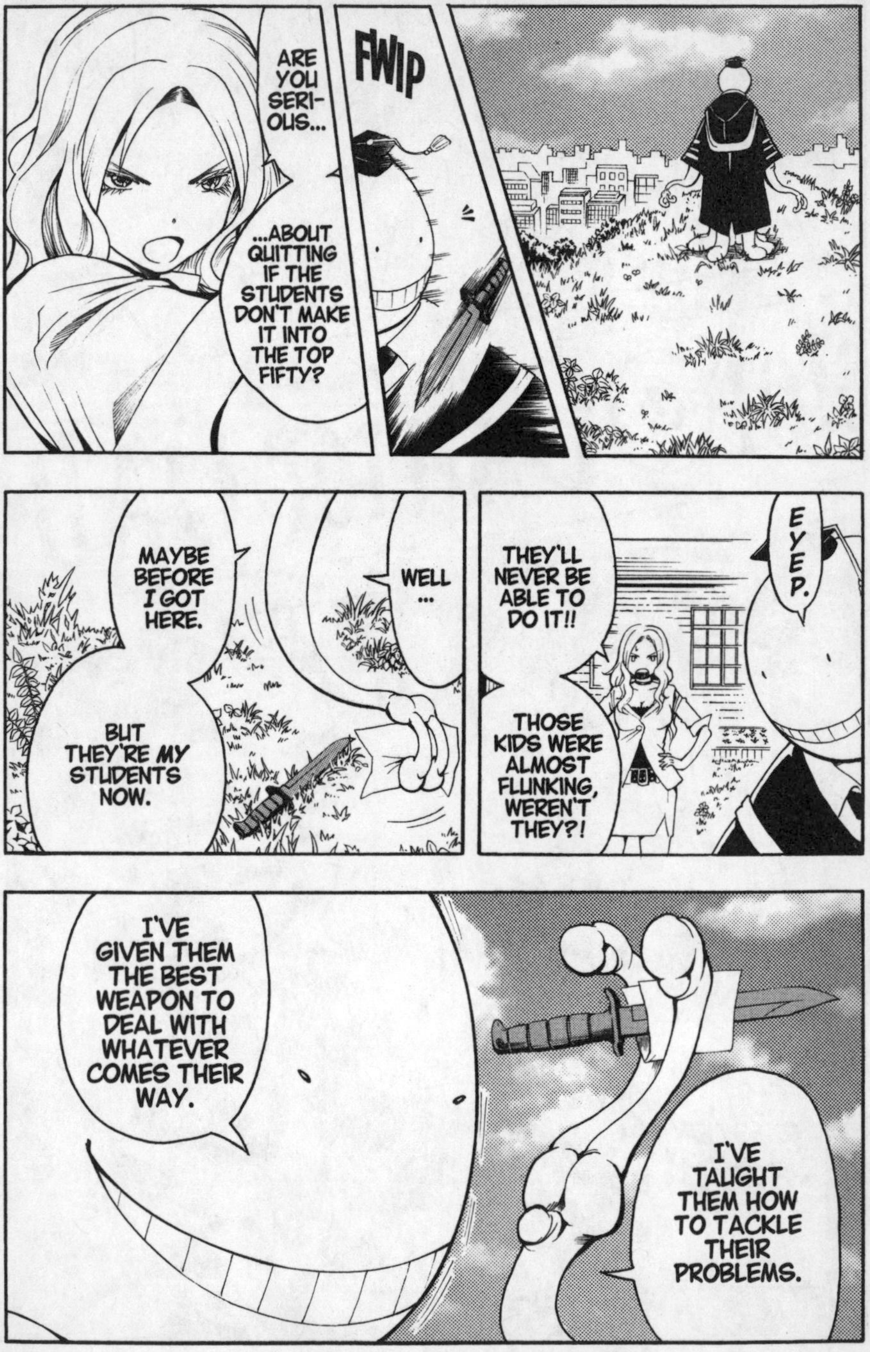
FWIP
ARE YOU SERIOUS...
...ABOUT QUITTING IF THE STUDENTS DON'T MAKE IT INTO THE TOP FIFTY?
EYEP.
THEY'LL NEVER BE ABLE TO DO IT!!
THOSE KIDS WERE ALMOST FLUNKING, WEREN'T THEY?!
WELL...
MAYBE BEFORE I GOT HERE.
BUT THEY'RE MY STUDENTS NOW.
I'VE GIVEN THEM THE BEST WEAPON TO DEAL WITH WHATEVER COMES THEIR WAY.
I'VE TAUGHT THEM HOW TO TACKLE THEIR PROBLEMS.

I'VE TAUGHT YOU WELL.

IT'S NOT SOME WEIRD MONSTER.

STRCH

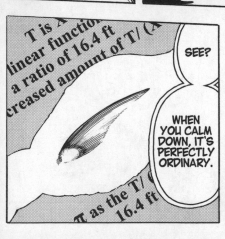

T is A linear function a ratio of 16.4 ft creased amount of T/ (X

SEE?

WHEN YOU CALM DOWN, IT'S PERFECTLY ORDINARY.

T as the T/ (16.4 ft

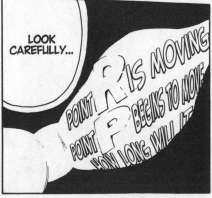

LOOK CAREFULLY...

POINT A IS MOVING POINT B BEGINS TO MOVE HOW LONG WILL IT

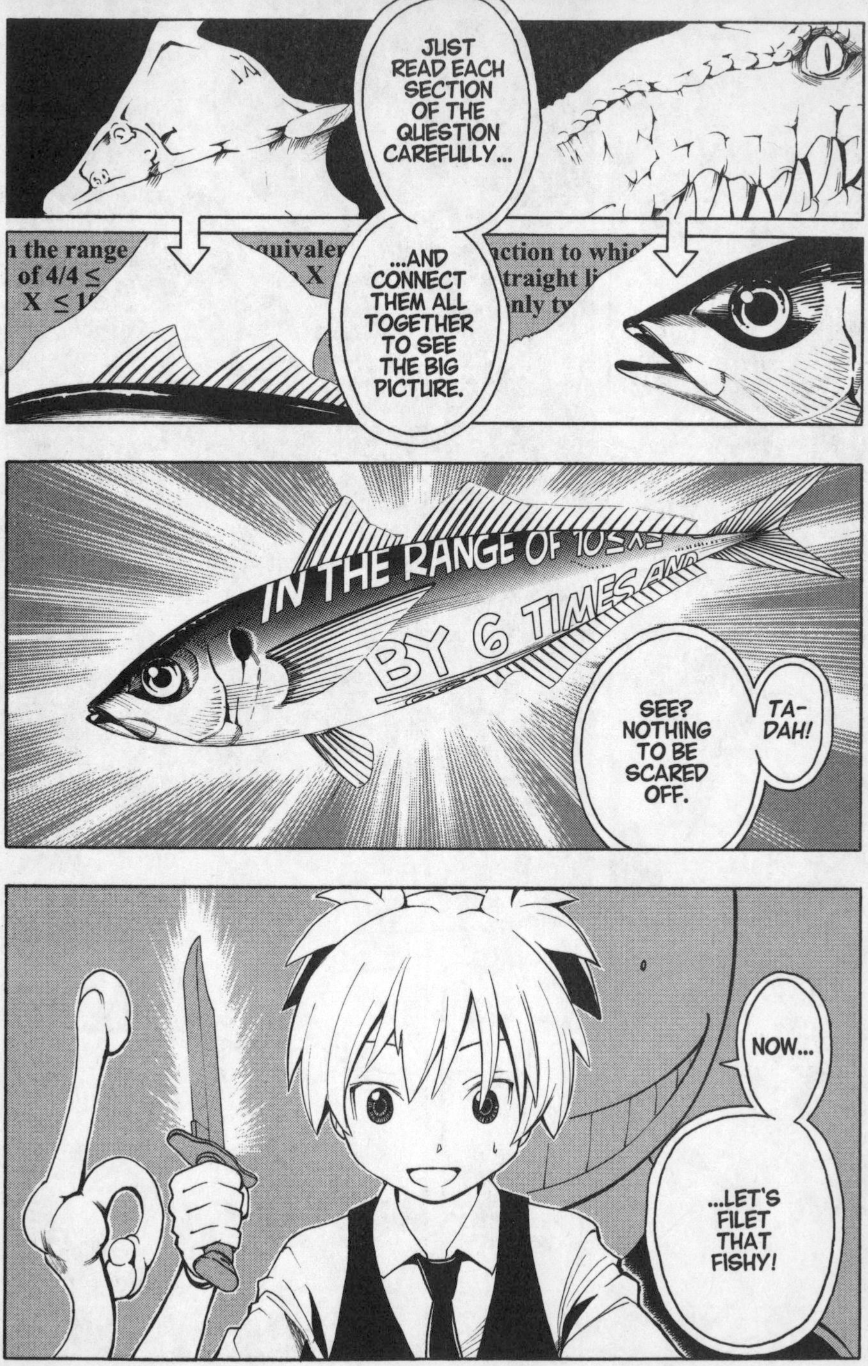
JUST READ EACH SECTION OF THE QUESTION CAREFULLY...
...AND CONNECT THEM ALL TOGETHER TO SEE THE BIG PICTURE.
IN THE RANGE OF
BY 6 TIMES AND
TA-DAH!
SEE? NOTHING TO BE SCARED OFF.
NOW...
...LET'S FILET THAT FISHY!

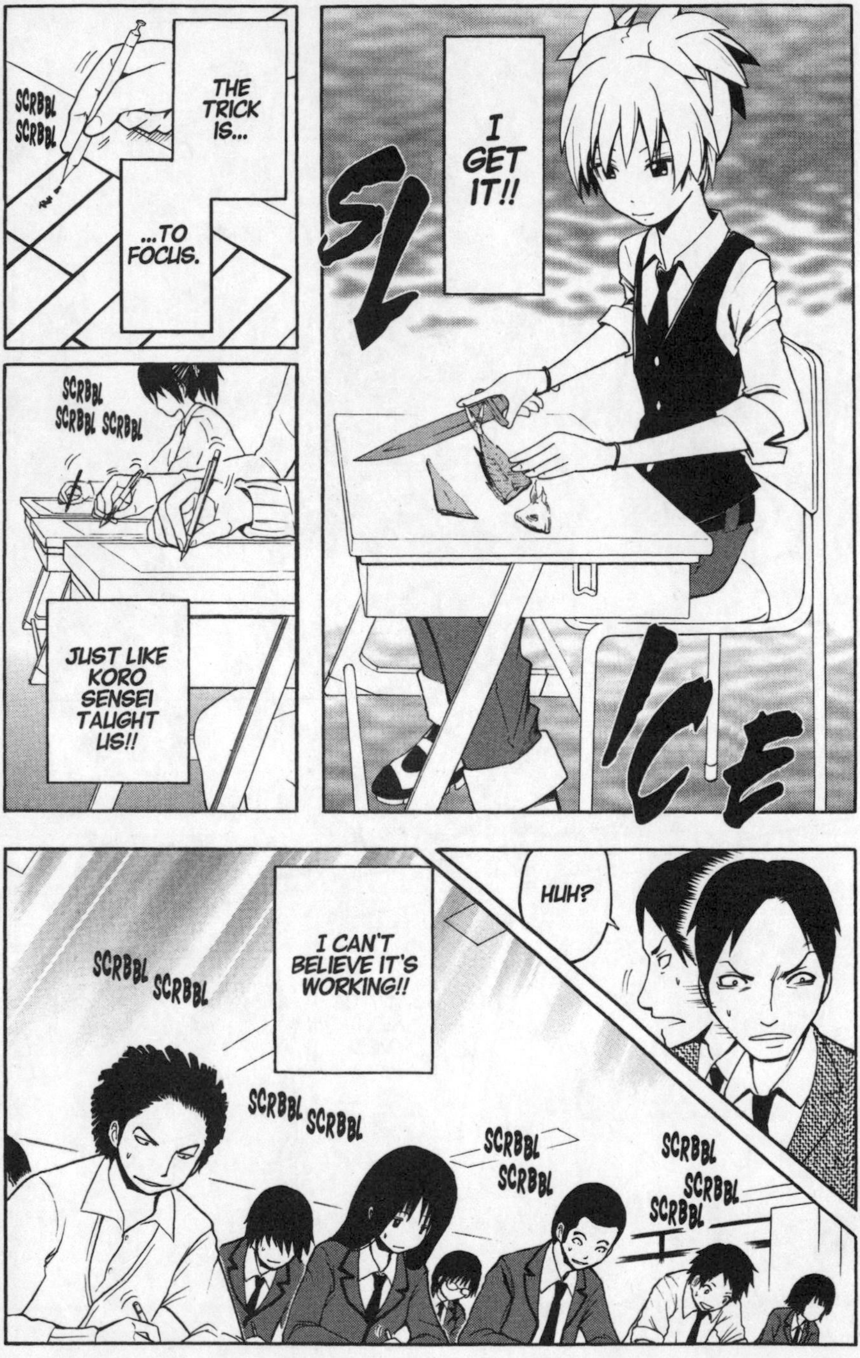
I GET IT!!
SLICE
THE TRICK IS...
...TO FOCUS.
SCRBBL SCRBBL
SCRBBL SCRBBL SCRBBL
JUST LIKE KORO SENSEI TAUGHT US!!
HUH?
I CAN'T BELIEVE IT'S WORKING!!
SCRBBL SCRBBL
SCRBBL SCRBBL
SCRBBL SCRBBL
SCRBBL SCRBBL SCRBBL

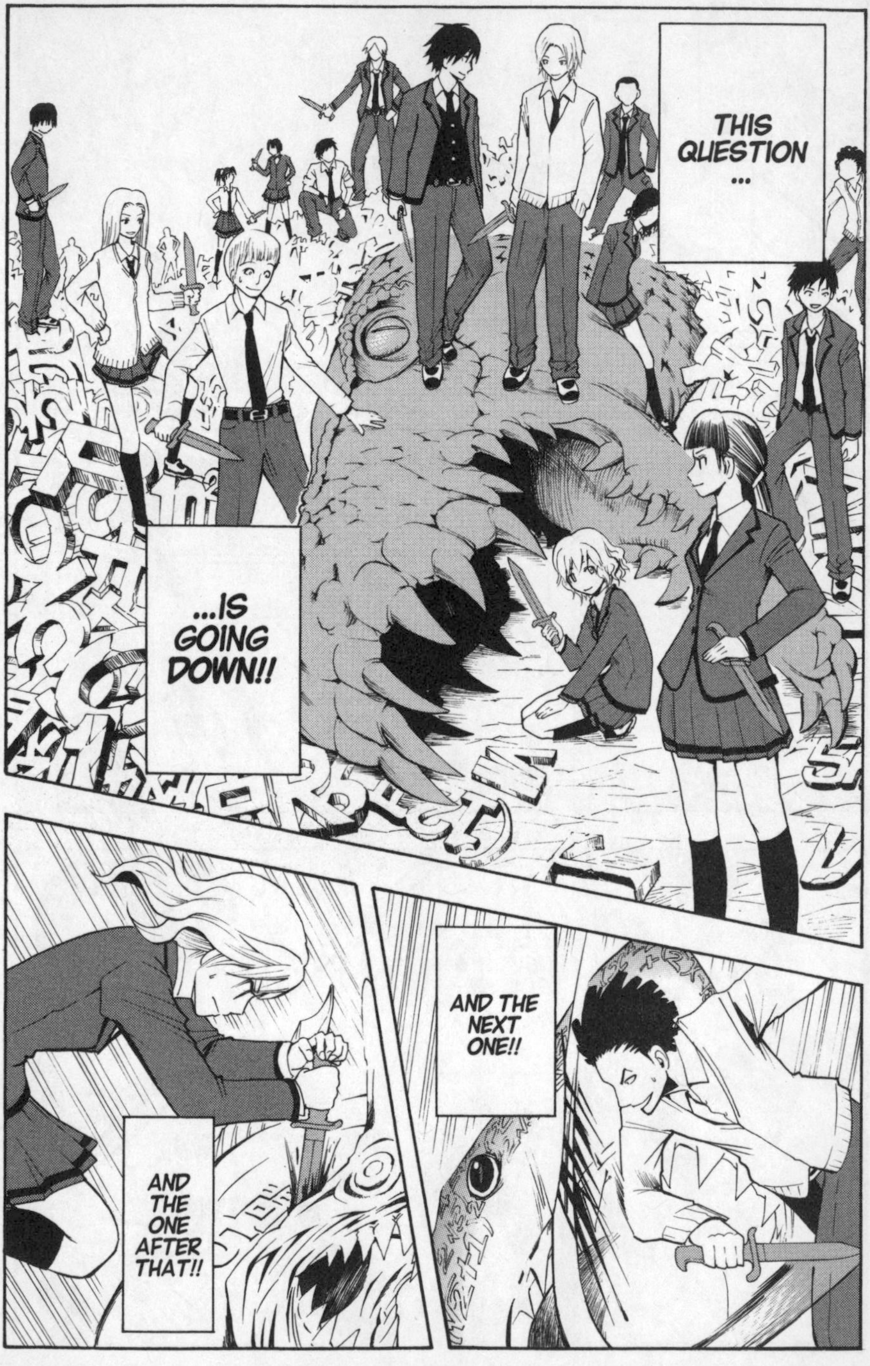
THIS QUESTION ...
...IS GOING DOWN!!
AND THE NEXT ONE!!
AND THE ONE AFTER THAT!!

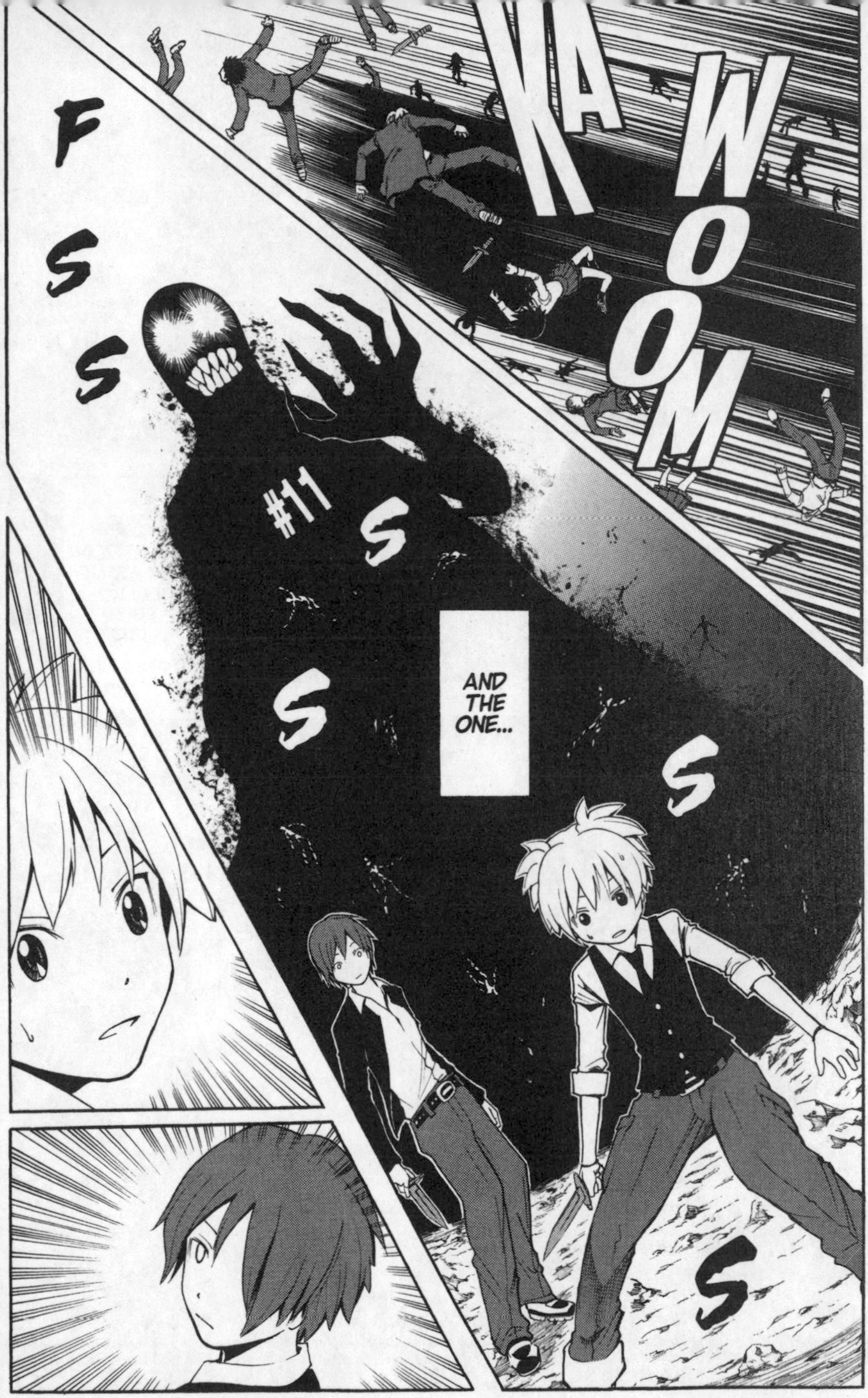
KA WOOM
F S S S S S S S
#11
AND THE ONE...

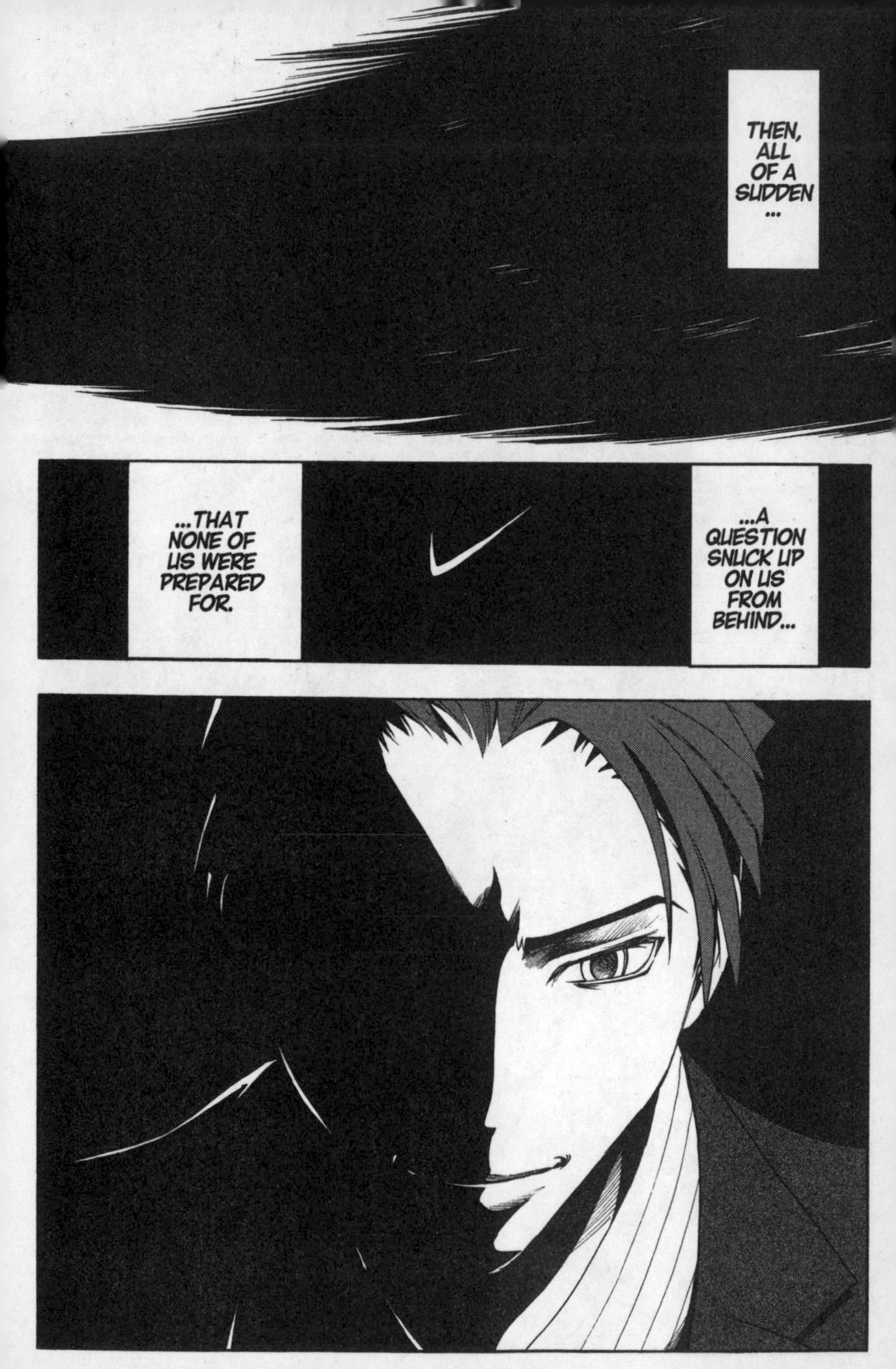
THEN, ALL OF A SUDDEN ...
...A QUESTION SNUCK UP ON US FROM BEHIND...
...THAT NONE OF US WERE PREPARED FOR.

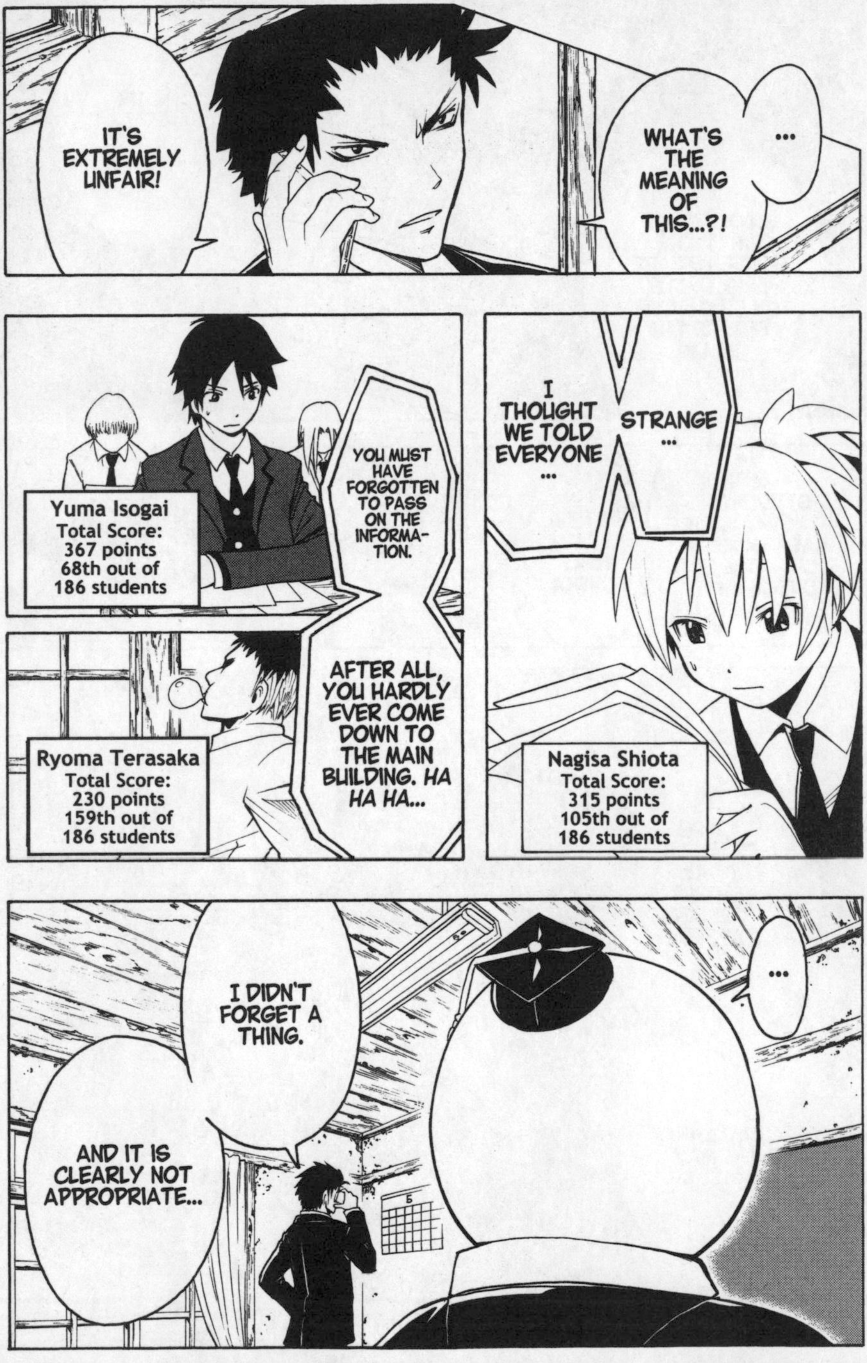
...
WHAT'S THE MEANING OF THIS...?!
IT'S EXTREMELY UNFAIR!
STRANGE...
I THOUGHT WE TOLD EVERYONE...
Nagisa Shiota Total Score: 315 points 105th out of 186 students
YOU MUST HAVE FORGOTTEN TO PASS ON THE INFORMATION.
Yuma Isogai Total Score: 367 points 68th out of 186 students
AFTER ALL, YOU HARDLY EVER COME DOWN TO THE MAIN BUILDING. HA HA HA...
Ryoma Terasaka Total Score: 230 points 159th out of 186 students
...
I DIDN'T FORGET A THING.
AND IT IS CLEARLY NOT APPROPRIATE...

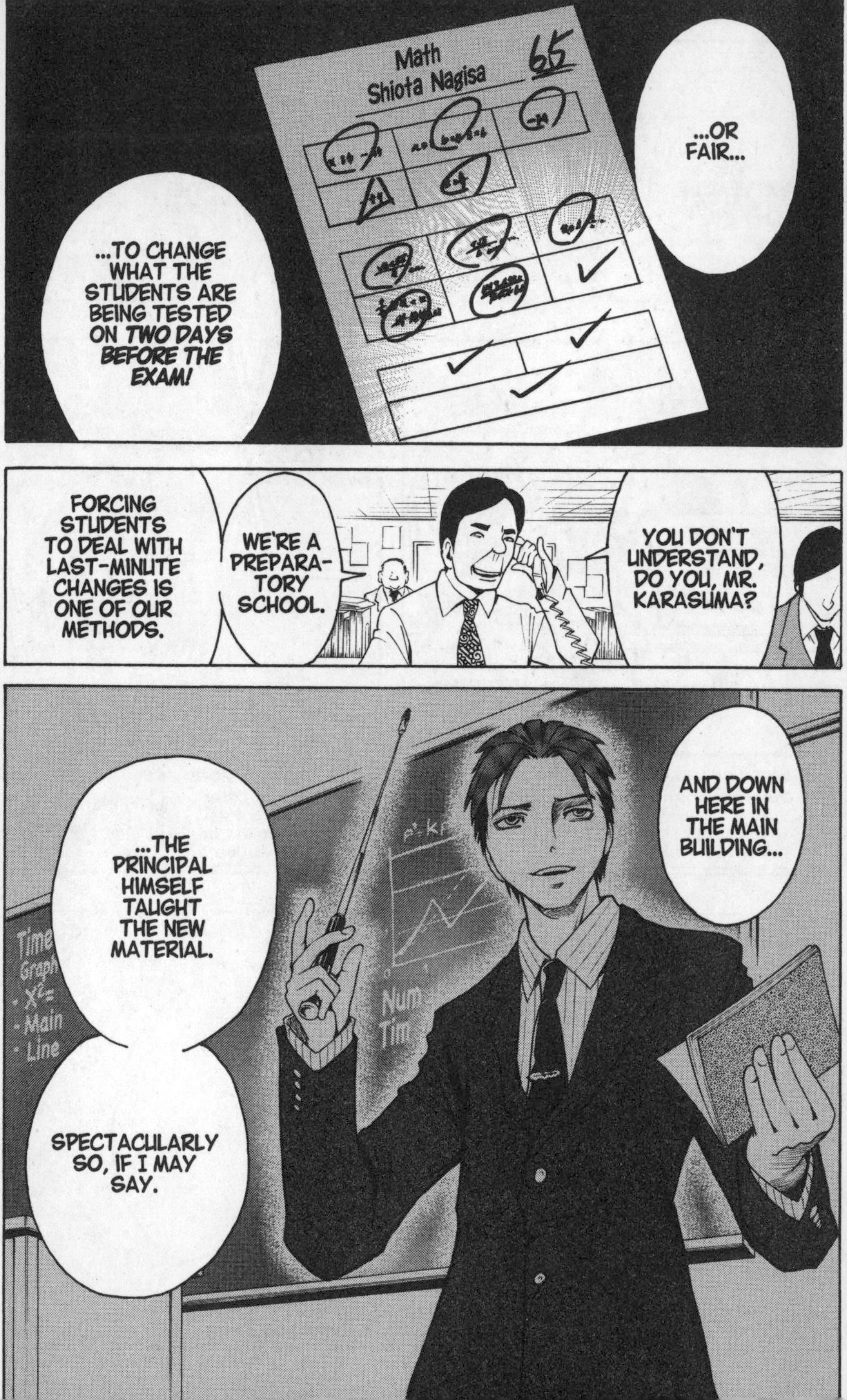
...OR FAIR...
Math
Shiota Nagisa
65
...TO CHANGE WHAT THE STUDENTS ARE BEING TESTED ON *TWO DAYS BEFORE THE EXAM!*
YOU DON'T UNDERSTAND, DO YOU, MR. KARASUMA?
WE'RE A PREPARATORY SCHOOL.
FORCING STUDENTS TO DEAL WITH LAST-MINUTE CHANGES IS ONE OF OUR METHODS.
AND DOWN HERE IN THE MAIN BUILDING...
...THE PRINCIPAL HIMSELF TAUGHT THE NEW MATERIAL.
SPECTACULARLY SO, IF I MAY SAY.

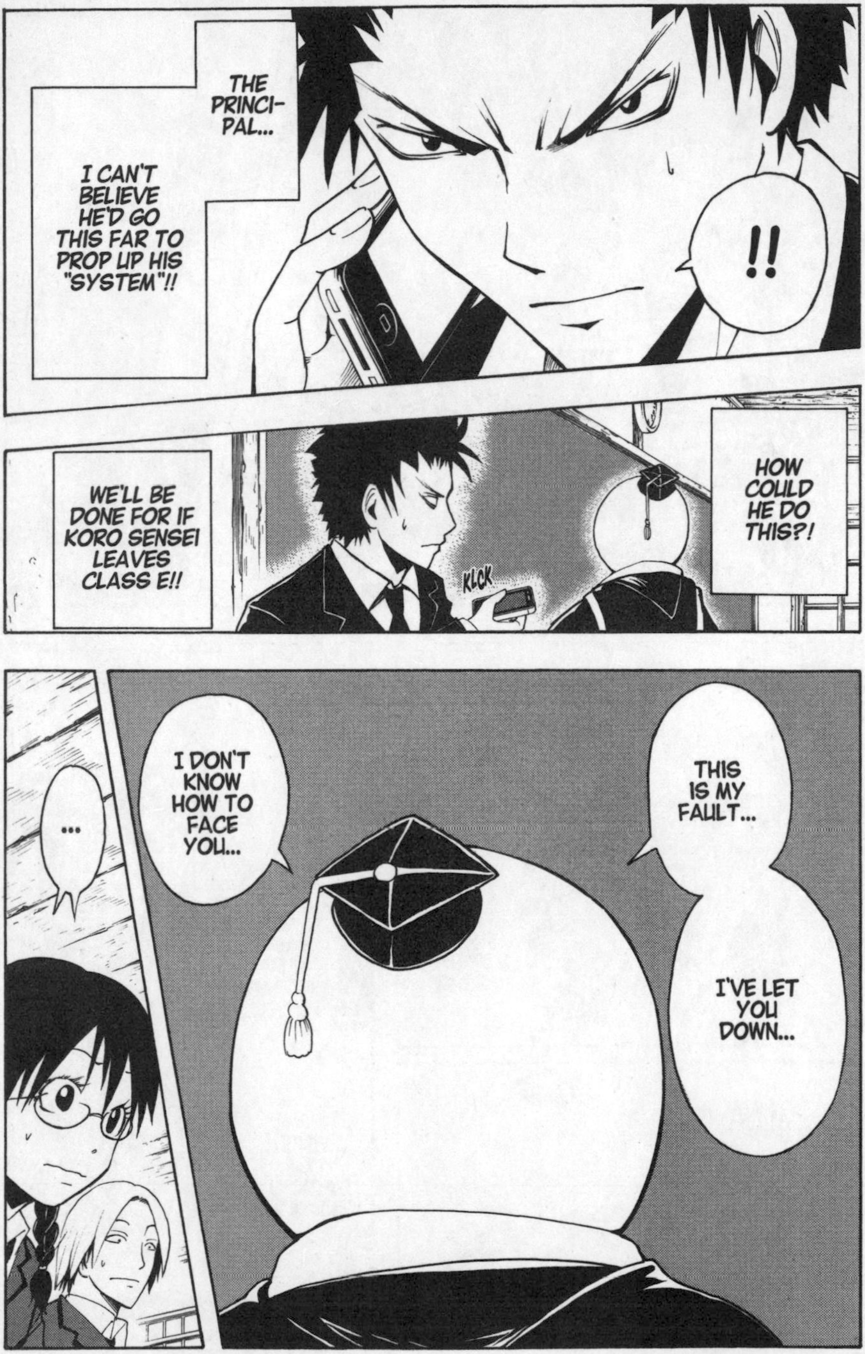
!!
THE PRINCIPAL...
I CAN'T BELIEVE HE'D GO THIS FAR TO PROP UP HIS "SYSTEM"!!
HOW COULD HE DO THIS?!
KLCK
WE'LL BE DONE FOR IF KORO SENSEI LEAVES CLASS E!!
THIS IS MY FAULT...
I'VE LET YOU DOWN...
I DON'T KNOW HOW TO FACE YOU...
...

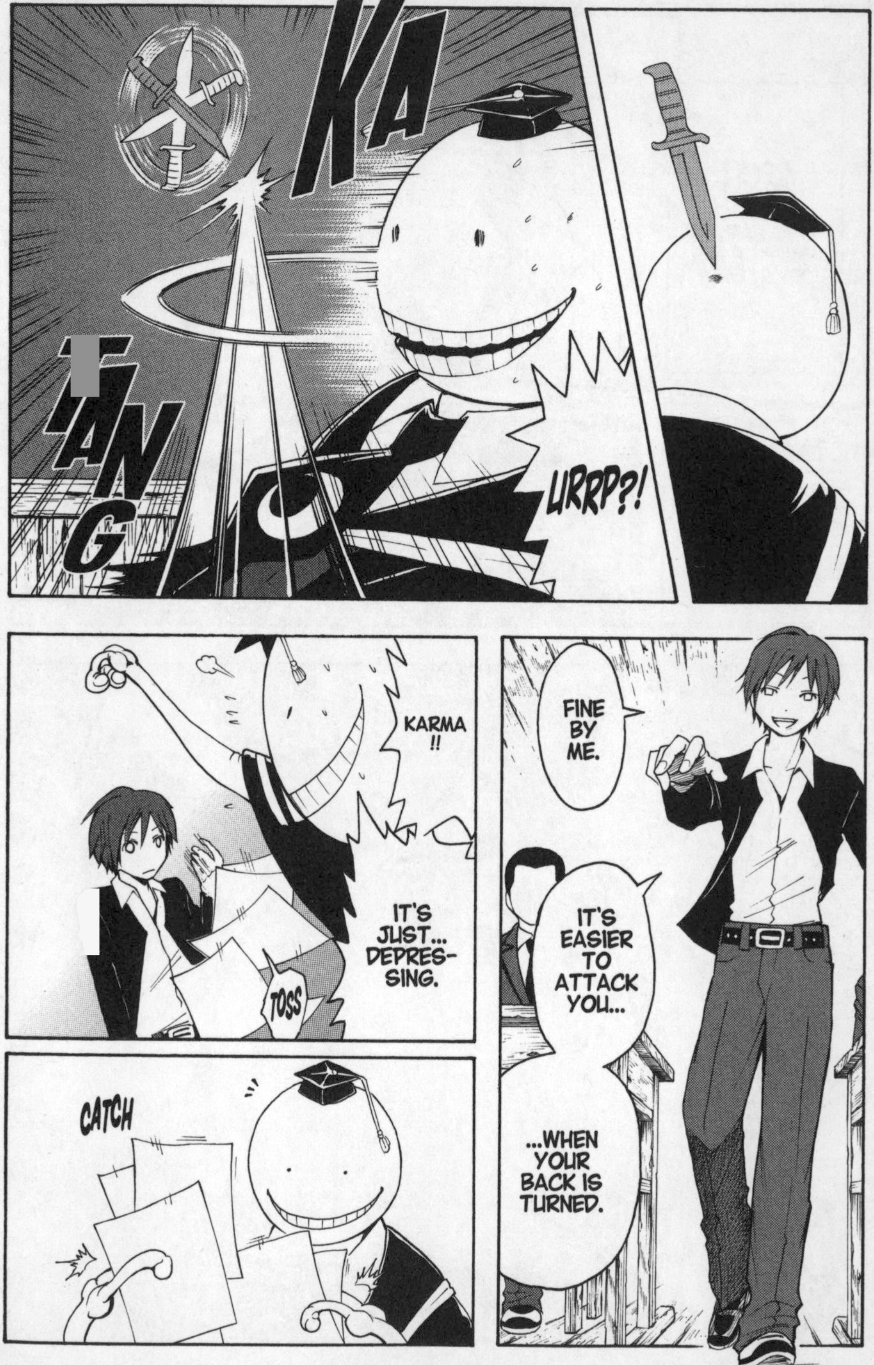
KA
TANG
URRP?!
FINE BY ME.
IT'S EASIER TO ATTACK YOU...
...WHEN YOUR BACK IS TURNED.
KARMA!!
IT'S JUST... DEPRES-SING.
TOSS
CATCH

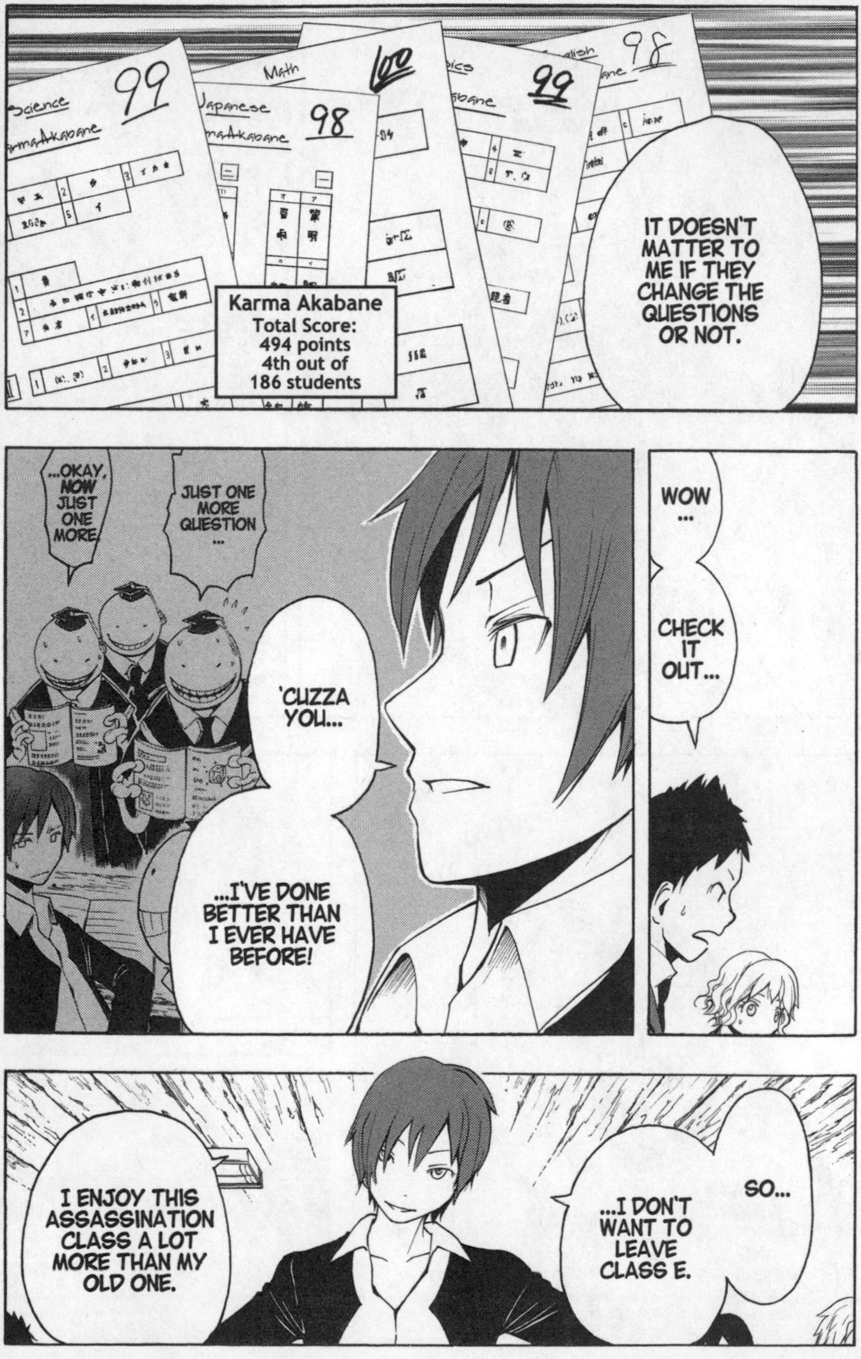
IT DOESN'T MATTER TO ME IF THEY CHANGE THE QUESTIONS OR NOT.
English 98
99
Math 100
Japanese 98
Science 99
Karma Akabane Total Score: 494 points 4th out of 186 students
WOW ...
CHECK IT OUT...
'CUZZA YOU...
...I'VE DONE BETTER THAN I EVER HAVE BEFORE!
JUST ONE MORE QUESTION ...
...OKAY, NOW JUST ONE MORE.
SO...
...I DON'T WANT TO LEAVE CLASS E.
I ENJOY THIS ASSASSINATION CLASS A LOT MORE THAN MY OLD ONE.

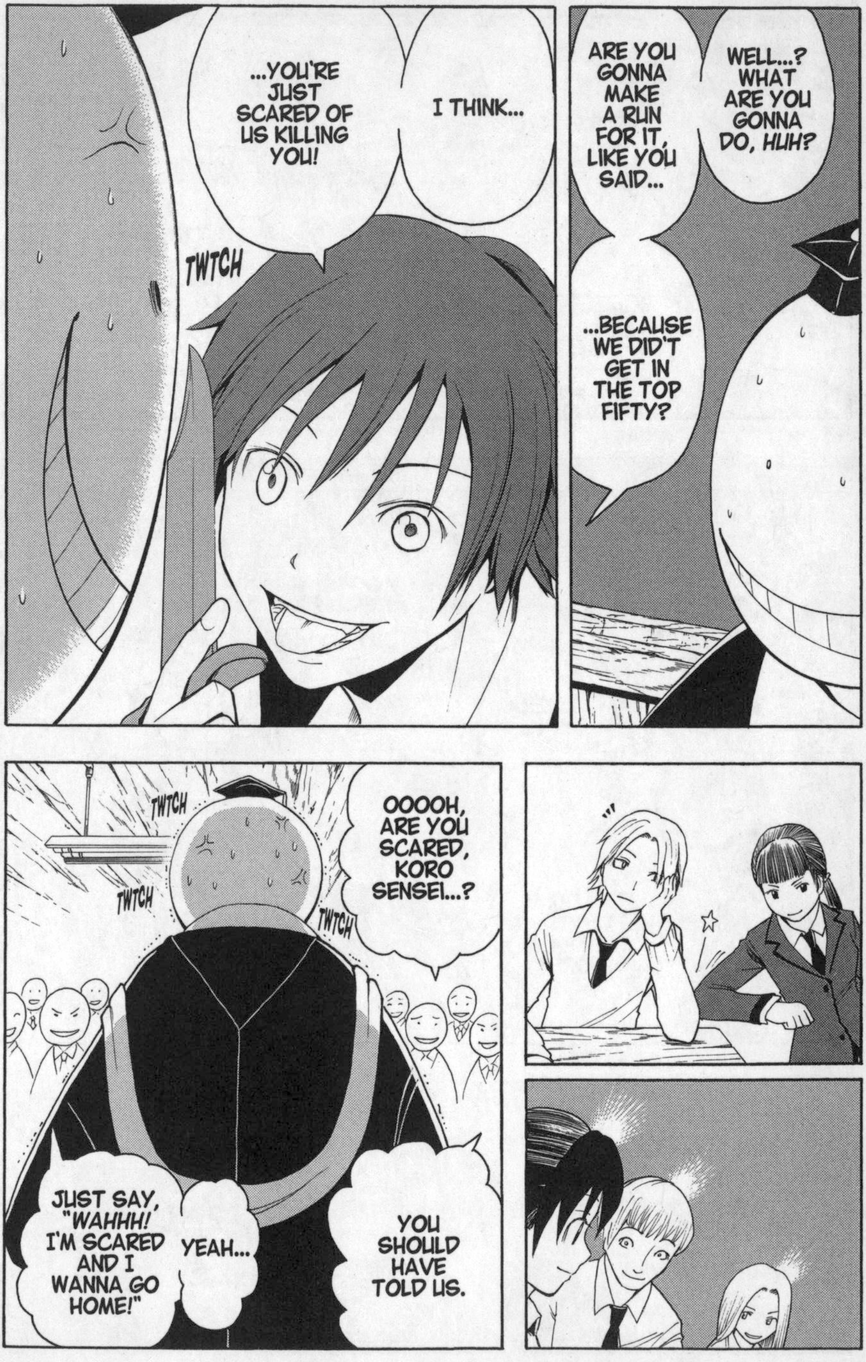
WELL...? WHAT ARE YOU GONNA DO, HUH?
ARE YOU GONNA MAKE A RUN FOR IT, LIKE YOU SAID...
...BECAUSE WE DID'T GET IN THE TOP FIFTY?
I THINK...
...YOU'RE JUST SCARED OF US KILLING YOU!
TWTCH
OOOOH, ARE YOU SCARED, KORO SENSEI...?
TWTCH
TWTCH
TWTCH
YOU SHOULD HAVE TOLD US.
YEAH...
JUST SAY, "WAHHH! I'M SCARED AND I WANNA GO HOME!"

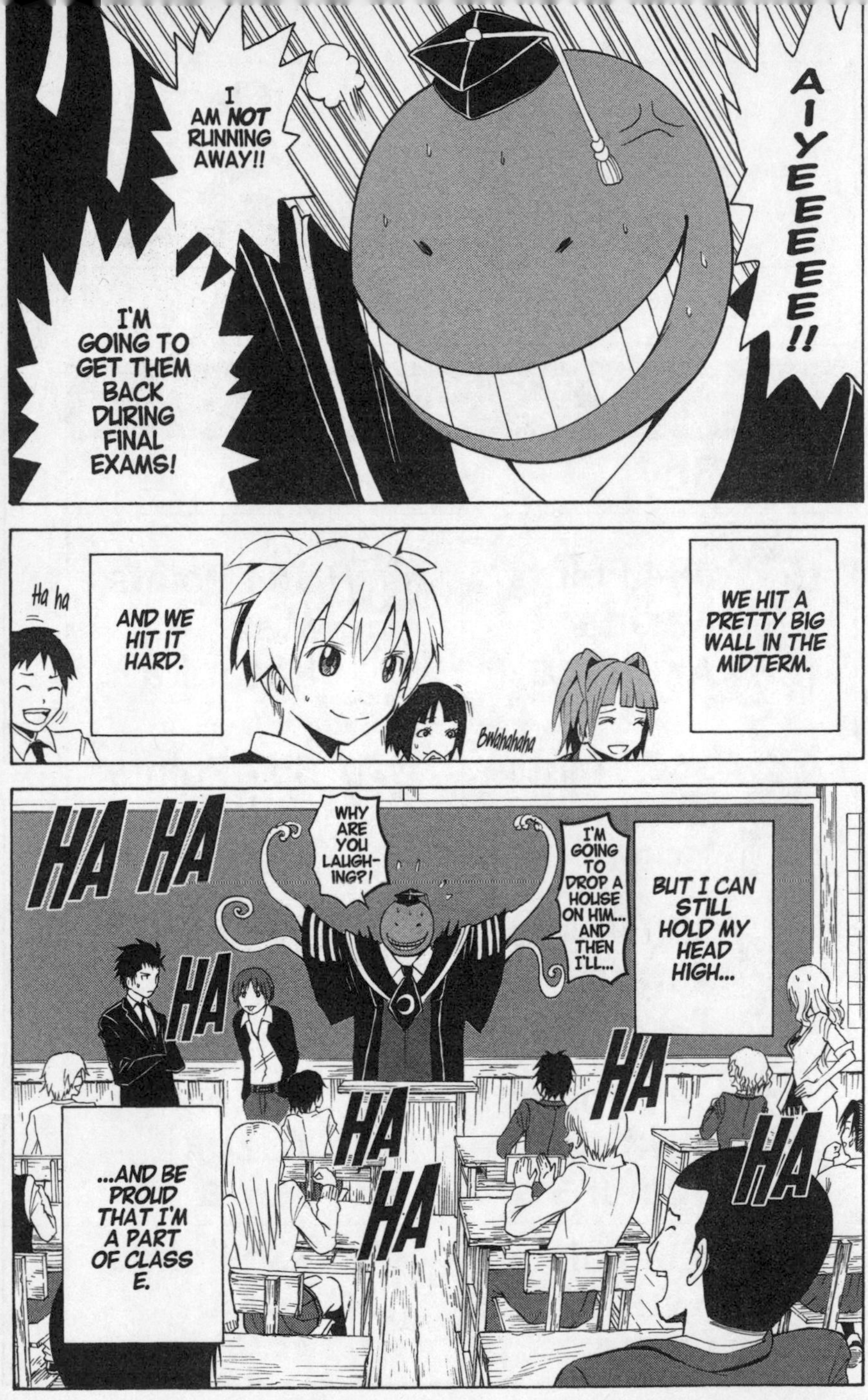
AIYEEEEE!!
I AM NOT RUNNING AWAY!!
I'M GOING TO GET THEM BACK DURING FINAL EXAMS!
WE HIT A PRETTY BIG WALL IN THE MIDTERM.
Bwahahaha
AND WE HIT IT HARD.
Ha ha
BUT I CAN STILL HOLD MY HEAD HIGH...
I'M GOING TO DROP A HOUSE ON HIM... AND THEN I'LL...
WHY ARE YOU LAUGHING?!
HA HA
HA
HA
HA
HA
HA
...AND BE PROUD THAT I'M A PART OF CLASS E.

Class 3-E

Best 5

Total Score

Total score of the first trimester midterm exam (Out of 500 points).

Rank	Boys	Girls
1	494 Points Karma Akabane	364 Points Meg Kataoka
2	367 Points Yuma Isogai	357 Points Yukiko Kanzaki
3	350 Points Kotaro Takebayashi	349 Points Rio Nakamura
4	341 Points Koki Mimura	339 Points Yuzuki Fuwa
5	338 Points Ryunosuke Chiba	335 Points Toka Yada

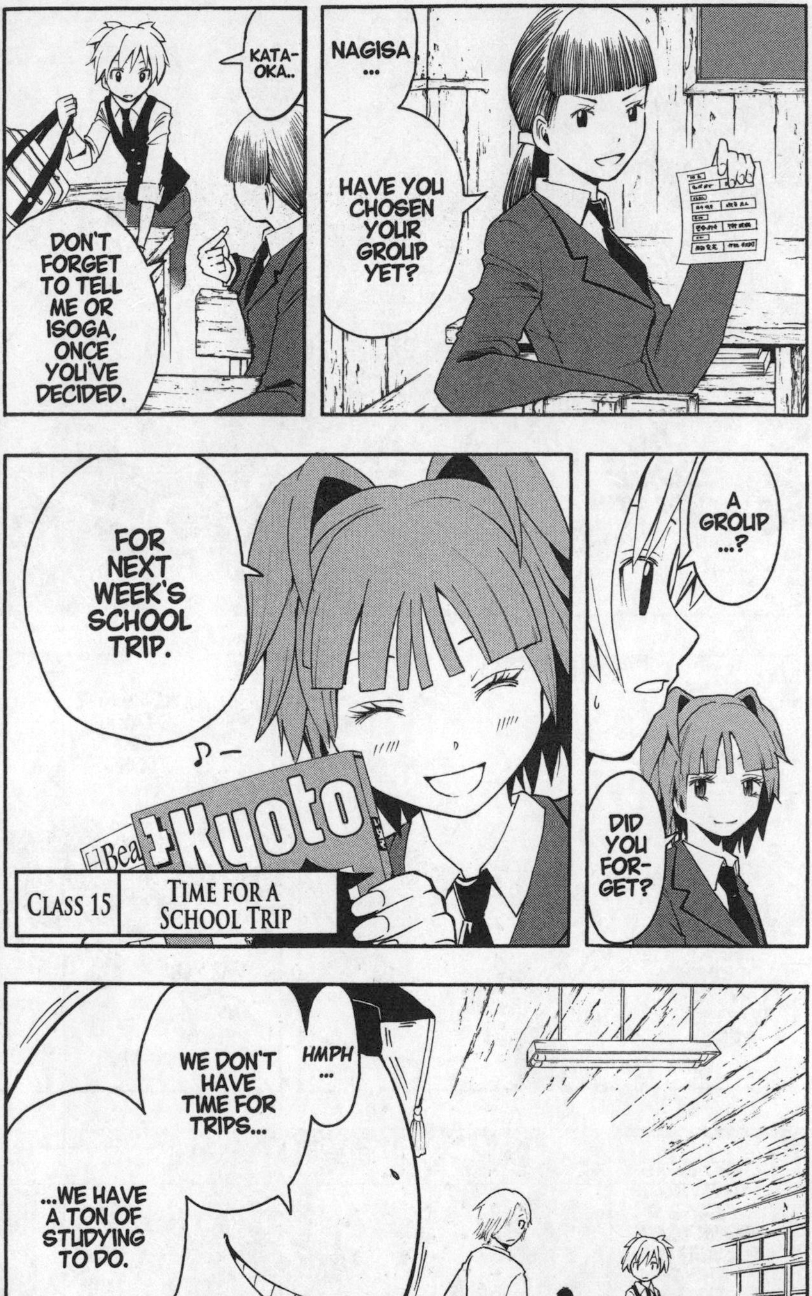
NAGISA ...
HAVE YOU CHOSEN YOUR GROUP YET?
KATA-OKA..
DON'T FORGET TO TELL ME OR ISOGA, ONCE YOU'VE DECIDED.
A GROUP ...?
DID YOU FOR-GET?
FOR NEXT WEEK'S SCHOOL TRIP.
Kyoto
CLASS 15
TIME FOR A SCHOOL TRIP
HMPH ...
WE DON'T HAVE TIME FOR TRIPS...
...WE HAVE A TON OF STUDYING TO DO.

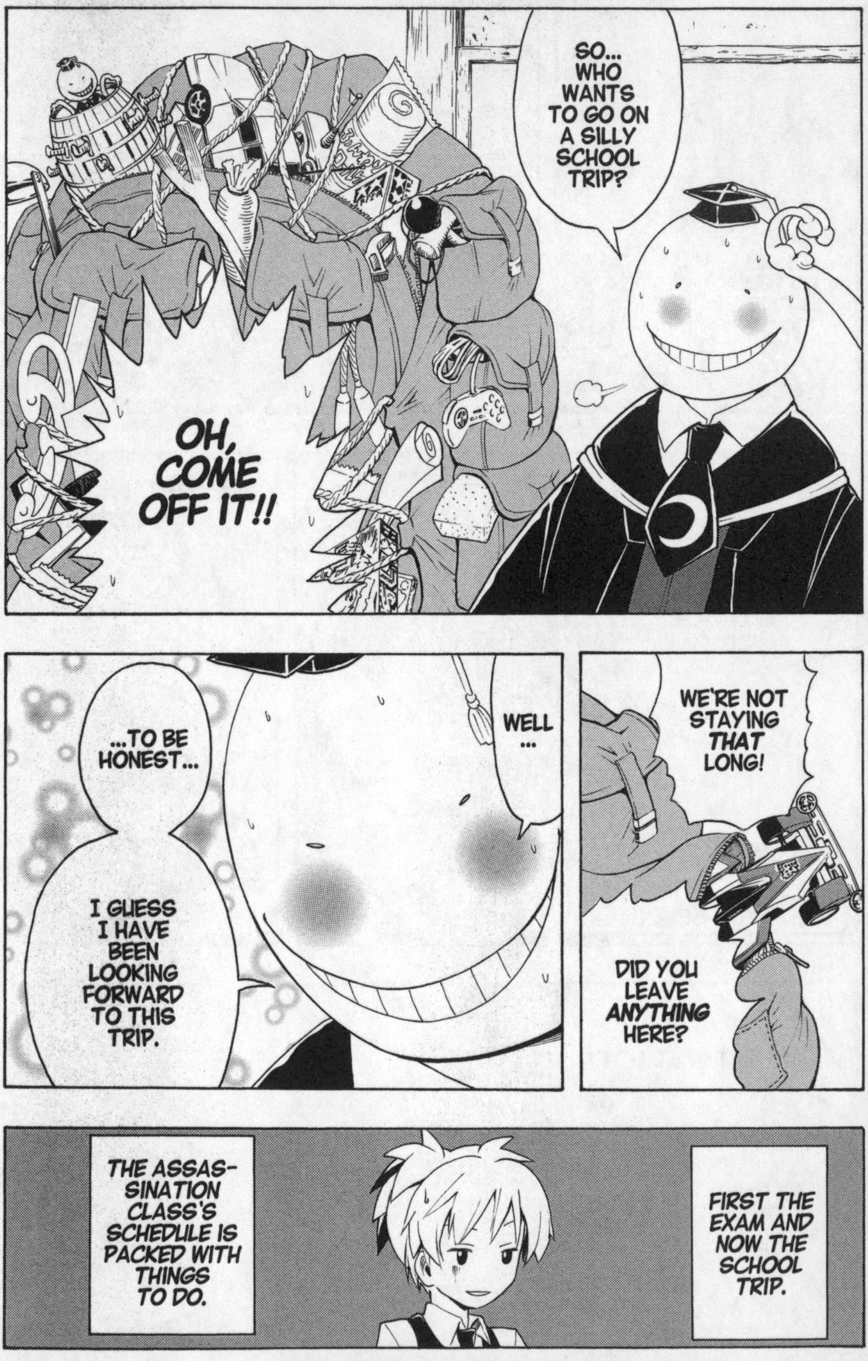
SO... WHO WANTS TO GO ON A SILLY SCHOOL TRIP?
OH, COME OFF IT!!
WE'RE NOT STAYING *THAT* LONG!
DID YOU LEAVE *ANYTHING* HERE?
WELL ...
...TO BE HONEST...
I GUESS I HAVE BEEN LOOKING FORWARD TO THIS TRIP.
FIRST THE EXAM AND NOW THE SCHOOL TRIP.
THE ASSASSINATION CLASS'S SCHEDULE IS PACKED WITH THINGS TO DO.

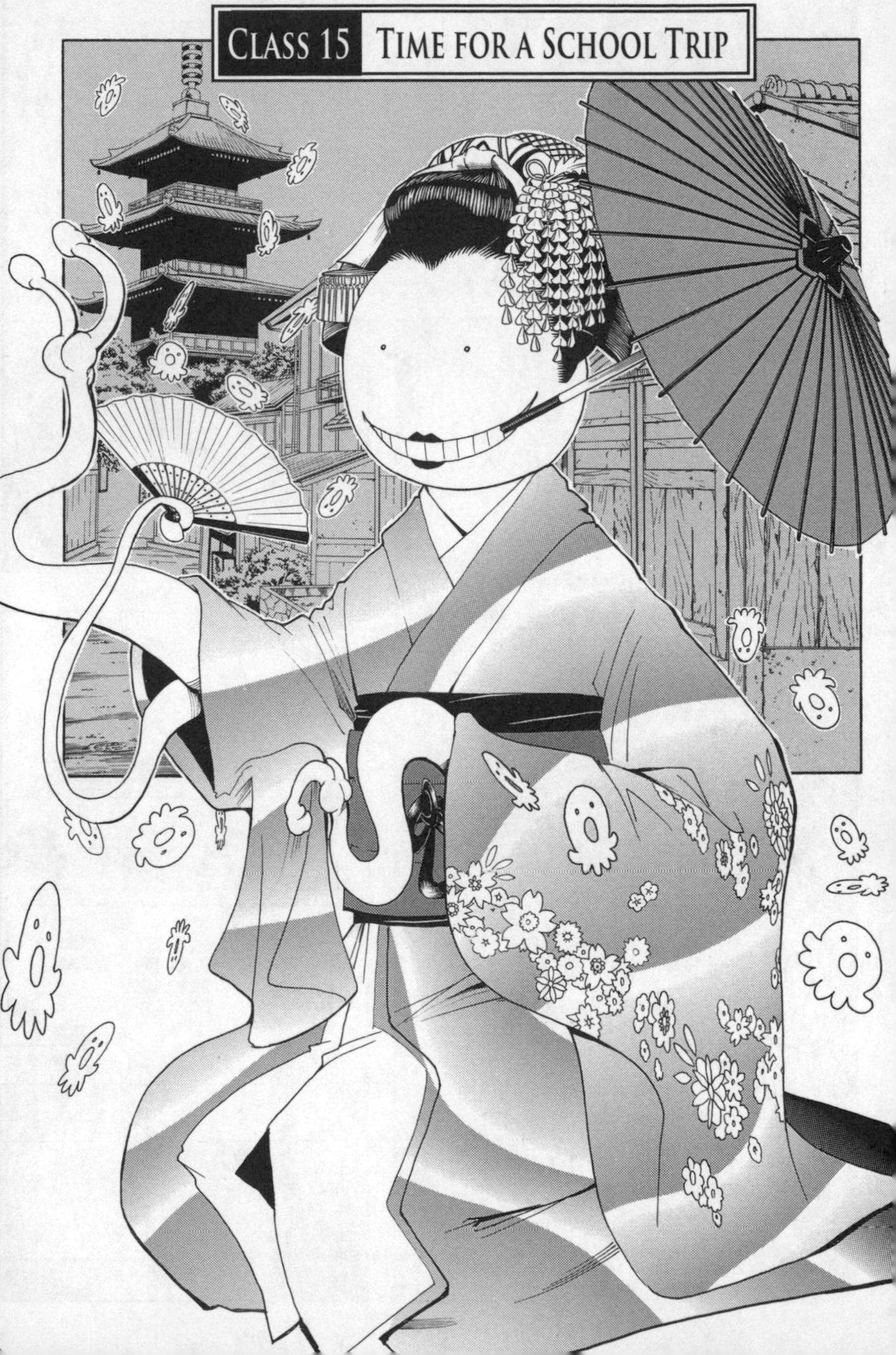
CLASS 15
TIME FOR A SCHOOL TRIP

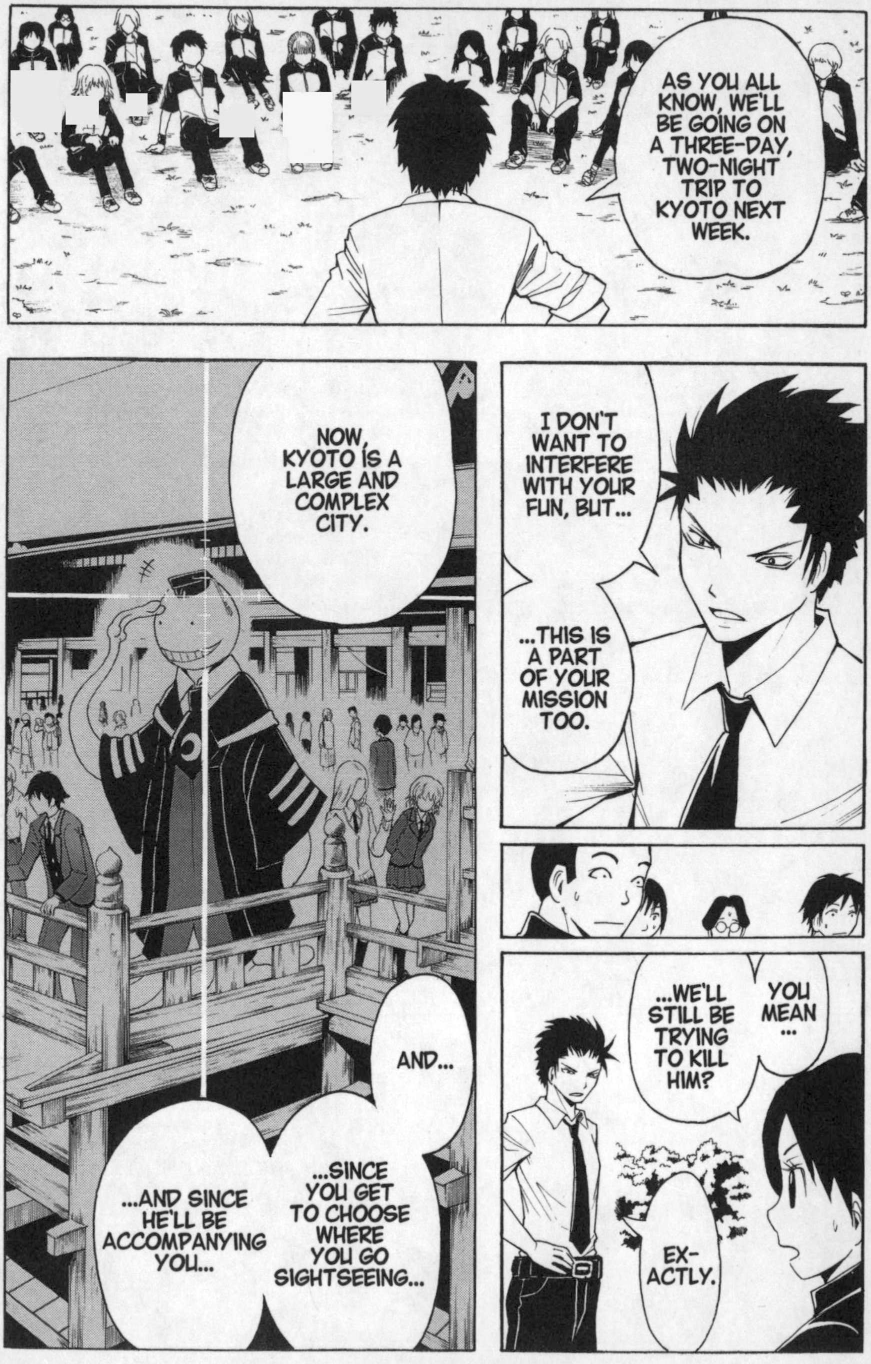
AS YOU ALL KNOW, WE'LL BE GOING ON A THREE-DAY, TWO-NIGHT TRIP TO KYOTO NEXT WEEK.
I DON'T WANT TO INTERFERE WITH YOUR FUN, BUT...
...THIS IS A PART OF YOUR MISSION TOO.
YOU MEAN...
...WE'LL STILL BE TRYING TO KILL HIM?
EX-ACTLY.
NOW, KYOTO IS A LARGE AND COMPLEX CITY.
AND...
...SINCE YOU GET TO CHOOSE WHERE YOU GO SIGHTSEEING...
...AND SINCE HE'LL BE ACCOMPANYING YOU...

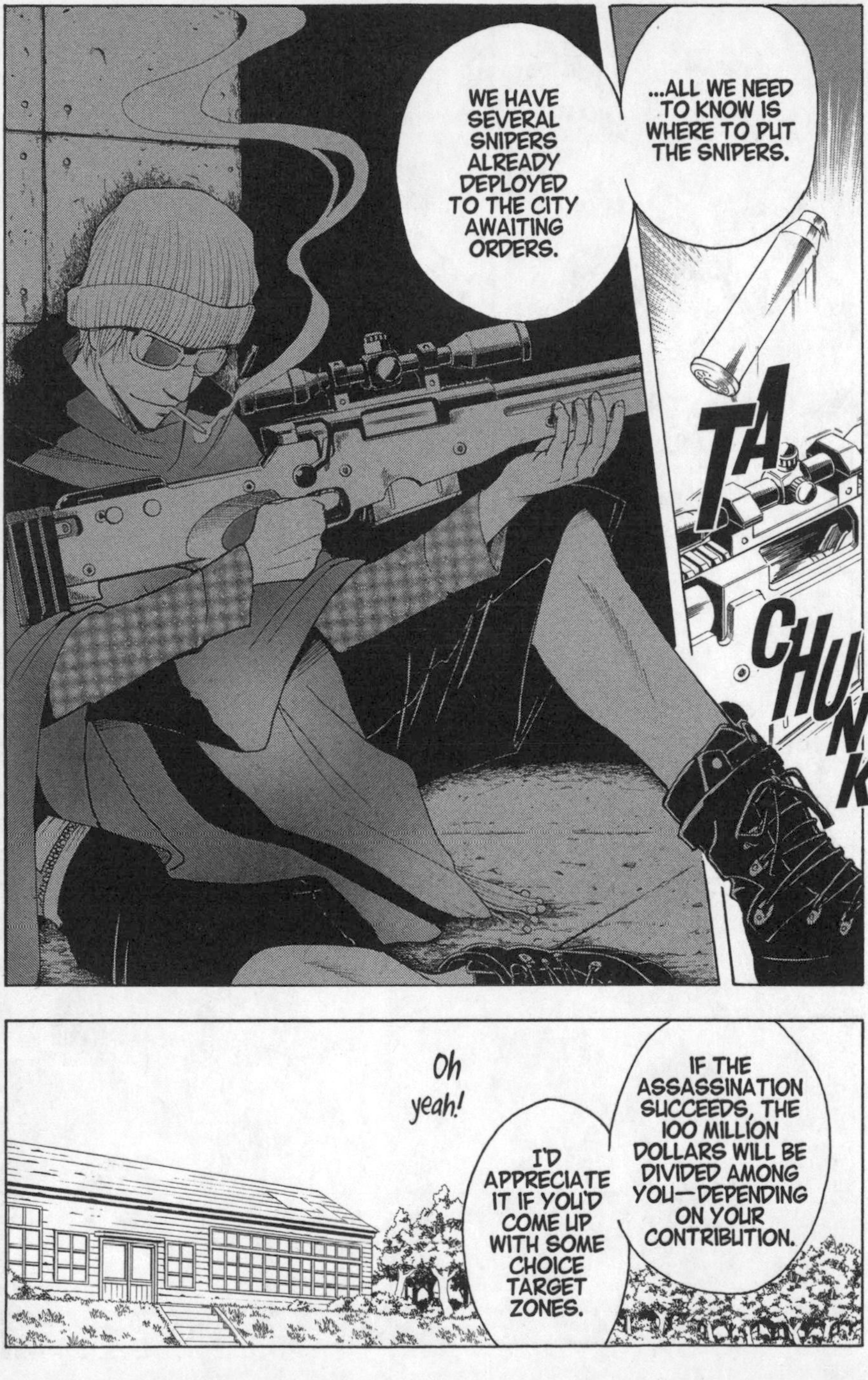
...ALL WE NEED TO KNOW IS WHERE TO PUT THE SNIPERS.
WE HAVE SEVERAL SNIPERS ALREADY DEPLOYED TO THE CITY AWAITING ORDERS.
TA CHUNK
IF THE ASSASSINATION SUCCEEDS, THE 100 MILLION DOLLARS WILL BE DIVIDED AMONG YOU—DEPENDING ON YOUR CONTRIBUTION.
I'D APPRECIATE IT IF YOU'D COME UP WITH SOME CHOICE TARGET ZONES.
Oh yeah!

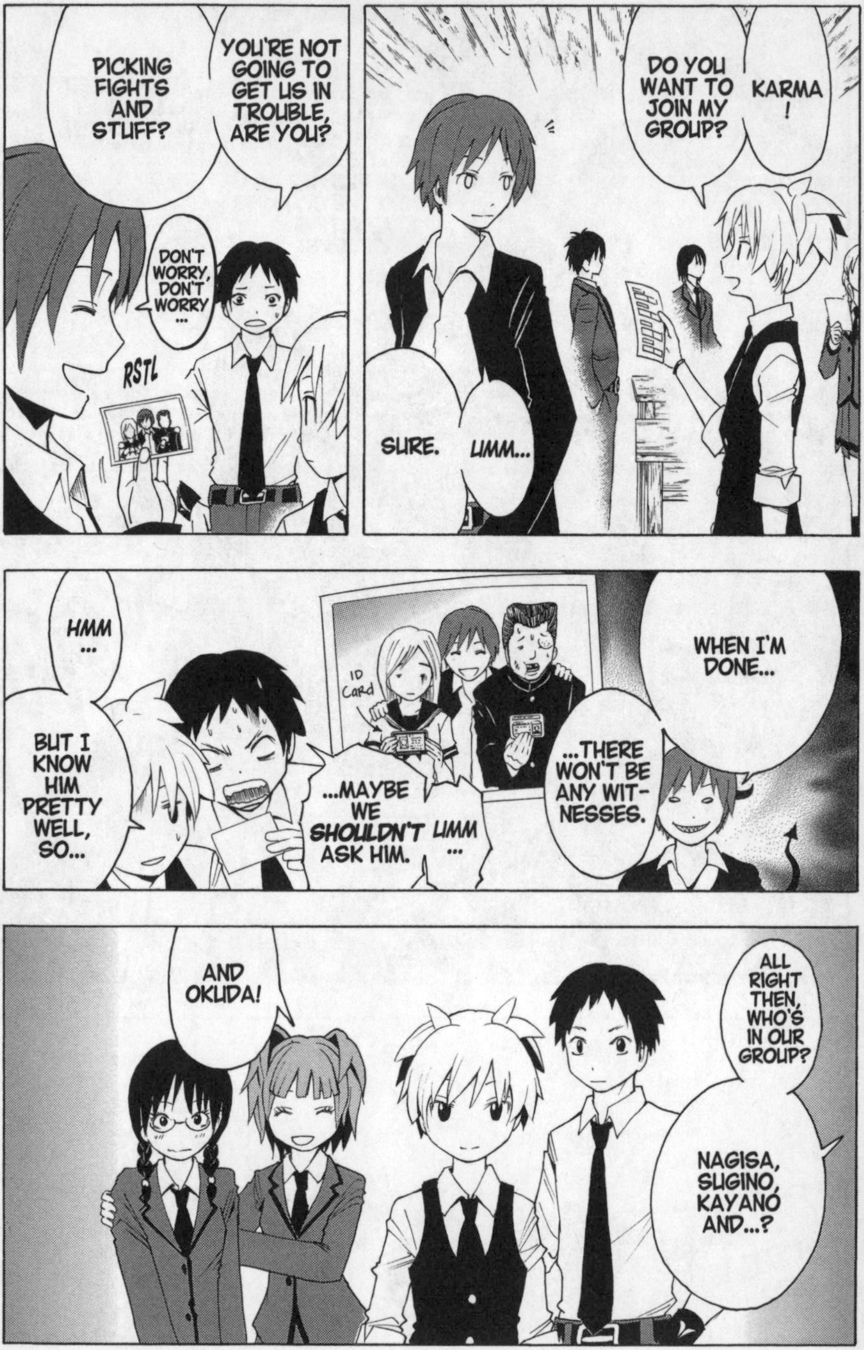
KARMA!
DO YOU WANT TO JOIN MY GROUP?
UMM...
SURE.
YOU'RE NOT GOING TO GET US IN TROUBLE, ARE YOU?
PICKING FIGHTS AND STUFF?
DON'T WORRY, DON'T WORRY...
RSTL
WHEN I'M DONE...
...THERE WON'T BE ANY WIT-NESSES.
ID Card
UMM...
...MAYBE WE SHOULDN'T ASK HIM.
HMM...
BUT I KNOW HIM PRETTY WELL, SO...
ALL RIGHT THEN, WHO'S IN OUR GROUP?
NAGISA, SUGINO, KAYANO AND...?
AND OKUDA!

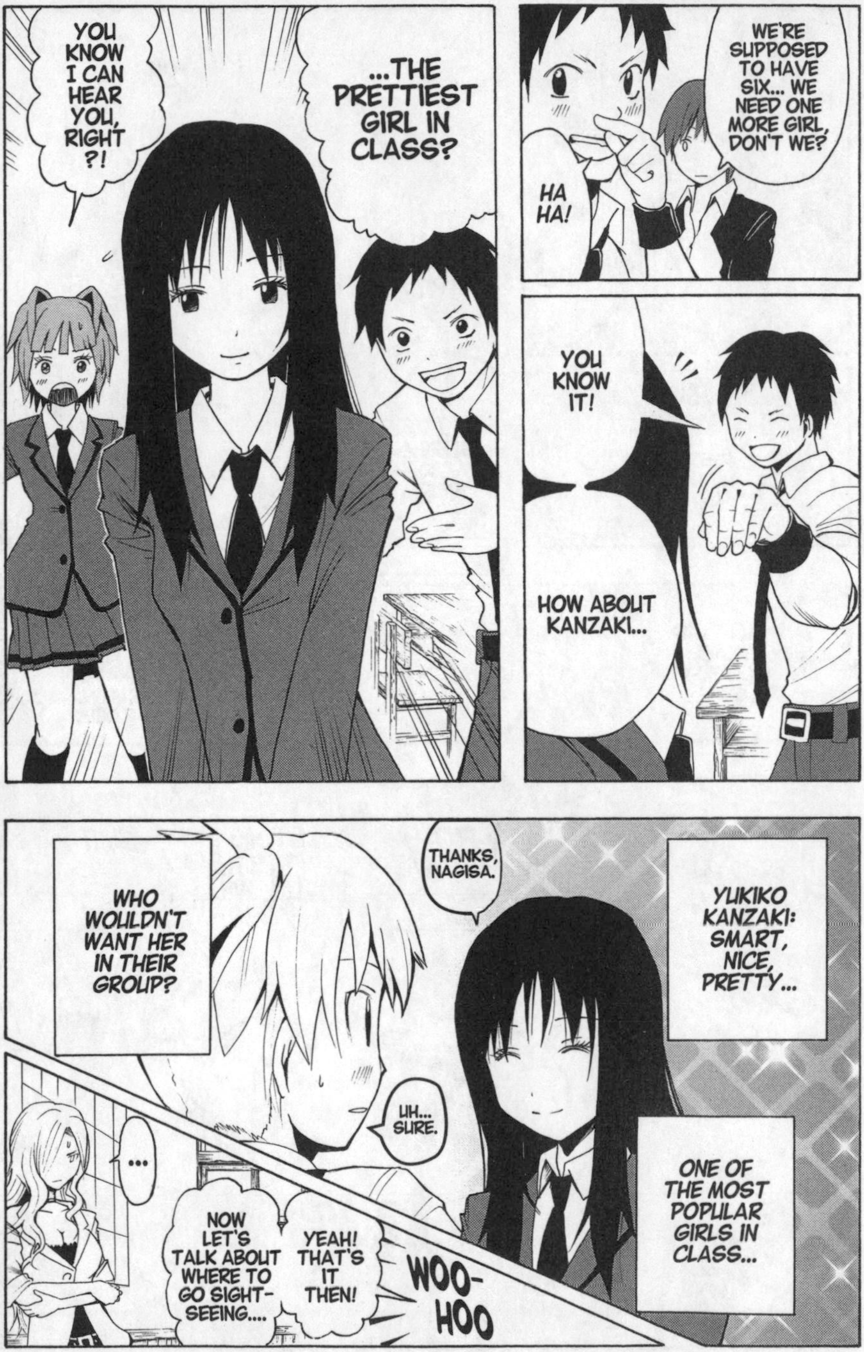
WE'RE SUPPOSED TO HAVE SIX... WE NEED ONE MORE GIRL, DON'T WE?
HA HA!
YOU KNOW IT!
HOW ABOUT KANZAKI...
...THE PRETTIEST GIRL IN CLASS?
YOU KNOW I CAN HEAR YOU, RIGHT?!
YUKIKO KANZAKI: SMART, NICE, PRETTY...
THANKS, NAGISA.
WHO WOULDN'T WANT HER IN THEIR GROUP?
ONE OF THE MOST POPULAR GIRLS IN CLASS...
UH... SURE.
WOO-HOO
YEAH! THAT'S IT THEN!
NOW LET'S TALK ABOUT WHERE TO GO SIGHT-SEEING....
...

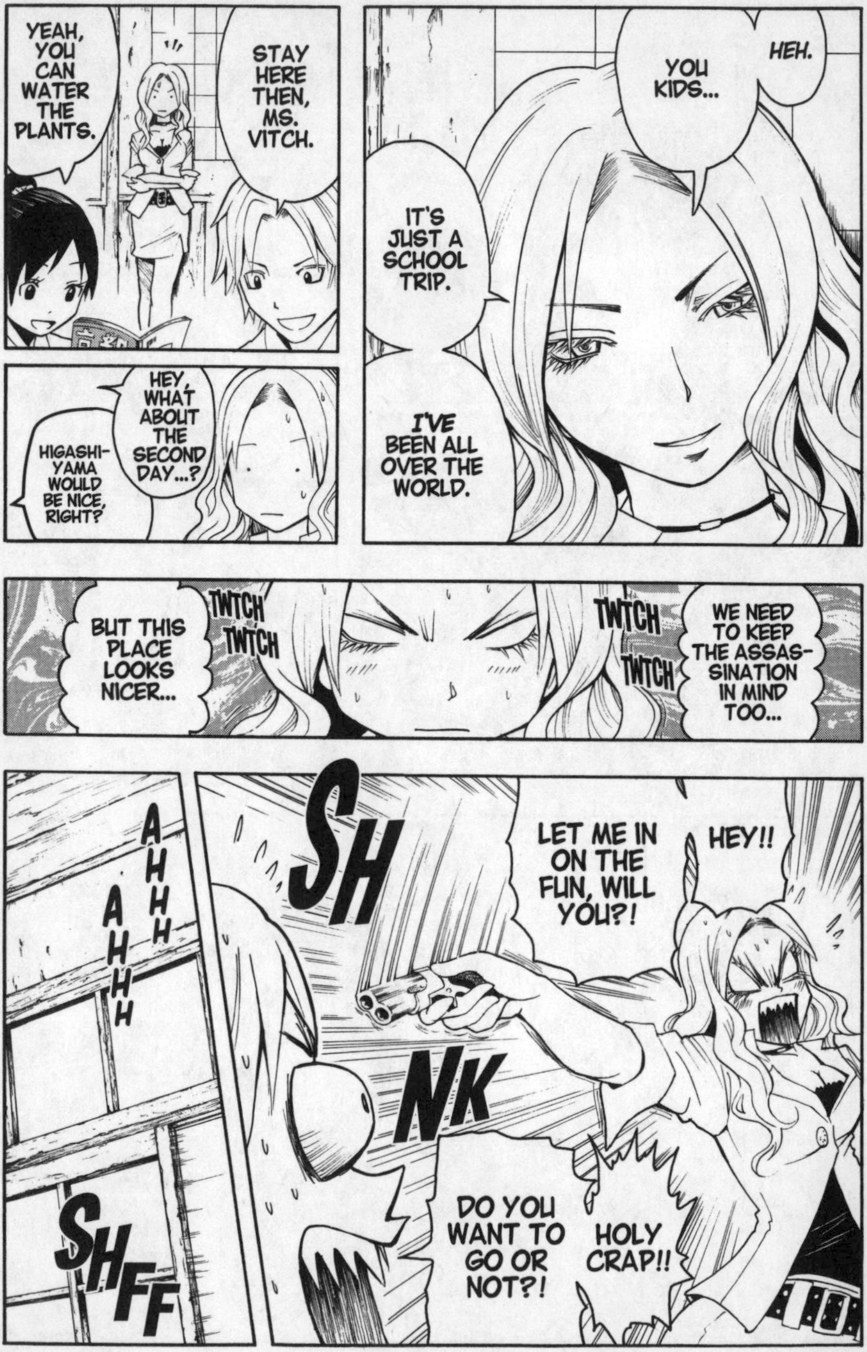
HEH.
YOU KIDS...
IT'S JUST A SCHOOL TRIP.
I'VE BEEN ALL OVER THE WORLD.
STAY HERE THEN, MS. VITCH.
YEAH, YOU CAN WATER THE PLANTS.
HEY, WHAT ABOUT THE SECOND DAY...?
HIGASHI-YAMA WOULD BE NICE, RIGHT?
WE NEED TO KEEP THE ASSAS-SINATION IN MIND TOO...
TWTCH
TWTCH
TWTCH
TWTCH
BUT THIS PLACE LOOKS NICER...
HEY!!
LET ME IN ON THE FUN, WILL YOU?!
SH
NK
HOLY CRAP!!
DO YOU WANT TO GO OR NOT?!
AHHH
AHHH
SHFF

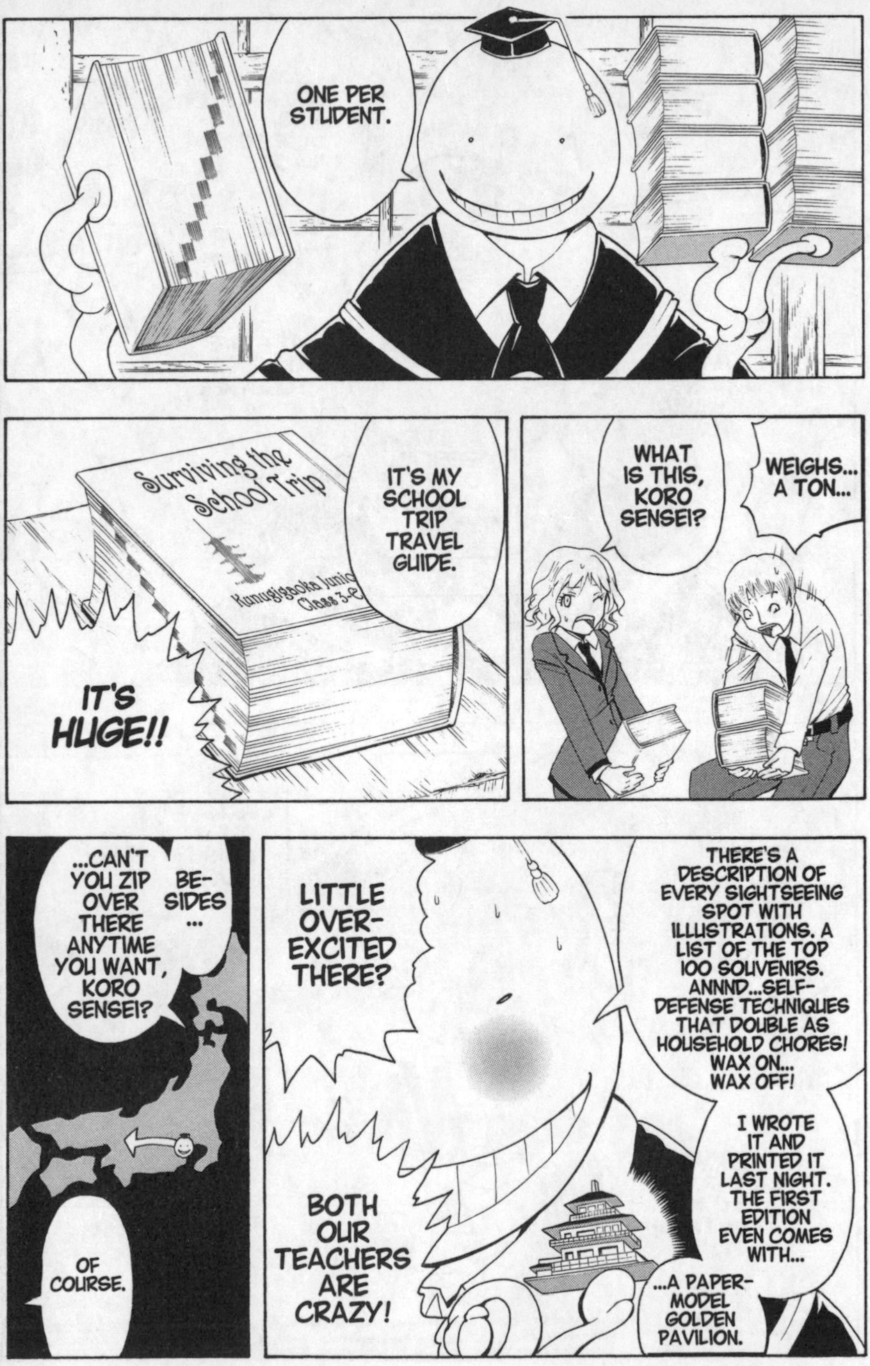
ONE PER STUDENT.
WEIGHS... A TON...
WHAT IS THIS, KORO SENSEI?
IT'S MY SCHOOL TRIP TRAVEL GUIDE.
Surviving the School Trip
IT'S HUGE!!
THERE'S A DESCRIPTION OF EVERY SIGHTSEEING SPOT WITH ILLUSTRATIONS. A LIST OF THE TOP 100 SOUVENIRS. ANNND...SELF-DEFENSE TECHNIQUES THAT DOUBLE AS HOUSEHOLD CHORES! WAX ON... WAX OFF!
LITTLE OVER-EXCITED THERE?
I WROTE IT AND PRINTED IT LAST NIGHT. THE FIRST EDITION EVEN COMES WITH...
...A PAPER-MODEL GOLDEN PAVILION.
BOTH OUR TEACHERS ARE CRAZY!
BE-SIDES...
...CAN'T YOU ZIP OVER THERE ANYTIME YOU WANT, KORO SENSEI?
OF COURSE.

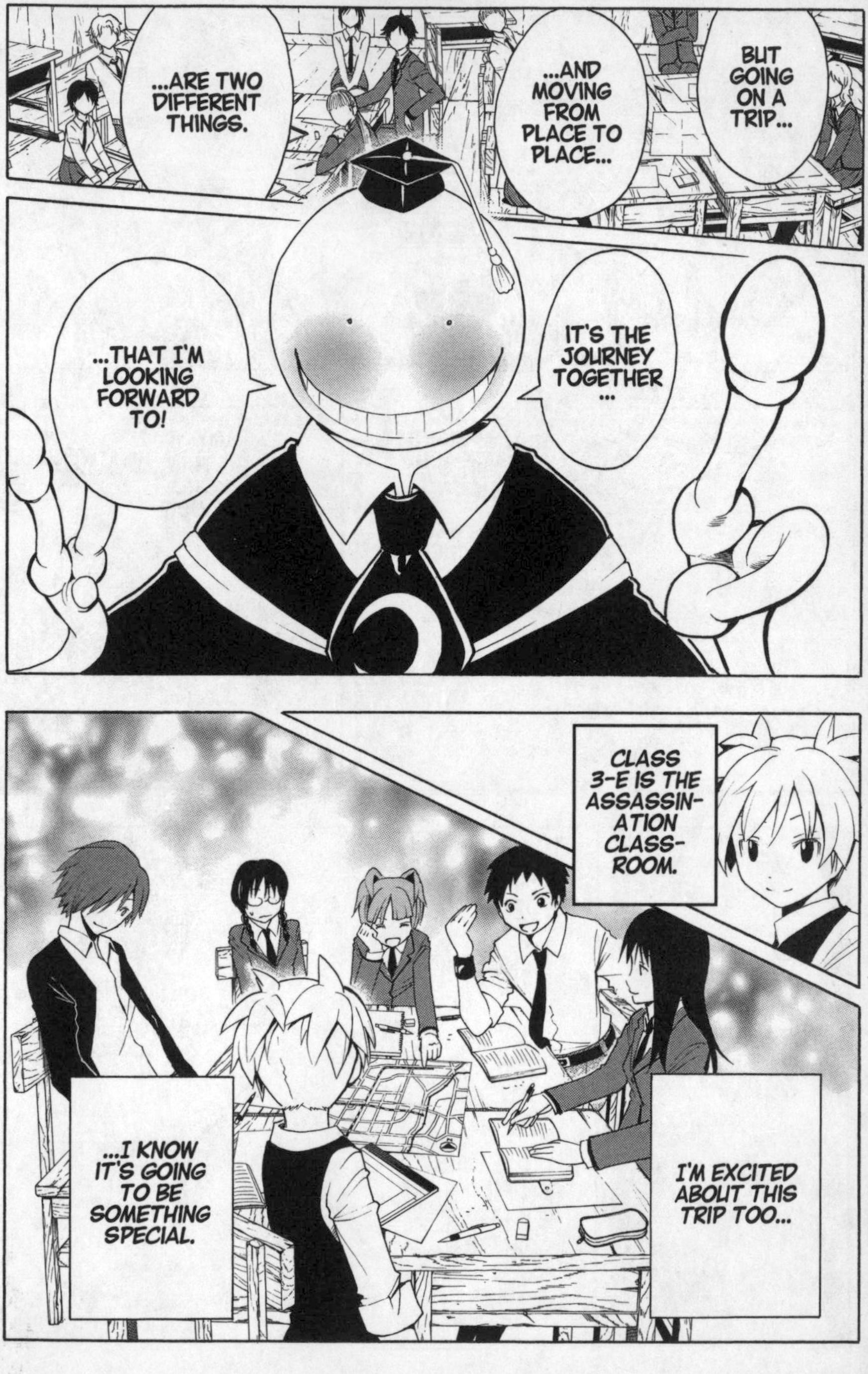
BUT GOING ON A TRIP...
...AND MOVING FROM PLACE TO PLACE...
...ARE TWO DIFFERENT THINGS.
IT'S THE JOURNEY TOGETHER ...
...THAT I'M LOOKING FORWARD TO!
CLASS 3-E IS THE ASSASSIN-ATION CLASS-ROOM.
I'M EXCITED ABOUT THIS TRIP TOO...
...I KNOW IT'S GOING TO BE SOMETHING SPECIAL.

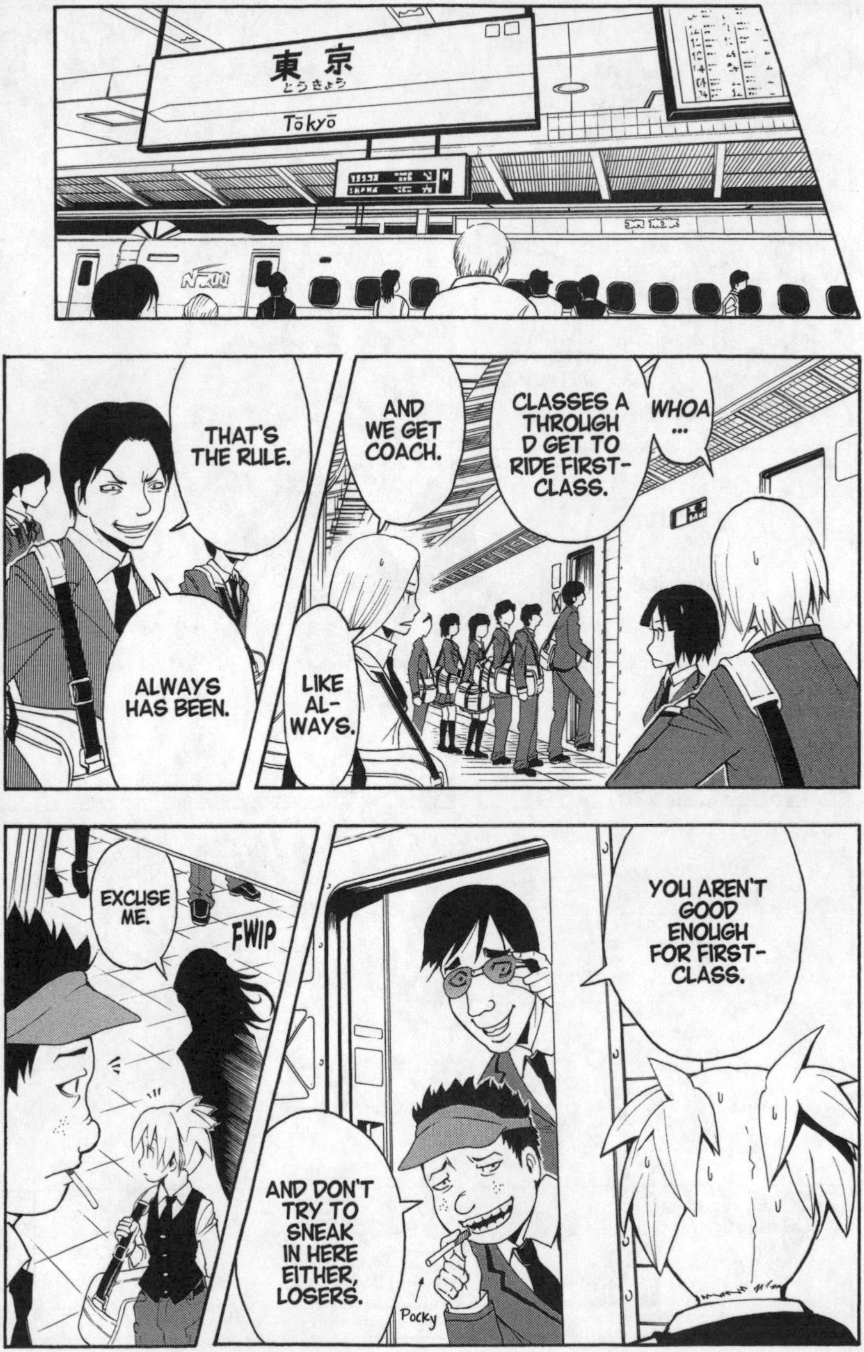
東京
とうきょう
Tōkyō
WHOA ...
CLASSES A THROUGH D GET TO RIDE FIRST-CLASS.
AND WE GET COACH.
LIKE AL-WAYS.
THAT'S THE RULE.
ALWAYS HAS BEEN.
YOU AREN'T GOOD ENOUGH FOR FIRST-CLASS.
AND DON'T TRY TO SNEAK IN HERE EITHER, LOSERS.
Pocky
FWIP
EXCUSE ME.

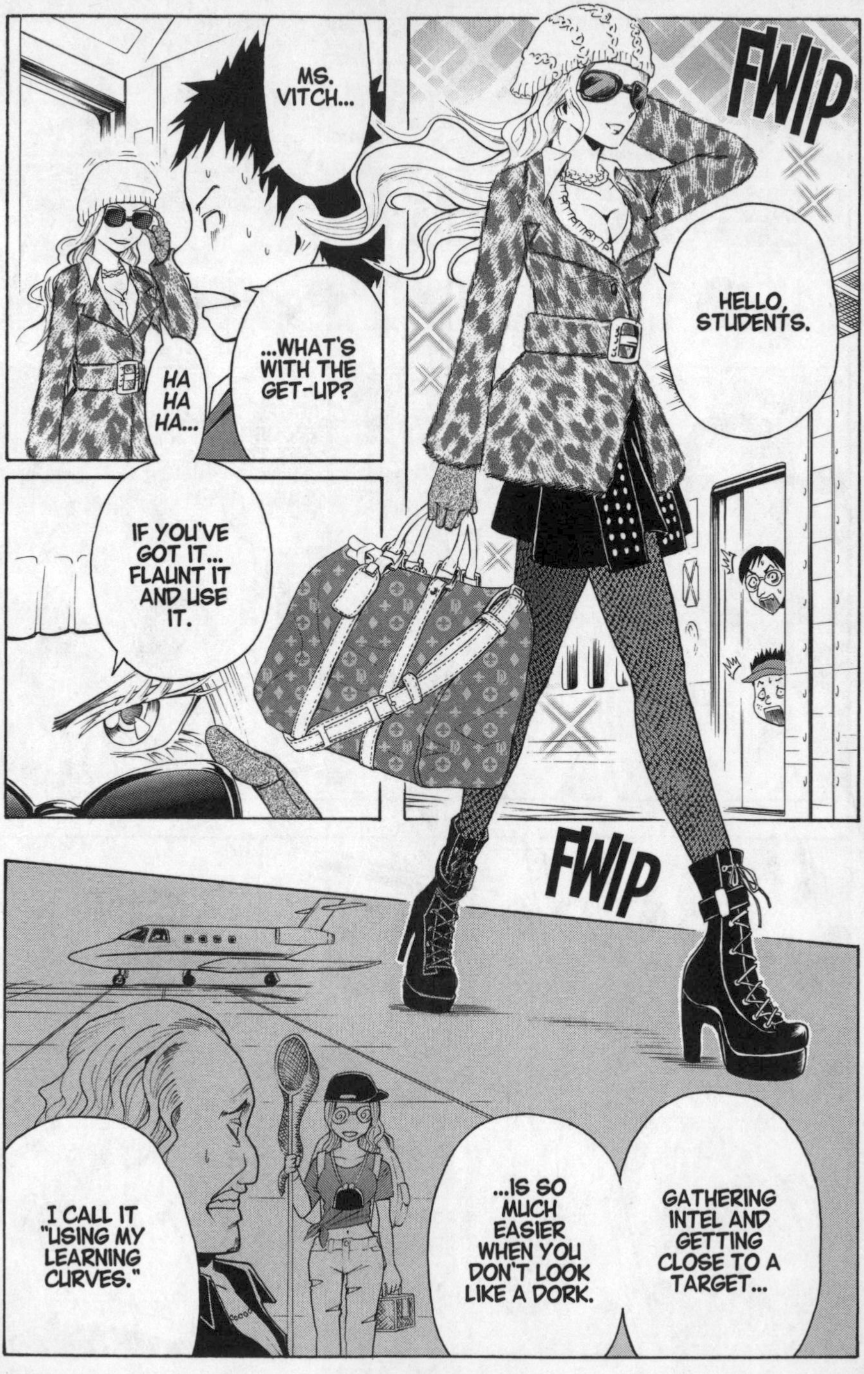
FWIP
HELLO, STUDENTS.
FWIP
MS. VITCH...
...WHAT'S WITH THE GET-UP?
HA HA HA...
IF YOU'VE GOT IT... FLAUNT IT AND USE IT.
GATHERING INTEL AND GETTING CLOSE TO A TARGET...
...IS SO MUCH EASIER WHEN YOU DON'T LOOK LIKE A DORK.
I CALL IT "USING MY LEARNING CURVES."

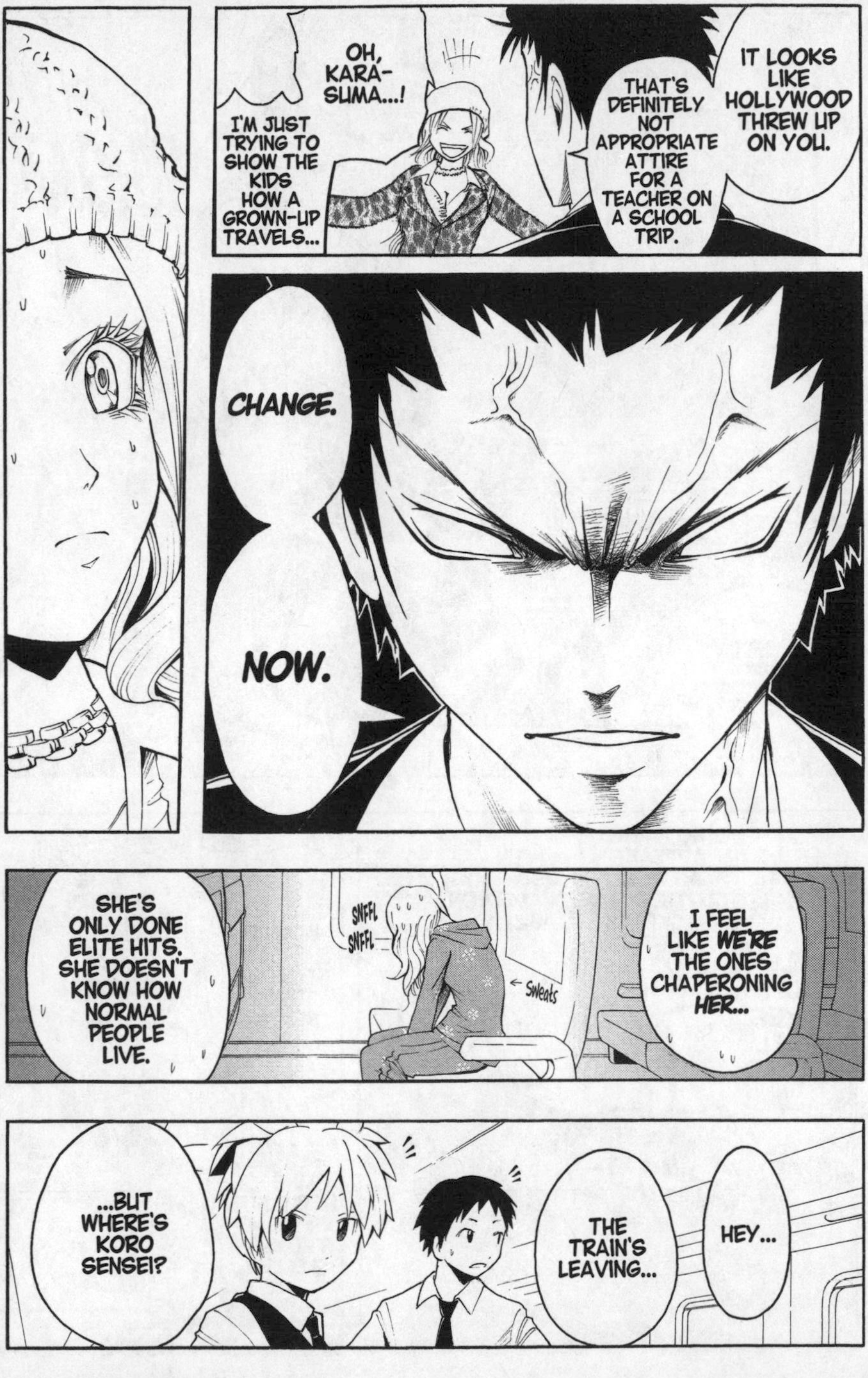
IT LOOKS LIKE HOLLYWOOD THREW UP ON YOU.
THAT'S DEFINITELY NOT APPROPRIATE ATTIRE FOR A TEACHER ON A SCHOOL TRIP.
OH, KARA-SUMA...!
I'M JUST TRYING TO SHOW THE KIDS HOW A GROWN-UP TRAVELS...
CHANGE.
NOW.
I FEEL LIKE WE'RE THE ONES CHAPERONING HER...
SNFFL
SNFFL
← Sweats
SHE'S ONLY DONE ELITE HITS. SHE DOESN'T KNOW HOW NORMAL PEOPLE LIVE.
HEY...
THE TRAIN'S LEAVING...
...BUT WHERE'S KORO SENSEI?

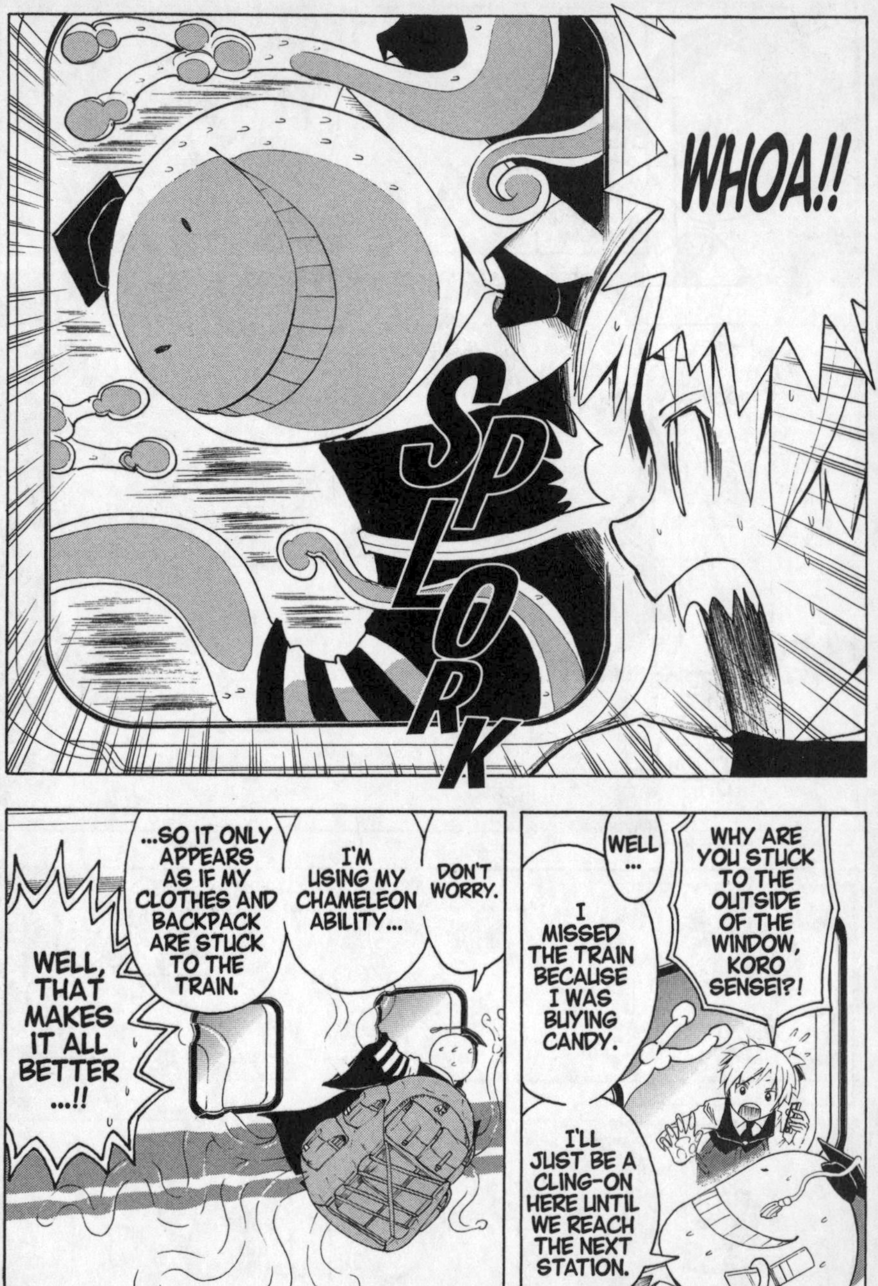
WHOA!!
SPLORK
WHY ARE YOU STUCK TO THE OUTSIDE OF THE WINDOW, KORO SENSEI?!
WELL...
I MISSED THE TRAIN BECAUSE I WAS BUYING CANDY.
I'LL JUST BE A CLING-ON HERE UNTIL WE REACH THE NEXT STATION.
DON'T WORRY.
I'M USING MY CHAMELEON ABILITY...
...SO IT ONLY APPEARS AS IF MY CLOTHES AND BACKPACK ARE STUCK TO THE TRAIN.
WELL, THAT MAKES IT ALL BETTER...!!

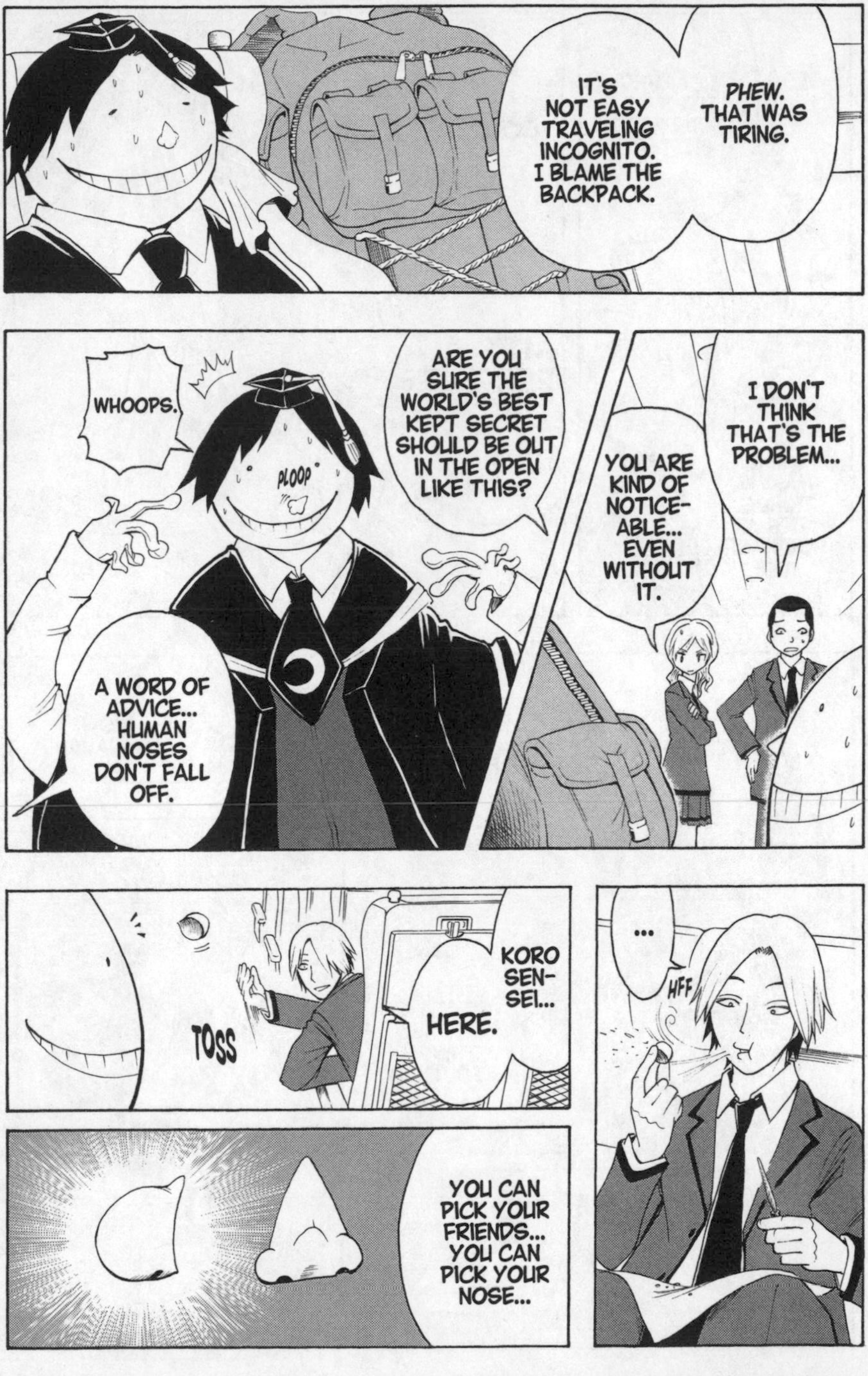
PHEW. THAT WAS TIRING.
IT'S NOT EASY TRAVELING INCOGNITO. I BLAME THE BACKPACK.
I DON'T THINK THAT'S THE PROBLEM...
YOU ARE KIND OF NOTICE-ABLE... EVEN WITHOUT IT.
ARE YOU SURE THE WORLD'S BEST KEPT SECRET SHOULD BE OUT IN THE OPEN LIKE THIS?
PLOOP
WHOOPS.
A WORD OF ADVICE... HUMAN NOSES DON'T FALL OFF.
...
HFF
KORO SENSEI...
HERE.
TOSS
YOU CAN PICK YOUR FRIENDS... YOU CAN PICK YOUR NOSE...

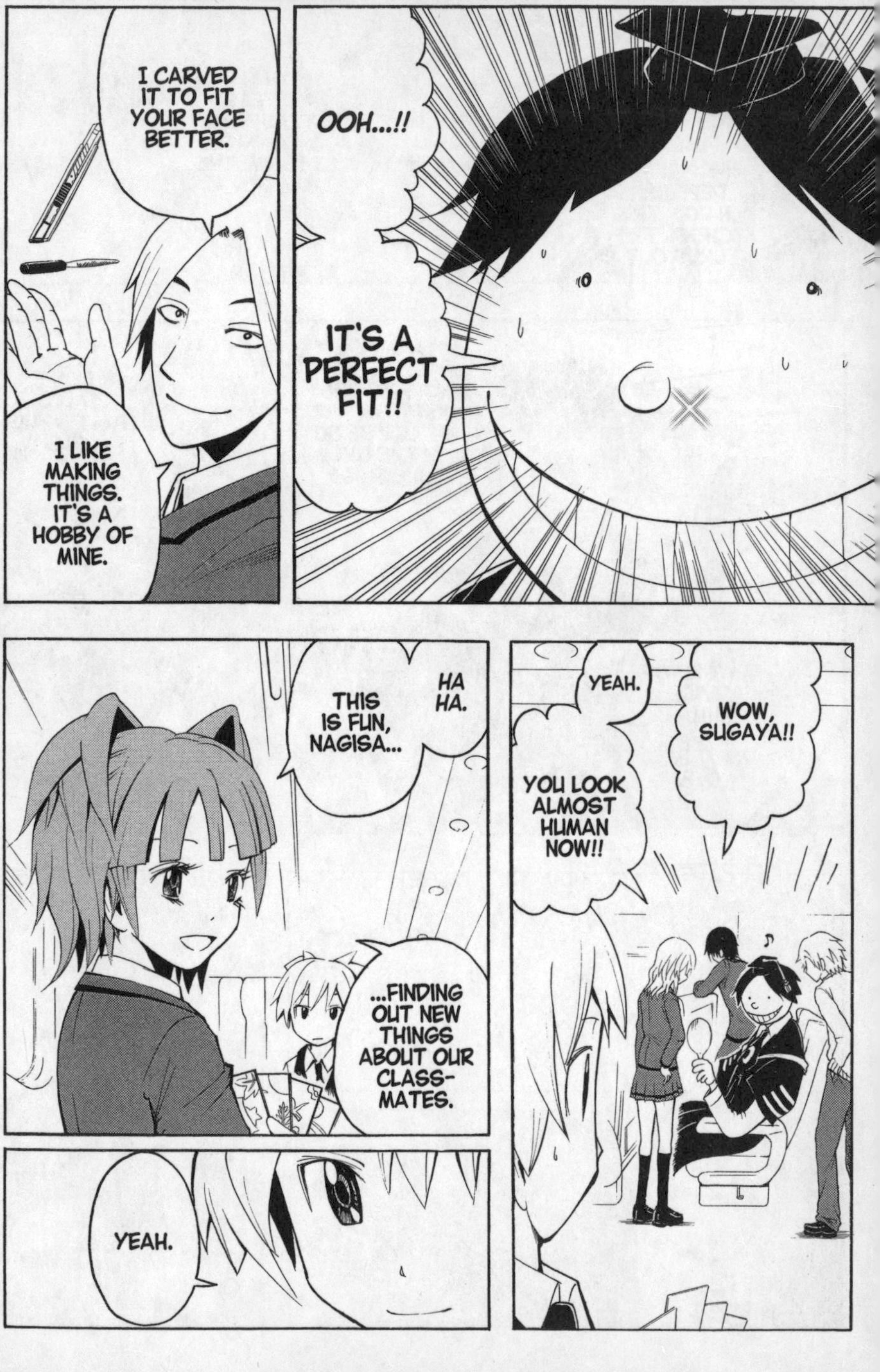
OOH...!!
IT'S A PERFECT FIT!!
I CARVED IT TO FIT YOUR FACE BETTER.
I LIKE MAKING THINGS. IT'S A HOBBY OF MINE.
WOW, SUGAYA!!
YEAH.
YOU LOOK ALMOST HUMAN NOW!!
HA HA.
THIS IS FUN, NAGISA...
...FINDING OUT NEW THINGS ABOUT OUR CLASSMATES.
YEAH.

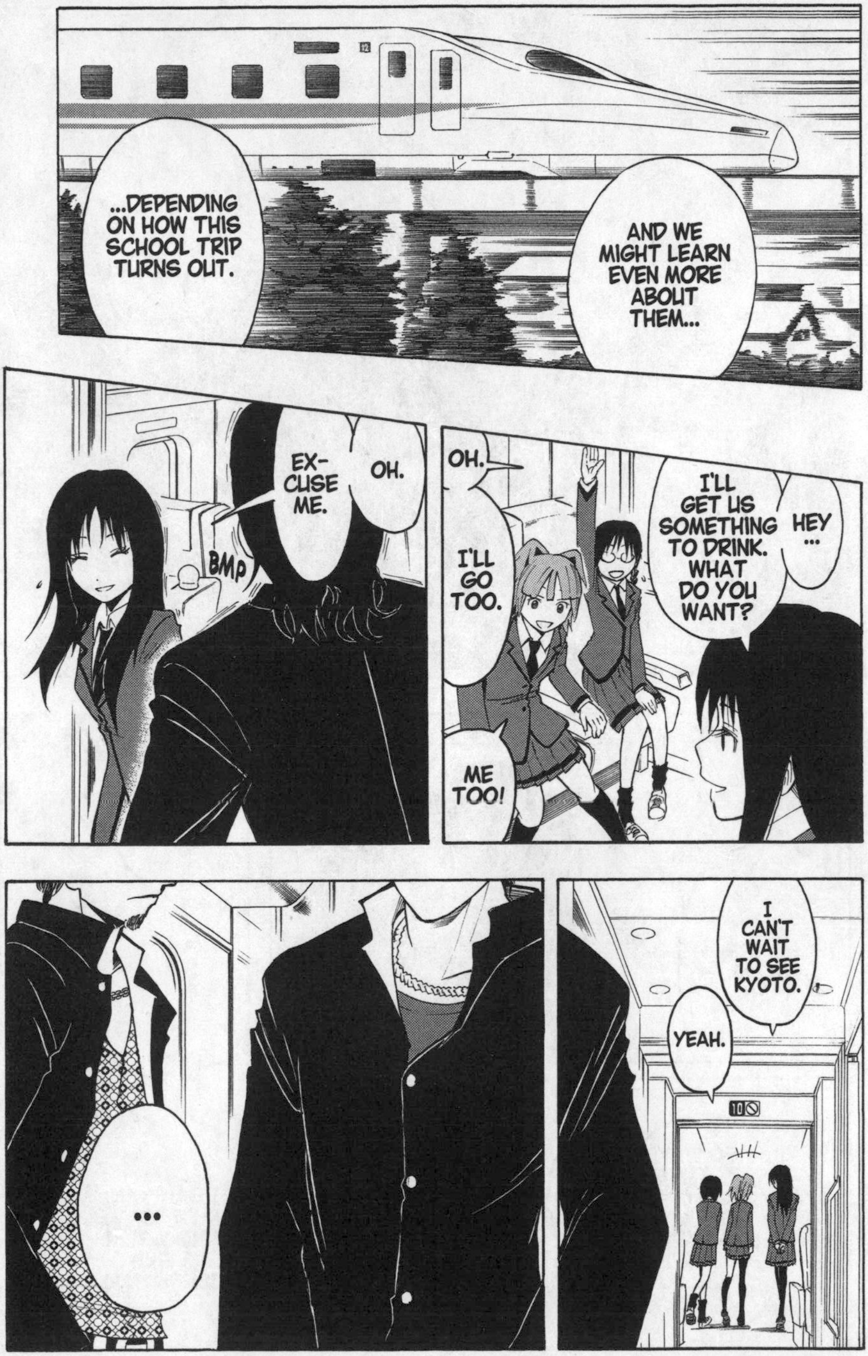
AND WE MIGHT LEARN EVEN MORE ABOUT THEM...
...DEPENDING ON HOW THIS SCHOOL TRIP TURNS OUT.
HEY ...
I'LL GET US SOMETHING TO DRINK. WHAT DO YOU WANT?
OH.
I'LL GO TOO.
ME TOO!
OH.
EX-CUSE ME.
BMP
I CAN'T WAIT TO SEE KYOTO.
YEAH.
...

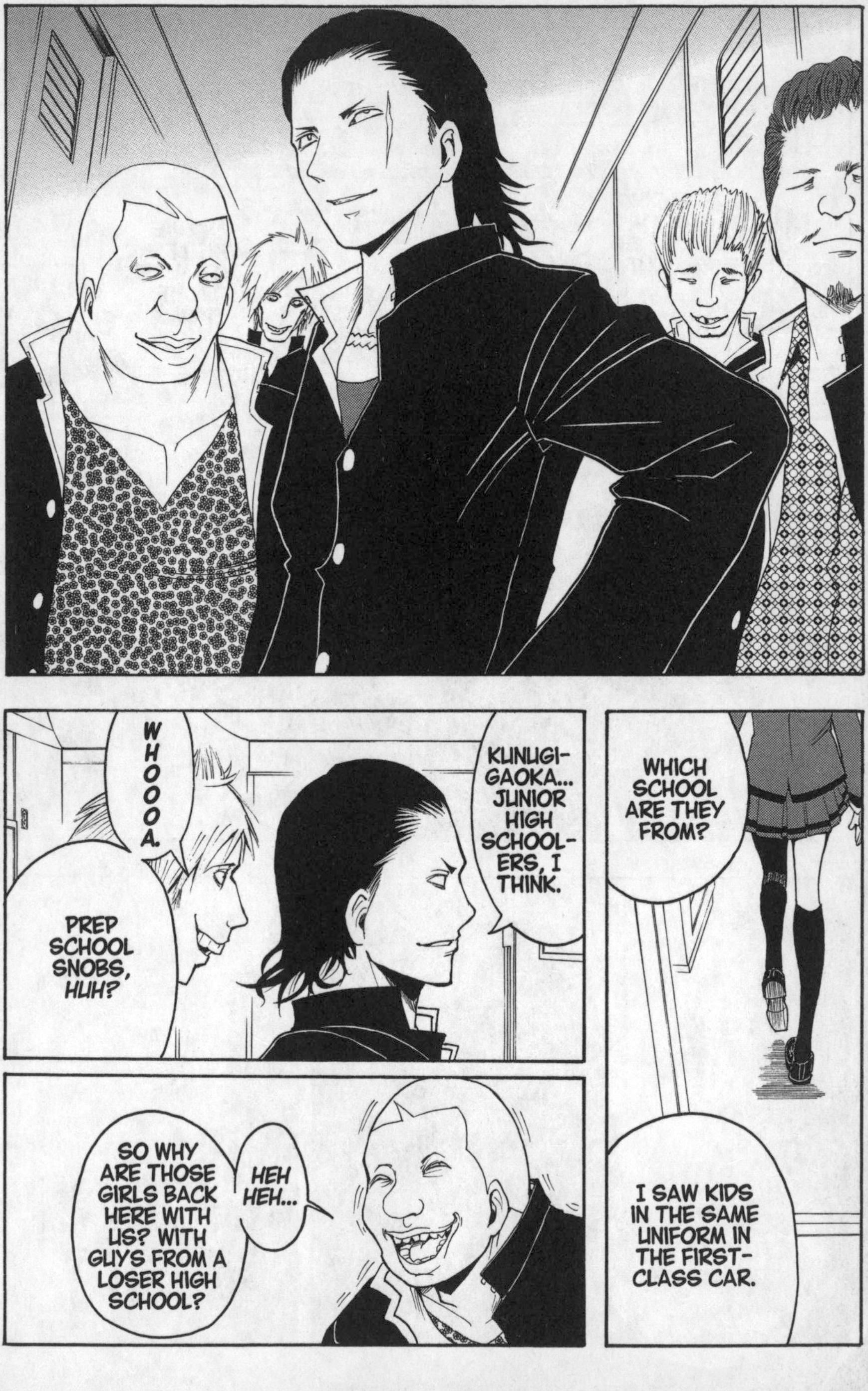
WHICH SCHOOL ARE THEY FROM?
I SAW KIDS IN THE SAME UNIFORM IN THE FIRST-CLASS CAR.
KUNUGIGAOKA... JUNIOR HIGH SCHOOLERS, I THINK.
WHOOOOA.
PREP SCHOOL SNOBS, HUH?
HEH HEH...
SO WHY ARE THOSE GIRLS BACK HERE WITH US? WITH GUYS FROM A LOSER HIGH SCHOOL?

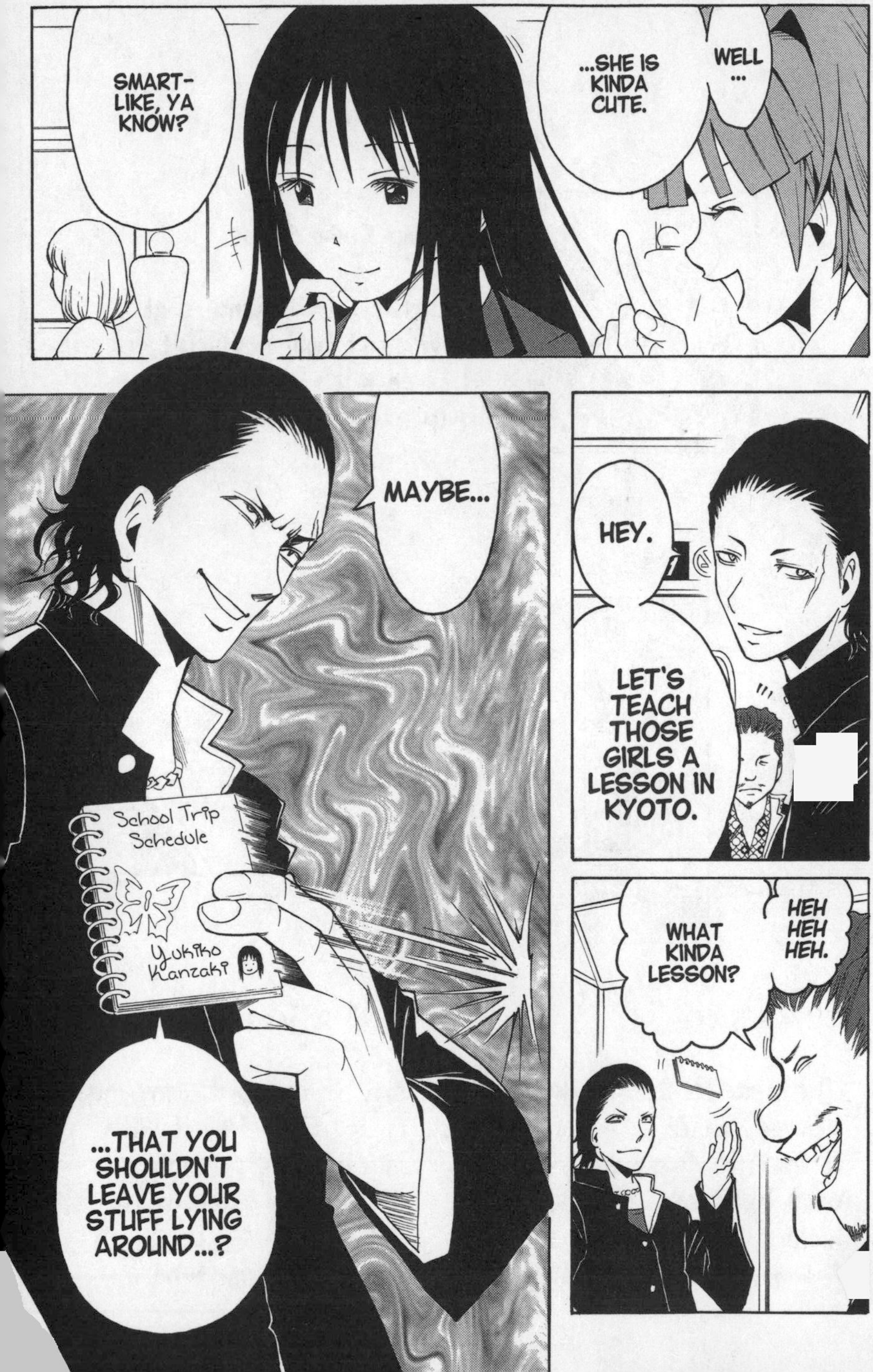
WELL ...
...SHE IS KINDA CUTE.
SMART-LIKE, YA KNOW?
HEY.
LET'S TEACH THOSE GIRLS A LESSON IN KYOTO.
HEH HEH HEH.
WHAT KINDA LESSON?
MAYBE...
School Trip Schedule
Yukiko Kanzaki
...THAT YOU SHOULDN'T LEAVE YOUR STUFF LYING AROUND...?

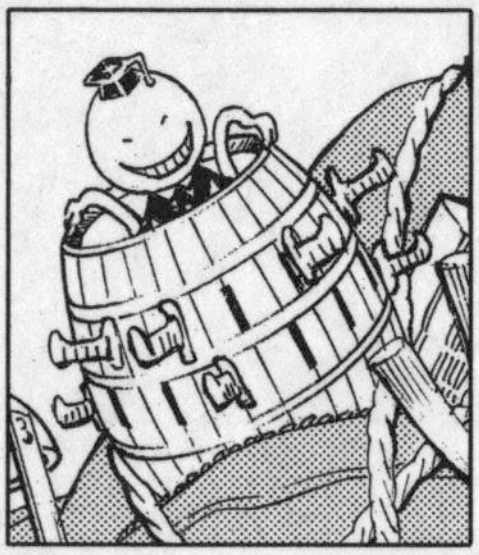

Pop-up Koro Sensei

A classic party game that shows just how difficult it is to kill him. A school trip must-have.

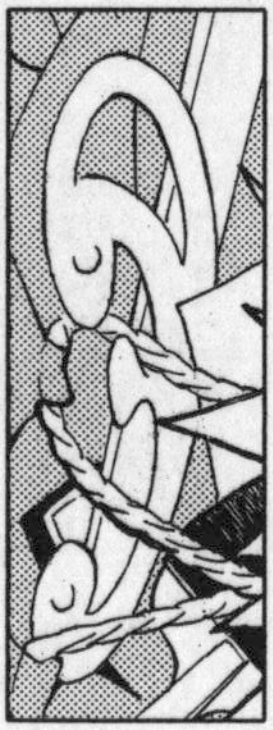

Curve Ruler

The perfect tool to draw curves, which are difficult to execute freehand. The best types are the ones that have an edge on both sides. A school trip must-have.

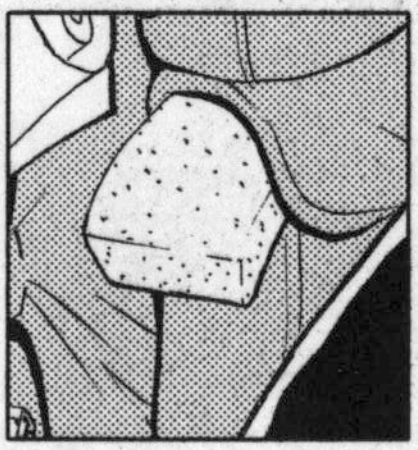

Devil's Tongue Jelly

Boil it and put some miso on it. Stir fry it with mildly spicy seasonings. Drop it in a broth, so the flavor settles in. A school trip must-have.

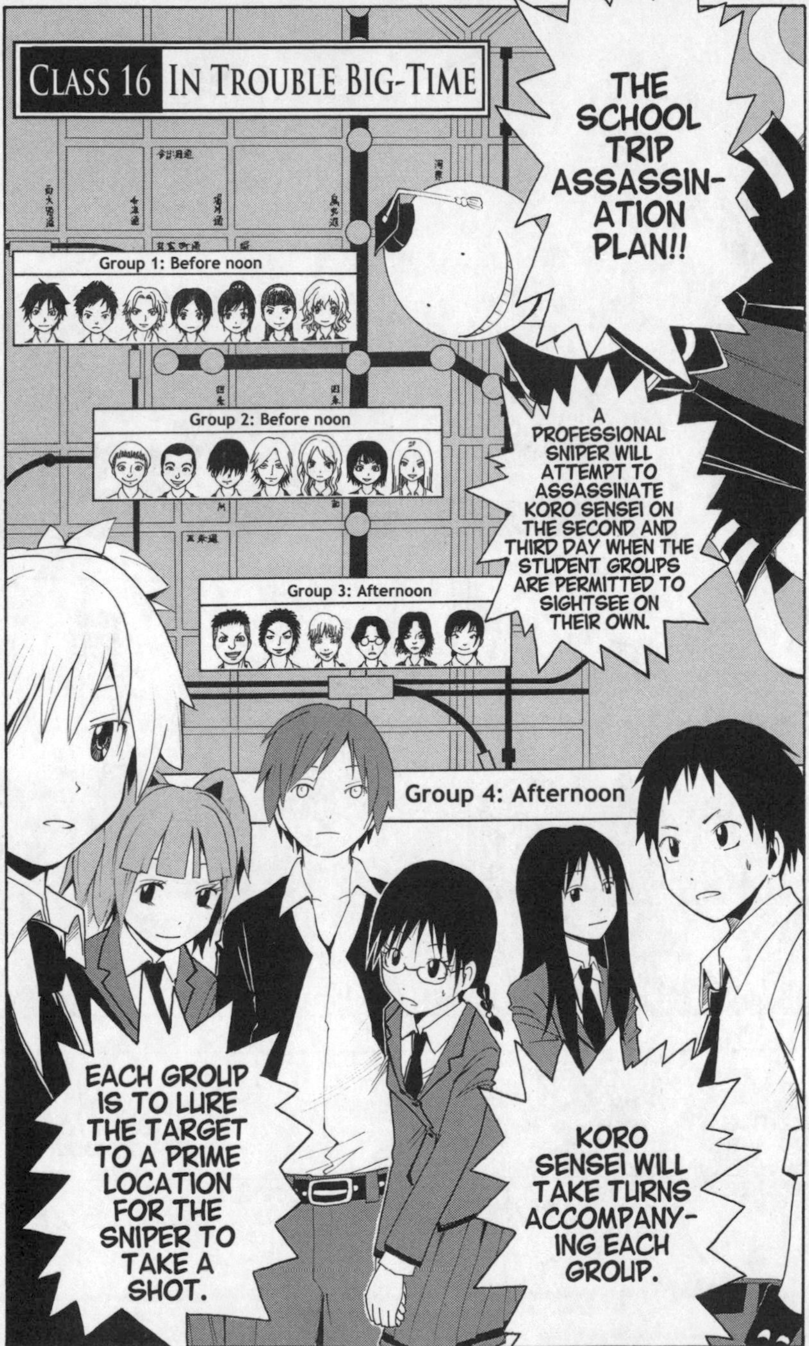
Class 16 In Trouble Big-Time
THE SCHOOL TRIP ASSASSINATION PLAN!!
Group 1: Before noon
Group 2: Before noon
Group 3: Afternoon
Group 4: Afternoon
A PROFESSIONAL SNIPER WILL ATTEMPT TO ASSASSINATE KORO SENSEI ON THE SECOND AND THIRD DAY WHEN THE STUDENT GROUPS ARE PERMITTED TO SIGHTSEE ON THEIR OWN.
KORO SENSEI WILL TAKE TURNS ACCOMPANYING EACH GROUP.
EACH GROUP IS TO LURE THE TARGET TO A PRIME LOCATION FOR THE SNIPER TO TAKE A SHOT.

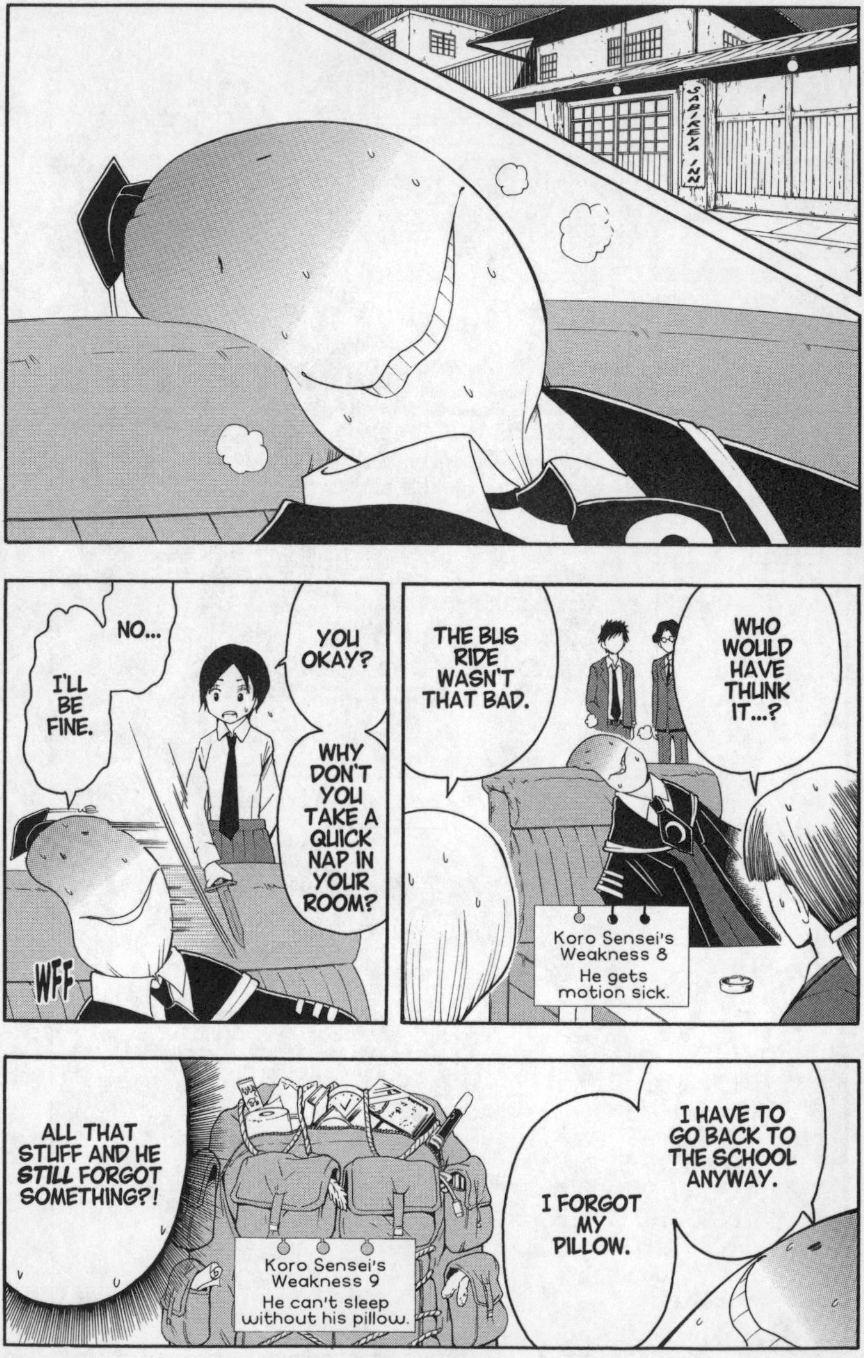
SABIREYA INN
WHO WOULD HAVE THUNK IT...?
THE BUS RIDE WASN'T THAT BAD.
Koro Sensei's Weakness 8
He gets motion sick.
YOU OKAY?
WHY DON'T YOU TAKE A QUICK NAP IN YOUR ROOM?
NO...
I'LL BE FINE.
WFF
I HAVE TO GO BACK TO THE SCHOOL ANYWAY.
I FORGOT MY PILLOW.
ALL THAT STUFF AND HE *STILL* FORGOT SOMETHING?!
Koro Sensei's Weakness 9
He can't sleep without his pillow.

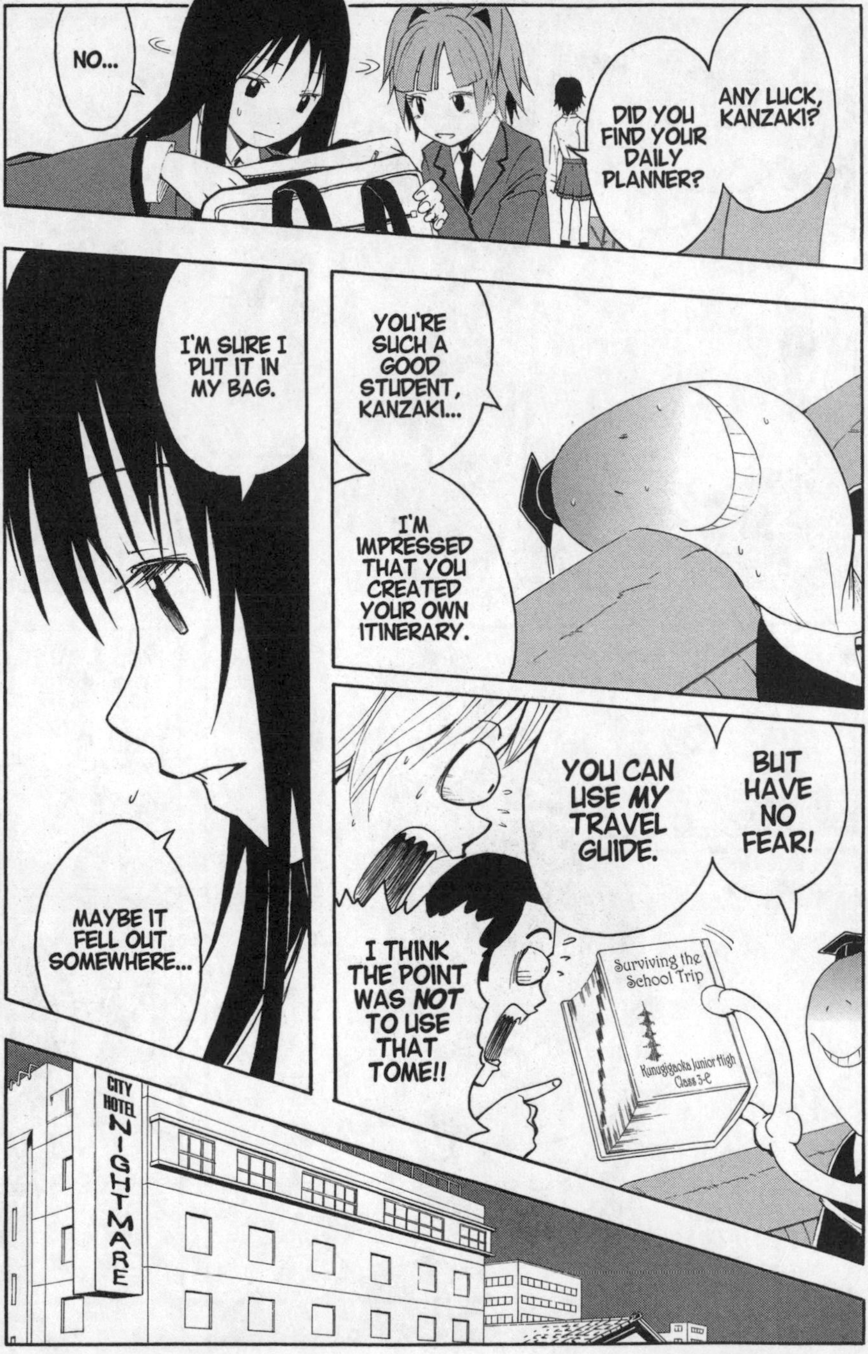
ANY LUCK, KANZAKI?
DID YOU FIND YOUR DAILY PLANNER?
NO...
YOU'RE SUCH A GOOD STUDENT, KANZAKI...
I'M IMPRESSED THAT YOU CREATED YOUR OWN ITINERARY.
BUT HAVE NO FEAR!
YOU CAN USE MY TRAVEL GUIDE.
Surviving the School Trip
Kunugigaoka Junior High Class 3-E
I THINK THE POINT WAS *NOT* TO USE THAT TOME!!
I'M SURE I PUT IT IN MY BAG.
MAYBE IT FELL OUT SOMEWHERE...
CITY HOTEL NIGHTMARE

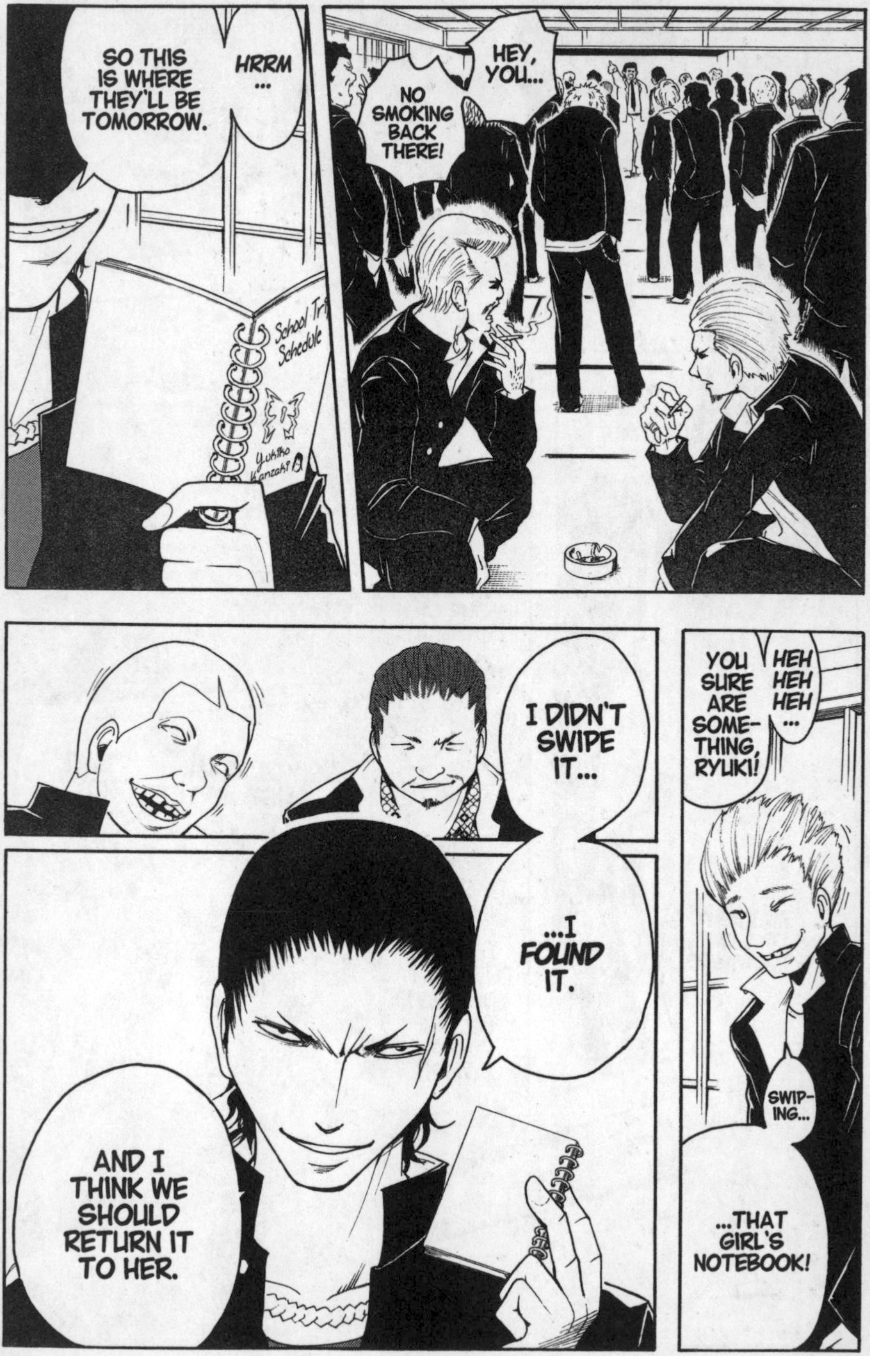
HEY, YOU...
NO SMOKING BACK THERE!
HRRM...
SO THIS IS WHERE THEY'LL BE TOMORROW.
HEH HEH HEH...
YOU SURE ARE SOMETHING, RYUKI!
SWIPING...
...THAT GIRL'S NOTEBOOK!
I DIDN'T SWIPE IT...
...I FOUND IT.
AND I THINK WE SHOULD RETURN IT TO HER.

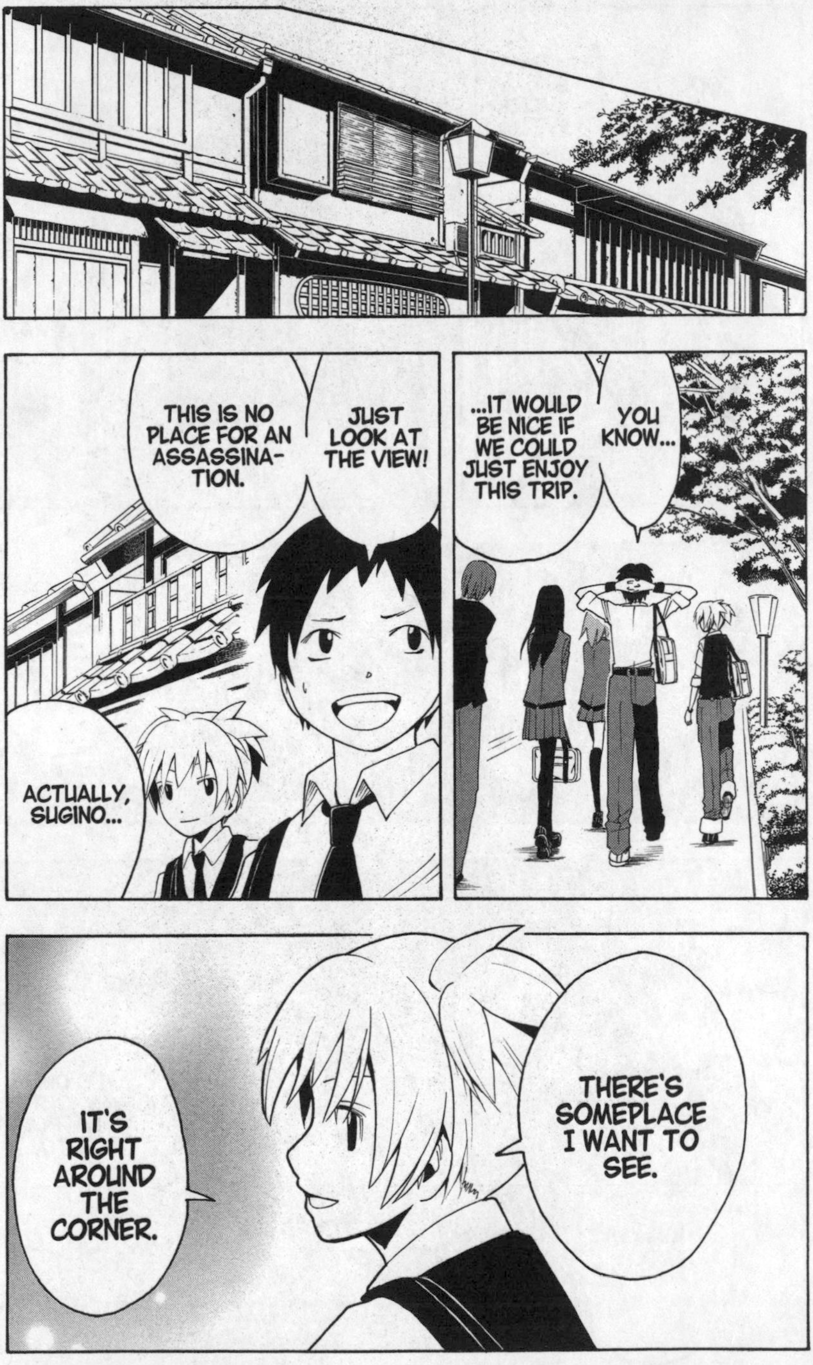
YOU KNOW...
...IT WOULD BE NICE IF WE COULD JUST ENJOY THIS TRIP.
JUST LOOK AT THE VIEW!
THIS IS NO PLACE FOR AN ASSASSINA-TION.
ACTUALLY, SUGINO...
THERE'S SOMEPLACE I WANT TO SEE.
IT'S RIGHT AROUND THE CORNER.

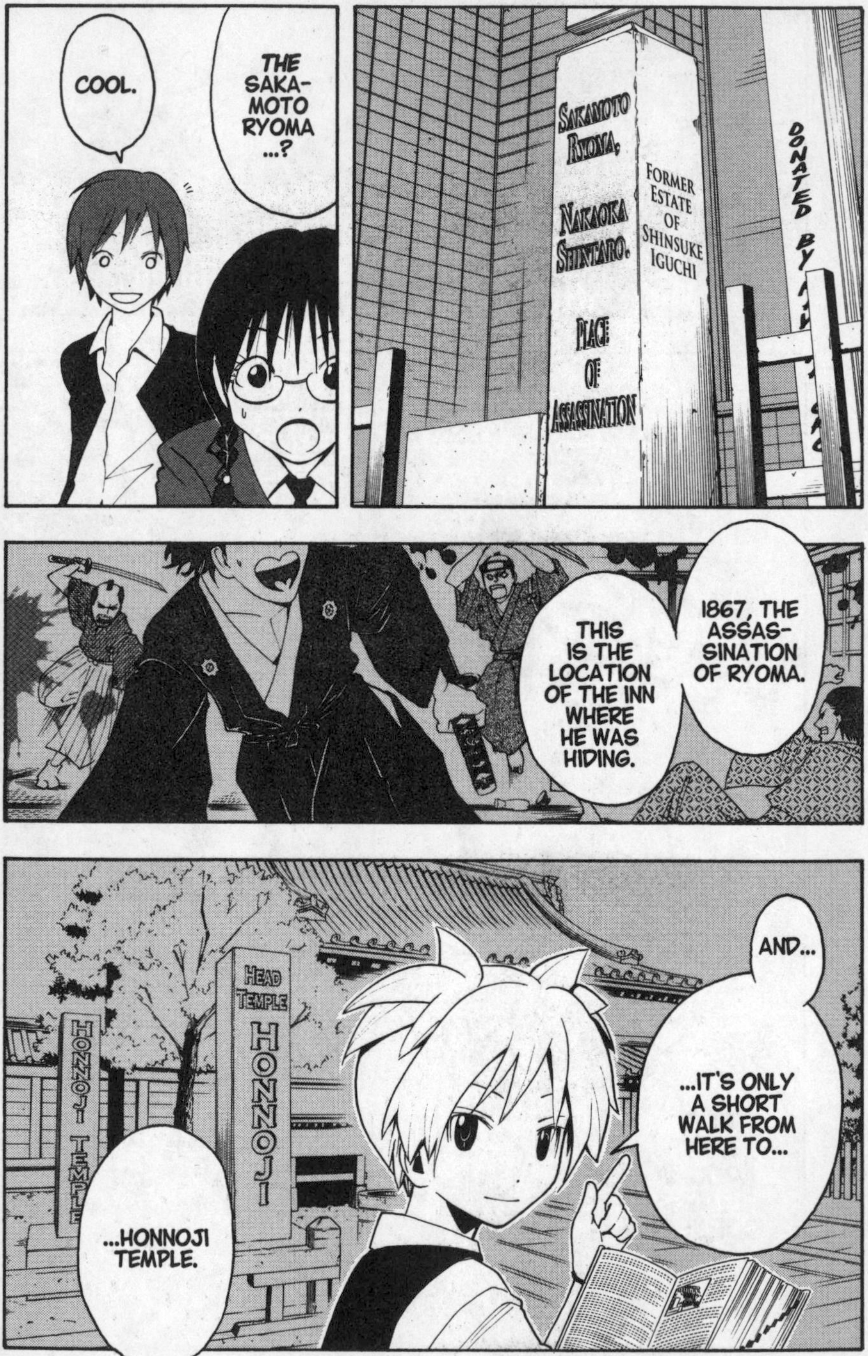
DONATED BY
FORMER ESTATE OF SHINSUKE IGUCHI
SAKAMOTO RYOMA, NAKAOKA SHINTARO. PLACE OF ASSASSINATION
THE SAKAMOTO RYOMA ...?
COOL.
1867, THE ASSASSINATION OF RYOMA.
THIS IS THE LOCATION OF THE INN WHERE HE WAS HIDING.
AND...
...IT'S ONLY A SHORT WALK FROM HERE TO...
HEAD TEMPLE HONNOJI
HONNOJI TEMPLE
...HONNOJI TEMPLE.

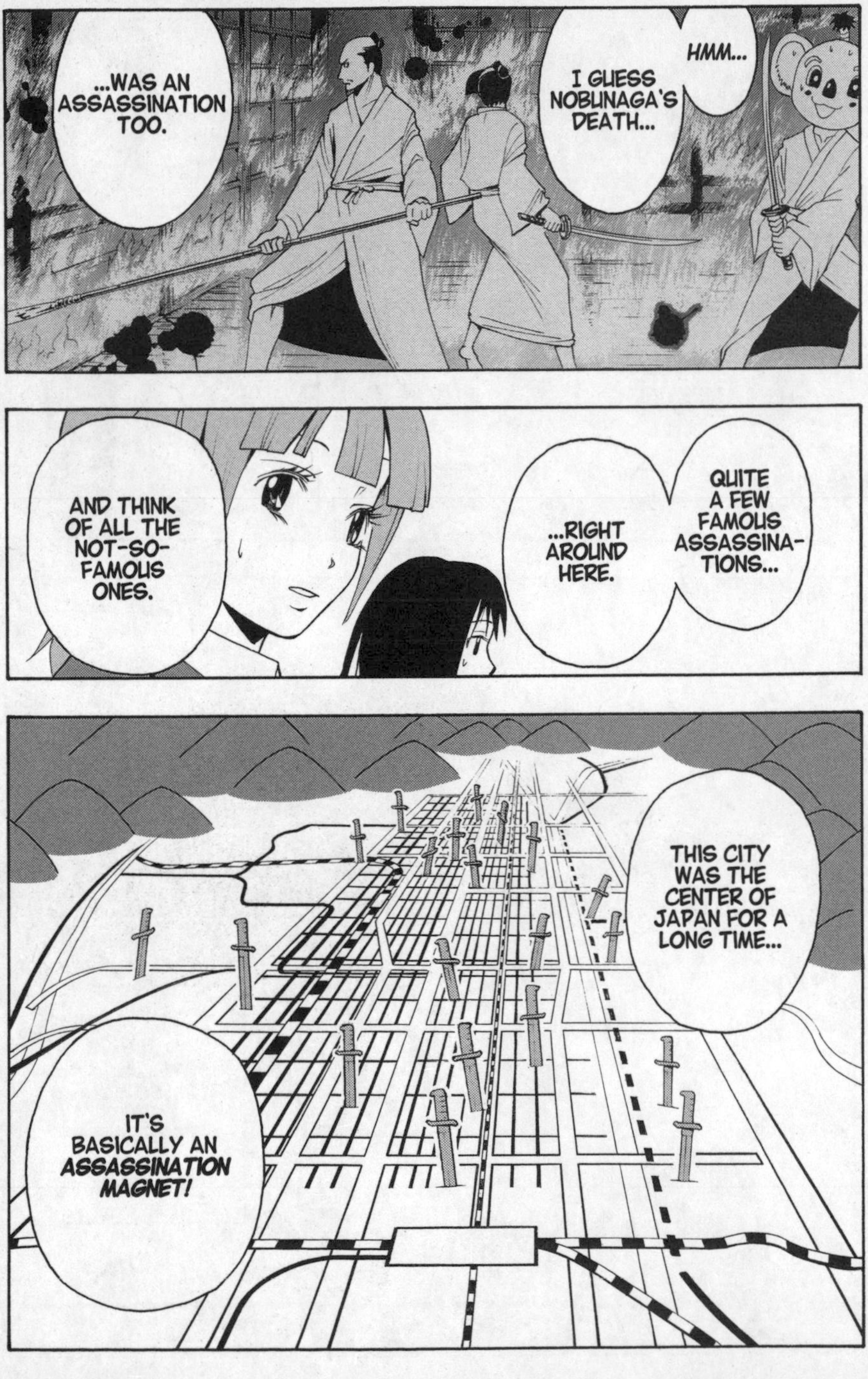
HMM...
I GUESS NOBUNAGA'S DEATH...
...WAS AN ASSASSINATION TOO.
QUITE A FEW FAMOUS ASSASSINA-TIONS...
...RIGHT AROUND HERE.
AND THINK OF ALL THE NOT-SO-FAMOUS ONES.
THIS CITY WAS THE CENTER OF JAPAN FOR A LONG TIME...
IT'S BASICALLY AN *ASSASSINATION MAGNET!*

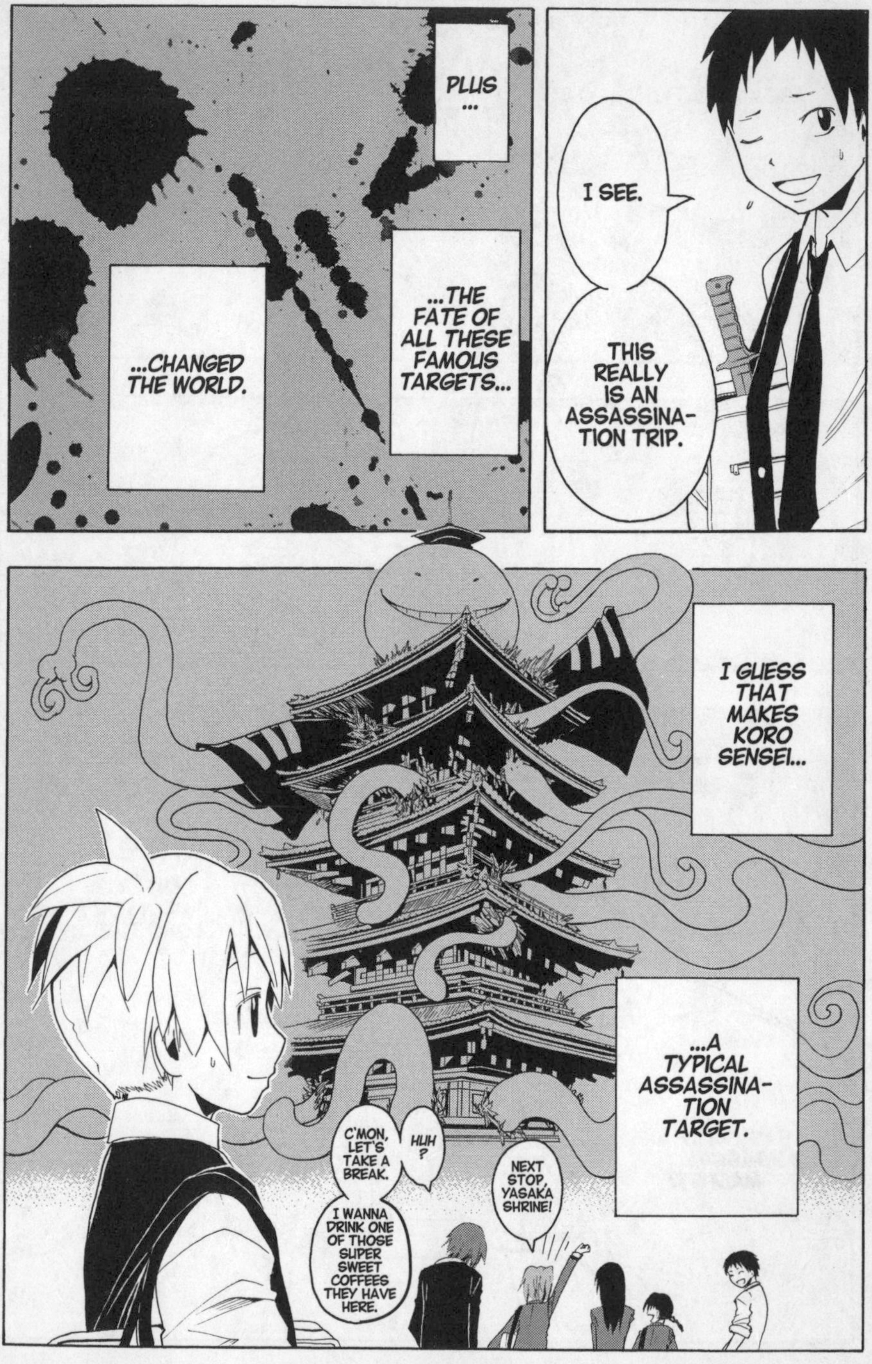
I SEE.
THIS REALLY IS AN ASSASSINATION TRIP.
PLUS...
...THE FATE OF ALL THESE FAMOUS TARGETS...
...CHANGED THE WORLD.
I GUESS THAT MAKES KORO SENSEI...
...A TYPICAL ASSASSINATION TARGET.
NEXT STOP, YASAKA SHRINE!
HUH?
C'MON, LET'S TAKE A BREAK.
I WANNA DRINK ONE OF THOSE SUPER SWEET COFFEES THEY HAVE HERE.

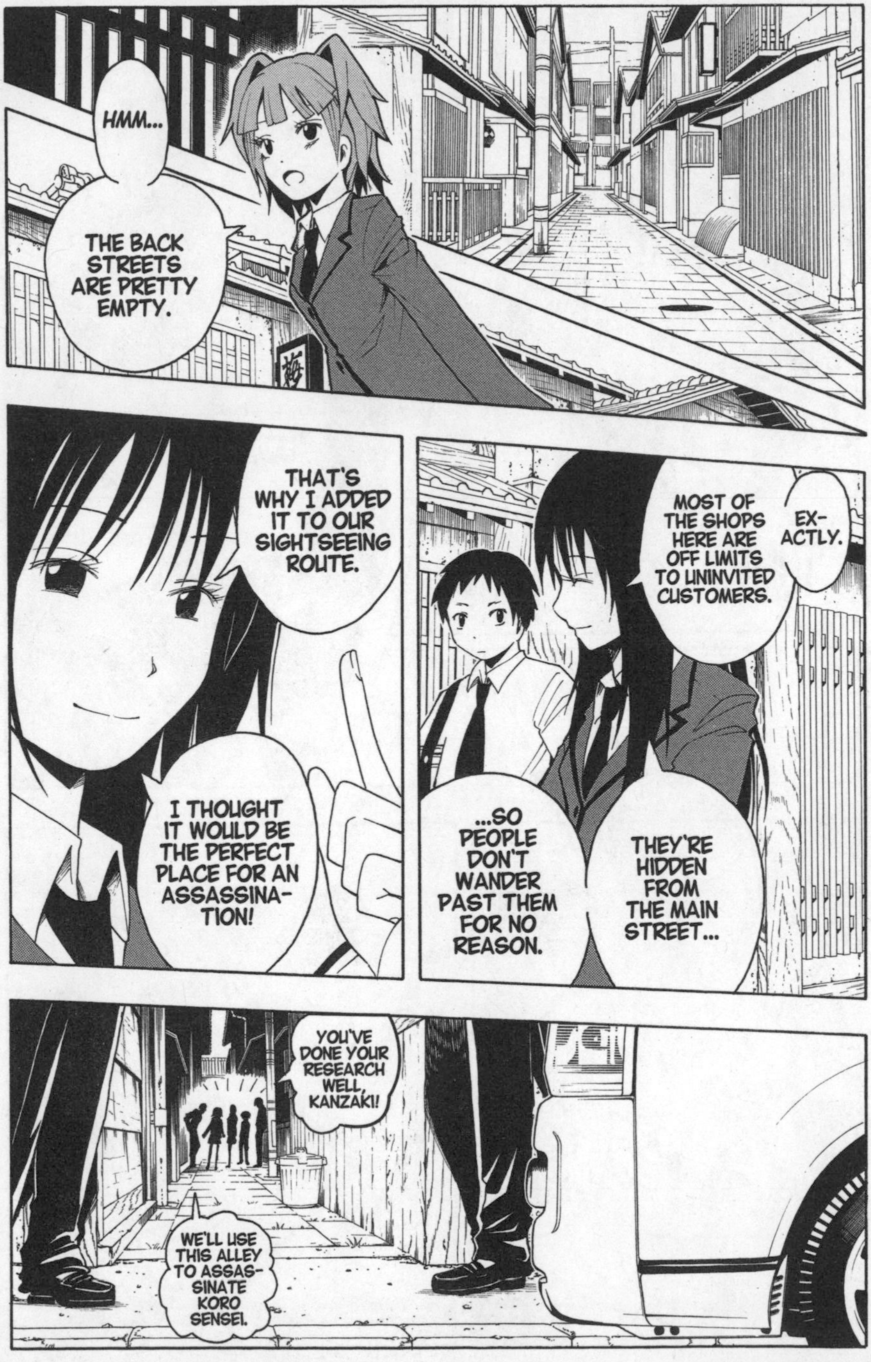
HMM...
THE BACK STREETS ARE PRETTY EMPTY.
EXACTLY.
MOST OF THE SHOPS HERE ARE OFF LIMITS TO UNINVITED CUSTOMERS.
THEY'RE HIDDEN FROM THE MAIN STREET...
...SO PEOPLE DON'T WANDER PAST THEM FOR NO REASON.
THAT'S WHY I ADDED IT TO OUR SIGHTSEEING ROUTE.
I THOUGHT IT WOULD BE THE PERFECT PLACE FOR AN ASSASSINATION!
YOU'VE DONE YOUR RESEARCH WELL, KANZAKI!
WE'LL USE THIS ALLEY TO ASSASSINATE KORO SENSEI.

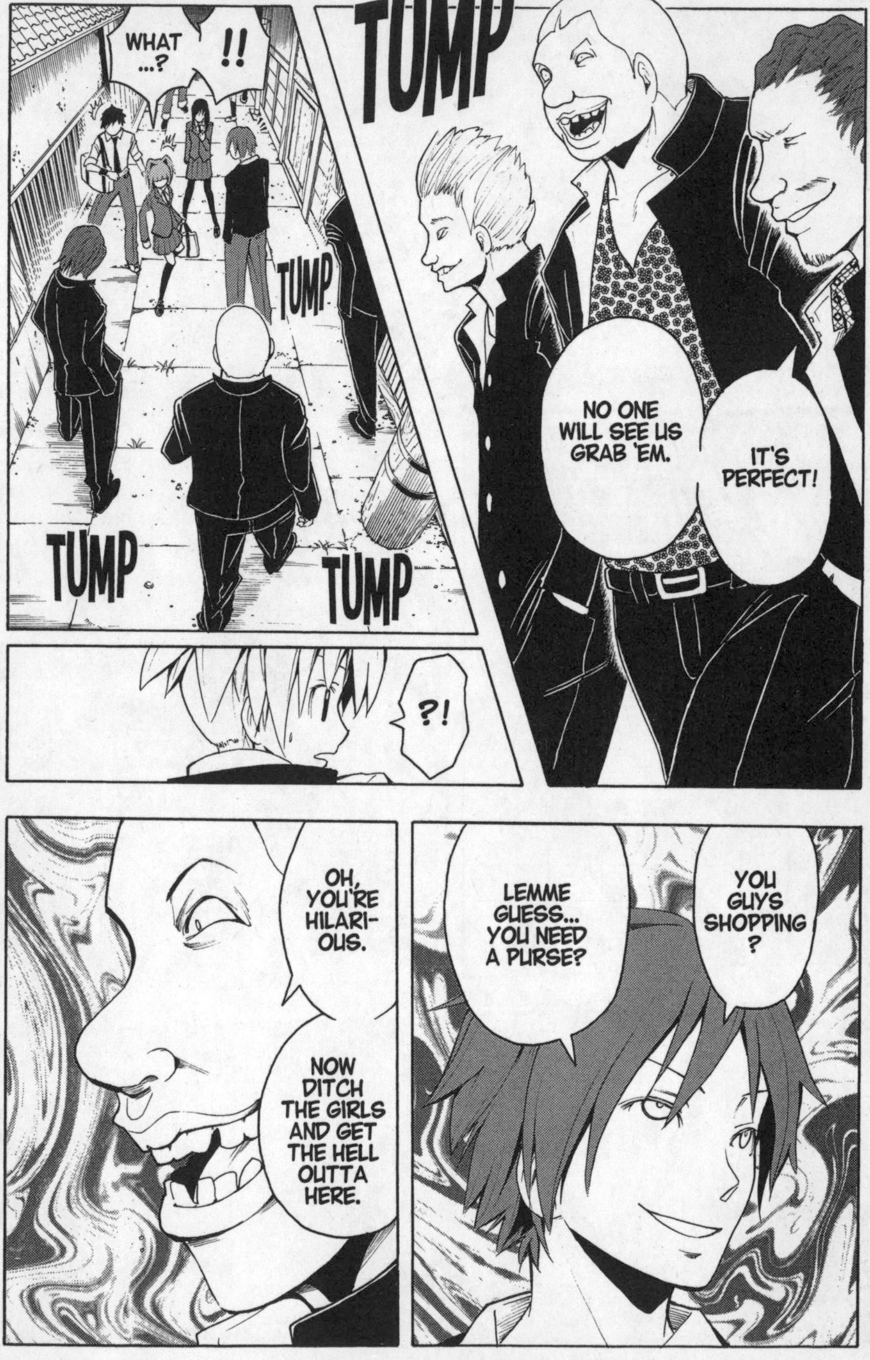
TUMP
NO ONE WILL SEE US GRAB 'EM.
IT'S PERFECT!
WHAT ...?
!!
TUMP
TUMP
TUMP
?!
YOU GUYS SHOPPING ?
LEMME GUESS... YOU NEED A PURSE?
OH, YOU'RE HILARI-OUS.
NOW DITCH THE GIRLS AND GET THE HELL OUTTA HERE.

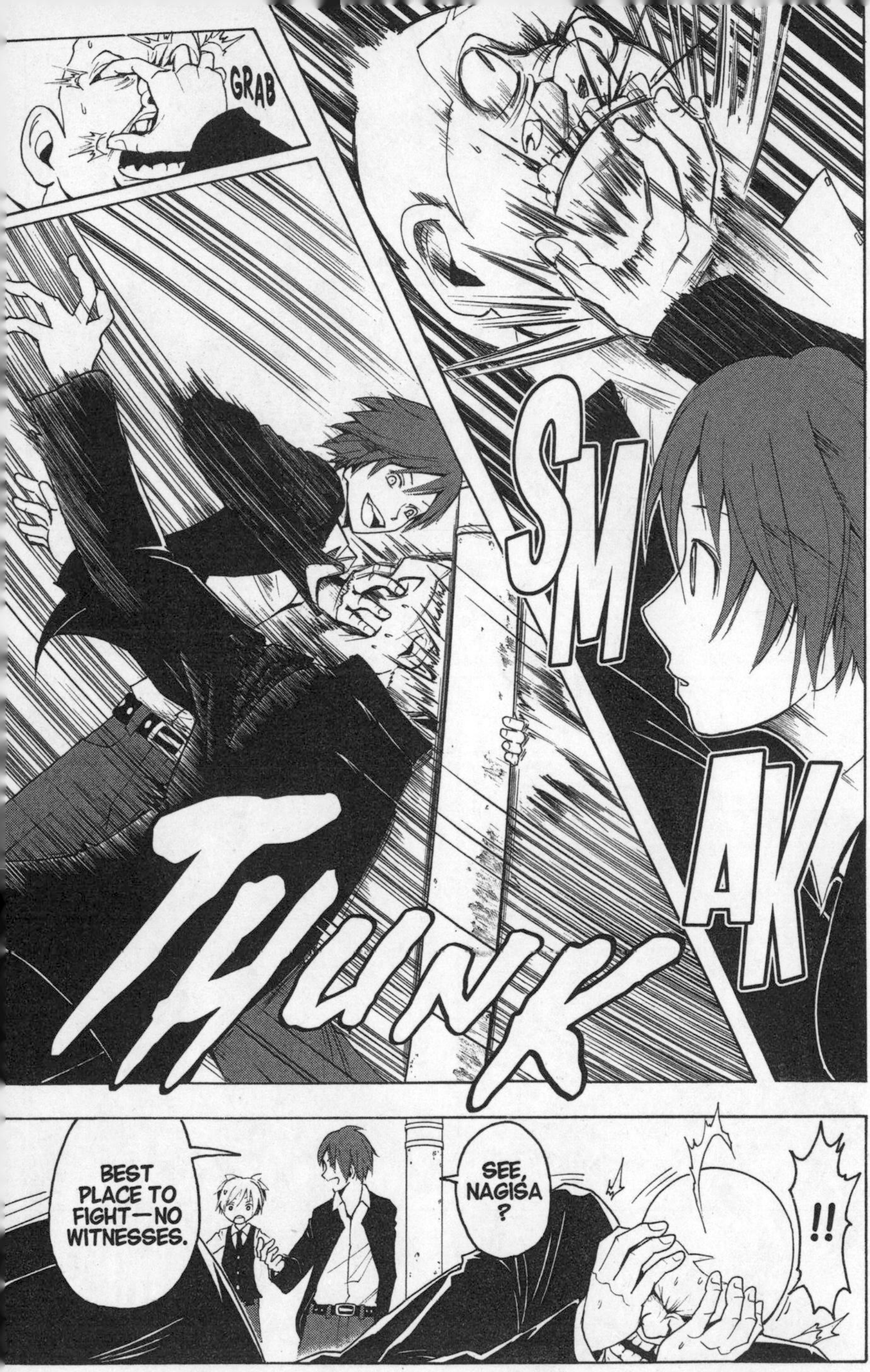
SMAK
GRAB
THUNK
!!
SEE, NAGISA?
BEST PLACE TO FIGHT—NO WITNESSES.

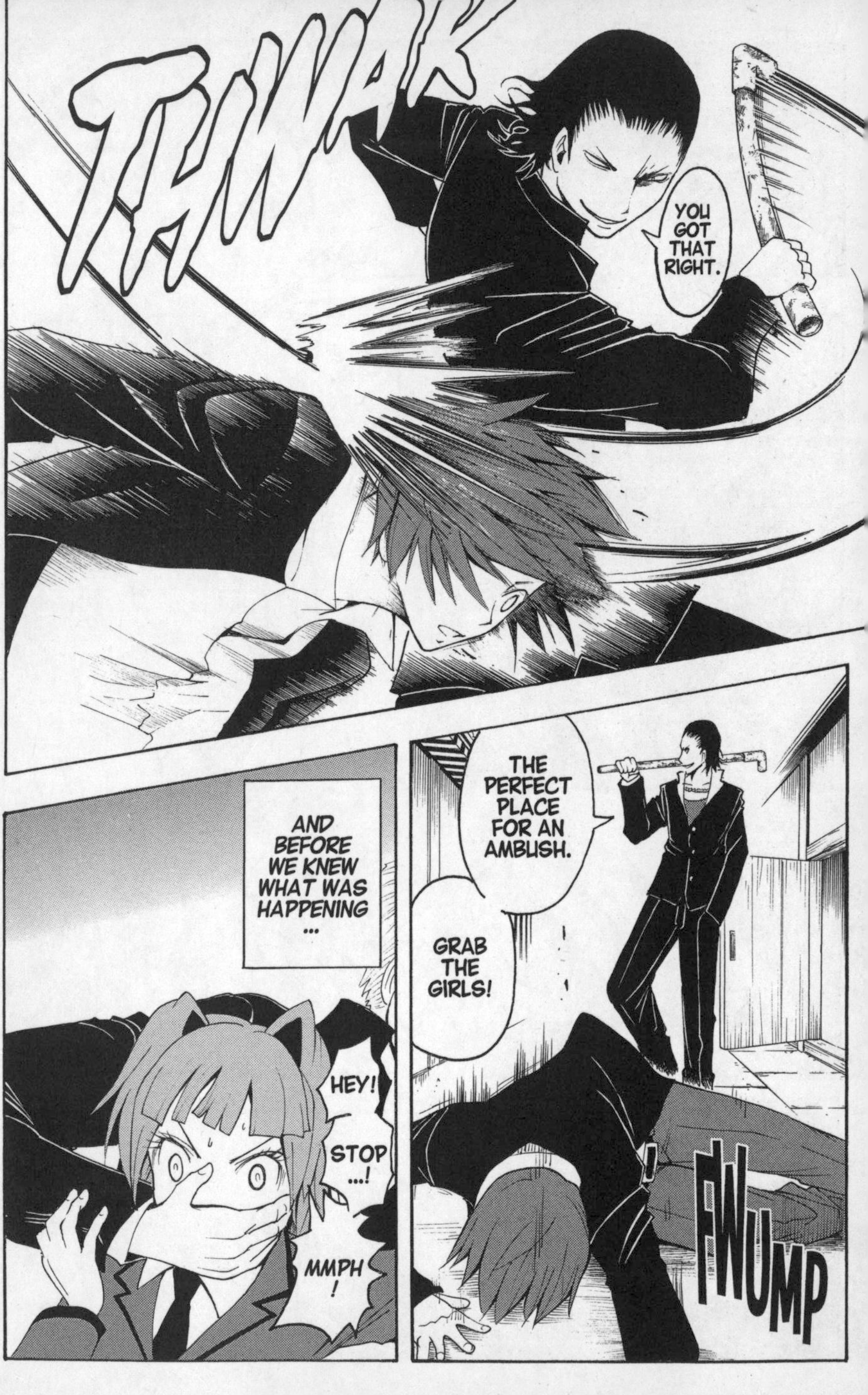
THWAK
YOU GOT THAT RIGHT.
THE PERFECT PLACE FOR AN AMBUSH.
GRAB THE GIRLS!
FWUMP
AND BEFORE WE KNEW WHAT WAS HAPPENING ...
HEY!
STOP ...!
MMPH !

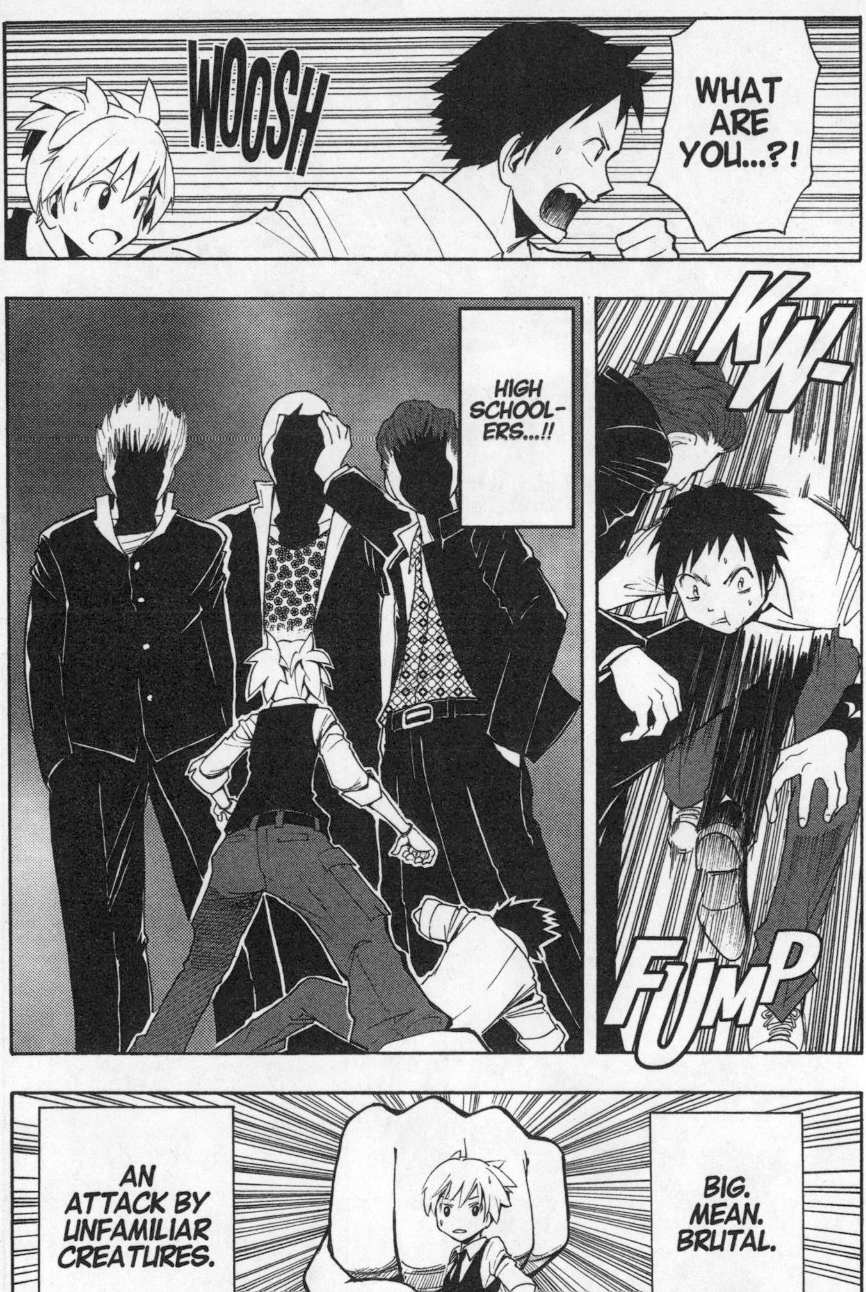
WHAT ARE YOU...?!
WOOSH
KW-
FUMP
HIGH SCHOOL-ERS...!!
BIG. MEAN. BRUTAL.
AN ATTACK BY UNFAMILIAR CREATURES.

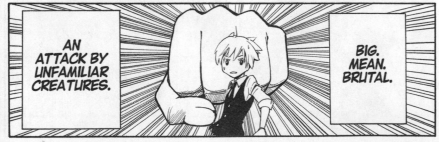

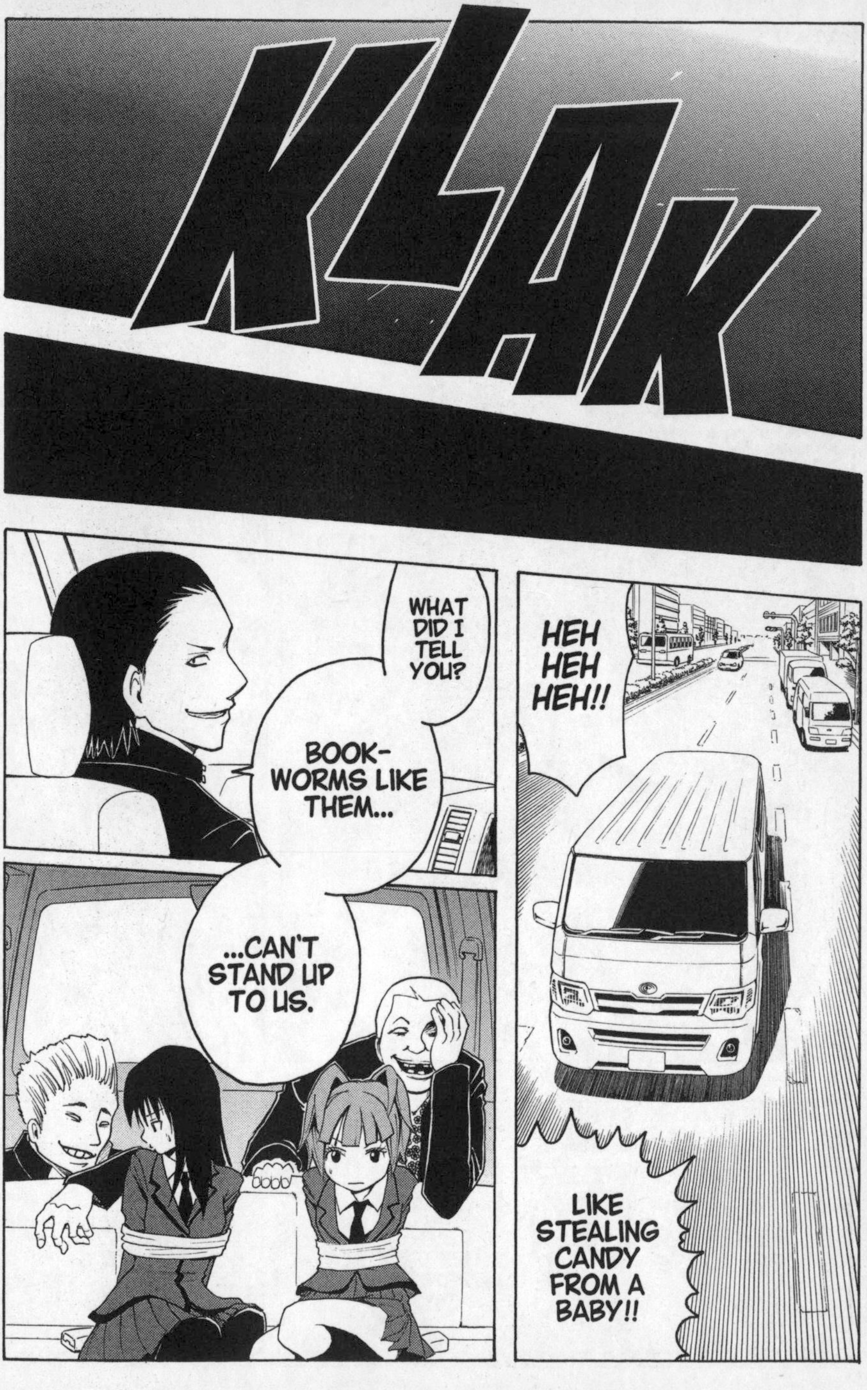
KLAK
HEH HEH HEH!!
LIKE STEALING CANDY FROM A BABY!!
WHAT DID I TELL YOU?
BOOK-WORMS LIKE THEM...
...CAN'T STAND UP TO US.

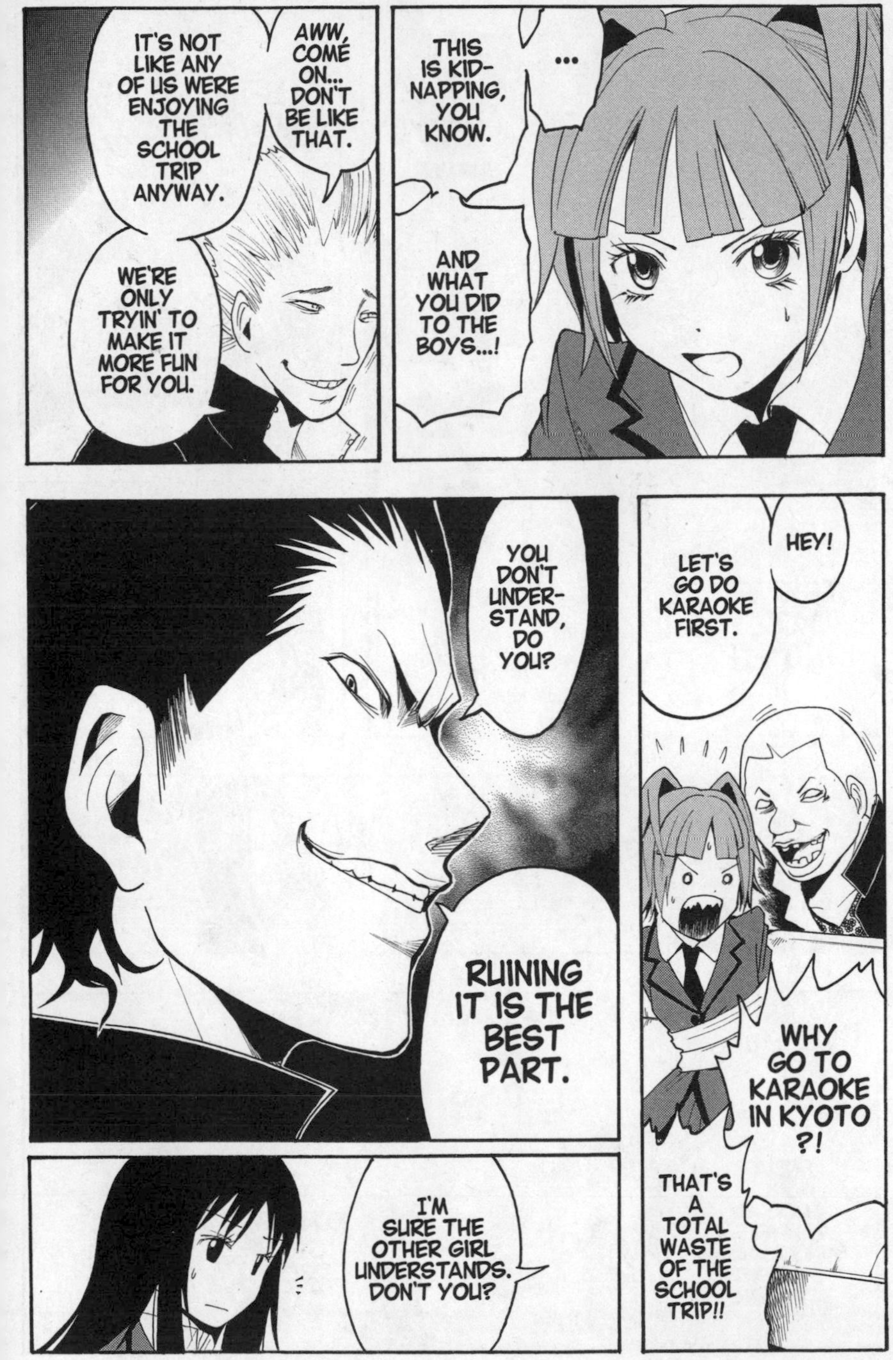
...
THIS IS KID-NAPPING, YOU KNOW.
AND WHAT YOU DID TO THE BOYS...!
AWW, COME ON... DON'T BE LIKE THAT.
IT'S NOT LIKE ANY OF US WERE ENJOYING THE SCHOOL TRIP ANYWAY.
WE'RE ONLY TRYIN' TO MAKE IT MORE FUN FOR YOU.
HEY!
LET'S GO DO KARAOKE FIRST.
WHY GO TO KARAOKE IN KYOTO?!
THAT'S A TOTAL WASTE OF THE SCHOOL TRIP!!
YOU DON'T UNDER-STAND, DO YOU?
RUINING IT IS THE BEST PART.
I'M SURE THE OTHER GIRL UNDERSTANDS. DON'T YOU?

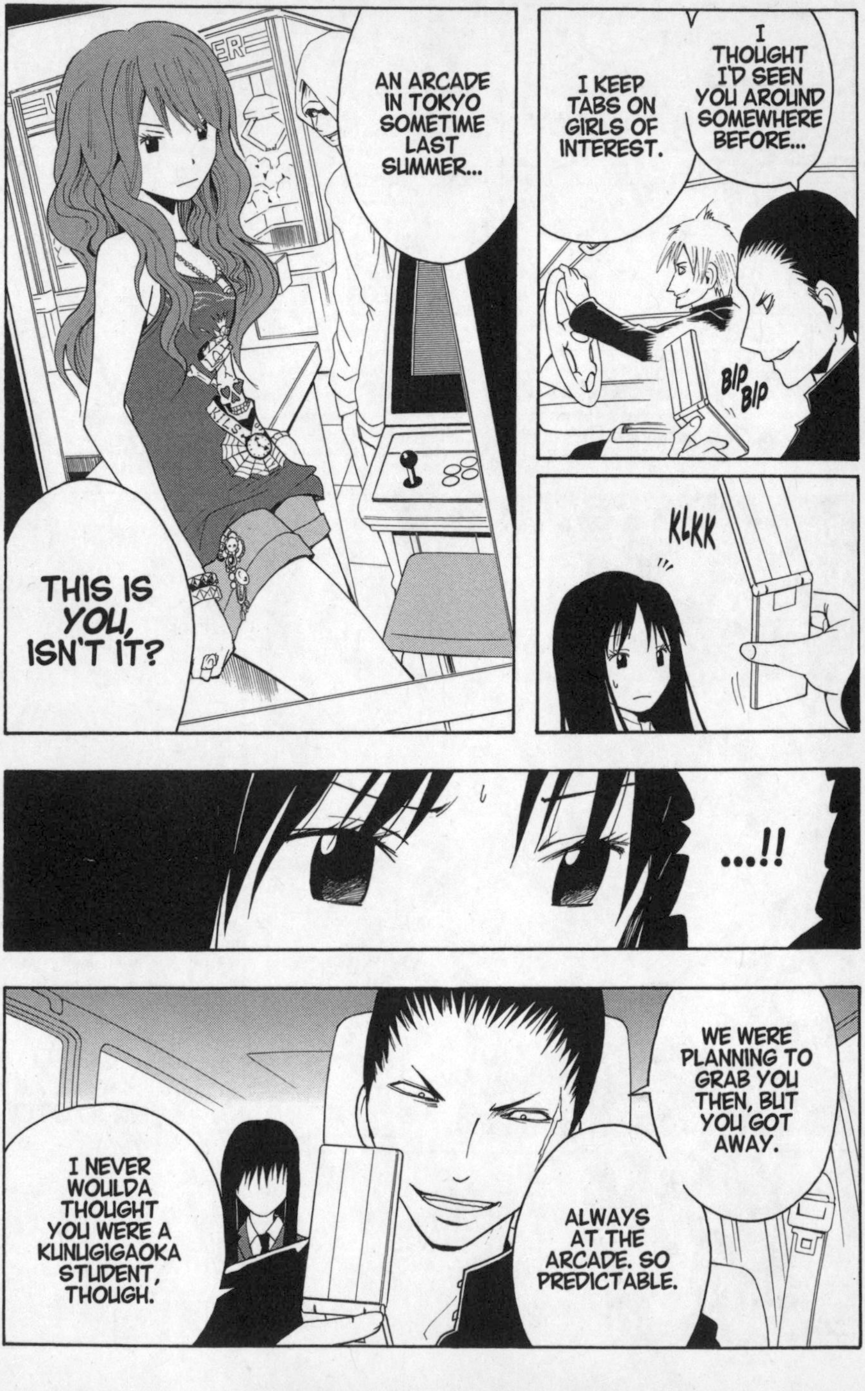
I THOUGHT I'D SEEN YOU AROUND SOMEWHERE BEFORE...
I KEEP TABS ON GIRLS OF INTEREST.
BIP BIP
KLKK
AN ARCADE IN TOKYO SOMETIME LAST SUMMER...
THIS IS *YOU*, ISN'T IT?
...!!
WE WERE PLANNING TO GRAB YOU THEN, BUT YOU GOT AWAY.
ALWAYS AT THE ARCADE. SO PREDICTABLE.
I NEVER WOULDA THOUGHT YOU WERE A KUNUGIGAOKA STUDENT, THOUGH.

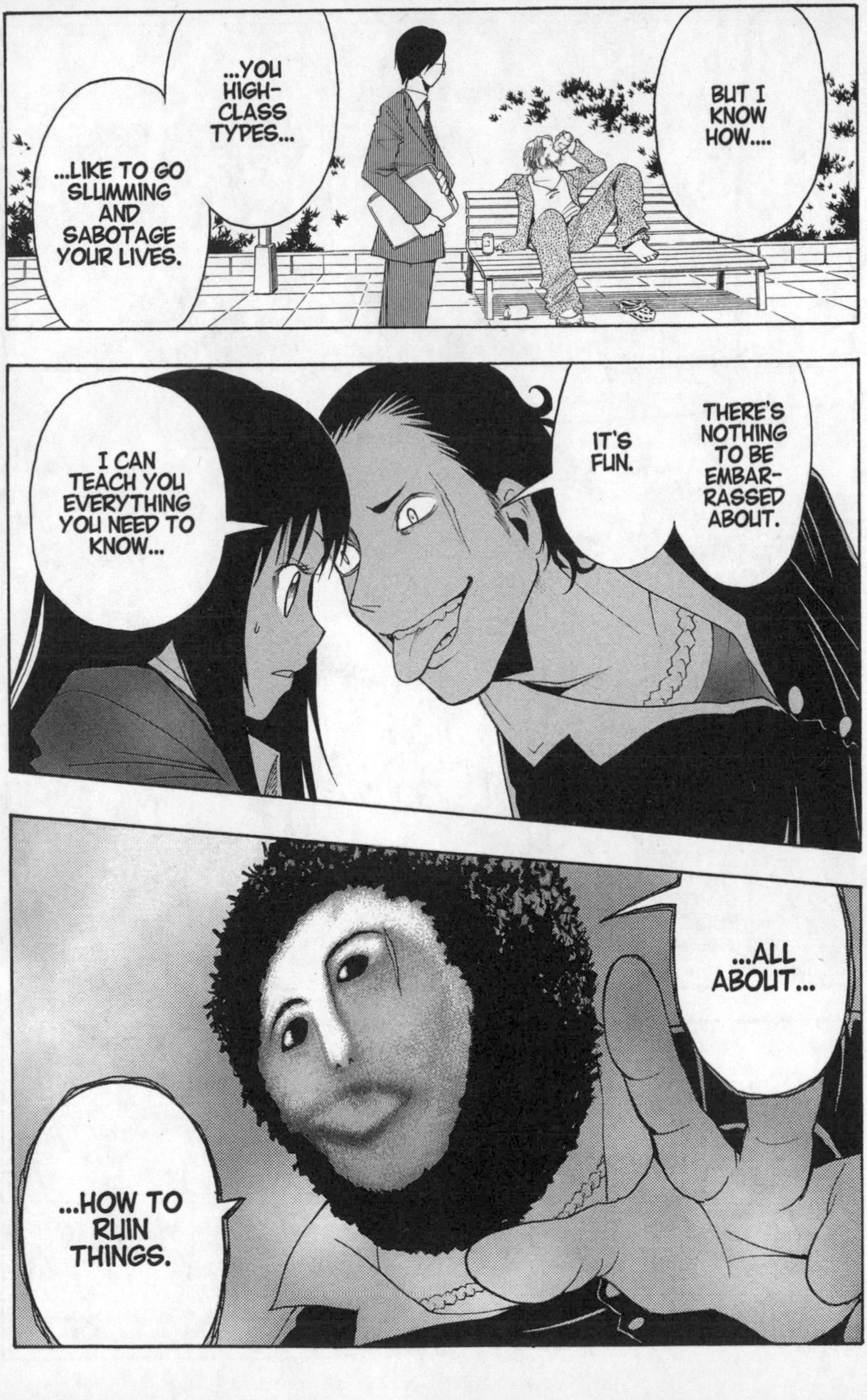

BUT I KNOW HOW....
...YOU HIGH-CLASS TYPES...
...LIKE TO GO SLUMMING AND SABOTAGE YOUR LIVES.
THERE'S NOTHING TO BE EMBARRASSED ABOUT.
IT'S FUN.
I CAN TEACH YOU EVERYTHING YOU NEED TO KNOW...
...ALL ABOUT...
...HOW TO RUIN THINGS.

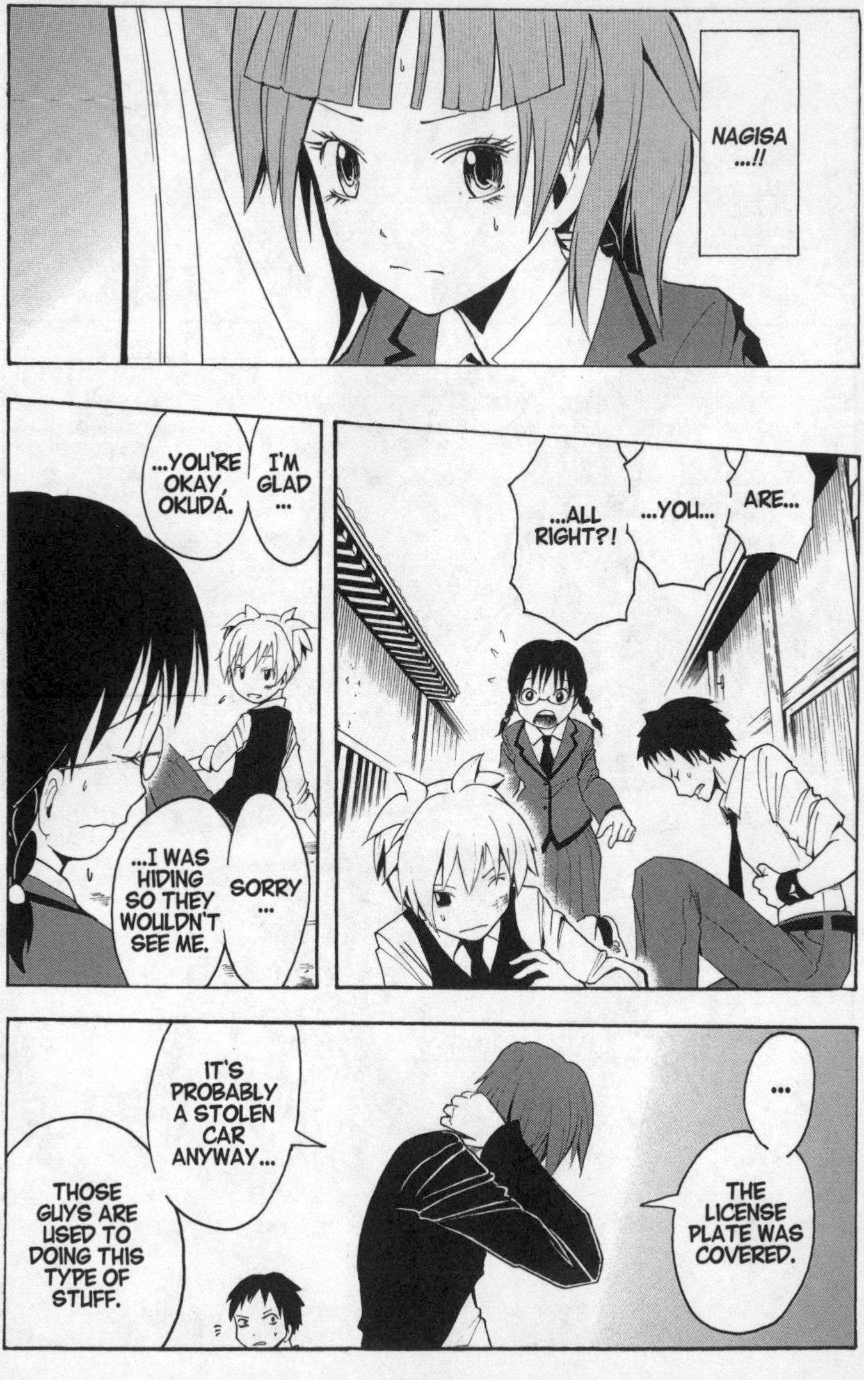
NAGISA ...!!
ARE...
...YOU...
...ALL RIGHT?!
I'M GLAD ...
...YOU'RE OKAY, OKUDA.
SORRY ...
...I WAS HIDING SO THEY WOULDN'T SEE ME.
...
THE LICENSE PLATE WAS COVERED.
IT'S PROBABLY A STOLEN CAR ANYWAY...
THOSE GUYS ARE USED TO DOING THIS TYPE OF STUFF.

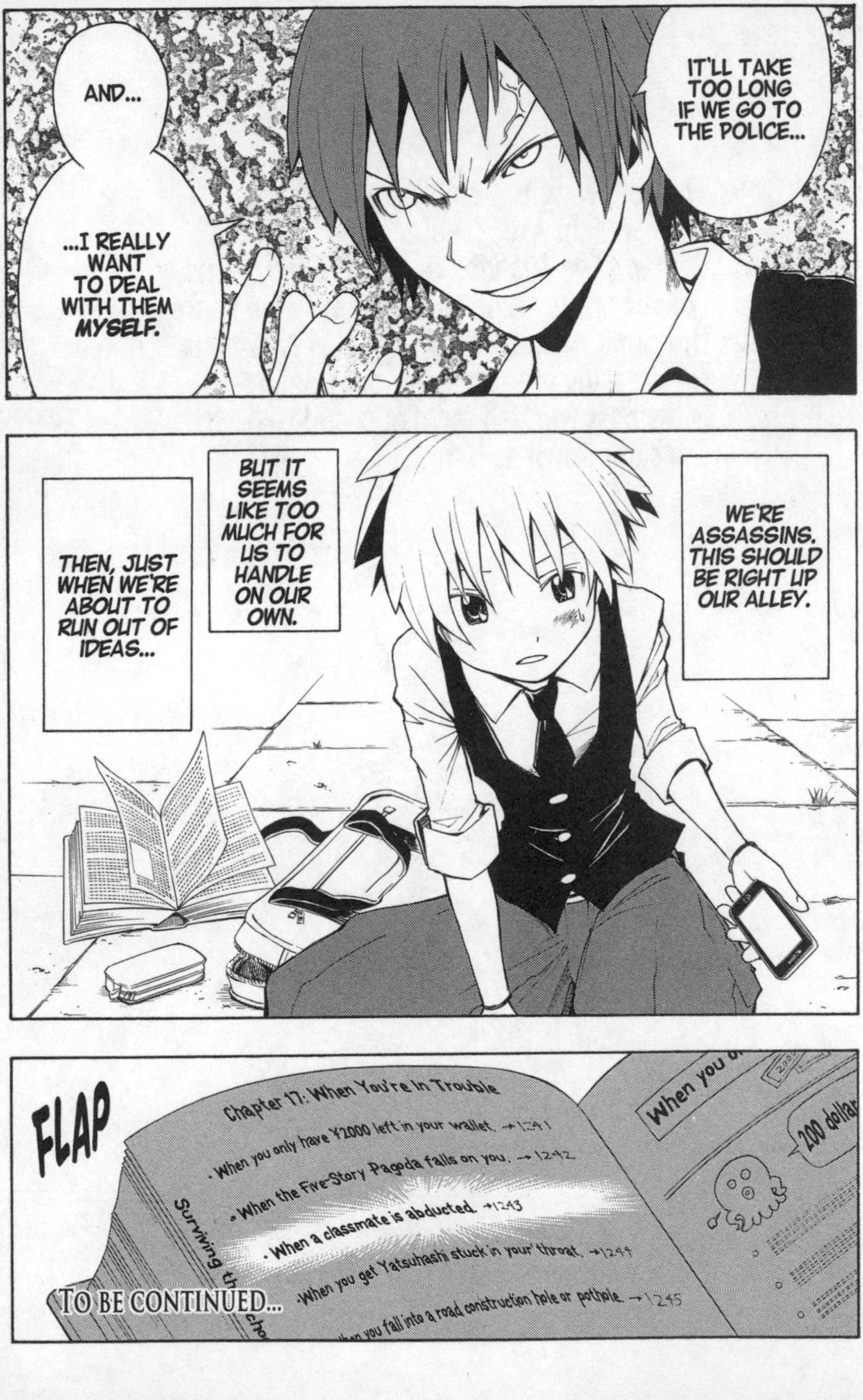
IT'LL TAKE TOO LONG IF WE GO TO THE POLICE...
AND...
...I REALLY WANT TO DEAL WITH THEM *MYSELF*.
WE'RE ASSASSINS. THIS SHOULD BE RIGHT UP OUR ALLEY.
BUT IT SEEMS LIKE TOO MUCH FOR US TO HANDLE ON OUR OWN.
THEN, JUST WHEN WE'RE ABOUT TO RUN OUT OF IDEAS...
FLAP
Chapter 17: When You're In Trouble
·When you only have ¥2000 left in your wallet. →1241
·When the Five-Story Pagoda falls on you. →1242
·When a classmate is abducted. →1243
·When you get Yatsuhashi stuck in your throat. →1244
hen you fall into a road construction hole or pothole. →1245
TO BE CONTINUED...

The following is a collaboration manga with Shuichi Aso, creator of *Saiki Kusuo No Sainan* (*The Mishaps of Kusuo Saiki*). This collaboration came to be because we share the same hometown. Aso Sensei is famous for creating great manga, but I believe this is his best work so far. I'm proud to be from the same town as him.

A change of uniform.

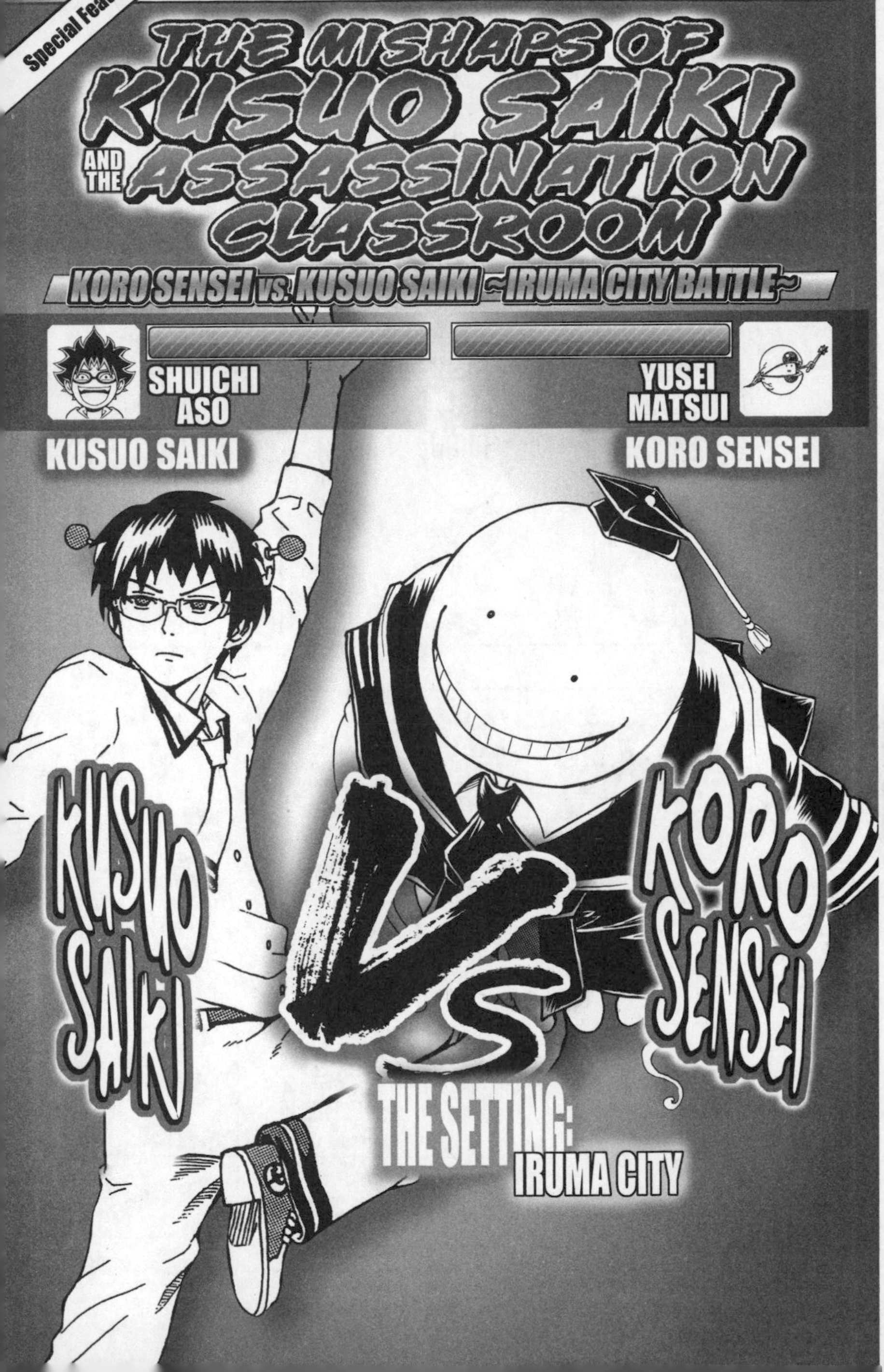
THE MISHAPS OF KUSUO SAIKI AND THE ASSASSINATION CLASSROOM
KORO SENSEI vs. KUSUO SAIKI ~IRUMA CITY BATTLE~
SHUICHI ASO
KUSUO SAIKI
YUSEI MATSUI
KORO SENSEI
KUSUO SAIKI
VS
KORO SENSEI
THE SETTING: IRUMA CITY

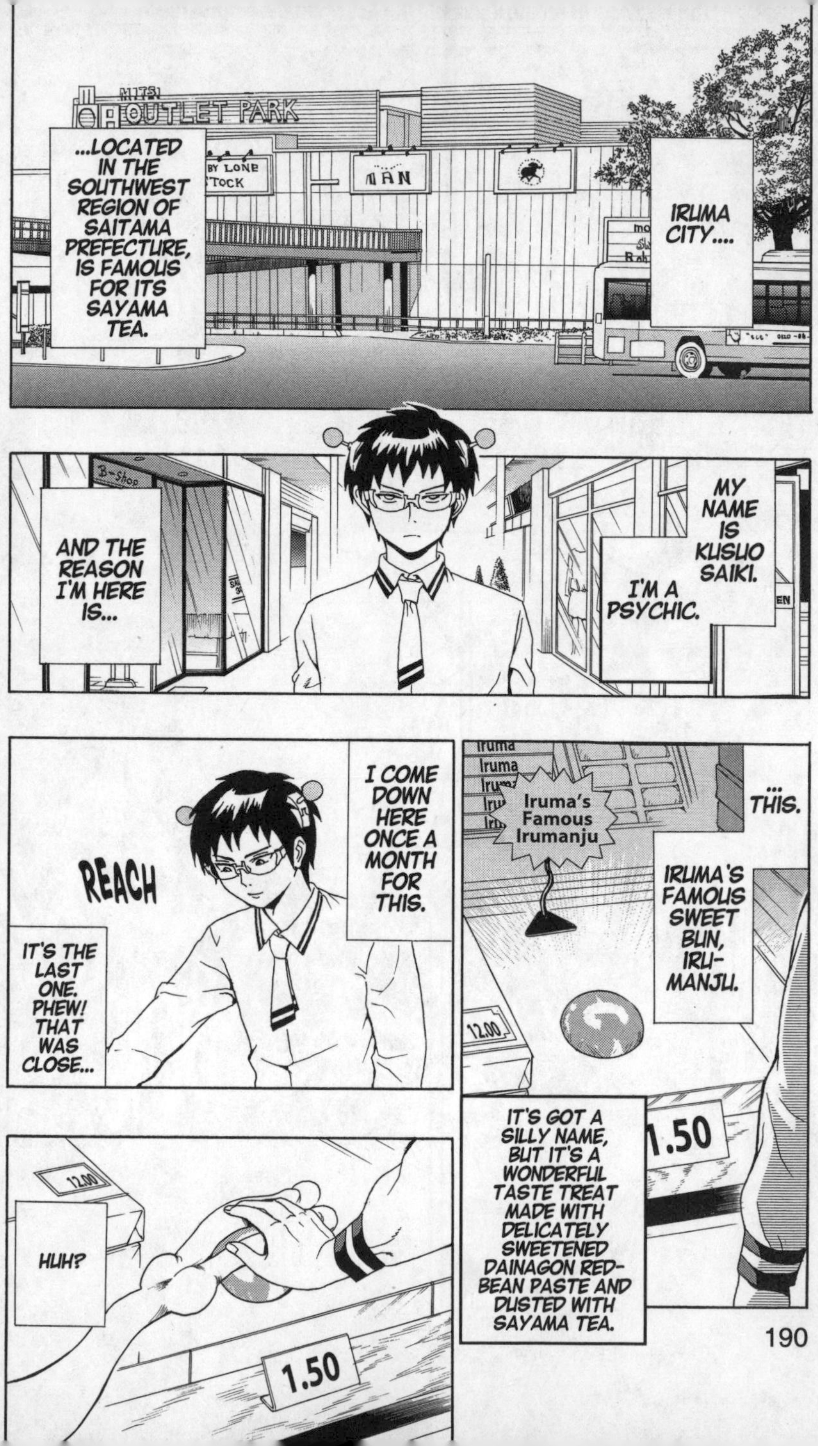
OUTLET PARK
IRUMA CITY....
...LOCATED IN THE SOUTHWEST REGION OF SAITAMA PREFECTURE, IS FAMOUS FOR ITS SAYAMA TEA.
MY NAME IS KUSUO SAIKI.
I'M A PSYCHIC.
AND THE REASON I'M HERE IS...
Iruma's Famous Irumanju
...THIS.
IRUMA'S FAMOUS SWEET BUN, IRU-MANJU.
12.00
IT'S GOT A SILLY NAME, BUT IT'S A WONDERFUL TASTE TREAT MADE WITH DELICATELY SWEETENED DAINAGON RED-BEAN PASTE AND DUSTED WITH SAYAMA TEA.
1.50
I COME DOWN HERE ONCE A MONTH FOR THIS.
REACH
IT'S THE LAST ONE. PHEW! THAT WAS CLOSE...
12.00
HUH?
1.50

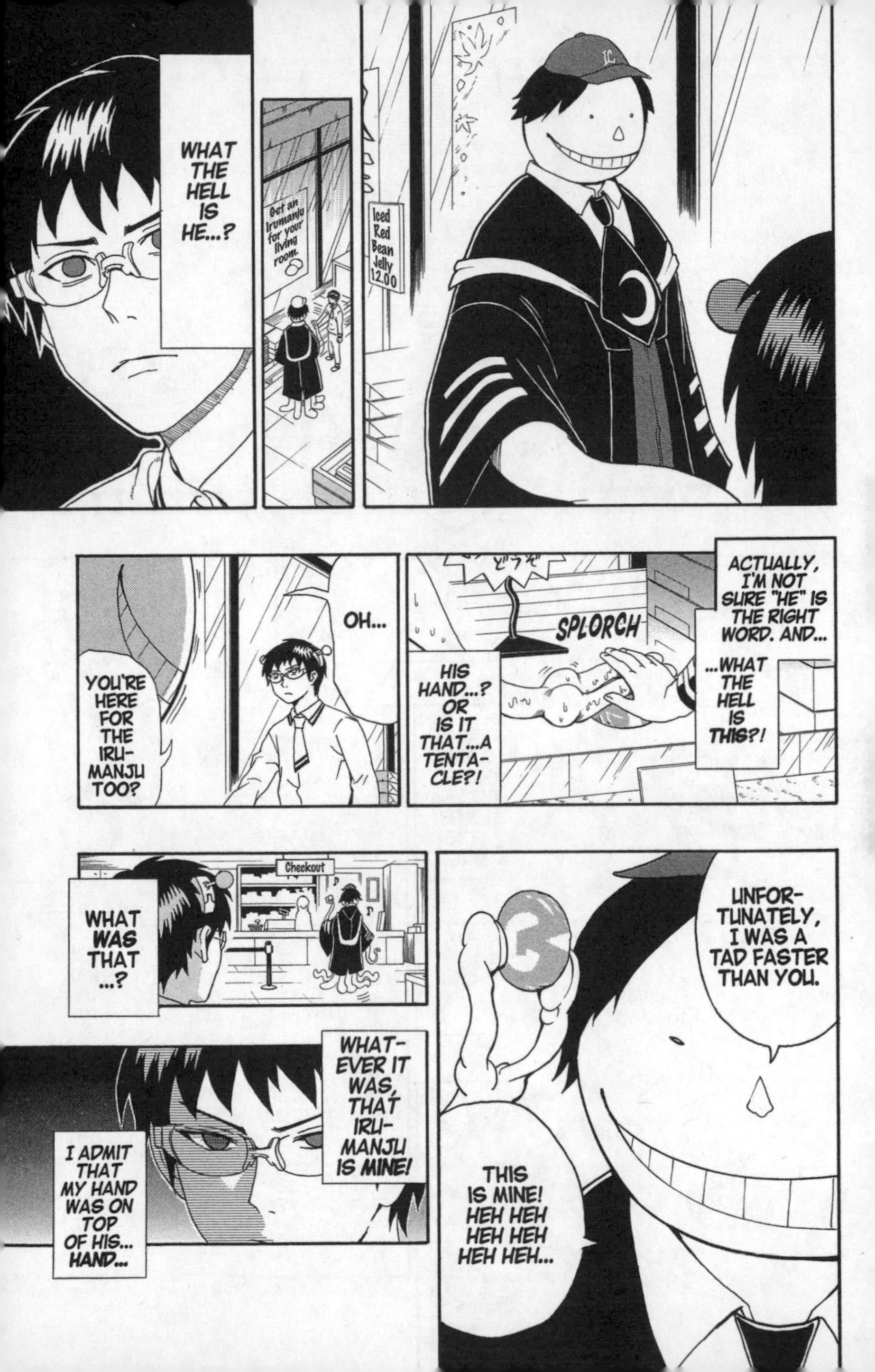
Get an Irumanju for your living room.
Iced Red Bean Jelly 12.00
WHAT THE HELL IS HE...?
ACTUALLY, I'M NOT SURE "HE" IS THE RIGHT WORD. AND...
...WHAT THE HELL IS THIS?!
SPLORCH
HIS HAND...? OR IS IT THAT...A TENTACLE?!
OH...
YOU'RE HERE FOR THE IRUMANJU TOO?
UNFORTUNATELY, I WAS A TAD FASTER THAN YOU.
THIS IS MINE! HEH HEH HEH HEH HEH HEH...
Checkout
WHAT WAS THAT...?
WHATEVER IT WAS, THAT IRUMANJU IS MINE!
I ADMIT THAT MY HAND WAS ON TOP OF HIS... HAND...

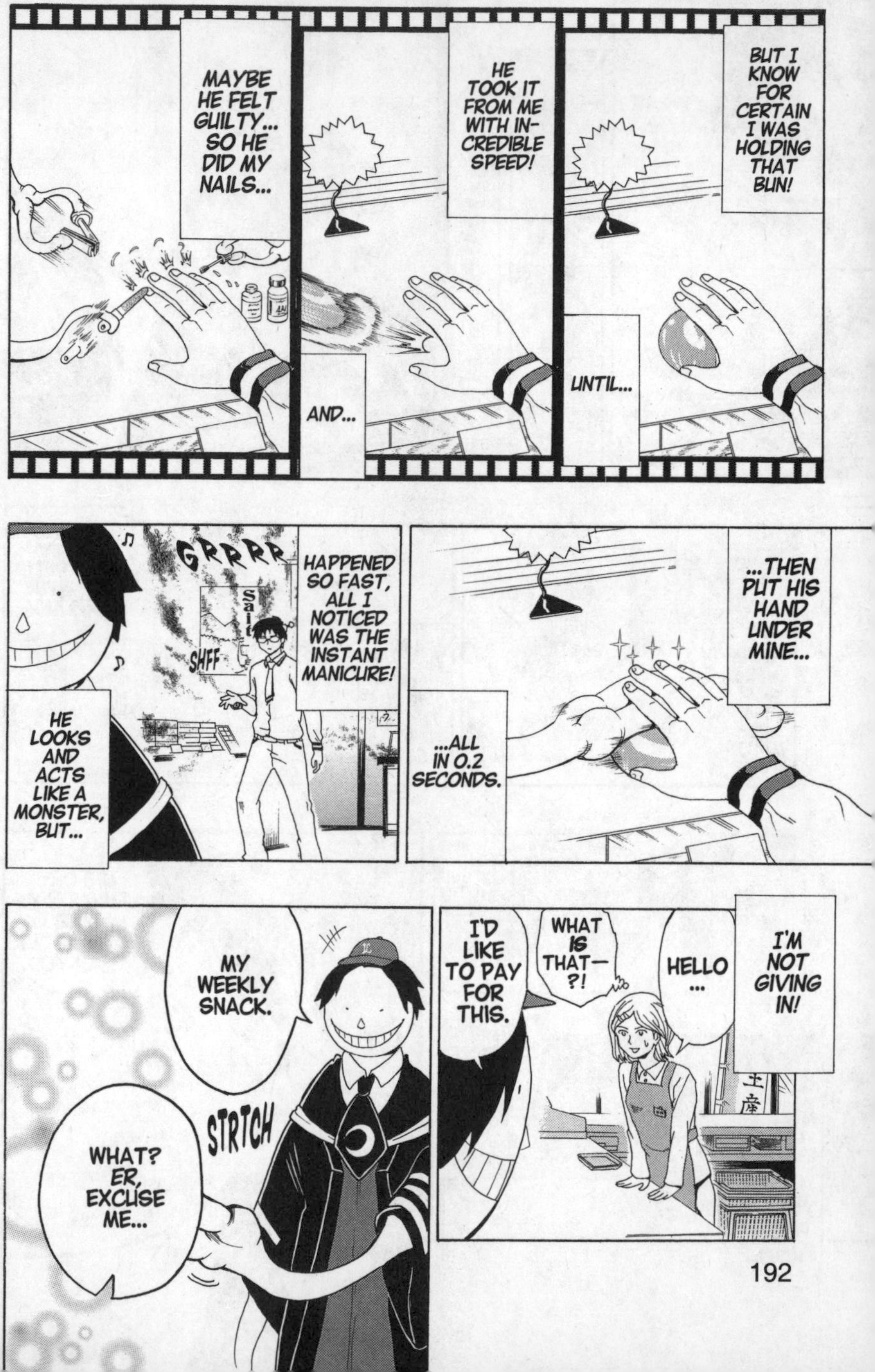
BUT I KNOW FOR CERTAIN I WAS HOLDING THAT BUN!
UNTIL...
HE TOOK IT FROM ME WITH INCREDIBLE SPEED!
AND...
MAYBE HE FELT GUILTY... SO HE DID MY NAILS...
...THEN PUT HIS HAND UNDER MINE...
...ALL IN 0.2 SECONDS.
HAPPENED SO FAST, ALL I NOTICED WAS THE INSTANT MANICURE!
GRRRR
SHFF
HE LOOKS AND ACTS LIKE A MONSTER, BUT...
I'M NOT GIVING IN!
HELLO...
WHAT IS THAT—?!
I'D LIKE TO PAY FOR THIS.
MY WEEKLY SNACK.
STRTCH
WHAT? ER, EXCUSE ME...

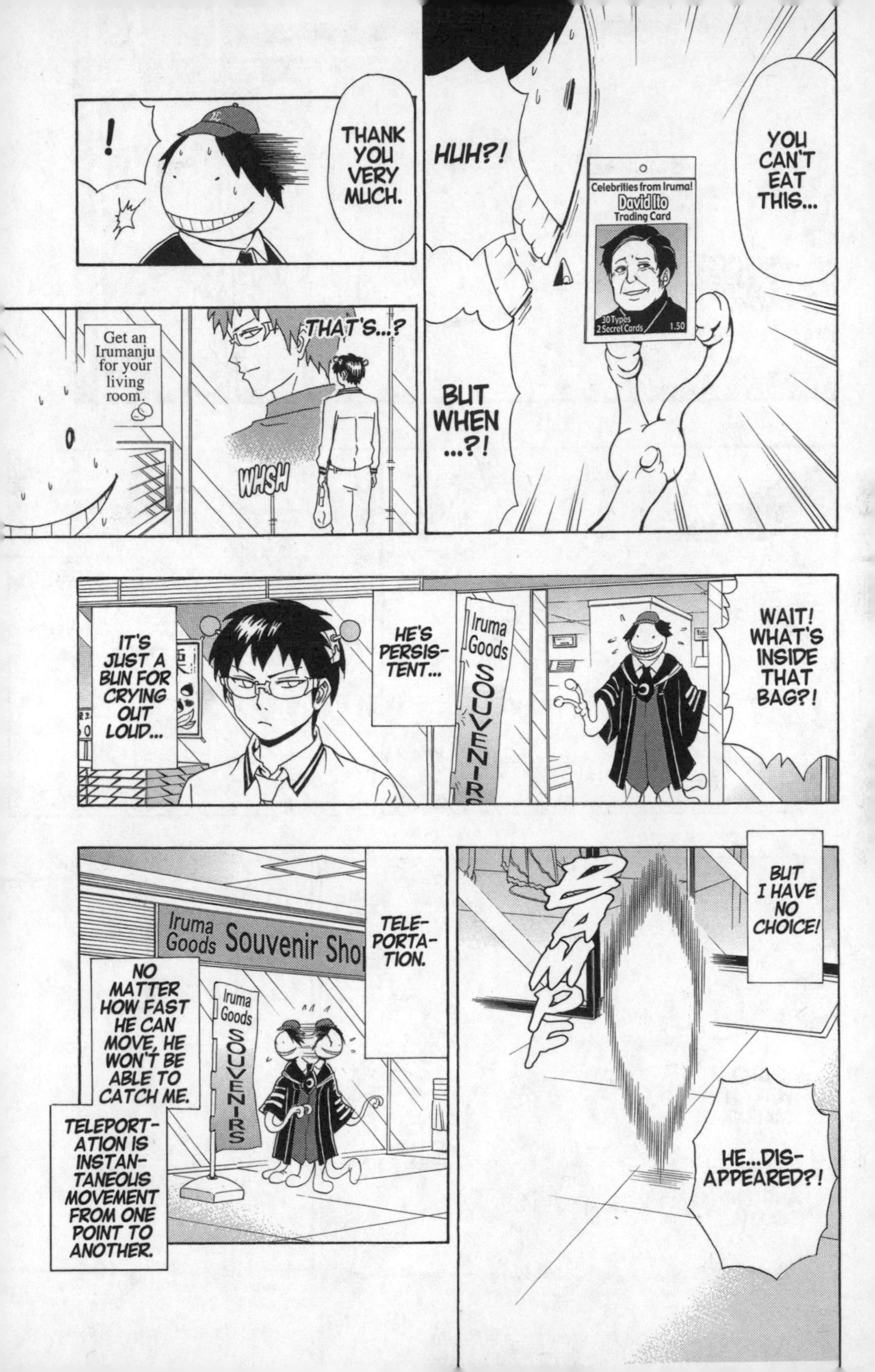
YOU CAN'T EAT THIS...
Celebrities from Iruma!
David Ito
Trading Card
30 Types
2 Secret Cards
1.50
HUH?!
BUT WHEN ...?!
THANK YOU VERY MUCH.
!
THAT'S...?
Get an Irumanju for your living room.
WHSH
WAIT! WHAT'S INSIDE THAT BAG?!
HE'S PERSIS-TENT...
Iruma Goods
SOUVENIRS
IT'S JUST A BUN FOR CRYING OUT LOUD...
BUT I HAVE NO CHOICE!
BAMPF
HE...DIS-APPEARED?!
TELE-PORTA-TION.
Iruma Goods Souvenir Shop
NO MATTER HOW FAST HE CAN MOVE, HE WON'T BE ABLE TO CATCH ME.
Iruma Goods
SOUVENIRS
TELEPORT-ATION IS INSTAN-TANEOUS MOVEMENT FROM ONE POINT TO ANOTHER.

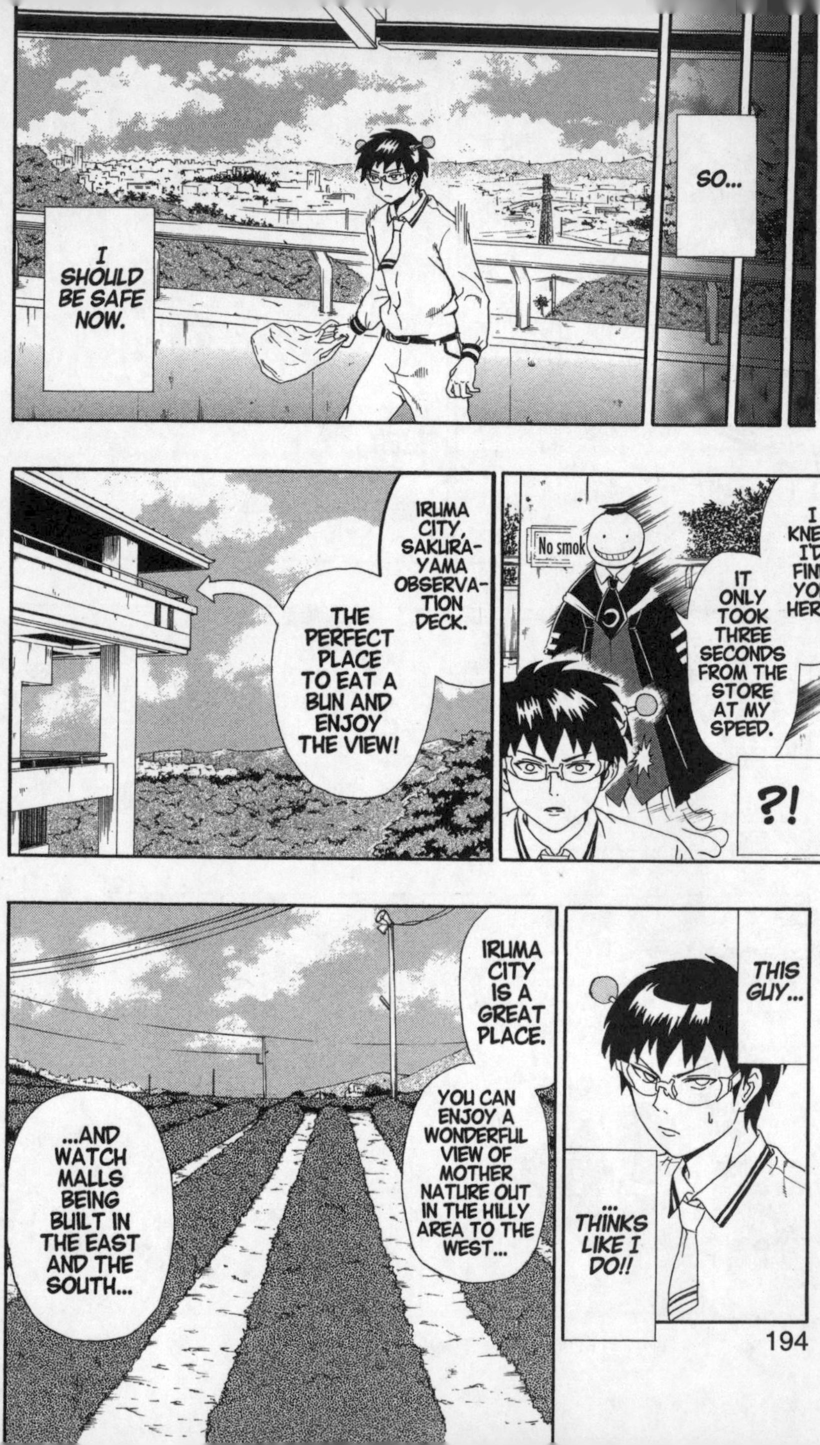
SO...
I SHOULD BE SAFE NOW.
No smok
I KNEW I'D FIND YOU HERE.
IT ONLY TOOK THREE SECONDS FROM THE STORE AT MY SPEED.
?!
IRUMA CITY, SAKURA-YAMA OBSERVATION DECK.
THE PERFECT PLACE TO EAT A BUN AND ENJOY THE VIEW!
THIS GUY...
...THINKS LIKE I DO!!
IRUMA CITY IS A GREAT PLACE.
YOU CAN ENJOY A WONDERFUL VIEW OF MOTHER NATURE OUT IN THE HILLY AREA TO THE WEST...
...AND WATCH MALLS BEING BUILT IN THE EAST AND THE SOUTH...

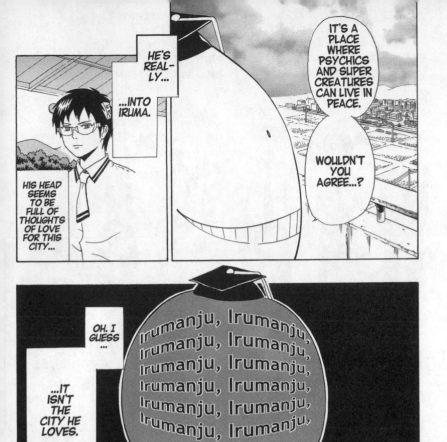

IT'S A PLACE WHERE PSYCHICS AND SUPER CREATURES CAN LIVE IN PEACE.

HE'S REAL—LY...

...INTO IRUMA.

WOULDN'T YOU AGREE...?

HIS HEAD SEEMS TO BE FULL OF THOUGHTS OF LOVE FOR THIS CITY...

OH, I GUESS...

...IT ISN'T THE CITY HE LOVES.

Irumanju, Irumanju, Irumanju, Irumanju, Irumanju, Irumanju, Irumanju, Irumanju, Irumanju, Irumanju, Irumanju, Irumanju, Irumanju, Irumanju, Irumanju.

YOU'RE GIVING ME HALF THE BUN?!

OH?!

SHFF

...

ME TOO.

IT'S LIKE YOU READ MY MIND!

-IRUMA CITY BATTLE- (THE END)

Character Designs

This is the illustration we use for the clothing and tones of the main characters. Their seating arrangement is also written here.

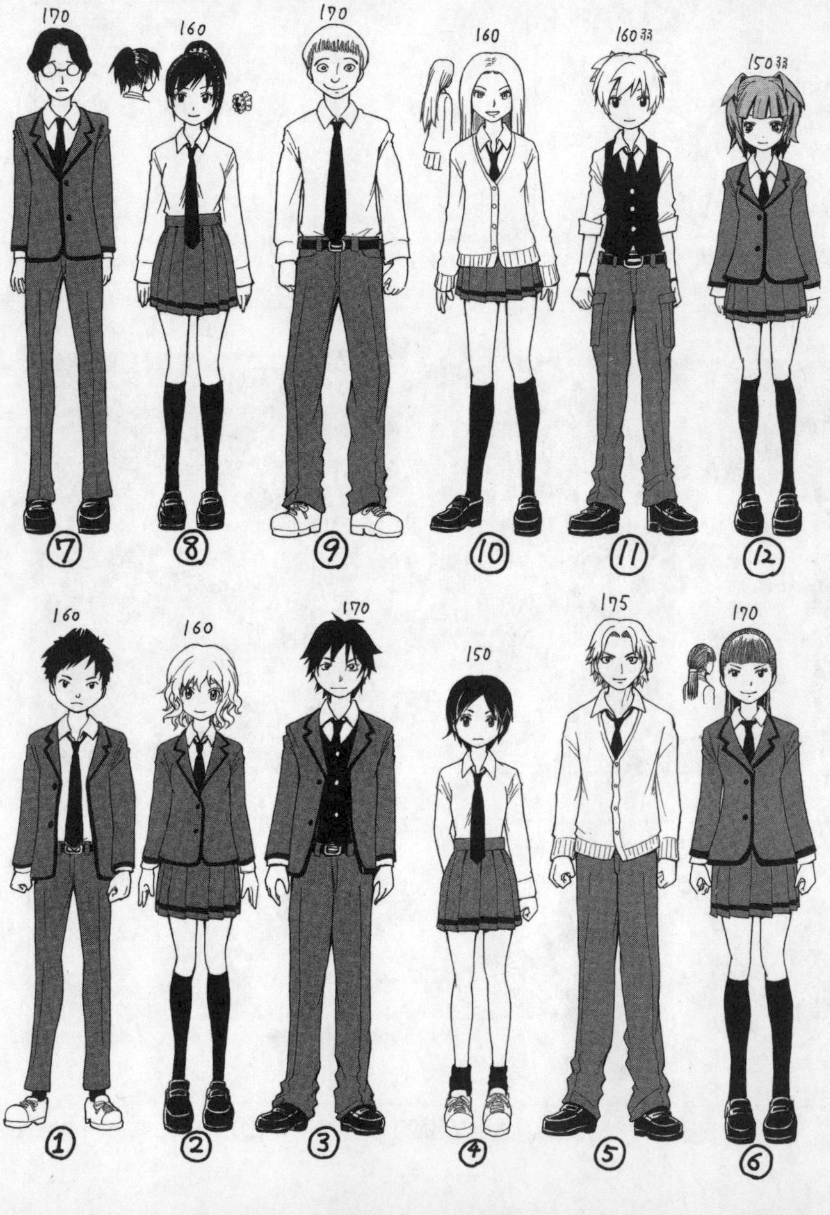

170
160
170
160
160
150
⑦
⑧
⑨
⑩
⑪
⑫
160
160
170
150
175
170
①
②
③
④
⑤
⑥

This is a story about the whole class, so creating a character sheet is a must. Many of the characters only appear as bit players, so I try to be careful not to give them too unique an appearance.

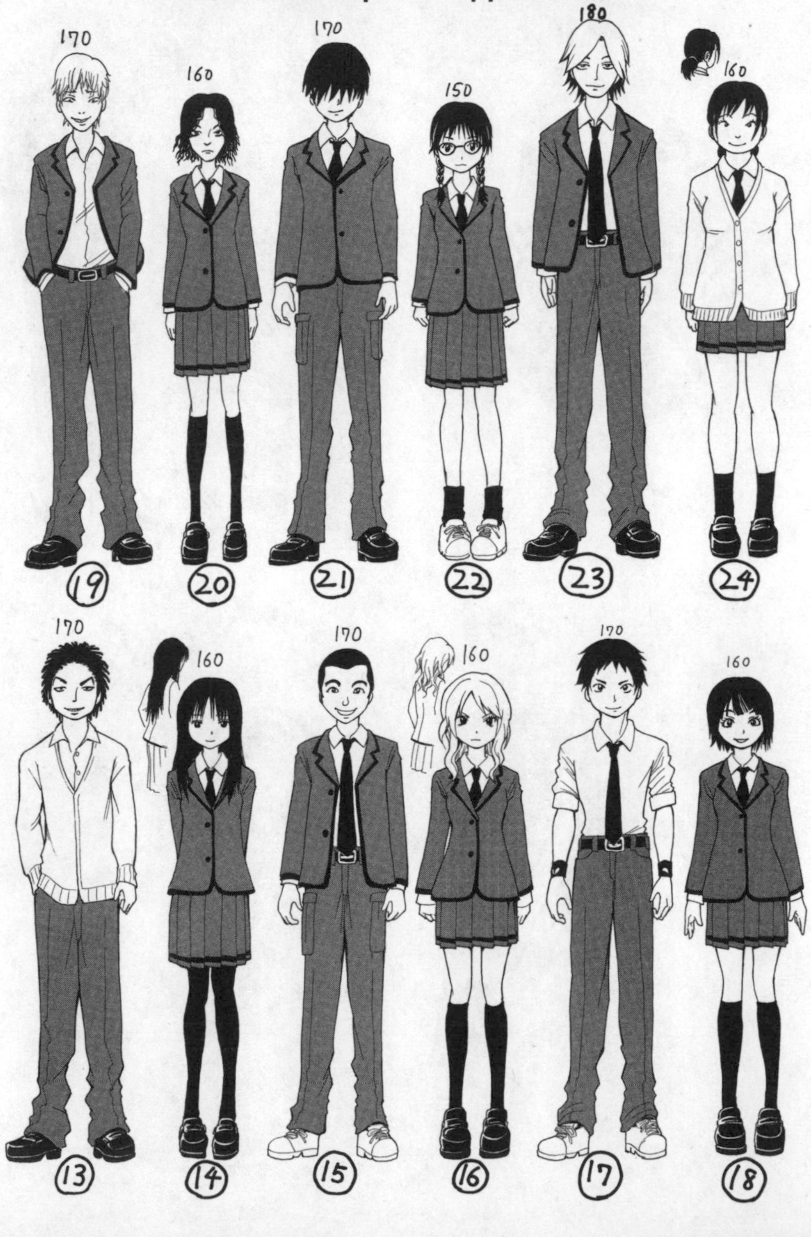
170
19
160
20
170
21
150
22
180
23
160
24
170
13
160
14
170
15
160
16
170
17
160
18

Koro Sensei has shoulders now!!
Some of the details of the characters
change as the story unfolds.

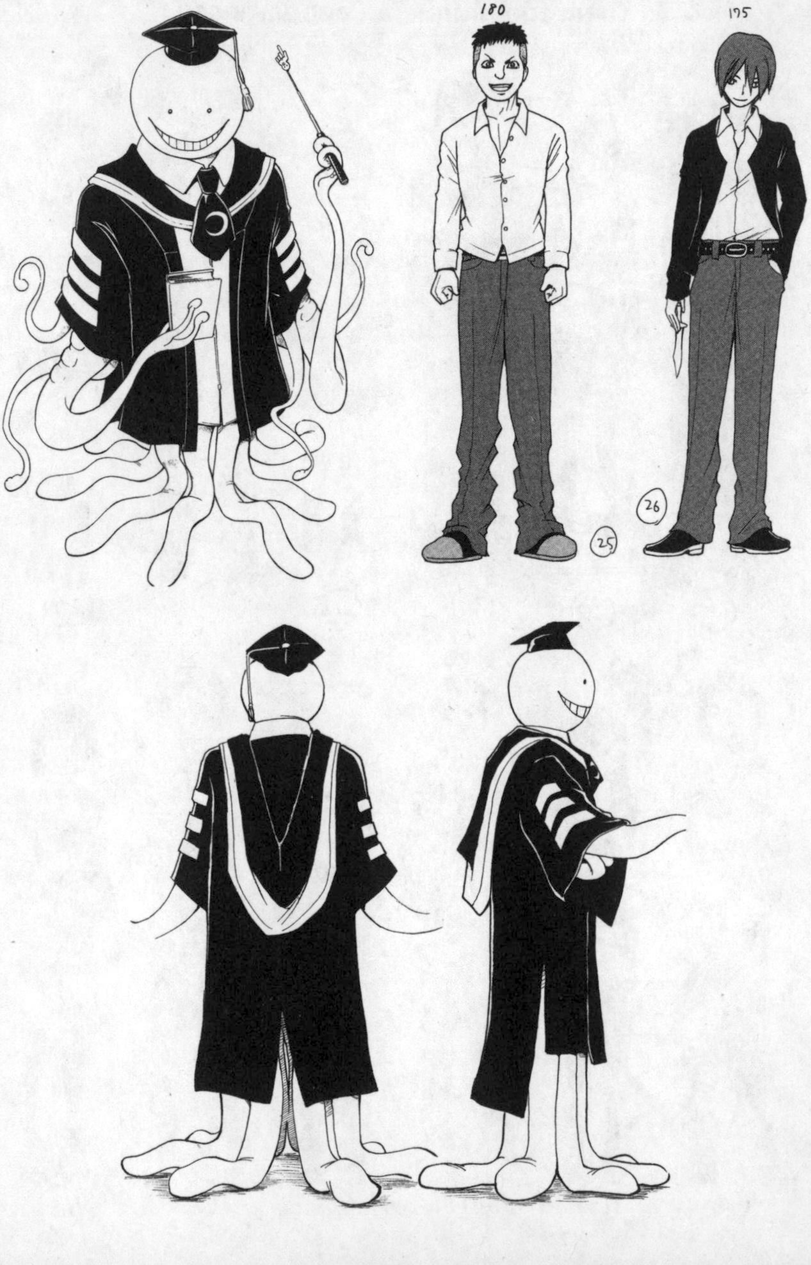
180
175
26
25

Props and whatnot. My assistants and I each have a copy of these files.

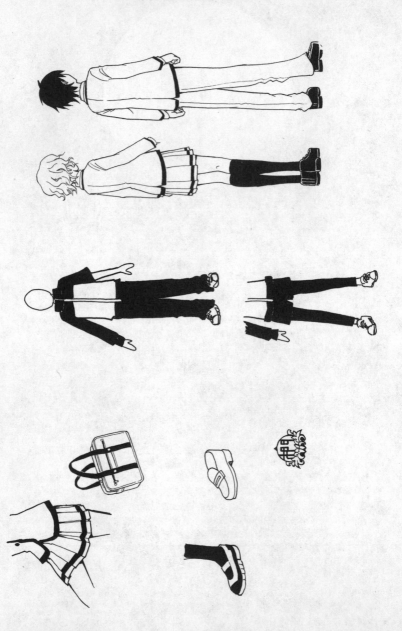

Vol. 1 was picked up by more people than I expected. I just can't thank you enough for that!

But what I write about in this series won't change based on sales. It'll be a story about the relationship between Koro Sensei and his students within the time frame of one school year.

I hope you're looking forward to reading about the students' school days...and imagining their future after they graduate.

—Yusei Matsui

Yusei Matsui was born on the last day of January in Saitama Prefecture, Japan. He has been drawing manga since elementary school. Some of his favorite manga series are *Bobobo-bo Bo-bobo*, *JoJo's Bizarre Adventure* and *Ultimate Muscle*. Matsui learned his trade working as an assistant to manga artist Yoshio Sawai, creator of *Bobobo-bo Bo-bobo*. In 2005, Matsui debuted his original manga *Neuro: Supernatural Detective* in *Weekly Shonen Jump*. In 2007, *Neuro* was adapted into an anime. In 2012, *Assassination Classroom* began serialization in *Weekly Shonen Jump*.

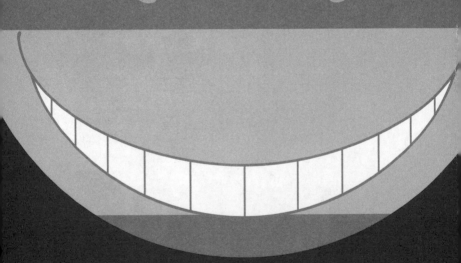

When his face is covered with yellow and green stripes, he's mocking you. And when
he really thinks you're an idiot...the stripes begin to revolve like a barber's pole.

ASSASSINATION
CLASSROOM

YUSEI MATSUI

TIME FOR GROWN-UPS

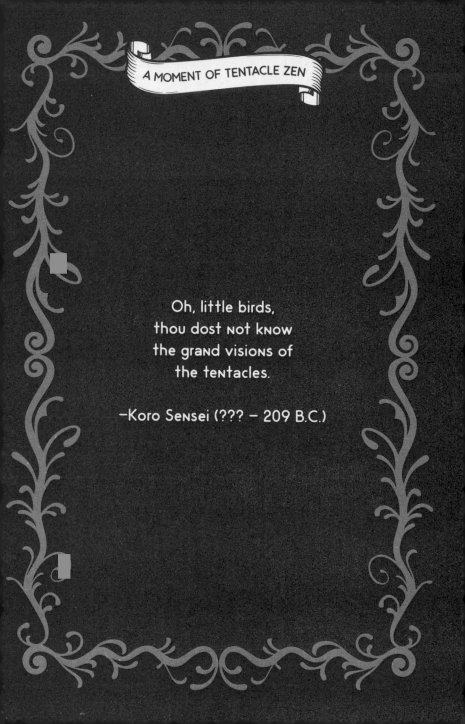

A MOMENT OF TENTACLE ZEN

Oh, little birds,
thou dost ɴoᴛ ᴋɴow
the grand visions of
the tentacles.

–Koro Seɴsei (??? – 209 B.C.)

ASSASSINATION CLASSROOM

Volume 2
SHONEN JUMP Manga Edition

Story and Art by YUSEI MATSUI

Translation/Tetsuichiro Miyaki
English Adaptation/Bryant Turnage
Touch-up Art & Lettering/Stephen Dutro
Cover & Interior Design/Sam Elzway
Editor/Annette Roman

First published in Japan in 2012 by SHUEISHA Inc., Tokyo.
English translation rights arranged by SHUEISHA Inc.

Printed in the U.S.A.

Published by VIZ Media, LLC
P.O. Box 77010
San Francisco, CA 94107

10
First printing, February 2014
Tenth printing, September 2020

viz.com
shonenjump.com

RATED T+ OLDER TEEN ratings.viz.com

PARENTAL ADVISORY
ASSASSINATION CLASSROOM is rated T+ for Older Teen and is recommended for ages 16 and up. This volume contains realistic violence and suggestive situations.

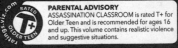

Syllabus for
Assassination Classroom, Vol. 3

The latest addition to the misfit students of Class 3–E is a Norwegian robot specially designed to assassinate their teacher—but sadly lacking in social skills. Nothing Koro Sensei can't cure with a little super-fast tentacle work! When playboy Maehara gets dissed by a girl for being in Class 3–E, revenge is clearly warranted—and Koro Sensei can help with that too! Then, Irina, the English language teacher/sexy assassin, gets a visit from her murder mentor. Plus, an intriguing secret about Koro Sensei's mysterious past is revealed...

Available Now!

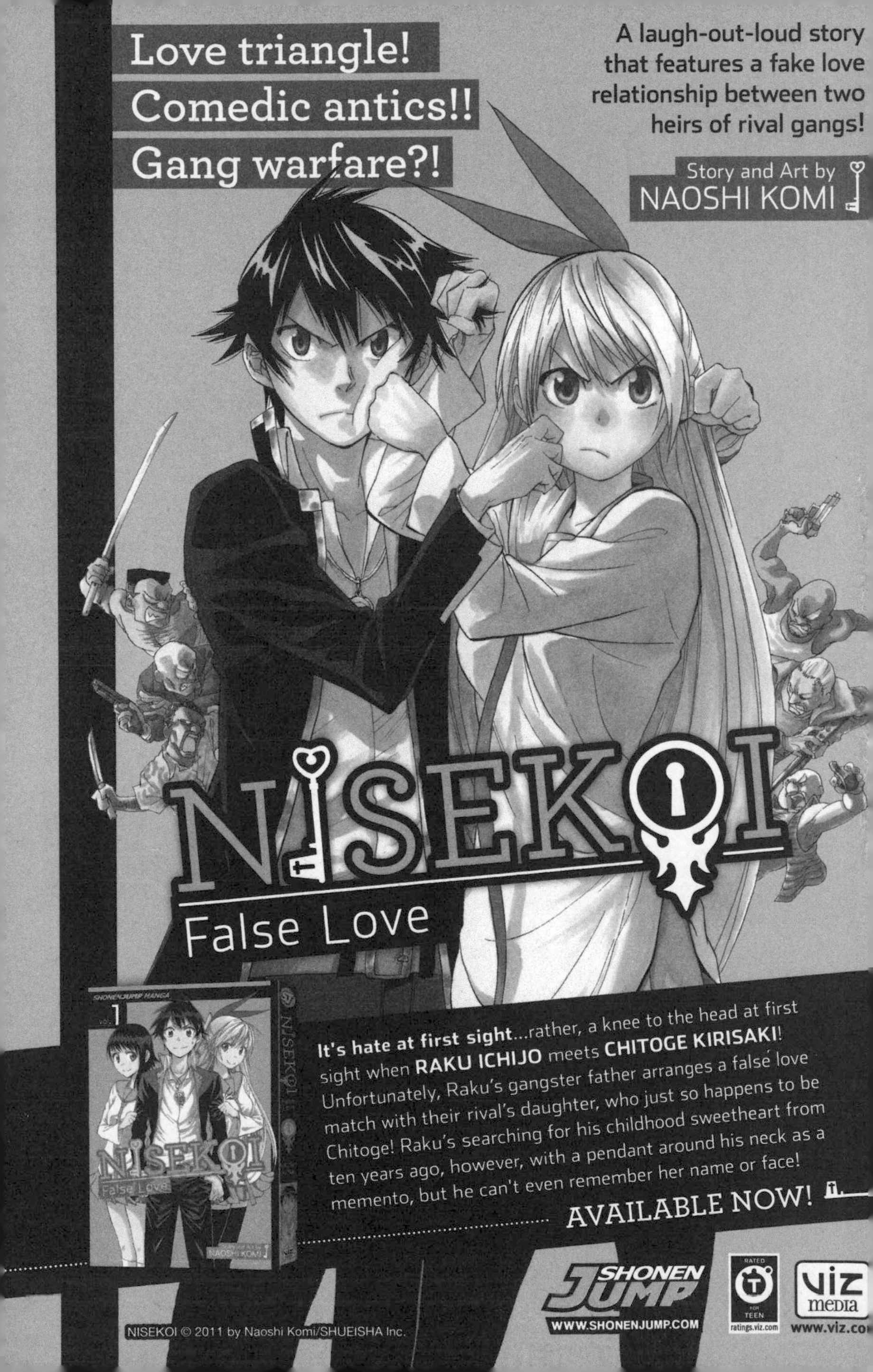

Love triangle!
Comedic antics!!
Gang warfare?!
A laugh-out-loud story that features a fake love relationship between two heirs of rival gangs!
Story and Art by
NAOSHI KOMI
NISEKOI
False Love
SHONEN JUMP MANGA
vol. 1
NISEKOI
False Love
NAOSHI KOMI
It's hate at first sight...rather, a knee to the head at first sight when **RAKU ICHIJO** meets **CHITOGE KIRISAKI**! Unfortunately, Raku's gangster father arranges a false love match with their rival's daughter, who just so happens to be Chitoge! Raku's searching for his childhood sweetheart from ten years ago, however, with a pendant around his neck as a memento, but he can't even remember her name or face!
AVAILABLE NOW!
SHONEN JUMP
WWW.SHONENJUMP.COM
RATED T FOR TEEN
ratings.viz.com
VIZ MEDIA
www.viz.com
NISEKOI © 2011 by Naoshi Komi/SHUEISHA Inc.

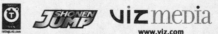

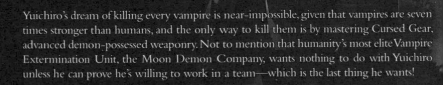

You're Reading in the Wrong Direction!!

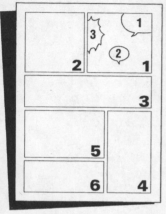

Whoops! Guess what? You're starting at the wrong end of the comic!

…It's true! In keeping with the original Japanese format, **Assassination Classroom** is meant to be read from right to left, starting in the upper-right corner.

Unlike English, which is read from left to right, Japanese is read from right to left, meaning that action, sound effects and word-balloon order are completely reversed… something which can make readers unfamiliar with Japanese feel pretty backwards themselves. For this reason, manga or Japanese comics published in the U.S. in English have sometimes been published "flopped"—that is, printed in exact reverse order, as though seen from the other side of a mirror.

By flopping pages, U.S. publishers can avoid confusing readers, but the compromise is not without its downside. For one thing, a character in a flopped manga series who once wore in the original Japanese version a T-shirt emblazoned with "M A Y" (as in "the merry month of") now wears one which reads "Y A M"! Additionally, many manga creators in Japan are themselves unhappy with the process, as some feel the mirror-imaging of their art skews their original intentions.

We are proud to bring you Yusei Matsui's **Assassination Classroom** in the original unflopped format.
For now, though, turn to the other side of the book and let the adventure begin…!

—Editor